**W9-ADP-794**

# MEDIA TECHNOLOGY AND SOCIETY

*Media Technology and Society* offers a comprehensive account of the history of communications technologies, from the telegraph to the Internet.

Winston argues that the development of new media, from the telephone to computers, satellite, camcorders and CD-ROM, is the product of a constant play-off between social necessity and suppression: the unwritten 'law' by which new technologies are introduced into society.

Winston's fascinating account challenges the concept of a 'revolution' in communications technology by highlighting the long histories of such developments. The fax was introduced in 1847. The idea of television was patented in 1884. Digitalisation was demonstrated in 1938. Even the concept of the 'web' dates back to 1945. Winston examines why some prototypes are abandoned, and why many 'inventions' are created simultaneously by innovators unaware of each other's existence, and shows how new industries develop around these inventions, providing media products for a mass audience.

Challenging the popular myth of a present-day 'Information Revolution', *Media Technology and Society* is essential reading for anyone interested in the social impact of technological change.

**Brian Winston** is Head of the School of Communication, Design and Media at the University of Westminster. He has been Dean of the College of Communications at the Pennsylvania State University, Chair of Cinema Studies at New York University and Founding Research Director of the Glasgow University Media Group. His books include *Claiming the Real* (1995). As a television professional, he has worked on *World in Action* and has an Emmy for documentary script-writing.

# MEDIA TECHNOLOGY AND SOCIETY

## A HISTORY: FROM THE TELEGRAPH TO THE INTERNET

*Brian Winston*

London and New York

First published 1998
by Routledge
11 New Fetter Lane, London EC4P 4EE

Simultaneously published in the USA and Canada
by Routledge
29 West 35th Street, New York, NY 10001

Reprinted 2000

*Routledge is an imprint of the Taylor & Francis Group*

Typeset in Perpetua and Bank Gothic by
J&L Composition Ltd, Filey, North Yorkshire
Printed and bound in Great Britain by
MPG Books Ltd, Bodmin

*British Library Cataloguing in Publication Data*
A catalogue record for this book is available
from the British Library

*Library of Congress Cataloging in Publication Data*
Winston, Brian.
Media technology & society : a history / Brian Winston.
p.   cm.
Rev. ed. of: Misunderstanding media. 1986.
Includes bibliographical references (p.  ) and index.
1. Mass media—Technological innovations—History.
2. Communication—Technological innovations—History.
3. Communication—Social aspects.  4. Mass media—Social aspects.
I. Winston, Brian. Misunderstanding media.  II. Title.
P96. T42W49  1998
302.23—dc21            97–34781

ISBN  0–415–14229–6 (hbk)
ISBN  0–415–14230–X (pbk)

For my wife and children – my 'angels of history'

# CONTENTS

# FIGURES

# ACKNOWLEDGEMENTS

This book is a reworking and updating of material originally published in 1986 (*Misunderstanding Media*). I then essayed a polemic against the rhetoric of the Information Revolution grounded in a history, necessarily both synthetic and revisionist, of the central technologies of that supposed event. This current work is the other way round in that it again offers that history, mainly of electronic communications from telegraphy to holography, but now does so centrally with the anti-technicist polemic in the supporting role.

From the 1970s on I was increasingly aware of a gap between the rhetoric of runaway technological change and the reality of my professional life as a media worker and teacher. Working with film and teaching film-making when videotape was supposed to have wiped out that technology spurred a central thought that change was occurring more slowly than was (and is) commonly believed.

In synthesising the histories of these technologies I have obviously relied extensively on the work of others but my understanding owes more than can be adequately footnoted to colleagues and friends at New York University a decade and more ago – especially William Boddy, Michelle Hilmes, Aaron Nmugwen, Mitchell Moss and Martin Elton. Svein Bergum and Jimmy Weaver, members of my seminar group on technology and ideology at that time, were especially supportive as were others both at NYU and elsewhere including Daniel Zwanziger, Bernard Abramson, Robert Horwitz, Herb Schiller, Janet Staeger, Michael Wreen, Steve Scheuer and Nick Hart-Williams. The Interactive Telecommunications Programme at NYU was a crucial forum, especially for testing the validity of early versions of the model proposed in the Introduction and applied throughout this book.

My two commuter friends on the AMTRACK Hudson Valley line, Wayne Barden and Frederick Houston, helped me refine the legal points I wanted to make. (I am still grateful to 'Mo' Fink and the other AMTRACK conductors for making that period of commuting when I was doing much of my early reading for the book so pleasant. I am also happy that much of the rewriting was done on Isambard Kingdom Brunel's still great railroad between Paddington and Cardiff.) More recent thanks too to Xavier Delcourt and Angelo Agostini for guiding me to some fresh thoughts.

Bertell Olhman, Patrick Watson and Ted Conant kindly read bits and pieces of the original manuscript. Bill Boddy (in 1985) and Dwayne Winseck (in 1997) tackled the whole text and I am very much in their debt. Lynne Jackson was my research assistant at NYU and without her help this project would have been stillborn.

I am also grateful to Martin Barker and Geoff Mulgan (among others) for suggesting *Misunderstanding Media* might be usefully revisited; and I am pleased that Rebecca Barden thought so too. To Peter Hopkins goes my thanks for commissioning the original work and to Lindsay Waters for buying it as well. To my wife Adèle goes my usual gratitude for undertaking correcting chores.

*Cardiff*
*June 1997*

# INTRODUCTION: A STORM
# FROM PARADISE

## TECHNOLOGICAL INNOVATION,
## DIFFUSION AND SUPPRESSION

### THE INFORMATION REVOLUTION AS HYPERBOLE

A Klee painting named 'Angelus Novus' shows an angel looking as though he is about to move away from something he is fixedly contemplating. His eyes are staring, his mouth is open, his wings are spread. This is how one pictures the angel of history. His face is turned towards the past. Where we perceive a chain of events, he sees one single catastrophe which keeps piling wreckage upon wreckage and hurls it in front of his feet. The angel would like to stay, awaken the dead, and make whole what has been smashed. But a storm is blowing from Paradise; it has got caught in his wings with such violence that the angel can no longer close them. This storm irresistibly propels him into the future to which his back is turned, while the pile of debris before him grows skyward. This storm is what we call progress.

(Benjamin 1969: 257–8)

An image of history as something other than a progressive chain of events informs this book. It is my contention that the received understanding of our current technological situation, the view that we are living in the midst of an 'Information Revolution' or at the start of an 'Information Age', can be seen rather differently if the histories of the technologies involved are considered. I am not necessarily suggesting, with Walter Benjamin and Paul Klee, that if we take their view we will agree that we are drowning in an ever-growing pile of debris; but I am agreeing with them that, certainly, the storm of progress blows so hard as to obscure our vision of what is actually happening. What is hyperbolised as a revolutionary train of events can be seen as a far more evolutionary and less transforming process.

The suggestion that we are not in the midst of monumental and increasingly frequent change in information (or better, communications) technology runs so

1

counter to our whole underlying philosophy of progress, as well as the particular rhetoric of the 'Information Revolution' itself, that it must surely be doubted by right-thinking people. But the position taken here, rather, is that Western civilisation over the past three centuries has displayed, despite enormous changes in detail, fundamental continuity – and that it continues to do so.

The concept of the 'Information Revolution' is implicitly historical, for how can one know that a situation has changed – has revolved – without knowing its previous state or position? Even the notion of a 'Digital Age' (to take another hyperbolic slogan) implicitly posits other preceding non-digital ages. It is therefore apposite to offer a critique of these ideas which is itself grounded in the past; in the historical circumstances surrounding the application of what may be broadly termed 'science', especially the science of electricity, to the human communication process.

Such an historical consciousness reveals the 'Information Revolution' to be largely an illusion, a rhetorical gambit and an expression of technological ignorance. The popular literature on these matters and the media resound with visions of techno-glory or apocalypse, the same set of phenomena being the source for both styles of pontificating. Curiously, more than a few supposedly scholarly works, again both the technophiliac as well as the jeremiads, exhibit the same traits – fervid but purblind imagination, unbalanced judgements and unidimensional insights.

This is the background against which I shall argue more specifically that there is nothing in the histories of electrical and electronic communication systems to indicate that significant major changes have not been accommodated by pre-existing social formations. The term 'revolution' is therefore quite the wrong word to apply to the current situation. Indeed, it is possible to see in the historical record not just a slower pace of change than is usually suggested but also such regularities in the pattern of innovation and diffusion as to suggest a model for all such changes. Repetitions can be seen across this diverse range of technologies and across the two centuries of their development and diffusion. Consider, for example, the ways in which ideas for devices occur, the importance of science and general knowhow, the relationship of prototypes to 'inventions' and the balance of forces pushing and inhibiting the technologies. A model to reflect these patterns implicitly suggests the primacy of the social sphere as the site of these activities, conditioning and determining technological developments. It allows us to go beyond a straightforward account of technological history to pose more general questions about how the pattern of innovation and diffusion of electrical and electronic communications illuminates the broader role played by such technologies in our civilisation.

## MODELLING CHANGE

To do this, the model treats the historical pattern of change and development in communications as a field (the social sphere) in which two elements (science and technology) intersect.[1] The detailed relationship between the field and these elements can be elucidated by reference to a conceptual figure, drawn from Saussurian linguistics.

Utterance is, for Saussure, the surface expression of a deep-seated mental competence. In Chomskyan terms, each utterance is a performance dependent on this competence. By analogy, then, these communication technologies are also performances but of a sort of *scientific competence*. Technology can be seen as standing in a structural relationship to science. Technologies are, as it were, utterances of a scientific language, performances of a scientific competence (Figure 1). The model thus suggests that we view discrete communications technologies within the social sphere as a series of performances ('utterances') by technologists in response to the ground of scientific competence.

'Science' here is being used very broadly, more in line with its original meaning of 'acquaintance with or mastery of any department of learning' rather than its

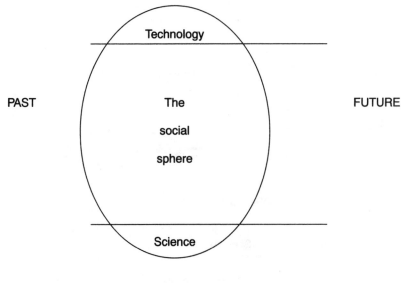

**PERFORMANCE**

Technology

PAST    The social sphere    FUTURE

Science

**COMPETENCE**

*Figure 1* Building the model: the social sphere

modern sense of 'a connected body of demonstrated truths' or 'observed facts systematically classified'. The ground of scientific competence for these communications technologies includes, for example, the centuries-old investigations of electromagnetic phenomena and photokinesics.

The possibilities of using electricity for signalling, including photoelectric phenomena, march, from the mid-eighteenth century on, virtually hand-in-hand with the growth of the scientific understanding of electricity itself. Similarly, the development of photography involved knowledge of the different effects light has on various substances, a scientific agenda item from at least the Middle Ages on. The propensity of certain solids to conduct sounds seems to have been known in ancient times and was certainly a well-observed phenomenon by the late eighteenth century. It is such knowledge and understandings that form the ground of scientific competence which can then be transformed into technology. (All examples are described more fully below.)

The first transformation – *ideation* – moves the technology from the ground of scientific competence up to the level of *technological performance* (Figure 2). Its effect is to activate the technologist. To continue with the linguistic metaphor, the ideation transformation is akin to the processes whereby a transformation at the

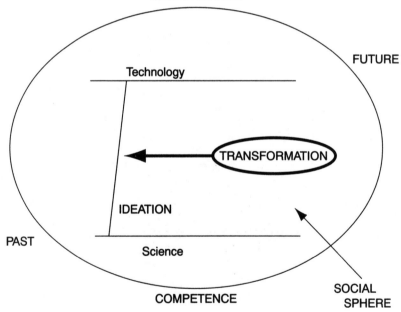

*Figure 2* Building the model: ideation

level of competence takes place in the human brain, so that utterance, performance, can be generated. Ideation occurs when the technologist envisages the device – gets the idea, formulates the problems involved and hypothesises a solution. Those mysterious mental forces – creativity, intuition, imagination, 'the will to think' – are subsumed by ideation as are the general constraints of culture and the limits imposed by social forces of all kinds on the technologist's mind.

Although the technological idea will be grounded in scientific competence, it will not necessarily relate directly to science any more than a conscious understanding of linguistic competence is needed to generate utterance. Rather, just as in language a formal understanding of the deep structure of linguistic competence is not a prerequisite of utterance, so too a lack of formal scientific competence is no bar to technological performance. But the technologist will, at some level, have absorbed the science; just as a speaker, at some level, has absorbed grammar.

A German thought of the telegraph in the last years of the eighteenth century, three decades before the first working device. A Frenchman hypothesised the telephone in 1854, more than 20 years before Bell. The idea of television, which depended on the identification of the phenomenon of photoemission (i.e. that certain metals produce electrons when stimulated by light) was suggested in 1877. Bell Laboratory workers began worrying about the transistor in the 1930s when solid state amplifiers had already been envisaged for a decade. Some of these thinkers went on to test their ideas 'in the metal'; many did not. But more often than not their work was known to those who set about building devices.

Ideation transforms the processes of science into the testing of solutions – that is, the building of devices which is the business of technological performance. This will go on until the device is widely diffused and even beyond, as spin-offs and refinements are developed. In the first stage the technologists begin to build devices working towards fulfilling the plans which emerged from the ideation transformation. The devices they now construct can be thought of as *prototypes* (Figure 3).

However, we need to remember at this point once again that the technologist is a social being and that all this is taking place within the social sphere. The social has obviously informed the model thus far. The scientists conceptualising necessary fundamental understandings are as much social beings, exponents of and prisoners of the culture that produced them, as are the technologists who have ideas for devices and build prototypes. Yet now it is important to consider the social in a less general but more direct and concentrated way to answer some recurrent and basic questions.

Why, for example, are some prototypes abandoned while others are not? Why are some devices classed as 'inventions' when they did not work in significantly better ways than did other devices classed as prototypes? Why are many 'inventions'

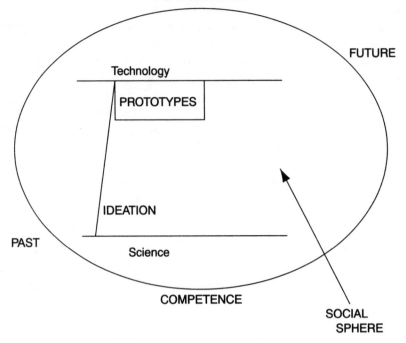

*Figure 3* Building the model: prototypes

created more or less simultaneously by technologists who had no contact with each other? The answers to such conundra are to be found in the operation of a second transformation impacting on, and transforming, technological performance, this time coming not so much from the (socially conditioned) minds of technologists as from society itself. This transformation is, as it were, a concentration of the generalised social forces which have hitherto been determining the process of innovation. Now these generalised forces coalesce to function as a transforming agency which I will call *supervening social necessities* (Figure 4). Just as ideation worked upon the ground of scientific competence to create prototypes, so more general supervening social necessities now work on these prototypes to move them out of the laboratory into the world at large. In the nature of the case this second transformation is more amorphous than the first. There is no limitation on the forces that can act as supervening social necessities. They can range from the objective requirements of changed social circumstances (such as the consequences of the introduction of one technology forcing the development of another) through to the subjective whims of perceived needs (such as the introduction of new

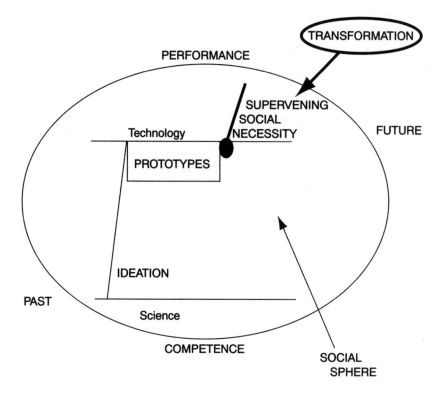

*Figure 4* Building the model: supervening social necessity

consumer technologies to fulfil essentially the same function as those filled by previously diffused consumer technologies).

It is supervening social necessities of one kind or another which define the various different sorts of prototypes discernible in the historical record and which transform such prototypes into inventions. First, let us consider the four classes of possible prototypes:

The prototype can be *rejected* because a supervening necessity has not yet operated and no possible use for the device is seen. Ronalds' demonstration of a working telegraph in 1816 would be an example of this. The British naval authorities, understanding that the semaphore was the only machine to use in long-distance signalling, simply refused to acknowledge the superiority of his electromagnetic technology. Nearly every technology has its Ronalds.

The prototype can be *accepted* because the early and incomplete operation of a supervening necessity has created a partial need which the prototype partially fills. The daguerreotype photographic process which was widely used in the mid-nineteenth century is among the clearest examples of this accepted group. The efficiency of Hollerith punch-card calculators, introduced at the turn of the century but made increasingly sophisticated in the years after the First World War, can be said to have been so well accepted that the development of the electronic computer was delayed.

*Parallel* prototypes: these will occur when the device which will become the parallel prototype is already in existence solving another technological problem. Its potential use for a secondary purpose is realised only after the operation of a supervening necessity. Various laboratory contrivances existed in the last two decades of the nineteenth century to demonstrate the validity of electromagnetic wave theory by detecting the presence of radio waves. Distinguished physicists such as Hertz and Lodge are associated with these demonstration machines. They were in fact a species of radio but were not seen as such. Their existence is, however, of importance in tracing the work of Marconi, Popov and others which led to radio. The cathode ray tube, before Rozing, would be another example.

Finally, in this stage of technological performance, there can be *partial* prototypes which are machines designed to perform effectively in a given area but which do not. The telephonic apparatus developed by Reiss in the 1860s and, arguably, Bell's earliest machines were of this type. Baird and Jenkins' mechanical televisions were also partial prototypes.

These then are the four prototypes – rejected, accepted, parallel and partial (and all the examples given are dealt with more fully below). This classification is without prejudice to the efficacy of the devices. Except for partial prototypes which simply did not work very well, the other three classes of prototype all work, more rather than less. The degree of their subsequent diffusion, though, depends more on the operation of the supervening necessity transformation than on their efficiency. An accepted prototype is a device which effectively fulfils the potential of the technology but, because the full power of the supervening necessity has not yet been called into play, there is still room for development. The rejected prototype might work just as well as the device eventually 'invented' but will achieve no measure of diffusion because there is no externally determined reason for its development. The parallel prototype is a similar case. The initial thrust of the technology is directed towards purposes other than those which eventually emerge. The effectiveness of this prototype in solving the problem for which it was originally designed has nothing to do with its effectiveness as a device in the second area. It is, in effect, a species of *spin-off*.

All these devices are then, as it were, impacted by those concentrations of social factors I have designated as supervening social necessities. These too can themselves be roughly classified into three sub-types:

The least difficult class of supervening social necessity to discern is that occasioned by the consequences of other technological innovation. For instance, it was the railway which transformed telegraphic prototypes into a widely diffused technology. Before railways, as Ronalds discovered, there was no demonstrable need for such devices. Single-track systems, however, required, as an urgent matter of safety, instantaneous signals. Similarly, the radio came into its own with the development of the ironclad battleship. With these, for the first time, naval battle plans called for ships to steam out of sight of one another, thus rendering the traditional signalling methods useless.

A concentration of social forces working directly on the processes of innovation, rather than being, as with the first sub-type, mediated through another technology, constitute a second, more difficult to discern, group of supervening necessities. The rise of the modern business corporation created today's office, the architecture of the building which houses it and the key machines – telephone, typewriter and calculator – which make it function. In the middle decades of the nineteenth century the possibility of the limited liability company was established for the first time in law. The legal development of the modern corporation thus, in this sense, engenders telephony. In the same way, the growing urban mass impacts on the technologies of print, photography, cinematography and then on the electronic mass media as I shall show below.

Strictly commercial, as opposed to these sorts of social, needs for new products and other limited marketing considerations would form a third type of necessity – less certain in guaranteeing diffusion and producing less significant innovation than either the consequences of social change or the effects of other technological advances. Super 8mm film, Polaroid movies, 16 rpm records and the CD can stand for the host of devices to which commerce makes us heir under this rubric.

## 'INVENTION'

The action of a supervening necessity does not account for the entire development and reception of a technology. Rather it transforms the circumstances in which the technologist labours creating fertile ground for innovation. It follows from this that there must be the possibility of a fifth class of 'prototype', as it were, one which is either synchronous with or subsequent to the operation of a supervening necessity. The production of such machines is the business of further technological performance and leads to what is commonly called the 'invention'. So within the laboratory the work continues as it did in the prototype stage but the supervening necessity transformation means the devices now produced are inventions (Figure 5).

Since the difference between such devices and the previous group of prototypes is the operation of a widespread transformation (social necessity), it is likely, and history reveals common, that such creations will occur in a number of places synchronously. The telephone is but the most extreme example of this because Bell and his rival Gray filed patents for a speaking electric telephone on the very

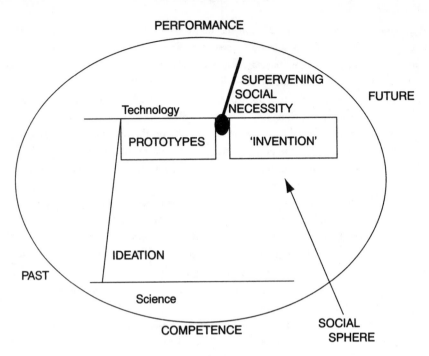

*Figure 5* Building the model: 'invention'

same February day in 1876. Since they were both responding to the same social necessity (the rise of the modern corporation and its office) there is thus no mystery in the synchronicity of this communication invention – nor indeed of any other.

The suggestion here is that the distinction between prototype and 'invention' is far less clear-cut than is often supposed to be the case. Given that arguments about innovation are quite frequently resolved in court, there is a tendency for the victors in such cases to obscure the failings of their own technologies with as much public relations hyperbole as they can muster even as they denigrate the strengths of their rivals' ideas and machines. Again, the telephone is a good case in point. Its early history is of endless court battles in which the rival prototypes were subjected to very thorough drubbings at the hands of Bell's lawyers, exactly because Bell's patented apparatus did not really work. It is possible that at least some of these other devices were as close or as far from the speaking telephone as was Bell's.

This stage in the model will be designated *technological performance - invention*. Of all the stages, this is the best known. Herein are to be found all the heroes of communication technology's Hall of Fame – Reiss, Rosen and Hoff, Mauchly and Eckert, Baran, Gabor and the rest.

The *invention* now moves into the market place. Yet acceptance is never straightforward, however 'needed' the technology. As a society we are schizo-phrenic about machines. On the one hand, although perhaps with an increasingly jaundiced eye, we still believe in the inevitability of progress. On the other hand we control every advance by conforming it so that it 'fits' to pre-existing social patterns. The same authorities and institutions, the same capital, the same research effort which created today's world is also trying to create tomorrow's. A tech-nologically induced hara-kiri on the part of these institutions, whereby a business 'invents' a device which puts it out of business, is obviously impossible. But what is equally true, although less obvious, is the difficulty of inventing something to put other businesses out of business; and the bigger the threatened business the more difficult it is. Progress is made while going down the up escalator (or, as optimists might argue, up the down). This jerky advance into the future can be seen constantly repeated in communications history. Its daily cavorting can be read in the trade press. It is theorised by historians such as Fernand Braudel as a conflict between historical 'brakes' and 'accelerators' being applied to technological pro-gress: 'First the accelerator, then the brake: the history of technology seems to consist of both processes, sometimes in quick succession: it propels human life onward, gradually reaches new forms of equilibrium on higher levels than in the past' (Braudel 1981: 430).

In this model, the 'accelerator' is the supervening social necessity transforming the prototype into an 'invention' and pushing the invention out into the world – causing its diffusion. But there is also a 'brake': this operates as a third transfor-mation, wherein general social constraints coalesce to limit the potential of the device radically to disrupt pre-existing social formations. I will refer to this particular 'concentration' of determining social factors as the *'law' of the suppression of radical potential* (Figure 6).

Understanding the interaction of the positive effects of supervening necessity and the brake of the 'law' of the suppression of radical potential is crucial to a proper overview of how communications technologies develop. Constraints operate to slow the rate of diffusion so that the social fabric in general can absorb the new machine and essential formations such as business entities and other institutions can be protected and preserved. Such a pattern, far from atrophying in the face of supp-osedly revolutionary change, persists. If anything, there has been a significant diminution in the cut-throat nature of the market place because the desire for stable trading circumstances, coupled with external restrictions and monopolistic tendenc-ies, works to contain the crudest manifestations of the profit motive.

Two caveats must be entered as to the chosen designation of this third and crucial transformation. Beyond the proper and necessary caution required when

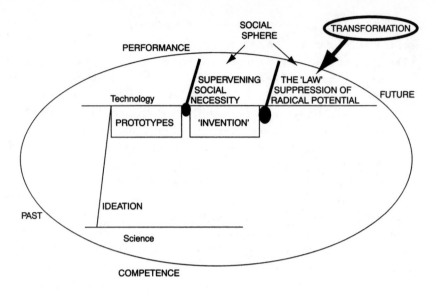

*Figure 6* Building the model: suppression of radical potential

postulating historical laws, '*law*' here is apostrophised to indicate that although the phenomenon under discussion can be found in the histories of all telecommunications technologies it is not so regular as always to manifest itself in the same form with equal force at the same point of development. It is recurrent enough to be a 'law' but not certain enough in its operation to be a law. Thus it is not a law, a universal hypothesis, in the Hempelian sense in that it does not assert that:

> In every case where an event of a specified kind *C* occurs at a certain place and time, an event of a specified kind *E* will occur at a place and time which is related in a specified manner to the place and time of the occurrence of the first event.
>
> (Hempel 1942: 35)

Second, *suppression* must be read in a particular way. As Lewis Carroll said, suppression is 'rather a hard word'. Here it is not meant to convey the idea of overt authoritarian prohibition or to indicate the presence of any form of conspiracy, conscious or unconscious; rather *suppression* is used in the more scientific senses given by the OED, i.e.: 'to hinder from passage or discharge; to stop or arrest the flow of; (in Botany) absence or non-development of some part or organ normally or typically present'. It is possible that even with these caveats the word is still too 'hard' to cover the sense of a technology's potential simply being dissipated by the actions of individuals and institutions. However a mere 'tendency' towards dissipation or retardation would be too soft to convey the strength of the forces at work.

The most obvious proof of the existence of a 'law' of suppression of radical potential, then, is the continuation, despite the bombardments of technology, of all the institutions of our culture in forms subject to alteration but not revolutionary change. To many, such changes as have occurred loom very large; but any sort of informed historical vision creates a more balanced picture of their true size and scope. It is the 'law' of suppression that ensures any new communications technology takes decades to be diffused.

Let me just add that the 'law' of suppression is conceived of as being far more powerful than the concept of 'development cycles' determining, through an examination of business alone, the factors and time involved in diffusing an innovation. It seeks to capture a far wider set of phenomena, which work in the broadest possible way to ensure the survival, however battered, of family, home and workplace, church, president and queen, and above all, the great corporation as the primary institution of our society. To offer one specific example, it is the 'law' of suppression which led the British Government in 1997 to ignore digital television's potential as a means of providing a new high definition 1000+ line standard. Instead it licensed the technology to established industrial entities, including, in effect, the comparative newcomer satellite broadcaster as well as the old terrestrial players. The 'law' was at work to stabilise the sector by both constraining the radical potential of the latest development and, at the same, bringing the exploiters of the previous 'new thing' into the fold.

This does not in any way mean that the technologists cease to produce devices. On the contrary, supervening necessity has transformed prototype into invention and supervening necessity now, despite the operation of the 'law' of suppression, continues to encourage technological performance in the form of production, spin-offs and redundancies. There follows a struggle, as it were, between the accelerator or the push of supervening social necessity and the brake or the pull of the 'law' of suppression. This conflict governs the nature and pace of the diffusion of the technology (Figure 7). Supervening social necessity guarantees that the 'invention' will be produced. The 'law' operates as a constraint on that production. This final transformation thus occasions a tripartite phase of *technological performance – production, spin-offs and redundant devices or redundancies,* which reflects the effects of the contradictions which are at work.

Of the three distinct activities covered in this stage, the least problematic is that of *production*. The acceptance of the device is to a certain extent guaranteed by the operation of the supervening necessity. Much attention has been paid by economists to the symptomatic study of diffusion at both a macro and micro level with the result that the most scholarly literature available on innovation is skewed away

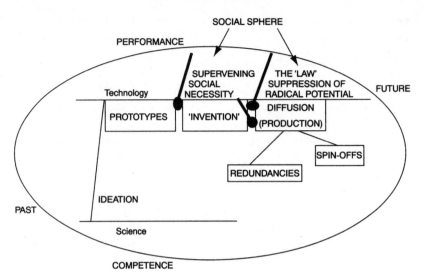

*Figure 7* Building the model: diffusion

from the processes previously described in our model in favour of a concentration on these production and marketing phases. The problems of moving prototypes into production and marketing will therefore be peripheral to this study.

However, in the course of this movement the device can be modified, extended or refined; alternative solutions can appear as rival technologies. Such developments can themselves, as in the prototype phase, either be accepted or rejected. If such a development is accepted, diffused, it is a *spin-off*. Videogames, for instance, are an accepted extension of microchip technology which was certainly not developed with that specific purpose in mind. Similarly the CD, initially a computer memory technology, largely failed as a video format, succeeded in audio form (not least because the record industry simply stopped pressing vinyl) only to also re-emerge in CD-ROM form as a memory store for computing. As an audio medium, then, the CD can be classified as an accepted spin-off. Spin-offs are products of technological performance synchronous or subsequent to the original device's diffusion.

If, on the other hand, the technological performances of this post-production stage are rejected, as the video CD (the laser disk) was by the domestic market, then the technology can be described as a *redundancy* which suffers the same fate as a partial prototype. Before the all-conquering videotape, laser videodisks made little headway; and non-laser videodisks as well as Polaroid instant movie film suffered the same fate for the same reason, redundancies all. Again, these cases are discussed below.

These, then, are the various elements proposed for modelling the processes of change in the technologies of communication. This is not the place to inscribe an account of the debate as to the efficacy of what Popper has called 'historicism' or the propounding of 'historical prophecies'. Many, in seeking to understand the pattern of Clio's garments, have been tempted into predicting, on the basis of that understanding, what she will wear tomorrow. When it comes to communication technology though, such efforts tend to be unfettered by much understanding of the past beyond the anecdotal. Indeed, there is a profound tendency to historical amnesia behind, for example, the oft repeated assertion that the pace of change is now so fast as to be uncontrollable or that 'nobody could predict' this or that development. The historical implications of the word 'revolution' are not denied by this amnesia; instead a supposed transformational movement from 'then' to 'now' is celebrated.[2]

The purpose of this book is not only to explicate the 'then' by inscribing a fuller account of what actually occurred in the telecommunications past but also to offer an interpretation, necessarily revisionist, of those occurrences. In attempting to do this, the model offers an understanding of the history and current position of communications in our culture which depends on an examination of the operation of the accelerators and brakes, or social necessities and constraints, rather than on the performance of technology considered *in vacuo*. In what follows I shall apply the model first to the electrical systems of communication, the telegraph and the telephone. Then, in Part II, radio and television are dealt with. Part III is concerned with computing while Part IV looks at the whole development of electrical and electronic networks from the telegraph to the Internet. The conclusion suggests, via a consideration of the current state of research into holography, that the model is still valid.

# Part I

# PROPAGATING SOUND AT CONSIDERABLE DISTANCES

# 1

# THE TELEGRAPH

## SCIENTIFIC COMPETENCE TO IDEATION: STATIC ELECTRICAL TELEGRAPHS

The application of the natural phenomenon we call electricity to the processes of human communication involves a line of electrical experimenters stretching back to Queen Elizabeth I's physician William Gilbert. The first Englishman to write, in *De Magnete*, a book based on direct observation, Gilbert coined the phrase *vis electrica* to describe the property, noticed in antiquity, possessed by amber (ελεκτρον) and some other substances which, when rubbed, attracted light materials such as feathers.

Further experimentation by the superintendent of the gardens of the King of France in 1733 revealed what Franklin was to call positive and negative charges. In 1745 Musschenbroek built the first device to produce an electric field, the Leyden Jar. His friend, Cunaeus, got a serious electric shock from it. The jar prompted the beginnings of a discussion as to the nature of the phenomenon and a parade of electricians, many of whose names are now immortalised in equipment or units of measure, elaborated, into the early nineteenth century, both the theory of and the laboratory apparatus for creating electrical phenomena.

There is another, even older strand of observation also involved in the ground of scientific competence leading to electrical communications systems. Robert Hooke, the experimental physicist, wrote in 1665:

> I can assure the reader that I have, by the help of a distended wire, propagated the sound a very considerable distance in an instant, or with seemingly as quick a motion as that of light, at least incomparably quicker than that which at the same time was propagated through air; and this was not only in a straight line or direct, but in one bended in many angles.
>
> (Moncel 1879: 11–12)

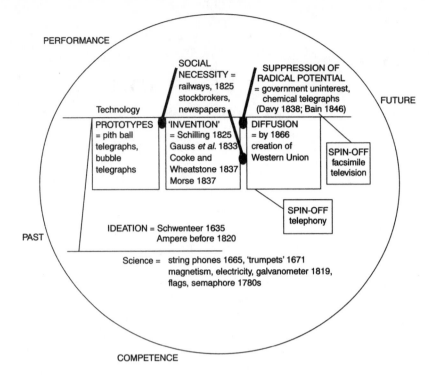

*Figure 8* Telegraphy

Hooke was describing a string telephone which enjoys, in the toy-box, a popularity that has persisted into the twentieth century (Landes 1983: 126). In the decade before the first demonstration of electrical telephones, these string toys were in vogue as an adult diversion, 'Lovers' telegraphs'. They worked up to a distance of 170 yards, the size and nature of the cord having some effect on their efficiency, silk being better than hemp. Such toys will also figure in the history of the telephone because they all depended upon the attachment of a thread or a wire to a stretched membrane (Moncel 1879: 33).

Finally, a third, long-observed phenomenon also comes into play as part of the ground of scientific competence leading to telegraphy. Applying magnetic force to move a piece of metal or needle was a trick known in antiquity. St Augustine mentions it in *De Civitate Dei*. Creating false oracles by, for instance, marking letters around a bowl of water in which floated a cork-born needle manipulated by a hidden magnet was considered an 'abuse', at least by della Porta (Fahie 1884: 5). He can, though, be credited with the first glimmer of the idea of the telegraph to appear in print: 'Lastly, owing to the convenience afforded by the magnet, persons can converse together through long distances. . . .we can communicate what we wish by means of two compass needles circumscribed with an alphabet' (ibid.). In 1635, Schwenteer, in his *Délassements physico-mathematiques,* describes a system using a magnetic needle along these lines, but the experiments which would demonstrate the viability of his idea were not to be conducted until 1819 (Braudel 1981: 434).

The idea of using magnetism and electricity for a signalling system was thus established early in the modern period. The elaboration of the idea as well as the first prototypes for such systems tended to propose the use of static electricity. In one, suggested by an anonymous correspondent of the *Scots' Magazine* writing from Renfrew in 1753, signalling was to be effected by twenty-six wires with twenty-six electroscopes in the form of mounted pith balls, each to represent one letter. Making the electrical circuit agitated the balls. This was the first of many such ideas, another, by Bozolus, a Jesuit, being explained in Latin verse. Devices along these lines existed in experimental form by the 1780s. One of the brothers Chappe had begun his telecommunication experiments with thoughts of such a friction telegraph, before perfecting his 'optical-mechanical' system.[1]

Optical mechanical systems, such as the Chappe semaphore, can be seen as a sort of precursor to the electrical telegraph, like the string telephones. They are part of the ground of competence rather than prototypes. Received opinion suggests that the supervening necessity for the semaphore was the needs of France's revolutionary armies. Patrice Flichy, however, goes further to point out that the Revolution itself required enhanced communication if 'the people' were to act all over the vastness of France with one mind. The semaphore system was used for civilian communications; for example, decrees of the Convention and clauses of the constitution as well as news of political events such as Bonaparte's *coup d'état* were all signalled to provincial centres. Strasbourg could communicate with Paris in 36 minutes. Overall, the effect of the semaphore was to help create a new sort of mental landscape which Flichy terms, 'l'espace national'. (Flichy 1991: 19–23). In France, by the 1840s, there were over 3000 miles of semaphore lines, all operated by the War Department. A law of 1837 established a French government monopoly in long-distance communication systems (Brock 1981: 136). Lines of semaphore stations were established all over Europe. Nicholas I connected St Petersburg to Warsaw and the German border, with a branch to Moscow, by towers five to six miles apart, 220 towers each with six men.

Pre-electric telegraphs, like any other technology, created a certain inertia, and research on electrical alternatives was inhibited. In fact, the existence of these elaborate, military systems operated to suppress the efforts of a number of early experimenters working in the static electrical tradition. For example, one of the Wedgwoods, Ralph, planned an electric telegraph for the benefit of the Admiralty in 1814 but was turned away. Their Lordships' lackeys wrote, 'the war being at an end, and money scarce, the old system [of shutter-semaphores] was sufficient for the country' (Fahie 1884: 124; brackets in original). The shutter-semaphore had been developed in an Admiralty competition by Lord George Murray to improve upon the French device. The inventor of the most elegant of these true electrical prototypes suffered a similar fate.

In 1816, Francis Ronalds demonstrated an electrical telegraph system that worked over eight miles of wire strung up on frames in his London garden. He mounted clock mechanisms at either end of the wire. In place of the clock hands he had an engraved disk with letters, numbers and other instructions inscribed and in place of the glass was an opaque disk in which an aperture was cut. The clocks being exactly synchronised, the operator waited for the required letter or instruction to appear in the aperture, made the circuit and moved the electroscope, a pith ball at the other end of the wire. The receiver, seeing what letter was in the second clock's aperture as the ball moved, could note it down. Within two days of receiving notice of this apparatus, Barrow, the secretary of the Admiralty wrote: 'Mr. Barrow presents his compliments to Mr. Ronalds, and acquaints him, with reference to his note of the 3rd inst., that telegraphs of any kind are now wholly unnecessary, and that no other than the one now in use will be adopted' (Fahie 1884: 124). Ronalds' is the classic rejected prototype. The last static electrical telegraph was proposed, a true redundancy, in 1873, forty-six years after the dynamic version was 'invented'.

Ronalds' experience does not so much reveal official blindness as a lack of supervening social necessity, the reason for such blindness. Ships had flags and armies (and governments) semaphores. They were accepted as partial precursors for the telegraph and they provided as much communication capacity as was required.

## PROTOTYPES, NECESSITY AND 'INVENTION': DYNAMIC ELECTRICAL TELEGRAPHS

Systems based on dynamic electricity were proposed in the first decade of the nineteenth century but these too required a discrete circuit for each letter of the alphabet. Instead of pith balls, the idea was to exploit the fact that water decomposes, giving off bubbles when electricity is introduced into it. Using a Voltaic pile and various arrangements of glass flasks, it was possible to indicate letters by these bubbles.

The ideation of the modern telegraph had occurred in Schwenteer's suggestion but this was clearly forgotten; for, 175 years later, Ampère had the same sort of thought and proposed that 'one could by means of as many pairs of conducting wires and magnetic needles as there are letters' establish a signalling system. In

1819, it was noticed that an electric current would deflect magnetic needles and Faraday discovered that a freely-moving magnetised needle when surrounded by a wire coil will respond to the power of the electrical current in the coil. A device, the Galvanometer, to measure currents was built and the would-be electrical telegraphers acquired a signalling instrument using dynamic electricity which was to disperse the bubbles and banish the pith balls. The prototype phase of telegraphy ended.

But there was still a question: Who needed a dynamic electrical system for distant signalling? Where was the social necessity to turn these experiments into an 'invention'?

In 1809, Richard Trevithick brought to London the latest wonder of the country's mining areas, an iron wagon-way upon which a steam locomotive ran. At Euston Square he built a round track within a wooden fence and charged 1 shilling for the ride (Briggs 1979: 90). In 1825, the first passenger train to go anywhere ran between Stockton and Darlington. The railway age began somewhat fitfully. Between 1833 and 1843 money was raised to build 2300 miles of railway in the UK, about a quarter of which was constructed during that time (Dyos and Aldcroft 1974: 124). Early railways were single-track affairs which necessitated, for the first time, instantaneous signalling methods. One of the many who can lay claim to having 'invented' the telegraph, Edward Davy, saw this clearly. In 1838 he wrote:

> The numerous accidents which have occurred on railways seem to call for a remedy of some kind; and when future improvements shall have augmented the speed of railway travelling to a velocity which cannot at present be deemed safe, then every aid which science can afford must be called in to promote this object. Now, there is a contrivance. . .by which, at every station along the railway line, it may be seen, by mere inspection of a dial, what is the exact situation of the engines running, either towards, or from, that station, and at what speeds they are travelling.
>
> (Fahie 1884: 407)

Here then is a real and pressing supervening necessity – railway safety. The history of telegraphy offers a clear example of how one technology, in this case the railways, creates a supervening necessity for another, the telegraph.

Davy (who is not to be confused with Sir Humphry Davy of the miner's lamp) was eager to have the railway interests exploit the 'contrivance', a dynamic telegraph of his design. He did not bother the Admiralty and he was right not to. In fact, the earliest telegraph wires did indeed run beside railway tracks and were used for operational purposes. That they could also be used for other messages was determined almost immediately. In 1840, the first telegram to excite London, that the Queen had given birth (thereby removing the unpopular King Ernest of Hanover as heir-presumptive), was carried from Windsor on the Great Western Railway's telegraph line, developed by Cooke and Wheatstone. Four years later, 'What hath God wrought', Morse's first public message, was carried down a telegraph wire running from Washington to Baltimore along the side of rail tracks. In May 1844, the Democratic National Convention was meeting in Baltimore and Silas Wright, its nominee for vice-president, declined the honour by telegram from Washington (Czitrom 1982: 6). A committee was dispatched by train to check the truth of this communication. The first French wire ran beside the tracks from Paris to St Germain (Thompson 1947: 15).

The same year which saw the emergence of a clear supervening necessity for the telegraph in the form of the Stockton and Darlington railway also witnessed its 'invention'. Baron Pawel Schilling, a Russian diplomat in Germany, had seen Sommering's apparatus. Using a battery-powered galvanometer, Schilling designed a device that worked in code. Right and left deflections of the needle indicated the letters – for example, A = RL, B = RRR, C = RLL and so on. However, Schilling was working in a repressive society which had anyway made a not inconsiderable investment in the previous optical technology of semaphores. Thus,

the Emperor Nicholas saw in it only an instrument of subversion and by an ukase it was, during his reign, absolutely prohibited to give the public any information relative to electric telegraph apparatus, a prohibition which extended even to the translation of the notices respecting it, which, at this time, were appearing in the European journals.

(Thompson 1947: 317)

Given that the idea of telegraphy had been widely mooted; that a system using a common scientific device, the galvanometer, had been demonstrated; and that the railways had a need for a signalling system, it is scarcely surprising that claimants for the honour of 'inventing' the telegraph are numerous. Apart from Schilling, Cooke and Wheatstone also used galvanometers to construct an elegant alphabetic system, which needed initially five, and later two wires to operate. The patent was granted on 12 June 1837 and eventually, by 1840, they had five galvanometers set in a line across the centre of a lozenge-shaped board on which were painted twenty letters. By deflecting any two needles, one letter could be isolated. A Scotsman, William Alexander, on the very day of their initial patent, wrote to Lord John Russell, the then Home Secretary, with a proposal for a telegraph between London and Edinburgh. Three days later an acknowledgement was sent but no action was taken. In December, somewhat unwillingly, Alexander inspected the Wheatstone telegraph and admitted its superiority to his own.

More seriously, there was also Davy, the man who had linked the telegraph to railway safety. Wheatstone was writing to his partner Cooke the January following Alexander's visit:

> Davy has advertised an exhibition of an electric telegraph at Exeter Hall. . .I am told he employs six wires, by means of which he obtains upwards of two hundred simple and compound signals, and that he rings a bell. I scarcely think that he can effect either of these things without infringing our patent.
>
> (Fahie 1884: 381)

Edward Davy, the son of a West Country doctor and inventor of 'Davy's Diamond Cement' for mending broken china and glass, had lodged a caveat against rumours of Wheatstone's work the previous March and it seems as if his was the superior scheme. His machine used a chemically treated paper strip which recorded the electrical impulse as a visible brown mark. It was the forerunner of a series of such devices which would eventually lead to the fax machine and television. Only the scientific inadequacies of the Solicitor General, who thought the devices were the same when in fact they were not, allowed Wheatstone and Cooke their patent. Davy strenuously struggled to have this decision overturned and to exploit his version with the aid of supporters among the railway men. But in the midst of this battle, which developed in the summer of 1838, he wrote to his father, 'I have notice of another application for a patent by a person named *Morse*' (Fahie 1884: 431; Emphasis in original).

Davy succeeded eventually in obtaining a patent but not in having his British rivals denied, and, upon his emigrating to Australia where he practised his father's profession of medicine, the diffusion of his design ceased although other researchers were to pursue the idea of electro-chemical signal indicators. Cooke and Wheatstone's model was adopted by many British railway companies but, despite seeing Davy off, in the wider world they were not to triumph. Their bane was to be the 'person named *Morse*'. And the reason for his victory over them was less to do with hardware than with what we would today call the software of his system.

Schilling's contribution, it will be remembered, was not just to use the galvanometer but also to understand that encoding the messages was the clue to efficiency. Binary codes were not new but again date back to antiquity; and in the sixth book of *The Advancement and Proficiency of Learning* (1604) Bacon gives an example of one, using the letters A and B as the binary base (Thompson 1947: 311). At the University of Göttingen, in 1833, Gauss and some colleagues rigged up a telegraph from the physics department offices to the University observatory and the magnetic lab, a distance of 1.25 miles. Using a system along Schilling's lines, the Göttingen faculty evolved a four-bit right/left code. In 1835 their apparatus became the first to be powered by a 'magneto-electric machine', a proto-dynamo, rather than a voltaic pile. Morse was to exploit all of these developments, and others.

S.F.B. Morse, 'the American Leonardo', was the son of a New England Congregationalist minister. After Yale, where he had exhibited a talent for art, he had become a professional portraitist and eventually a professor of painting at the forerunner of New York University, the University of the City of New York. A daguerreotypist who took the first photographic portrait in the USA, he was also a child of his time, rabidly anti-immigrant, i.e. anti-Irish and anti-Catholic. His best-known paintings were *Lafayette* and *The House of Representatives* and his under-standing of electricity informal. Crucial to his interest in telegraphy were the fame and proximity of Joseph Henry, subsequently secretary of the Smithsonian but then, in the late 1820s, a professor at the Albany Institute.

By substituting numerous small voltaic cells for the large one usually employed in such experiments, Henry had been able to create an electromagnetic pull sufficiently strong to move an arm with a bell attached. Henry, who was called to the chair of Natural Philosophy in the College of New Jersey (later Princeton) in 1832, publicly demonstrated bell-ringing from afar but did not patent the device. Morse, using Henry's apparatus as a starting point, and the expertise of two of his friends who possessed a broader grounding in electrical studies, built a contrivance wherein the electrical current deflected a marker across a narrow strip of paper, a recording telegraph. The sender used notched sticks which were pulled across the electrical contact to transmit the impulses. In September 1837, some two years after he had first made a working model and five years after he began his experiments, he filed a caveat; the Morse system, with its code, was ready.

Morse's contribution to codes was simple and crucial. He dispatched his assistant Vail and a backer to a printer where the relative frequency of the letters was gauged by examining type-fonts. Previous systems, such as Schilling's, seemed to rely on common sense with the vowels represented by the shortest number of impulses but little further refinement. Morse understood, with Schilling and others, that it was easier to train people to learn a code than to find enough different circuits for electricity to display letters. But Morse's crucial insight was that printers' experience would reveal the most efficient way to construct such a code. It is for this reason that his system prevailed.


## SUPPRESSION AND DIFFUSION: OWNING THE TELEGRAPH

The diffusion of the telegraph was to be a rather vexed affair since the initial supervening necessity, railroad safety, although sufficiently strong to bring the device to the 'invention' stage was not so sustained as to ensure diffusion. Other electrical signalling systems for track control came to be developed and telegraphy was relegated to carrying internal operational messages. The initial need was dissipating even as other factors, including the existence of the semaphore, were working to constrain the diffusion of the new system. The telegraph was saved because new uses were immediately discovered and rapidly developed by the stock market and, especially in North America, newspapers.

In all this, the telegraph reveals how the 'law' of the suppression of radical potential works, even as a series of supervening necessities labours to push the technology out into the world. The first factor to note is a patent war, always a raw expression of the power struggle involved in technological diffusion. In the case of the telegraph such battles were inevitable, given the widespread availability of the technology being deployed by the various systems. The Morse patent was denied altogether in England; the apparatus, unenthusiastically received by the French government, was nationalised there. Even in the US, Morse, who had raised government funds to build the experimental Washington-Baltimore line, had considerable difficulty in diffusing the system further. Morse came close to libelling Henry when the latter began to give expert evidence against him in various patent cases.

Beyond the question of patent, there was also the issue of system ownership. Again, ambiguities and uncertainties work to slow diffusion. In 1845, the Morse line had been operated by the US Post Office and in the first six months of the year it had cost $3284.17 and had brought in $413.44. The Postmaster General asked the crucial question:

> How far the government will allow individuals to divide with it the business of transmitting intelligence – an important duty confided to it by the Constitution, necessarily and properly exclusive. Or will it purchase the telegraph, and conduct its operations for the benefit of the public?
> (Brock 1981: 63)

But the public had thus far shown very little interest in benefiting from the telegraph and the Congress demurred at further involvement with such an economic white elephant. Despite the Postmaster General's talk of 'an instrument so powerful for good or evil' which could not 'with safety be left in the hands of private individuals uncontrolled by law', a crucial privatising precedent was set in American public communications policy. The telegraph was returned to Morse and his backers. This failure to find non-railway uses for it in 1845 thus had profound repercussions. In the USA, the transmission of intelligence was to be neither necessarily nor exclusively a government function. Others, the press and business, could also be involved. After that crucial hesitancy in the first year, stock speculators began to see the utility of the telegraph and the beginnings of that process which today allows global simultaneous participation in a multitude of international money and commodity markets to be demonstrated for the first time. Newspapers became avid consumers of telegrams, which had a considerable effect on their contents. No longer, as in the eighteenth century, was it possible to scoop a rival with 'late intelligences'; now, the telegraph rendered news, like soft fruit, perishable – useless if delayed.

The policy of privatisation thus created was not reversed when such uses made the telegraph into a commonplace a year or so later and private enterprise was creating a system racked with patent disputes, geographical dislocations and redundant duplicated wires. Nor did Congress feel moved to involve itself in either the emergence of the great national private monopoly (Western Union) or the international developments that followed. The principle established with the telegraph was to hold good through all the subsequent technologies until a century and a quarter later Congress allowed commercial corporations into space. What had initially been adopted to avoid wasting taxpayers' dollars became a self-denying ordinance – the government would not engage in profitable communications enterprises. In time, this would help underpin the received opinion that government enterprises in telecommunications (and indeed elsewhere) cannot, by their very nature, be profitable. (This then becomes self-fulfilling: if such enterprises are profitable, then they should be, and are, privatised.)

Henry O'Reilly, significantly himself a newspaperman, secured the rights to exploit the Morse patents in the West on terms which the patentors subsequently regretted and sought to annul. In more sparsely populated country the wires were soon seen as necessities by everybody and O'Reilly did better than anticipated. To escape from the Morse patent, he turned to other telegraphic instruments of which there were a number available. Cooke and Wheatstone, for example, had a prior patent to Morse's in America and there was another machine, that of House, also on the market; but it was Bain's chemical telegraph, a facsimile prototype patented in 1843 along the same lines as the one proposed by Davy, which O'Reilly chose to exploit (Hubbell 1942: 55). The basic principles was to use chemically treated paper in the receiver to interact with the electrical signal. In 1847 an even more sophisticated device, a 'copying telegraph' relying on scanning, was introduced by Bakewell.

By this date, in certain sections, between Louisville and Nashville for instance, O'Reilly and Morse's licensees raced side by side to complete the line. By 1849 there were rival Bain and Morse lines between Boston and Washington and New York and Buffalo. The American courts intervened and in 1851, in a rerun of the struggle between Cooke and Wheatstone and Davy in 1838, held for Morse. The judgement prevented further chaos by declaring the Bain patent invalid and his machine an infringement of Morse's.

With this declaration, the Bain telegraph is removed from the history of this technology but it remains, with Davy's, a pioneering element in the development of the fax and television. There were other prototypes for these as well. Photo-telegraphy, for example, begins with a device, developed by the Abbé Caselli and introduced in 1862, which could transmit daguerreotypes or a facsimile of the sender's handwriting. He sent a picture by wire from Amiens to Paris and with the support of Napoleon III, Caselli established a number of commercial stations, but the slowness of the system prevented him from mounting a real challenge to Morse (Handel 1967: 128). Elisha Gray, the telegraph engineer who was to be beaten to the Washington patent office by Bell, had designed a device which could, with rheostats, electromagnets and styluses, copy a written document telegraph-ically. The facsimile languished for lack of a supervening social necessity. Why send a fax when sending a letter, with multiple daily deliveries at least in the big cities, was so efficient?

In Europe the telegraph, a substitute for the imperial semaphore, was seen as an extension of postal, i.e. state, services. The American Postmaster General's position on the necessity of governmental control was implicitly accepted.

The telegraph is the model of all the electrical signalling systems which follow. Not for the last time was the widespread availability of the technology eventually used to create a working system to lead to disputes in the courts. And, again not for the last time, was flamboyance, charisma and flair to secure for one of many pioneers the accolade 'inventor'. Morse, although by no means the telegraph's 'inventor' in any eureka sense, was nevertheless responsible for the form in which it was eventually diffused. (Only certain extremely conservative English railway companies stuck with alphabetic Cooke and Wheatstone telegraphs beyond the midpoint of the century.) Moreover, the effect of the struggle for control of telegraphy, which worked to limit its disruptive potential, raised the crucial question of public versus private ownership which was also to be heard again and again in the debates about subsequent communication technologies.

# 2

# BEFORE THE SPEAKING
# TELEPHONE

## SCIENTIFIC COMPETENCE: THE TELEPHONE

The earliest practical telephone transmitter consisted of a diaphragm attached to a wire. The end of the wire was dipped into a bowl containing an acid solution and an electrical contact fixed to the bowl. As the voice vibrated the diaphragm so the wire moved. This created a variable resistance in the solution which was registered through the contact. The device was used by Alexander Graham Bell to utter the immortal words 'Mr Watson, come here I want you' on 10 March 1876. Bell did not design this contrivance.

Its specification had been deposited in a caveat – 'a description of an invention not yet perfected' – in the Washington Patent Office nearly a month earlier on 14 February 1876 by Elisha Gray, the co-owner and chief scientist of a Chicago telegraphic equipment manufacturing company. That same day, some two hours earlier it would seem, although no record was kept, Bell patented an 'Improvement in Telegraphy' using electromagnets and a vibrating diaphragm of a kind he had been experimenting with for many months. For the previous couple of years he had been in competition with Gray, both of them in the footsteps of many others, to produce a device which could increase the capacity of telegraph wires by allowing a multiplicity of signals to be carried simultaneously. It is perhaps no wonder then that that evening at 5 Exeter Place, Boston, when it must have dawned on Bell that Gray's design might well transmit sound better than his own, he spilt the acid on his clothing. Bell's patent – US No. 174465 – had been allowed but a week. It had been issued a mere three days before. Yet Gray's machine was clearly superior (and more fully described) than the one Bell had sketched in his deposition. Watson's was not the only help Bell would need.[1]

The line of enquiry which gives rise to the word 'telephone' dates from the seventeenth century. Ear trumpets were developed as signalling systems. For example, Samuel Pepys tried a version of this new invention but noted that it 'was only a great glass bottle broke at the bottom'; nevertheless he put the neck to his ear 'and there did plainly hear the dancing of the oars of the boats in the Thames at Arundel Gallery window, which, without it, I could not in the least do' (Pepys 1953: 205, dated 2 April 1668). Such crude devices worked as transmitters as well. One, 5 feet 6 inches long, 'was tried at Deal Castle by the Governor thereof, the voice being plainly heard off at Sea as far as the King's ships usually ride, which is between two and three miles, at a time when the wind blew from the shore' (Kingsbury 1915: 2).

At the end of the eighteenth century, mindful of the limitations inherent in visual signalling systems such as the then popular semaphore, Huth proposed a system of megaphones for long-distance work. He wrote that the difference between visual and acoustic methods of signalling 'might deserve a different name and it might become necessary to give a different name to telegraphic communication by means of speaking tubes. What would be more appropriate here than a word derived also from the Greek: Telephon or *Fernsprecher*' (Rhodes 1929: 226)? During the next century the word *Telephon* came to denote in German all speaking-tube devices whether electrical or not. Similar usages can be found in French, a communication code using the tonic sol-fa musical scale being described as *téléphonie* in 1828. Sound-from-afar, in that classically educated age, was then more likely than not to be named telephony if any acoustic element was involved in the communication process, irrespective of the hardware used. These devices and systems did not involve the human voice. In 1858 a telegraph device was designated *téléphonie-électrique* in a Paris publication (ibid.: 229–30). The English, being every bit as well educated as the continental Europeans in the classical languages, adopted the same nomenclature. By the mid-nineteenth century in German, and to a lesser extent in French and English, all devices which relayed sound through whatever medium were known in both scientific and popular literature as telephones.

And then, of course, there were the 'Lovers' telegraphs'. They arrived, as the latest fad, in Chicago in December 1875 and Elisha Gray was well aware of them (Prescott 1972: 425). It is also curious that, following the demonstration of the electric telephone in 1876 a number of reputable scientists, including Heaviside (of the layer), devoted their energies to improving the string telephones, one getting a device to operate over nearly half a mile of wire (Moncel 1879: 35–6).

String phones, megaphones, speaking tubes and ear trumpets as well as sound resonators and the telegraph are part of the ground of scientific competence in the broad sense for the modern telephone. In the more usual, limited meanings of science the wave theory of electromagnetic phenomena was also of significance.

In the eighteenth century a number of different concepts explaining the range of electrical phenomenon then known were in circulation. The most potent of these, articulated by the French physicist Dufay after 1733, held electricity to be of two distinct types: 'vitreous' as when glass is rubbed with silk and 'resinous' as when sealing wax is rubbed with fur. Franklin proposed the terms 'positive' and 'negative' for these phenomena and suggested that a single electric fluid was at work but only flowed when positive. The fluid theory, which is still remembered whenever we talk of 'current', was adequate to explain the basic performance of static electricity. With any scientific concept, there are always what Thomas Kuhn would call anomalies – events unexplained by the dominate theory or paradigm (Kuhn 1962: 90–1) – and that was the case here, increasingly as experimental work in dynamic electricity progressed during the century from 1750 on and especially after the introduction of the voltaic battery in 1800. Anomalies unexplained by eighteenth-century electrical theory started accumulating. The experimental work, of course, went forward despite this – as it always does – and with it the development of devices to detect and measure electromagnetic phenomena to which we shall return when considering the development of radio and television.

In 1845, the then dominant Franklin paradigm for electricity was crumbling. By this time, Michael Faraday had been working with electricity for more than a decade. He yoked what he knew of magnetic waves together with Young's 1801 demonstration of light waves (p. 88) to observe that 'magnetic force and light were proved to have a relation to each other'. (Dr Thomas Young was a polymath, now unjustifiably neglected, whose scientific work was of particular importance to the developments of communications and whom we shall therefore meet again in this history.) Faraday hypothesised that light waves might be transverse vibrations travelling along the lines of magnetic and electrical force he was studying. He produced evidence that the electric fluid was made up of particles and theorised that there were lines of force surrounding electrified or magnetised bodies. He added 'This fact will most likely prove exceedingly fertile' (Wilson 1935: 86).

The great experimenter was right. His lines of enquiry foreshadowed the unified electromagnetic wave theory of James Clerk Maxwell which was, a generation later, to bring all these strands together, replacing Franklin's paradigm and absorbing Young's observations. Maxwell's work and its experimental verification by Hertz in the late 1880s lies at the heart of all electronic communications systems.

In 1865, Maxwell broke with eighteenth-century concepts by proposing a wholly new explanation, or paradigm, for electromagnetism:

> The theory I propose may therefore be called a theory of the *electromagnetic field*....The electromagnetic field is that part of space, which contains and surrounds bodies in electric or magnetic conditions. It may be filled with any kind of matter, or we may endeavour to empty it of all gross matter. There is always, however, enough of matter left to receive and transmit the undulations of light and heat, and it is because transmission of these radiations is not greatly altered when transparent bodies of

measurable density are substituted for the so called vacuum, that we are obliged to admit the undulations are those of an ethereal substance, and not of gross matter. . . . We have therefore some reason to believe that there is an ethereal medium filling space and permeating bodies, capable of being set in motion and transmitting that motion from one part to another.

(Maxwell 1865: 460)

Maxwell's mathematisation of these waves is, for all post-telegraph telecommunications technologies, a crucial element in the ground of scientific competence.[2]

These different strands of acoustic and electrical enquiry combine. Sir Charles Wheatstone, who came from a family of musical instrument makers, gave the world the concertina as well as the alphabetic telegraph noted above and was interested in the acoustic aspects of long-range signals. In 1821 he demonstrated the Enchanted Lyre. If the sounding boards of two instruments were joined together Wheatstone showed that notes played on one would be reproduced on the other. For about two years the machine was exhibited in London; and 'so perfect was the illusion [wrote Sir Charles] in this instance from the intense vibratory state of the reciprocating instruments, and from the interception of the sounds of the distant exciting one, that it was universally imagined to be one of the highest efforts of ingenuity in musical mechanism' (Kingsbury 1915: 4). In fact it was an extension of a physical phenomenon known to anybody who had ever put ear to ground, which, as that procedure is described in Pliny, means considerable numbers of people. The relationship between such resonance experiments and the development of the electric telegraph is twofold. Both are concerned with distant signalling. Second, the discovery of certain acoustic phenomena, held to be of the resonance type but connected with electromagnets, promised considerable practical advantage in melding sound with electricity.

The first electromagnetic device which converted electrical waves into sound is credited to a Dr C.G. Page of Massachusetts in 1837. He achieved this effect, which he called 'Galvanic Music' (but which the rest of the world named for him 'the Page effect'), by revolving the armature of an electromagnet in front of a negative and positive electrical pole. Loud sounds were emitted which could be varied by altering the strength of the current in the poles (Fagen 1975: 83). In 1846, M Froment of Paris showed a device which was designed not to create sounds but to analyse those made by Page's effect. His vibrating bar arrangement was a direct precursor of the great physicist Helmholtz's experiment the following decade to show that electrical impulse could be sent down a line and cause a tuning fork to resonate on the principle of sympathetic vibration. A similar acoustic phenomenon using capacitors where different notes were produced as the charge was varied was demonstrated in 1870.

These investigations were seen as having important economic consequences for telegraphy. If a number of Morse senders and receivers could be variously tuned, it was theoretically possible that all these signals, sounding different notes, could be sent down the same wire simultaneously but independently of each other. Increasing the capacity of the wires without physically stringing more of them was obviously economically desirable. Since, although the message was still encoded in dots and dashes, an acoustic element was involved, all the devices for the improvement of telegraphy along these lines were referred to as *telephones* – harmonic or musical telephones.

To move from harmonic telephones to the speaking or articulating telephone required an understanding of another electrical phenomenon, variable resistance. Variable resistance to electricity was found in substances, from sulphuric acid to carbon, under different physical conditions. The Comte Du Moncel, telephony's first historian, had experimented with this from 1856 on and had published his results (Moncel 1879: 144). In 1866, M Clarac of the French telegraphic administration 'constructed tubes containing powdered carbon, the electrical resistance of which could be regulated by increasing the pressure upon it by means of an adjusting screw'. The purpose of the device was simply to demonstrate the variable resistance phenomenon and it flowed from work by Sir William Thomson (Lord Kelvin) which showed that resistance to current in a wire could be varied by putting the wire under tension (Kingsbury 1915: 114–15).

Finally, the move from devices where signalling was accomplished with discrete electrical pulses (e.g. telegraphy) to systems which offered electrical analogues of sound waves (e.g. telephony) required an understanding of human speech. Helmholtz is of importance to this strand of competence too, for contributions to what today would be called psycholinguistics. He published, in 1862, his seminal work *Sensations of Tone* and the fixed pitch theory of vowel tones he enunciated was part of the underpinning of the experiments with harmonic telephones. This work was a facet of an ongoing and widespread interest in the production and reception of human speech.

Alexander Graham Bell was an elocution teacher concerned with deafness. The received impression is that such a man invents the telephone as the very pattern of an inspired nineteenth-century amateur; and further his amateur status is in complete contrast to the way in which things are done these days, not least at the mighty research laboratories that bore his name. But this impression is wrong. There was a continuum between the scientific investigation of electromagnetic phenomena and human communication, as Helmholtz's interests indicate. Bell's father and grandfather, both in the same profession as Alexander, had made distinguished contributions to the psycholinguistic literature of the day (at least in its practical elocutionist aspect). Bell from his childhood was aware of this work, the theory of speech production and the creation of machines to produce human sounds.

Work on speech synthesisers goes back to the eighteenth century. In 1779 the St Petersburg Academy offered a prize for a machine which could reproduce vowel sounds and a number of contrivances were developed, none good enough to win the prize. Bell was not only immersed in this tradition, he also contributed to it, albeit in a small way. His father offered the three Bell boys prizes, after the fashion of the Academy of St Petersburg, for speaking machines. Alexander apparently produced a crude version using the model of a human skull stuffed with India rubber and cotton. His father was acquainted with Sir Charles Wheatstone and borrowed scientific literature from him. Wheatstone himself demonstrated the most successful of the automaton 'speaking machines' to the young Bell. In the 1860s after meeting Alexander Ellis, the man who was to translate Helmholtz into English, Bell also developed an interest in electricity. He read Helmholtz himself in French in 1870, five years before the Ellis translation appeared (Bell 1908: 7, 206–7).

Bell was also aware of the attempts to render speech visible as various systems for translating musical sound pressure waves into a visible form had been proposed in the eighteenth century (Nmungwun 1989: 15). Moreover, his father had invented a universal system of orthography called 'visible speech' as an aide to teaching the deaf. Mechanical devices were designed to the same end or for purer acoustic and linguistic research reasons. For example, acoustic experiments conducted in the early nineteenth century by Young prompted Léon Scott de Martinville to introduce, in 1855, the phonautograph, or sound-writer, a contrivance designed to listen (as it were) rather than to talk. It was to be of considerable consequence both for the telephone and the phonograph.

> This [phonautograph] consisted of a cone over the smaller end of which was tightly stretched a membrane, and hinged at the end of this was a long wooden lever. At the other end of the lever a short pig's bristle was attached and suspended just above the surface of a sheet of glass covered with lampblack. By speaking into the cone and moving the glass, the pig's bristle would trace the pattern of the sound waves.
>
> (Blake 1928: 13)

By 1872 Bell was experimenting along Helmholtzian lines. In the summer of 1874, while immersed in the problems of the harmonic telephone, he took time to build a macabre version of Scott's phonautograph. He obtained the ear of a deceased man and rigged it up to a metal horn with the armature and stylus attached to the ossicles. He got very good tracings from the device (Blake 1928: 15). He was also aware of Koenig's manometic capsule. In this machine the voice acting on a membrane caused a gas flame to flicker. The flame was reflected in a continuously revolving mirror which converted the flickerings into seamless bands of light. Both these devices, like his father's 'visible speech' system of writing, were part of a search to allow the deaf to 'see' speech. Since the patterns produced by these two contrivances differed radically, Bell gave up on them as potentially useful tools in his professional work as a teacher of the deaf. And anyway, as his harmonic telephone researches indicated, his mind was on other matters (Fagen 1975: 2–3).

## IDEATION: SPEECH TRANSMITTED BY ELECTRICITY

The ideation transformation works on elements within the ground of scientific competence. This then leads to devices in the metal during the technological performance phase. Ideation without devices is the technological equivalent of poems lying unread in the bureau drawer. However, the record of the idea does not necessarily have to be clearly articulated. This was certainly the case with the development of the telephone, where no recorded theoretical notions (including those of Bell himself) envisage a fully practical machine. But, as with the telegraph, the wherewithal for the technology was so much to hand that numerous scientists and technologists came close to describing how a speaking telephone might work.

For example, in 1831, Wheatstone wrote:

> When sound is allowed to diffuse itself in all directions as from a centre, its intensity, according to theory, decreases as the square of the distance increases; but if it be confined to one rectilinear direction, no diminution of intensity ought to take place. But this is on the supposition that the conducting body possesses perfect homogeneity. . . .Could any conducting substance be rendered perfectly equal in density and elasticity so as to allow the undulations to proceed with uniform velocity without any reflections or interferences, it would be as easy to transmit sounds through such conductors from Aberdeen to London as it is now to establish communication from one chamber to another. . . .The almost hopeless difficulty of communicating sounds produced in air with sufficient intensity to solid bodies might induce us to despair of further success; but could articulations similar to those enounced by the human organs of speech be produced immediately in solid bodies, their transmission might be effected with any required degree of intensity. Some recent investigations lead us to hope that we are not far from effecting these desiderata.
>
> (Kingsbury 1915: 12–13)

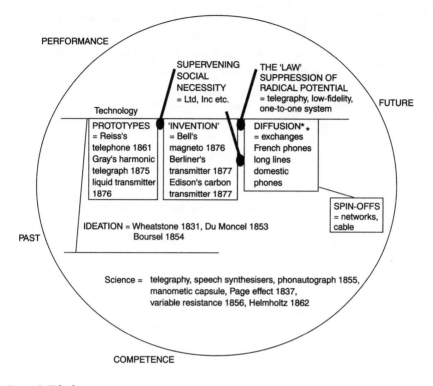

*Figure 9* Telephony

Although Wheatstone, less than a decade away from his telegraph and in the midst of his success with the Enchanted Lyre, did not seem to have electrical signalling in mind, the references to undulations and the notion of creating an analogue of the human voice are essential to the idea of the telephone.

By the mid-eighteenth century, the connection to electricity was being made (Figure 9). Du Moncel, in 1853, envisaged using Page's effect to create with different tunings on various metal plates 'an electric harmonica' (Moncel 1879: 23). A year later Charles Bourseul published the following in Paris:

> I have, for example, asked myself whether speech itself may not be transmitted by electricity – in a word if what is spoken in Vienna may not be heard in Paris. The thing is practical in this way:
>
> We know that sounds are made by vibrations. . . .Suppose a man speaks near a moveable disk, sufficiently flexible to lose none of the vibrations of the voice, that this disk alternately makes and breaks the currents from a battery; you may have at a distance another disk, which

will simultaneously execute the same vibrations. . . .It is, at all events, impossible in the present condition of science to prove the impossibility of transmitting sound by electricity. Everything tends to show, on the contrary, that there is such a possibility. . . .I have made some experiments in this direction: they are delicate, and demand time and patience, but the approximations obtained promise a favourable result.

(Moncel 1879: 13–14)

It is fairly clear that Bourseul's 'approximations' did not amount to an actual machine, but the idea of electric telephony is clearly enunciated. Omitted is the need to impress an analogue of the voice on the current; Bourseul's 'makes and breaks' suggest a digital mode, as in the telegraph.

There was one non-technical impediment to this work. The notion of electrically based voice communication was, from the 1840s on, regarded as chimerical – 'a sort of term of reproach' – and an indication, in any searching for it, of a measure of mental disturbance. Thus when Cooke and Wheatstone went to arbitration to determine which of them should have the credit for their telegraph, it is Cooke's solicitor who constantly uses the word 'telephone' to emphasise, as it were, the impracticality of Wheatstone's ideas (Kingsbury 1915: 11). The telephone sacrificed its respectability as an object of proper scientific inquiry not only because of a succession of more or less non-speaking devices between Bourseul and Bell of the harmonic telephone type but also because of the long tradition of subterfuge associated with remote-controlled speaking figures going back, perhaps, to the oracles of the ancient world. In such a tradition, 'assertions of ventriloquism' continued to find their mark. This factor certainly affected Bell who was inhibited by a fear of ridicule. He was working on the harmonic telephone but he claimed he was thinking about a speaking telephone – the harp – as a sort of piano-sized musical box comb with between 3000 and 5000 tines to replicate the hair-like organ of Corti within the human ear. He explained his failure to construct such a contrivance in the summer of 1874 in part thus: 'Fearing ridicule would be attached to the idea of transmitting vocal sounds telephonically, especially by those unacquainted with Helmholtz's experiments, I said little or nothing of this plan' (Kingsbury 1915: 11).

The following winter, having secured some backing, he continued to pursue the commercially attractive harmonic telephone and began to have his prototypes built for him at a professional telegraphic equipment manufacturers in Boston, where he was assigned the services of a young electrician, Thomas Watson. Watson attests to Bell's continued hesitancy about telephony and its dubious status in 1875.

We discussed the possibility of constructing [a telephone], but nothing was ever done about it for Thomas Sanders and Gardiner G. Hubbard, the two men who were financially and otherwise supporting Bell in his experiments, were urging him to perfect his telegraph, assuring him that then he would have money and time enough to play with his speech-by-telegraph vagary all he pleased. So we pegged away at the telegraph and dreamed about the other vastly more wonderful thing.

(Watson 1926: 62–3)

Clearly, Bell felt confident enough about Watson to share his thinking with him in some detail (even if we may be permitted to doubt a little Watson's claim of total recall):

Bell had a remarkable power for clear and terse explanation. The words he used in giving me the essence of his great idea have remained with me ever since. 'Watson', he said, 'if I can get a mechanism which will make a current of electricity vary in its intensity, as air varies in intensity when a sound is passing through it, I can telegraph any sound, even the sound of speech.' He went on to describe a machine which he thought might do this. It was an apparatus with a multitude of tuned strings, reeds and other vibrating things, all of steel or iron combined with many magnets. It was big, perhaps, as an upright piano.

(Watson 1926: 63)

This account is less lucid than it appears and its inconsistencies find expression first in the patent Bell was awarded a year later and subsequently in the more than 600 legal actions he and his partners fought to defend it.

The 'multitude of tuned strings' has nothing to do with the eventual solution and does not imply a need for a 'mechanism which will make an electric current vary in its intensity'. In fact the rationale Bell gave Watson is somewhat at odds with the device he described, crucially in this matter of variable resistance. Variable resistance was to be at the heart of the telephone transmitter in its *invented* form, but Bell and his supporters had some considerable difficulty laying claim to the concept prior to February 1876. The record yields only one conclusive mention of variable resistance before this date, in a letter written by Bell in May 1875.

Another experiment has occurred to me which, if successful, will pave the way for still greater results than any yet obtained. The strings of a musical instrument in vibrating undergo great changes of *molecular tension*. In fact, the vibration represents the struggle between the tension of the string and the moving force impressed upon it. I have read somewhere that the resistance offered by a wire to the passage of an electric current is affected by the *tension of the wire*. If this is so, a *continuous current of electricity* passed through a vibrating wire should meet with varying resistance, and hence a pulsatory action should be induced in the current. If this turns out to be the case, the oscillations of the current should correspond in *amplitude*, as well as in the rate of movement, to the vibrations of the string. One consequence would be that the *timbre* of a sound could be transmitted.

(Bell 1908: 53; italics in original)

It is curious that Bell should refer to an experiment by Kelvin, later to be one of his most influential supporters and already a famous scientist, in such vague terms: 'I have read somewhere. . . '; but that he did not conduct any experiments with wires under tension for four years and, most importantly, makes only glancing reference to variable resistance in the first patent, is even stranger and of extreme significance.

By 1875 it is clear that Elisha Gray was conceptually closer to the telephone than Bell. Eight years earlier, Gray had made his first experiments in the area of Page's effect and he claimed to conceive then of

the idea of a telephonic system based on the differences of resistance effected in a circuit completed by a liquid where the layer of liquid interposed between the electrodes varies in thickness under the influence of the telegraphic plate which is in connection with one of the electrodes.

(Moncel 1879: 86)

It would seem reasonable to suggest that Gray too was being tendentious here. The concept is most unlikely to have been so well formed at the early date claimed, especially since Gray, by his own account, did not pursue the idea for some years. Gray went on to achieve a great deal with his harmonic telephone researches, but he also continued with less focused work. In 1874 he was conducting some experiments with a battery and the zinc lining of a bathtub which demonstrated that he could amplify the galvanic noise by friction and pressure (Prescott 1972: 452).

Then the following December, in Milwaukee, he saw the lovers' telegraph which he stated:

proved to my mind that the movements of a single point on the diaphragm corresponded accurately with the movements of the air produced by any spoken word or sound. I saw that if I could reproduce electronically the same motions that were made mechanically at the centre of the diaphragm by speaking upon it, such electrical vibrations would be reproduced upon a common receiver in the same manner that musical tones were. . . .The fact that the longitudinal movement (in water or other fluid of poor conducting quality) of a wire or some good conductor of electricity, with reference to another wire or metal conductor, produced variations in the resistance of an electric circuit proportional to the amplitude of movement, was old in the art of that time; so that the last link of knowledge necessary to solve the problem in my mind was furnished in the capabilities of the longitudinal vibrations of the string in the before mentioned so called lovers' telegraph.

(Prescott 1972: 452–3)

Without any experimentation in the metal, Gray simply, in February 1876, designed a system along these lines and filed it as a caveat – an incomplete 'invention' but a warning to others that an investigation was under way – a few hours (apparently) after Bell filed for his patent. The caveat was quite clear that the object of the device was 'to transmit the tones of the human voice through a telegraphic circuit and reproduce them at the receiving end of the line, so that actual conversations can be carried on by persons at long distances apart' (Prescott 1972: 453). The transmitter consisted of a tube, in the shape of a flat-bottomed flask, the bottom of which was covered with a membrane. A platinum wire ran from the centre of the membrane into a small container of sulphuric acid which was connected to a battery. The other battery terminal was a button set into the bottom of the container. His planned receiver was an electromagnetic device of less sophistication than that which Bell had already built. Because of this, although it was clear that the transmitter was better than Bell's (as was proved by Bell's building one virtually identical to it on 10 March 1876) it was equally true that Gray, like Bell, was some way away from a system.

Apart from the simultaneous arrival of the plans at the patent office, there is a distinction of style between the two men. Bell patented a telegraphic device, which was finished as such and had been built but was not a fully practical speaking telephone system. He described it as an improvement in telegraphy not only because that was what it was but also presumably because he needed to satisfy his backers that he was not wasting their money on a 'speech-by-telegraph vagary'. Nevertheless there was a certain boldness about his approach:

I was so satisfied in my own mind that I had solved the problem of the transmission of articulate speech, that I ventured to describe and claim my method and apparatus in a United States patent, without waiting for better results; in full confidence that the problem had been solved, and that my instruments *would turn out to be* operative speaking telephones. I was more concerned about taking out a caveat or patent than about further experiments. I believed I had experimented sufficiently to entitle me to a patent.

(Bell 1908: 339; emphasis added)

In the event, Bell's confidence was somewhat misplaced. His instruments turned out to be operative *listening* telephones, i.e. receivers. They were never to work very well as transmitters.

Gray, on the other hand, built nothing but was on conceptually sounder ground, at least as far as the transmitter was concerned, and was clear about his telephonic intentions. There was no talk of harmonic telegraphy in the caveat. It can be strongly argued that as far as telephony was concerned Bell too should have petitioned for a caveat. These confusions were confounded when a year later Gray wrote, to Bell in words he was increasingly to regret: 'I do not, however, claim even the credit of inventing it [the telephone], as I do not believe a mere description of an idea that has never been reduced to practice – in the strict sense of that phrase – should be dignified with the name of invention' (Prescott 1972: 458).

It is true that originally patents were granted to people who, in terms of the oldest statute on this matter, that of the republic of Venice, 1474, '*build* any new and ingenious device in this City' (Congress 1964: 11; emphasis added). The statute was designed to give to practical innovators exactly the protection given by copyright to authors (or rather publishers). It arose simultaneously with the introduction of printing and the earliest surviving patent was granted to John of Speyer exactly for the introduction of movable type into Venice. A century later the concept reached the Common Law, was conformed to the pre-existing English system of grants from the crown, in the form of an open (or patent) letter for a monopoly, and was first codified in 1623 as the Statute of Monopolies. As the law developed, Patent Offices were established – that of the United States in 1790 – and *build* was glossed to include processes. The patent system under which Gray and Bell were operating required either partial or full specifications of the contrivance, not the contrivance itself nor proof that it really worked. Gray's scrupulous disclaimer was therefore quite unnecessary in law. His was not 'a mere description', although such would have sufficed, but a rather more fully described system than Bell's, yet he chose to register it as a partial innovation while Bell claimed his partial innovation was complete. Boldness (and, as is explained below, some bureaucratic help) was to carry the day.

Both Bell and Gray met one essential patent requirement, that the contrivance be useful. The issue is which of them met the other essential, that it be novel. It is obvious from this account that the ideation of telephony was within the state of art at this time and not dependent on advances in any technological or scientific area.

It should therefore come as no surprise that the indefatigable Du Moncel, in his exhaustive catalogue of early workers, mentions that neither Bell nor Gray was first with the liquid version of variable resistance:

> It is a curious fact worth recording here, that Mr. Yates of Dublin, in 1865 when trying to improve Reiss's telephone, realised to a certain extent Mr. Gray's concept of the liquid transmitter for he introduced into the platinum contacts of Mr. Reiss's instruments a drop of water, which adapted it for the reproduction of articulate sounds. However no notice was then taken of this result.
>
> (Moncel 1879: 59)

So much for the idea of the telephone. What of actual machines?

## PROTOTYPES: ELECTRICAL SPEAKING TELEPHONES BEFORE 1877

Mr Yates was tinkering with the device that was to cause Bell even more trouble than Gray's caveat, a widely known apparatus called a 'telephone', the creation of Philip Reiss. 'Probably the physics laboratory of every well-equipped college in the world had one in 1870', according to Thomas Watson (Watson 1926: 167).

During the prototype phase, apparatus will often already be to hand, serving other purposes – a parallel prototype, in my terminology. This would be the case with radio, where Marconi first utilised Hertz's coherer, or television when Rozing adapted the oscilloscope. Here in telephony Reiss's contrivance is a parallel prototype of the same type. It is in fact a kind of 'invention' in a line of devices, technological performances, all designed to demonstrate one or another aspect of wave theory. The supervening necessity for these machines was the need to validate Helmholtz's theoretical discussion of waves.

In 1860, by putting together the noise-emitting electromagnets of Page with the vibrating diaphragm of Scott's phonautograph, Philip Reiss created, for the advanced study of electromagnetic phenomena, a 'telephone'. He was a teacher in Frankfurt who seemed to have been aware of both Helmholtz's early formulation of a sound wave theory, knowing perhaps of a popular lecture given by Helmholtz three years previously, and Bourseul's outline of an electric telephone on 'makes and breaks' principles. Reiss built a sounding box with a speaking tube attached to one side. In the top of the box was a large circular opening, across which was stretched a membrane. At the centre of this was fitted a thin disk of platinum. A metallic point rested above the platinum – a hinged 'movable lever touching the membrane'. At its other end the lever acted upon a morse key whose impulses were sent via an electromagnet to a receiver (Moncel 1879: 16, Kingsbury 1915: 128–30).

Reiss knew about waves but did not know how to impress sound waves on an electrical current. He did not in effect understand the need to vary the carrying current by means of a variable resistance mechanism. Nevertheless, the Reiss transmitter had a number of sophisticated features, the most important of which was that it relied on a single diaphragm. It also used electromagnets to create a constant current upon which the endlessly making-and-breaking signals of the morse sender could react. Despite these severe limitations, it was close to being a working telephone and a rich source of inspiration. Reiss himself made three other variations and Mr Yates was but one of many copyists. In 1868 a refined Reiss telephone was demonstrated by a singer at the Cooper Union, New York: 'The vocal airs were faithfully reproduced but rather weak and nasal' (Moncel 1879: 21). Throughout the 1860s other scientists improved the device, normally by doubling the coils in the receiving box or increasing the reverberations in the sending box by means of partitions. Elisha Gray was among this number.

Gray had a distinguished career as an innovator, with major advances in facsimile telegraphy to his credit. In 1869, he founded Gray and Barton, a telegraphic equipment manufacturing firm in Cleveland, which was to become Western Electric of Chicago. Obviously as a supplier to the telegraphy industry, Gray would gain tremendous commercial advantage with the marketing of a multiple harmonic telephone and Reiss's apparatus seemed an attractive jumping-off point. Backed by an entrepreneur who had made his fortune in dental supplies, Gray began serious work on this project in 1874. In April he constructed a transmitter on a diatonic scale, which he began demonstrating in May. By December 1874, Gray had sold the device to William Orton of Western Union, with whom he anyway had a close working relationship, and had filed for a patent on this harmonic or musical telegraph (or 'telephone'). The patent was granted in February 1875. Apart from its telegraphic importance, it was complex enough, when fitted with a range of vibrating disks arranged in a scale, to be 'a new kind of instrument' upon which a piece of music, at least from the accordion or harmonium repertoire, could be played.

So important to Gray was this harmonic telephone that its exploitation distracted him in his patent battle with Bell. He had been told in February 1876 of the existence of a rival telephone scheme, as the law on caveats required, and had learned in March its details and that Bell was the patentee. In May 1876, he took his harmonic telephone to the Philadelphia Centennial Exhibition where he met Bell. The following month he constructed a model of his speaking telephone and in November finally made the one exactly specified in his caveat (Prescott 1972: 457). Gray's inactivity is difficult to explain. Perhaps the fact that Orton and therefore Western Union were uninterested in telephony at this point contributed and perhaps he, like Bell in 1874, was inhibited because of telephony's poor reputation. For instance his Western Electric partner, Enos Barton, went on record as saying: 'I well remember my disgust when someone told me it was possible to send conversation along a wire' (Brooks 1976: 83).

Bell, who had emigrated from Scotland and had established himself in Boston as a teacher of the deaf in 1871, knew that Gray was demonstrating a machine. He produced an alternative harmonic telegraph which worked well enough for him to convince the parents of two of his deaf pupils that he might have a device in sight. Thomas Sanders, in whose mother's house he was lodging and whose son he was teaching, joined the lawyer Gardiner Hubbard in an informal arrangement backing Bell. (The relationship went beyond business. Hubbard's daughter, Mabel, then a teenager and also deaf, eventually married Bell.) Money in support of the project was forthcoming following Hubbard's search of the patents in October 1874, because Gray, despite growing publicity, had still not yet filed on the musical telegraph. Bell was well aware of the threat that Gray posed to his work and he wrote to Hubbard and Sanders in November 1874 that 'It is a neck and neck race between Mr. Gray and myself who shall complete the apparatus first' (Brooks 1976: 43) This is again a little disingenuous since Gray was many months further advanced. However, Bell did manage to patent an harmonic device. More importantly in the course of subsequent development work, on 2 June 1875, an accident occurred that was to lead directly to the first telephone patent.

Despite the references in the May 1875 letter to a continuous current and variable resistance, nothing of the sort had been built into the devices with which Bell and Watson were tinkering. Then Watson accidentally created such a current when one of the tuning reeds malfunctioned and he flicked it manually – and in the other work room Bell heard the echo of the twang. Watson's account will serve to indicate the importance attached to this event by the Bell interests:

> The twang of that reed I plucked on June 2nd, 1875, marked the birth of one of the greatest of modern inventions, for when the electrically carried ghost of that twang reached Bell's ear his teeming brain shaped the first electric speaking phone the world has ever known. The sound of that twang has certainly been heard round the world and its vibration will never cease as long as man exists.
>
> (Watson 1926: 68)

Bell thought again of the single membrane of the phonautograph he had been working on in 1874 and overnight Watson built to Bell's specification the gallows telephone, so called because of the shape of its wooden frame. In it an armature was mounted so that one end was attached to an electromagnet while the other rested in the middle of a stretched membrane. In the transmitter a cone directed sounds towards the membrane; in the receiver the cone was reversed to collect sounds coming from the membrane. Using this apparatus Watson 'could unmistakably hear the tones of his [Bell's] voice and *almost catch a word now and then*. Bell was disappointed with this "meagre result" ' (Watson 1926: 71; emphasis added). By July, according to Bell, 'Articulated sounds were. . .unmistakably transmitted, but it was difficult to make out what was said' (Bell 1908: 338).

But Bell was under considerable pressure. Gray was marketing the device Bell was supposed to be inventing and his backer, Hubbard, was denying him Mabel, with whom he had fallen in love, until he came up with something. After the day of the twang, Bell and Watson abandoned tuned reeds and switched to magnets, thereby producing the contrivance which was patented as an 'Improvement in Telegraphy' the following year. Patent #174465 issued on 7 March 1876 proclaimed:

> My present invention consists in the employment of a vibratory or undulatory current of electricity in contradistinction to a merely intermittent or pulsatory current and the method of, and apparatus for, producing electrical undulations upon the line wire. . . .The advantages I claim to derive from the use of an undulatory current in place of a merely intermittent one are, first, that a very much larger number of signals can be transmitted simultaneously on the same circuit.
>
> (Bell 1908: 458)

No mention of speech. The fact that Bell claimed this as the first speaking telephone is contained in the following, some pages further on in the patent:

> I desire here to remark that there are many other uses to which these instruments may be put, such as the simultaneous transmission of musical notes, differing in loudness as well as in pitch, and the telegraphic transmission of noises or sounds of any kind.
>
> (Bell 1908: 458–9)

Again, no specific reference to speech. Indeed why would there be, since 'no really convincing demonstration of the transmission of audible and recognisable speech was made before the deposit of the specification' (Kingsbury 1915: 46).

As it was lodged, the body of Bell's text contained no reference to variable resistance either. Instead Bell thought to produce 'undulations in a continuous voltaic battery circuit by gradually increasing and diminishing the power of the battery (Bell 1908: 460). It is only in a 'For instance', added in the margin, that the clearest reference to variable resistance and a liquid is found:

For instance, let mercury or some other liquid form part of the voltaic circuit, then the more deeply the conducting wire is immersed in the mercury or other liquid, the less resistance does the liquid offer to the passage of the current.

(Bell 1908: 457)

The most serious attack mounted against Bell questioned the validity of these crucially important marginalia some years later when the official concerned, Zenas Wilbur, confessed before a congressional inquiry that he had illegally informed Bell's Washington attorneys of the contents of Gray's caveat, not just, as was required, of its existence. But the supposition that Bell had added the references to variable resistance after receiving this information remained, in a case involving Gray that went to the Supreme Court, unsubstantiated.

Yet Bell never really satisfactorily explained why he had not even toyed with liquid transmitters earlier, nor had he included a fuller description of variable resistance in the body of the patent. Bell told the court: 'Almost at the last moment before sending this specification to Washington to be engrossed, I discovered that I had neglected to include in it the variable resistance mode of producing electrical undulations, upon which I had been at work in the spring of 1875' (Bell 1908: 86). But the May 1875 letter was concerned with stretched wires, not mercury. Moreover, Bell had been summoned to the Patent Office on 26 February to explain certain points of similarity between his latest January patent application and the one he had been awarded for the harmonic telegraph a year earlier. After this visit at the latest, Bell knew, and admitted as much in a letter to Gray dated 2 March 1876, that the latter's caveat 'had something to do with the vibration of wire in water [sic]' (Bell 1908: 433). Bell satisfied the Examiner that his current application was wholly new, which resulted in the grant of 7 March; but the presumption remains that Bell re-examined the document he had signed the previous January after he knew of Gray's vibrating wire. What has never been established is whether or not he actually added the variable resistance note at that time.

Bell could have avoided the implication of fraudulent practice if he had had another copy of the document with the variable resistance clause inscribed, which antedated the disclosure of the Gray caveat. There was indeed another such document, the copy prepared for deposit in Britain. Bell's application had been returned to him by his lawyers for signature on 18 January 1876 and he handed over the copy to a friend, George Brown, in New York a week later. Brown was to take it to London yet Bell, 'by some accident' forgot to add the variable resistance clause to this version as well. (The copy was never deposited because of Brown's 'fear of ridicule' which caused him not only to fail to lodge the document but to lose it altogether.)

In short, Bell had patented mercury 'or some other liquid' but had then abandoned the entire liquid transmitter technology, although it worked while his magnetos did not. He had never conducted a liquid transmitter experiment prior to March 1876, when he had learned of Gray's idea. He had never mentioned the possibility of such a transmitter anywhere except in the margin of Patent #174465, supposedly written before 18 January. He had forgotten to include variable resistance twice, in both the original and the English copy. He was in Washington in the Patent Office late in February and had the opportunity to amend his submission. Finally, the combination of liquid transmitter and magneto receiver dramatically improved the meagre results achieved with magnets alone. The upset acid was quite forgotten by Bell 'in his joy over the success of the new transmitter when I told him how plainly I had heard his words, and,' wrote Watson, 'his joy was increased when he went to the end of the wire and heard how distinctly my voice came through' (Watson 1926: 78).

Yet, despite this success, in the late spring of 1876, work resumed on magneto transmitters alone. The developed contrivance looked in section somewhat like a squat revolver of enormous bore, its barrel being the speaking cone (Fagen 1975: 12). A new receiver was also built. It was in the form of a cylindrical iron box wherein a coil of wire was wound round a central core, making an electromagnet. An iron lid fixed to the top acted as the diaphragm. These devices were demonstrated in May to the American Academy of Arts and Sciences and at MIT. The decision was made to take the apparatus to the Philadelphia Centennial Exhibition. Watson made a number of instruments, a membrane transmitter (which became known thereafter as the Centennial single pole telephone), a variant designated the Centennial double pole telephone, an iron box receiver and the liquid transmitter which was also taken to the show (Kingsbury 1915: 49). On 25 June 1876 (the day of Custer's last stand), the speaking telephone was demonstrated for the first time to the public which fortuitously included Dom Pedro, the Emperor of Brazil, and Kelvin. It worked well enough for messages to be understood, but the distance was short and the utterances needed to be clichés like 'Mary had a little lamb'.

As Norbert Wiener pointed out, clichés contain less information than great poems and, being largely redundant (in Information Theory terms – see p. 153), can be effectively guessed at (Wiener 1954: 31). Bell understood this too:

> familiar quotations – like 'To be or not to be,' etc., – counting – like 1, 2, 3, 4, 5, etc., – were very readily understood. But expectancy had a good deal to do with this, as language read from a book was not, I think, as a rule, understood, although a few words could be made out here and there.
>
> (Bell 1908: 93)

Kelvin, speaking in Glasgow upon his return, attested that he heard 'To be or not to be? There's the rub' [sic] and 'some extracts from the New York papers'. 'This discovery,' he went on, 'the wonder of wonders in electric telegraphy, is due to a young fellow-countryman of our own, Mr. Graham Bell, a native of Edinburgh, and now naturalised in New York' (Moncel 1879: 37).

Most of the cases fought over the Bell master patent were worthless, the protagonists, naked adventurers who came forward claiming, typically, to have produced a telephone out of tin cans and broken cups at one point or another in the 1850s (Rhodes 1929: 207–10). Given its shaky technological base and its eventual enormous value, it is scarcely surprising that the patent should have been so hard pressed; it was to the Bell empire, the world's richest enterprise, what the Decretals of Constantine were to the Roman Church. The patent war is the first element of the operation of the 'law' of the suppression of radical potential as it applies to telephony. It was occasioned not by technology *per se* but more because the patent had been awarded to a partial prototype system. It was a premature licence and that alone encouraged litigation. Since 'lack of novelty is fatal to a patent', Gray's caveat and Philip Reiss's apparatus were the greatest dangers.

Gray was, in effect, bought out. In the first years of Bell's publicising the telephone, he abided by his letter and never claimed the technology. Eventually he made his personal peace with the National Bell Company, with the receipt of an *ex gratia* payment of $100,000. Even more significantly, he contracted his company, Western Electric, to become Bell's sole equipment manufacturer, an arrangement which was to survive the better part of a century's anti-monopoly attacks by the US Justice Department. Only patent official Wilbur's revelations more than a decade later stirred him to contest the issue. But by then it was too late and his claim failed.

The efficacy of the Reiss device as a speaking telephone was most extensively examined in a case brought in 1881 by the Bell Company against Amos Dolbear, Professor of Physics at Tufts College, for infringement of Bell's patents. Dolbear had assigned his own patents for a telephone to the American Speaking Telephone Company, a subsidiary of Western Union (Rhodes 1929: 210). Dolbear's defence to the suite was that Bell's patent of February 1876 was improperly awarded since the device described would not work and that Reiss's unpatented device of 1860 would work just as well. The Reiss machine was tried in open court and was generally reported as an utter failure. But this must be placed in context. In court, of the hundred things uttered into the Reiss telephone, only about fifteen could be guessed at and only about half of those were right. Poor though this was, it was not an 'utterly unintelligible rattle' as Watson (and most others) would have it (Rhodes 1929: 210). Equally, the other Dolbear contention, that the gallows telephone did not work, has, as I indicated above, some considerable merit.

All this is not to claim that the Reiss device worked and the first Bell telephone did not. Rather, it is to call attention to the somewhat overstated claims as to the difference in performance of the two machines which was no doubt engendered by lawyers representing interests which were already worth millions by the 1880s. National prejudice in this age of high imperialism also played a role. For instance, the great scientist Lord Kelvin (who although born in Belfast had lived in Glasgow from the age of 8) claimed Bell for Scotland and pronounced his machine a 'daring invention' (Moncel 1879: 37). One US judge, convinced of the superiority of the Caledonian/American over the German device, ruled that 'a century of Reiss would never have produced a speaking telephone by mere improvement in construction'. This overstated and modern experimentation with the Reiss telephone reveals just how close he had come.

The essential question is, 'How close did he want to come?' That he called his device a telephone means very little given the common German usage of that term in the nineteenth century. It does, though, seem likely, that (as some Bell partisans claimed) 'Reiss was not looking for the small still voice'. Instead he was seeking to demonstrate the reproduction of an undulatory sound wave by electricity, possibly with a view to amplifying it. Be that as it may, the point is that Reiss's telephone, the various harmonic telephones (or telegraphs), Bell's and Gray's liquid transmitters, the Centennial single pole telephone, the double pole and the iron box receiver were all prototypes, and partial prototypes at that, for the speaking telephone.

# 3

# THE CAPTURE OF SOUND

It is unlikely that Philip Reiss, researcher into Helmholtz's wave theory, was particularly looking for a system to transmit the human voice. Physics, as the supervening social necessity in play, did not require it. Indeed, there was no clearly defined need for such a thing in any sphere, although as the middle decades of the century progressed one did emerge. The single major factor impacting on a whole range of technological developments in these years, including telephony, was the legal creation of the modern corporation.

The limited liability company first came into its own in the years after the Civil War in America or, in Britain, after the Companies Act of 1862. These refined commercial operations necessitated the modern office and the building to house it. Up to the 1870s, even in the USA, five-storey streetscapes were the norm. The tallest building in the world in 1873 was the Tribune office in New York. It had eleven floors (Leapman 1983: 50). The seventeen-storey Mondanock building was erected in 1881.

> This age found its form, as early as the 1880s in America, in a new type of office building: symbolically a sort of vertical human filing case, with uniform windows, a uniform facade, uniform accommodations, rising floor by floor in competition for light and air and above all financial prestige with other skyscrapers. The abstractions of high finance produced their exact material embodiment in these buildings.
>
> (Mumford 1966: 609)

This in turn accelerated the introduction of the geared hydraulic passenger elevator (C. 1885),[1] the typewriter (patented first in 1714 but only appearing in its modern shift-key form in 1878), the modern mechanical desk calculator (1875) and the telephone (finally perfected between 1876 and 1879). In step with all these developments was the emergence of the legal entity called the limited company.

In the common law, chartered joint stock companies first appeared in the 1390s as the legal creations of the crown. Charters were difficult to obtain, costly and, from the point of view of the partners, difficult to control. By the eighteenth century such companies were seen as a 'common nuisance' tending to 'the common grievance prejudice and inconvenience of His Majesty's subjects or great numbers of them in trade, commerce or other lawful affairs' but markets in their shares were well established. The need for something more efficient was another consequence of the coming of the railway and the insatiable need for capital thereby created: 'The railways greatly advanced joint-stock company development both by their example and by the demand they induced in potential investors in other enterprises for railway-type security of investment' (Dyos and Aldcroft 1974: 203). In 1837 a report on the law of partnership proposed that all companies which so wished could be incorporated by publishing their objects and constitution in a register established by the state for that purpose (Harding 1966: 376). This was implemented in 1844 at the onset of the first major railway boom. The concept of limited liability was introduced in 1856 and the entire law of companies was consolidated in an act of 1862 which remains the basis of modern English practice.

Much the same pattern can be noticed in America, although the legal aspects of the developments were somewhat more rapid. A charter of incorporation was regarded as a privilege (or *franchise* in the Norman-French) in the first century of the republic and franchises were awarded to run railways and ferries or to have sole rights to trade in particular areas. Incorporation for 'any lawful business' was allowed first in Connecticut in 1837, the pressure for such an opportunity coming from the New England textile industry. However, before the Civil War, companies were still held by relatively few shareholders. The consolidation of small railways, which began in 1853 with the creation of the New York Central, led to more diffused ownership and, indeed, stock market battles for control in the 1860s. 'Since the Civil War, the quasi-public corporation has come to dominate the railroad field almost completely. . . . Following the lead of the railroads, in the last part of the Nineteenth Century and in the early years of the Twentieth, one aspect of economic life after another has come under corporate sway' (Berke and Meons 1932: 23, 129, 137). From the 1850s, the joint stock company was also to be found in Europe as well as 'a new kind of finance house' which used the savings of investors too small to engage in the stock market directly to buy shares in these new enterprises (Henderson 1969: 31).

The telephone, and all the other office devices, were born into a 'Great Depression', an economic downturn which was to last until the early 1890s.

Nevertheless, these technologies were also born into a world where industrialis-ation was continuing apace. These were the years when cities in both the US and UK got running tap water and gas lighting for the first time. In Birmingham the mayor, Joseph Chamberlain, began the processes of municipal socialism – slum clearance, sewage, water, street lighting, free libraries and art galleries. In America between 1871 and 1881 the number of federal employees doubled to more than 100,000 (Brock 1973: 418). By 1876 the American countryside no longer dominated the economy. And, everywhere, the great age of imperial expansion dawned, funded by the capital the limited companies facilitated. Between 1875 and 1900 the British Empire, the leader of this process, increased by 5 million square miles and 90 million people (Cole and Postgate 1961: 403).

The first telephone wire was erected in April 1877 by Charles Williams Jr to connect his home in Somerville to his factory in Boston (Stehman 1925: 4) (Williams had employed Watson and owned the electrical workshops where Bell conducted his 1875 experiments.) Although obviously the social uses of the telephone were appreciated from the very beginning (Marvin 1988: 87–92), the relative utility of the technology for business as opposed to pleasure was reflected in the lease terms. In the advertisement announcing the availability of the telephone, the Bell Telephone Association stated: 'The terms for leasing two telephones for social purposes connecting a dwelling house with any other building will be $20 a year; for business purposes $40 a year, payable semi-annually in advance' (Stehman 1925: 7).

The first use of a telephone for news reporting was on 3 April 1877 when word of one of Bell's lectures was transmitted from Salem to the *Boston Globe*. The proprietor of a burglar alarm system installed telephones so that his customers could summon messengers and express service. Another early telephone exchange (central office) connected a Boston drugstore with twenty-one local doctors. Bell himself, in seeking investors, downplayed the private home and pushed the telephone 'as a means of communication between bankers, merchants, manufac-turers, wholesale and retail dealers, dock companies, water companies, police offices, fire stations, newspaper offices, hospitals and public buildings, and for use in railway offices, in mines and (diving) operations' (Fagen 1975: 17).

Prominent among the first 778 telephone users in the spring of 1877 were those New York stockbrokers who, after they had realised its potential, had become early customers of the telegraph companies and whose support had created Western Union's highly profitable Gold and Stock Telegraph Company subsidiary. In Manhattan fifty years later, in the late 1920s, there were twice as many private switchboard attendants in businesses as there were Bell central exchange operators (Brock 1981: 93). 'Although we accept the telephone as a basic component of US households, it was primarily a business tool during the first 50 years of growth. It was not until after World War II that most households leased a telephone' (Carey and Moss 1985: 4). The pace is even slower in other industrialised nations. For all its obvious usefulness in the home, the telephone is a child of commerce, specifically of mid-nineteenth century commercial developments.

## 'INVENTION': CREATING THE TELEPHONE TO ORDER

The publicity at the Philadelphia Exhibition, the accident of the interest of Dom Pedro of Brazil and Kelvin's advocacy, as well as Bell's not inconsiderable effectiveness as a lecturer, inscribed the speaking telephone on public consciousness as the latest technical marvel, but in terms of science and practicality it was, throughout 1876, barely more than a toy. In the aftermath, Bell did nothing less than set about 'inventing' a more practical, less toy-like system, one that would operate efficiently but eschew any liquid variable resistance mechanism.

Using an improved metal diaphragm and more powerful magnets, Watson and Bell created the magnet telephone which Bell patented, still as an 'Improvement in Electric Telegraphy', in January 1877. Bell was offering it for sale by the following spring (Fagen 1975: 17). This further patent provided a securer foundation for the Bell empire by clearly stating that, after multiple telegraphic transmission, the invention's secondary object was 'the electrical transmission . . .of articulate speech and sound of every kind' (Bell 1908: 464). Bell had now produced a viable receiver which was to prove a real obstacle to his rivals, none of whom was able to develop an alternative; yet, as a transmitter, it was still quite deficient. Some sense of its limitations can be gleaned from the circular announcing its availability:

> The proprietors of the telephone, the invention of Alexander Graham Bell, for which patents have been issued by the United States and Great Britain, are now prepared to furnish telephones for the transmission of articulate speech through instruments not more than twenty miles apart. Conversation can easily be carried on after slight practice and with occasional repetition of a word or sentence. On first listening to the telephone, although the sound is perfectly audible, the articulation seems to be indistinct, but after a few trials the ear becomes accustomed to the peculiar sound and finds little difficulty in understanding the words.
>
> (Stehman 1925: 6)

This, it should be emphasised, is no hostile account of the apparatus but Bell's own advertisement. The race for a transmitter was still wide open.

Thomas Edison claimed independently to have noticed the variable resistance of substances under pressure in 1873, some years after the result was reported by the French. It was not until January 1877, prompted by the work of Bell and Gray, that Edison recalled his 1873 experiment. By mounting the diaphragm above a layer of one of these substances – plumbago initially, although in Edison's usual fashion many materials were tried – which formed part of an electric circuit, Edison impressed the sound wave form on to the electrical wave. The sensitivity of the telephone transmitter was much improved. It was not, as was the case with Bell's magnetos, voice driven, as it were; one did not need to bellow, but it was even less distinct than were the magnetos. Throughout 1877, Edison tried to improve performance and at least ten other devices, variations of this technical theme, were produced and included, since the technology is cognate, some which might be better described as microphones (Prescott 1972: 119–21).

The term microphone was adapted from an acoustical usage of Wheatstone's (for a species of stethoscope) by David Hughes. Hughes constructed a primitive machine which consisted of nothing but two nails mounted on a wooden base-board, attached to the poles of a battery, with a third nail loosely laid across them which was sensitive enough to acoustic vibrations to vary a current. He also experimented with a carbon pencil mounted vertically in between conical depress-ions made in two carbon blocks. A paper describing these experiments was read before the Royal Society in London in May 1878 and 'microphone' was adopted as the term of art for any acoustically sensitive loose contact device (Fagen 1975: 66–7; Prescott 1972: 142). That he was working on these lines at the same time as Edison was to be of importance in the patent battle. Edison was to claim bitterly that the credit for the microphone should be his.

Edison filed patents on the plumbago transmitter in 1877 and on the lampblack version early in 1878. Now Orton, having spurned Bell exactly because he saw telegraphy and telephony as distinct technologies and did not want Western Union to be in the telephone business, changed his mind. He was driven by the threat encapsulated in the enthusiasm of the New York stockbrokers, some of his best telegraphy customers, for the new technology. In 1878, he moved to add Edison's carbon transmitter patents to the arrangements he had previously made with Gray and Dolbear. Using these other patents and devices Orton established the Amer-ican Speaking Telephone Company to rival the emerging Bell Companies. Orton made considerable inroads into Bell's nascent business. On 1 May, the *Telegraphic Journal* published the results of a test which found Edison's device worked best and was least subject to interference on the 106-mile long line between New York and Philadelphia, thus confirming what the small market in telephones was also demonstrating – carbon transmitters were superior. Before the patent interference examiner, Edison went on record swearing that: 'he never conceived the possibility of transmitting articulated speech by talking against a diaphragm in front of an electro magnet.' He went on that 'he did most emphatically give Mr. Bell the

credit of the discovery of the transmission of articulated speech by that principle'
(Prescott 1972: 460). In other words, he had produced something different – and
better. He might as well be generous to Bell on this point (Bryan 1926: 76).

But the system involved pirating Bell's receiver via Dolbear's improvements. A
legal attack on the telegraph company was mounted by the telephone company,
grounded both on the unlicensed use of magnetos and Bell's marginal references to
variable resistance in the original 1876 patent. The fledgling Bell firm took on
Western Union, then one of the world's biggest enterprises, and at the same time
sought a device that would use the variable resistance principle in a transmitter
without copying either Gray or Edison. Watson was deputed, in a manner
normally considered to be peculiar to the twentieth century, to 'invent' a non-
liquid transmitter. National Bell's counsel advised that although he thought the
master patent could withstand Edison, using carbon would give hostages to
fortune. Watson had to produce a non-liquid *and* carbon-less variable resistance
transmitter. This daunting task, however, was less problematic than it seemed, for
Watson had seen the answer to Edison the previous summer.

Emile Berliner had arrived in the United States in 1870 as a 19-year-old. Six
years later, he was a clerk in a Washington DC dry-goods store. Among his
acquaintances was the chief operator at the fire alarm telegraph office. One night,
while practising 'sending', his friend told him, 'You must press down the key, not
simply touch it.'

> Then the telegraph man explained that in long-distance transmission,
> where the resistance is high, the sending key must be pressed down
> rather forcibly if efficient reception is to be assured.
>
> 'That's why we use men exclusively for long-distance telegraphy . . .
> because they naturally press down hard. They have a strong touch.
> Women wouldn't naturally press down hard and are therefore not
> adaptable to long-distance work'.
>
> (Wile 1926: 74–5)

Berliner hypothesised that the greater the pressure, the more current passed over
the contact.

Early in April 1877, even as Edison was working with the plumbago apparatus,
Berliner built a soap-box telephone. He knocked the bottom out of a wooden box,
7 x 12 inches, nailing in its place a sheet-iron diaphragm. Above this was secured a
cross bar and a screw with a polished steel button on its end which passed through
the bar to rest on the diaphragm. On 14 April 1877, he filed a caveat, although
the apparatus clearly worked well enough to warrant a patent; but the caveat cost
$10 and the patent $60. For a $12-a-week clerk there was no option. He began
negotiating with the local Bell Company in New York, which was not interested,

so he saved enough money himself to file for his patent by June. Watson arrived at Berliner's Washington rooming house, examined the soap-box and pronounced: 'We will want that, Mr. Berliner. You will hear from us in a few days' (Wile 1926: 112). Watson was quite clear as to why he was so enthusiastic: 'I thought he might antedate Edison . . .and advised Mr. Hubbard to make some agreement with Mr. Berliner for the use of his invention. . . . We tried to make each other believe that carbon transmitter wasn't essential to our welfare but we all knew it really was' (ibid.: 143). Berliner joined the National Bell Telephone Company in September and was sent to work in Bell's Boston lab. The soap-box was unstable but Berliner perfected it while working with another scientist at the lab, Francis Blake, who had himself been experimenting with microphones (Fagen 1975: 70). Bell history acknowledges that the patent is Berliner's, but the transmitter is named for Blake rather than for his more exotic colleague (Wile 1926: 129). Berliner was to establish himself as an independent researcher and, as such, went on to produce a sound recording system he called the gramophone (see p. 61).

By 1879, progress was also being made on the other side. Dolbear, using a condenser developed by Kelvin in 1863, produced a viable non-magneto receiver (Blake 1928: 18). Western Union and National Bell were in a stand-off position. National Bell had the superior receiver, the real source of its strength, and had acquired a comparable transmitter to Edison's which might or might not be sustained in the courts. Western Union had the advantages of its size and resources, Gray's caveat and a superior transmitter from Edison. Although it was relying on Dolbear's shakier claim to the magneto, it also had his condenser receiver. In November 1879 the two companies reached an agreement. For the life of the Bell master patents, i.e. until 1893 and 1894, the American Speaking Telephone Company agreed to drop all actions against those patents and to hand over to National Bell its own telephone patent rights. Western Union was not to enter the telephone business. In return, National Bell agreed to drop its cases and to buy out all the American Speaking Telephone's subscribers and equipment, 56,000 'stations' in fifty-five cities, as well as paying 20 per cent of each rental to Western Union. In the fifteen years of the contract approximately $7,000,000 was to be handed over (Stehman 1925: 17n). In addition, Elisha Gray received his $100,000 and Western Electric its monopoly deal.

## SUPPRESSION AND DIFFUSION: THE TELEPHONE AFTER 1900

The suppression of the disruptive potential of any new communications technology contains many elements – inertia, lack of vision, institutional constraints such as those imposed by the patent system. The operation of the 'law' of the suppression of radical potential in telephony exhibits all of these at work, even inertia. Although the Edison device was now available to it, the Bell system stuck with the Black transmitter, making 340,000 of them in the 1880s. (Only 6000 magneto box telephones, as described in Bell's 1877 patent, were made.) The standardised device, virtually the contemporary telephone, using carbon granules in a technique patented by Edison in 1886, was developed by both Edison and Blake but only came into production in 1895 (Fagen 1975: 82–3).

Even more significant was the brake applied by the limitations of entrepreneurialism. At the outset, thanks to the income generated by Bell's lectures, his backer, Hubbard, was able to make the momentous decision to rent rather than sell the 'station' equipment, an idea he took from the practice of a company he represented at law which rented shoe-sewing machinery to cobblers and collected on every shoe processed (Langdon 1935: 9). Yet overall, Hubbard, like most others, saw the telephone business in a limited way as the installation of single point-to-point pairs. Following the lead of Charles Williams Jr, 10,754 Bell phones, largely in pairs, were placed in service by the end of the first year. Nevertheless, most of those whom Hubbard approached to invest in telephony saw little future in it.

Beyond this failure of vision, the most effective suppressive factor was the law of patent. The original patent association of Bell, Watson and their two backers was turned into the first Bell Telephone Company. Hubbard appointed agents who placed the telephones, collected a percentage of the rental and often built the lines connecting them as independent contractors. Western Union, the organisation most directly threatened, took steps (as we have seen) to suppress its new rival with a superior product: better Edison telephones. Hubbard was forced to sue. He was rapidly running out of capital and finding it hard to attract more. He created National Bell and secured the services of Theodore Vail to be its general manager. Cousin to the Vail who had been Morse's assistant, this Vail was to be a critical figure in the development of American telephony. He arrived in the summer of 1878 and immediately and dramatically improved the legal situation. Exploiting the claimed priority of the recently acquired Berliner patent, he brought a second legal action, an 'interference' against the Edison device. This allowed Bell Telephone to begin to use its Berliner/Blake transmitters without fear of a Western Union injunction.

Bell, who had finally been allowed to marry Hubbard's daughter, Mabel in July 1877, went on a protracted European honeymoon. He was clearly uneasy about these various legal battles and, on his return from Europe to give evidence in the first of these in November 1878, Watson had to go to Quebec to escort him personally to Boston, where he was promptly admitted to the Massachusetts General Hospital for an operation (Watson 1926: 151–3). He was uninterested in corporate details and obviously had no reason to relish the legal attacks on his work and integrity. In the event he was to spend the next three decades defending himself.

Orton, on the other side, also had difficulties and could not give his undivided attention to the destruction of National Bell. Western Union itself was under attack from one of the archetypal entrepreneurs of the period, Jay Gould. Moreover, Bell did hold the master patents to at least half the system and, under Vail, was being as deft as the telegraph company in acquiring rights to the other half. It was also becoming clear that the telephone and the telegraph could live together, the one being used for short distances and the other on longer routes. The corporate situation by autumn 1879 therefore matched the technological one: It was a stand-off. The deal detailed above, made out of court in November of that year, is a classic expression of the 'law' of suppression in that it gave the established technology a real interest in the exploitation of the new, melded the patents so that they could be exploited effectively and rewarded Gray. The patents also worked to create a 15-year breathing space.

The problems of technological diffusion after the operation of the 'law' of suppression of radical potential are peripheral to this study. The disruptive potential of the telephone in the world of communications was contained during the period of the patent, as we shall see when we consider the development of the telephone network (p. 248). So too were the social threats to the established order which many commentators thought were posed by the telephone. Breaches of the rules of propriety in conversation; the promiscuous possibility of the lower orders, unseen, cheeking their betters; even the dangers of catching colds and other diseases down the wire (Marvin 1988: 81–97) – none of these came to pass. As a destroyer of societal norms, the telephone was as nothing when compared with the First World War. Socially as well as corporately, the telephone's radical potential was curtailed.

For example, in the late 1870s, microphones and loudspeakers were attached to telephone wires for experimental purposes. A church service was brought to the bedside of a sick person. In Switzerland an engineer relayed Donizetti's *Don Pasquale* (Moncel 1879: 172). In 1884 a London company offered, for an annual charge of £10, four pairs of headsets through which a subscriber would be connected to theatres, concerts, lectures and church services. In 1889, following the successful transmission of a comic opera, a Chicago telephone company offered the same (Marvin 1988: 212). In Paris and Budapest, all-day news services were available. The London experiment lasted until 1904, but the telephone news channels persisted into the inter-war years (Hollins 1984: 35). There were many other examples (Marvin 1988: 209 -231), but these services were technologically futile, exploiting a potential that had actually already been designed out of the system. The responsiveness of the telephone, once it worked at all, was deliberately limited in the interests of economy. The less bandwidth taken, the more conversations could be accommodated on a single wire at a more economically efficient cost. It was discovered that the human brain needs remarkably little information in order to recognise a voice, a fact of which telephones were to take maximum advantage.

Coupled with the non-provision of hi-fidelity (or anything remotely close to it) was the failure to expand the interconnectability of stations even after the development of the central office exchange; instead each subscriber could only talk to one other station at a time. Making it possible for one subscriber to talk to many others would have enhanced the telephone as a non-hierarchical means of communication. It was not to be and the very construction of the network system to limit telephony to one-to-one communication is therefore a mark of its repression. That we allow broadcasting, a very much more inherently centralised, undemocratic and controllable technology, to do this is the obverse of that mark. Today, it is still by no means easy to establish multi-party telephone link-ups. The telephone was a device designed to aid commercial intercourse, not to redress imbalances in information power within society. Indeed, as events in Poland during the communist counter-*coup* against Solidarity in the early 1980s revealed, even the spin-off social use of the phone, in which unsupervised conversations between only two stations can take place, are sometimes too dangerous for the state to allow. The whole phone system was shut down.

## 'INVENTING' A SPIN-OFF: THE RECORD

There is a most intimate relationship between the technologies of telephony and recorded sound:

> Mr Edison had a telephone diaphragm mounted in a mouth-piece of rubber in his hand, and he was sounding notes in front of it and feeling the vibration of the centre of the diaphragm with his finger. After amusing himself with this for some time, he turned round to me and said: 'Batch [Charles Batchelor], if we had some point on this, we could make a record on some material which we would afterwards pull under the point and it would give us the speech back'.
>
> (Chew 1981: 2)

As he proceeded late in 1877 to put this idea into practice and, using waxed paper as the recording medium, thereby 'invent' the phonograph, Edison was thinking of message systems along the lines of the telegram. After all, some early telegraph systems had relied on visible chemical tracing. Perhaps waxed paper recordings could be used by people without actual telephones to take advantage of the new system via a network of central offices?

On 27 November, Edison produced a new design which was built during the following week by mechanic John Kruesi. In it the wax paper had been replaced by tin-foil and it was operational by 6 December and demonstrated to the editor of the *Scientific American* on the following day. The first words, according to tradition, were 'Mary had a little lamb' and the first recorded voice was Kruesi's. The device was entirely mechanical. A drum, covered with tin-foil, was mounted on an axle which could be cranked. As the handle turned the drum moved under a stylus which was connected to a diaphragm. The diaphragm was mounted in a crude speaking/hearing tube. Speaking into the tube while cranking the handle produced an helical indentation in the tinfoil, an analogue of the sound pressure waves, via the diaphragm and stylus. Playback simply required cranking the drum back to the start position and allowing the indentations to vibrate the other way; that is, via the stylus against the diaphragm.

There was not very much 'eureka' about all this. The usual seventeenth-century savant had dreamed about capturing the human voice in hollow cylinders and, as we have seen, making sound visible was a well-established agenda item in a number of research traditions. Most significantly, since 1855, the same essential principle which Edison used for his phonograph had been applied in Scott's phonautograph. Even the term Edison used, 'phonograph', dated from 1863 (Chanan 1995: 24). These elements (and wave theory, of course) could be said to constitute the ground of scientific competence for the phonograph.

It is therefore no surprise to note also that Charles Cros, an important photography pioneer, published proposals for a non-electrical phonograph in Paris on 10 October 1877, almost perfectly in synchronisation with Edison. Although Cros patented the machine in May 1878, he never managed to make it work (Chanan 1995: 23). Emile Berliner, however, did. He worked for five years, living on his Bell royalties. Using a thinly waxed platter of polished zinc, he applied acid as the stylus cut the groove in the wax. This ate immediately into the zinc. On 12 November 1887, he obtained a patent for a gramophone, his term. He demonstrated this system on 16 May 1888. The device with a library of 7-inch platters was first marketed in Germany as a toy by Kämmer and Reinhardt (Chew 1981: 17–19).

As this illustrates, there was some confusion as to what these machines were for. Berliner's, in its public guise, was a playback device only. (The children were, of course, not trusted with the acid.) Edison's machine, essentially a recording device, was also something of a parlour toy rather than a serious medium and public attention wandered. The telephone message idea was never really viable and, as an alternative, by 1878, Edison was envisaging the phonograph as a substitute for a stenographer. He also foresaw books for the blind, music, the preservation of language and pronunciation for various purposes and audio family records. Recording telephone messages was now bottom of the list (Chanan 1995: 3).

Bell agreed about the technology's primary purpose as a business dictating machine. The social need would then be the same as that driving the introduction of the telephone, the calculator, the typewriter and the elevator – the modern business corporation. Bell and a new colleague Charles Tainter improved the Edison design in various ways. They returned to wax as the recording medium, but this time on cardboard rather than paper and they introduced an electric motor to drive the axle (Chanan 1995: 25). (It was during this period of experimentation that the idea of modulating light waves for signalling purposes was also explored giving rise to a persistent rumour that Bell was 'inventing' television.) Bell's backers had bought into Edison's phonograph patents but their approaches to Edison with a view to establishing a joint venture were rebuffed and the Bell-Tainter American Graphophone Company was founded instead. The first machines were sold in 1886 to Congress and Supreme Court reporters and a new front in the Edison-Bell wars was established (Chew 1981: 10–12).

These talking machines, though, lacked the self-evident advantages of the other technologies of the office. For one thing, the mechanisation of stenography was by no means a self-evident necessity, given the comparatively low cost of labour; and for another thing, the machines were, when compared with stenographers, crude and inefficient and still required transcription. This was still the case when the next generation of dictating machines was developed in 1898 by Valdemar Poulsen. Poulsen chose wire as his recording medium, following a suggestion which had been published in 1888 (Nmungwun 1989: 36). Poulsen returned to using electromagnetic fields to impress the sound wave analogue on the recording medium. The wire ran through the device at 10 feet per second. All in all, the Poulsen Telegraphone (or Telephonograph, as it was patented in America) was a great advance on the Edison/Bell-Tainter dictation machines, especially after 1902 when Poulsen and his partner, Peder Pedersen, discovered that applying a direct current to the recording head, the principle of DC bias, greatly reduced distortion.

Poulsen was a telephone engineer and his motivation had been to produce a device which could transmit recorded telephone messages at high speeds, thereby improving efficiency. Hence the various names he gave his device. But this emphasis on the recorded telephone call alerted AT&T to what that corporate mind perceived as a real threat. If telephone conversations could be recorded, the company's reasoning apparently went, then people would become wary about making them with disastrous results for the business. In one of the most extreme cases of the suppression of radical potential noted in these pages, there is evidence that the telephone company suborned Poulsen's man in America, Charles Rood, so that in the years up to the First World War and beyond he actively worked to destroy the business he was supposed to be running (Nmungwun 1989: 43–8). The American Telegraphone Company failed and it was not until after the Second World War that American interest in magnetic recording was revived with the importation of Nazi magnetophon recorders built on Poulsen's basic principles.

However, even without such chicanery, the stenographic use of recording technologies was not a powerful supervening necessity. That the telegraphone was never widely adopted is the final proof of this. Instead, it was a phonograph agent, Louis Glass of San Francisco, who demonstrated a real social need for a recorded sound device. In 1889, he attached coin-operated listening tubes to a phonograph thereby both 'inventing' the jukebox and demonstrating that the real supervening social necessity was not the office but the amusement requirements of the urban masses. The Bell-Tainter people (The Columbia Graphophone Company) stepped up the production of music cylinders and Edison became interested again, having more or less given up in the 1880s.

It was into this American environment that Berliner introduced his gramophone, the first grown-up versions of which were on sale by 1894. His initial design was very much more in line with the emerging dominant function of the technology, i.e. the playback of prerecorded music. In 1896, the first spring-driven gramophones appeared and it was with the engineer who produced the motor, Eldridge Johnston, that Berliner founded the Victor Company in 1901. Berliner and Eldridge clearly understood, as Chanan puts it, that 'a model of consumption' was being established 'which treated the record like a book, and not like, say, a photograph' (Chanan 1995: 28–9).

Partly because of this, the inevitable patent conflicts were quite easily solved. Edison and Bell had not fought each other very hard over the stunted dictation machine market and clearly Berliner had something of an edge. The patent pool phase was reached in 1902, the year Caruso recorded the first 'genuinely complete satisfactory gramophone records to be made' (Gelatt 1977: 38). The non-electric technology produced a limited acoustic response which favoured the strong human voice and it is no accident that the earliest hit records were of singers. Caruso, who was to make $2 million from his records by the time he died in 1921, had the first million-selling disc in 1904 (Chanan 1995: 5, 30).

These recording devices were spin-offs from the telephone research project but they produced in the first decades of the twentieth century a major industry which had profound cultural effects. The reasons were the strong push offered by the basic supervening necessity, urban entertainment, and the excellence of the phonograph/gramophone's cultural 'fit'. The gramophone extended the social circumstances in which music could be consumed. As with the radio, the next technology to come on line, recorded sound systems privatised the musical experience but did so in a context where home music making, at least for the upper orders of society, had long been established. Between 1902 and 1917 the US

Victor Company's value went from $2.72 million to $17 million. By 1914 there were eighty record companies in the UK and nearly 200 in the US (Chanan 1995: 54). Yet the 1920s were to some extent to puncture this pre-electric bubble. Worsening economic conditions hit the record industry particularly hard as did competition from radio, whose main attraction, certainly at the outset, was exactly the same provision of music in the home as records provided – but with rapidly emerging superior acoustic quality. Without electricity these were all partial but accepted prototypes.

# Part II

# THE VITAL SPARK AND
# FUGITIVE PICTURES

# 4

# WIRELESS AND RADIO

## SCIENTIFIC COMPETENCE TO IDEATION: FROM SPARK TO WIRELESS

The radio is the clearest example in these histories of a machine already in existence – 'invented' – but not recognised as such. We have seen that the physicists of the world were intent on demonstrating the truth of theories promulgated by Maxwell and Helmholtz in the 1860s by using a variety of laboratory devices and how these had impacted on the development of the telephone, the phonograph and the gramophone (Figure 10). Their importance to radio is even more pronounced.

Hertz had conducted a series of experiments between 1886 and 1868 to demonstrate the existence of Maxwellian electromagnetic waves. He built a spark transmitter (or inductorium) and another device variously described as a resonator, responder, revealer, cymoscope or, more prosaically, a spark gap detector to detect them. In the transmitter, two rods with a small ball at one end and a large plate or ball at the other were connected to the terminals of a sparking coil. A spark was created which jumped the gap between the two smaller balls creating an oscillating current. The current produced electric and magnetic fields causing radio wave emission. The detecting device was nothing more than a bent wire in either a circular or square shape with a small break in it. The width of the gap could be adjusted using a screw arrangement. When the inductorium sparked, a small visible spark could be seen in this gap in the ring resonator (Phillips 1980: 4–6). Despite the crudeness of the apparatus, Hertz was able to demonstrate that these 'aetheric radiations' did have wave-like properties and could, for instance, be reflected or refracted.

Hertz was not, of course, alone in this work. Curious electrical effects, the distant magnetising of needles following a Leyden jar discharge or a lightening strike had been noted in the 1840s. In 1875, Elihu Thomson of Philadelphia had detected a spark between a sharp pencil point and a brass door knob whenever a

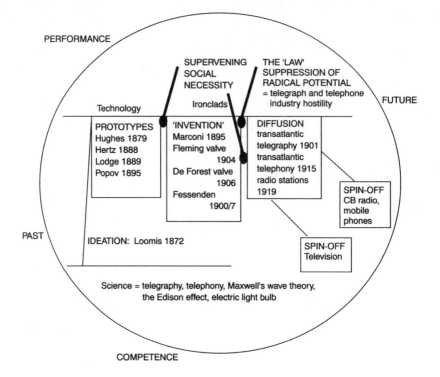

*Figure 10* Wireless telegraphy/radio

sparking coil was operated about 100 feet away in another room. But the most important and significant of these precursors to Hertz was David Hughes, the man who created the microphone. Conducting a series of experiments in London between 1878 and 1880, he had been working on one piece of apparatus, an induction balance circuit, when he noticed that a faulty contact on this circuit produced an audible noise in a microphone lying on the other side of the room. Eventually he was transmitting 500 yards along Great Portland Street. On 20 February 1880, he demonstrated the phenomenon to T. H. Huxley, G.G. Stokes and W. Spottiswoode, the president of the Royal Society. Stokes 'rather pooh-poohed all results' and told him that his experiments revealed induction, which was well understood, rather than the related and more mysterious phenomenon of radiation and 'left very coldly'.

Hughes, whose doctorate was in music not physics, was deterred by this snub but his notebooks show that he was well aware of wave theory and the ether concept. However, overawed by Stokes, he neither pursued the matter nor published his findings. His work had been a by-product of other investigations.

He himself was not otherwise rejected by the scientific establishment, being made an FRS that same year (Blake 1928: 39; Phillips 1980: 2–4; Beck 1967: 96–7). What had happened in Hughes's lab was the result of a radio wave being received in a device with a poor electrical contact – his microphone. In the microphone, the loose contact between the two conductors causes a very high resistance but an electrical current will dramatically decrease this. This phenomenon, in connection with currents rather than radiation, had been observed independently by scientists in 1835, in 1852 and again in 1884. Hence Stoke's disdain.

The most telling factor against the Hughes demonstration was that nobody had thought of using radiation phenomena for signalling, or indeed for any purpose other than theoretical physics experiments. Why would they, in a world blessed with telegraphy where the telephone was a recent wonder? Radio was about as useful in such an environment as the telegraph had been in a world of semaphores. There was no supervening social necessity and, in consequence, Hughes is the Ronalds of radio and all these machines are parallel prototypes – that is to say, they are perfectly good physics research tools, fully 'invented' as such, but they are also prototypes for the radio (or wireless) telegraph.

Over the next decade numerous researchers refined these experiments by producing devices of ever greater sophistication as regards the adjustability of the gaps. It was soon discovered that effective transmission of the radio wave depended exactly on such adjustment – tuning – so that both parts of the apparatus were, in the terminology of the day, 'syntonised', that is, tuned to the same frequency. At Bologna University, to take one example of this work among many, Augusto Righi created an elegant multiple spark gap using silvered glass (Phillips 1980: 10). Such contrivances were given a variety of names until Sir Oliver Lodge coined the term 'coherer' and, in the English-speaking world, that prevailed (Phillips 1980: 19). Lodge built his first coherer with A. Muirhead in 1889; but he was still responding to a purely scientific research agenda only. There was no other identified need and nobody had, at least in public, suggested their usefulness as signalling machines.[1]

The first published record of the idea of radio, specifically a radio telegraph, was articulated by Sir William Crookes in 1892. A colleague of Lodge's, he envisaged 'telegraphy without wires, posts, cables, or any of our present costly appliances'. He saw it as a person-to-person system and announced that 'all the requirements . . . are well within the possibility of discovery' (Marvin 1988: 156; Beck 1967: 95). As Lodge's coherer was already to hand, this was clearly the case. Nevertheless, nothing happened for another two years. Ideation had occurred but a supervening social necessity had not – or rather had not yet come into focus.

In August 1894, Lodge demonstrated a radio telegraph using his coherer at a meeting of the British Association in Oxford. He sent a signal from the Clarendon Laboratory some 150 yards to the University Museum. The University celebrated the centenary of this event with a plaque claiming, somewhat tendentiously as is often the case with such things, that the Museum was 'the site of the first public demonstration of wireless telegraphy' (Anon (Oxford) 1994: 39). Yet, despite the heavy prompt from Lodge's friend Crookes, Lodge (who failed to patent the coherer) and his audience did not appear to realise they had 'invented', or witnessed the 'invention' of, any such thing. They were merely detecting radio waves, a quite different matter altogether.

The honour of 'inventing' radio therefore goes to Marconi, not least because he was consciously working on a signalling system. Although like Morse and Bell, Gugliemo Marconi garnered other men's flowers, nevertheless, as a student of Righi's, he was by that fact alone more of a scientist than were the 'inventors' of the telegraph or the telephone. His one contribution to the development of radio was also more grounded in science than was Morse's code or any of Bell's initial devices. Following a hint of Mahlon Loomis, made as early as 1872, that electrical signalling over long distances if possible would involve very tall aerials, in 1894 Marconi experimentally demonstrated that this was indeed the case. Using his professor's spark gap device and a Lodge-style coherer he had built himself, he sent a signal over 1.5 miles through dint of raising the aerial he was using. As a result of his experiments he was eventually able to articulate a law for distance in radio: 'I find that, with parity of other conditions, vertical wires twenty feet long are sufficient for communicating one mile, forty feet four miles, eighty feet sixteen miles, and so on' (Fahie 1901: 260). Wires attached to kites would probably allow for messages to be sent transoceanically. His crucial contribution was not the 'invention' of radio as is conventionally understood but rather the discovery that Loomis' hunch was right: the taller the transmitting mast, the further the signal radiated.

But Marconi did more than this. He also discovered a supervening necessity.


## NECESSITY, DIFFUSION AND SUPPRESSION:
## IRONCLADS AND TELEGRAMS

Marconi had British connections via his Irish-born mother and so decided to patent his advances (as, accurately, 'Improvements in transmitting electrical impulses and signals') in London, which he did in June 1896 (Beck 1967: 95). According to the fiftieth anniversary publication of the company that was to bear his name, this was because he already realised the potential value of his device to shipping and he wished to launch it in the country with the world's largest fleet (Sturmey 1958: 17). His mother arranged for him to meet one of the most prominent scientists in the field (then known as 'electricians'), A.A. Campbell Swinton, who in turn led him to the Chief Engineer of the Post Office, William Preece. After an initial demonstration on Salisbury Plain arranged by Preece, Marconi began talking to the Admiralty.

In marked contrast to its attitude towards Ronalds' telegraph, the Admiralty was very interested in radio. Indeed, Captain H.B. Jackson was already experimenting with coherers at sea. By September, he had met with Marconi and, within two years, testing the wireless was an integral part of summer naval manoeuvres (Beck 1967: 96). The navy of the day, with its fleets of ironclads, had so serious a need for long-distance wireless signalling that the usual conservatism could not withstand it.

The first armour-plated vessel was a French wooden ship of the line refitted with metal protection, La Gloire, in 1859. The USS Monitor followed in 1860 and by 1863 the British were engaged in rebuilding the fleet along these lines. The first British armour-plated battleship, the Devastation was laid down in 1869. It was also the first naval vessel to have no sails. The third ship of this class was the Dreadnought. Over the next few decades, such ironclads all over the world became larger, faster and were ever more heavily armoured, increasing in size from 10,000 to 20,000 tons. Their guns had a range of up to 7000 yards and to avoid collisions they needed to steam into action 800 yards apart. This meant twelve ships of the line stretched over 6 miles of sea which in turn caused a major communications problem. Moreover, between 1815 and 1914, the only serious naval engagements were between Russia and Japan and the USA and Spain. Although these involved ironclads, they were one-sided encounters, so it was difficult to know from experience what these developments might mean in an actual open-seas encounter between the European imperial fleets. One thing, though, was clear. The admiral could no longer sail in the van and communicate by flag.

The development of the ironclad therefore created a signalling problem exactly as the development of the railway had; and just as the telegraph began as a solution to the railway's problem, so the wireless telegraph began as a solution to the ironclad's. The only difference was that, if anything, the naval need was stronger. In fact, of all the supervening necessities discussed so far, this was the clearest and the most compelling. Naval machismo and imperial posturing had produced enormous ships without any real consideration being given as to how to fight them. Without the wireless, their usefulness in an actual battle would have been very much curtailed. No wonder the Admiralty abandoned its traditional obscurantism in favour of investigation and support. Jackson was First Sea Lord by 1915.

Marconi and Jackson began intensive field trials and by the summer manoeuvres of 1898 they were communicating across 60 miles of water. As these experiments were being undertaken aboard British battleships, so A.V. Popov was doing the same in the Russian fleet. Like most of his fellow researchers, Popov's project initially had more to do with natural science than with communications. He had built a very elegant device for the purpose of researching natural electric phenomena, such as the detection of natural radio waves caused by distant storms. Nevertheless by 1896 he too was using his coherer to send messages between the Tsar's ironclads (Blake 1928: 65,119).

This is not the end of wireless telegraphy's watery connections. The earliest widespread diffusion of the technology was at sea. In the first years of the twentieth century, ships' wireless was becoming common. It was used for weather reports and, after 1901, by Lloyds to gather maritime intelligence. Marconi's endeavoured to maintain a monopoly over the technology by prohibiting intercommunication between its stations and others using different equipment. Lloyd's was not alone in challenging this effort. They did it in court but other nations resorted to diplomacy. The Germans summoned a convention which met in Berlin in 1903 and agreed on the principle of free intercommunication (Sturmey 1958: 52–6).

The wireless telegraph served other more dramatic nautical purposes. The most celebrated was the capture of the poisoner, Dr Crippen, fleeing to Canada aboard the S S *Montrose* with his mistress Ethel Le Neve, after the ship received a telegram about him at sea (Birkenhead n.d.: 240–1).[2] Equally dramatic was the transmission of distress signals by ships themselves. A second world congress on wireless telegraphy held in Berlin in 1906 agreed, among other standardisation matters, that S O S would be the call signal. On the night of 14 April 1912, the *Titanic*'s S O S was received not just by neighbouring vessels but by the Marconi station on Long Island. The company's young manager in Manhattan passed it on to the White House. The publicity further enhanced the wireless as the communication wonder of the age. (It also launched the career of David Sarnoff, the manager in question, who was to be the founder of the Radio Corporation of America and the father of NBC.)

By the time of the *Titanic* disaster, the wireless was a fully diffused maritime technology. Indeed, the fact that an international congress had met to standardise its use six years earlier is proof of that. Of course, it was without competition since no other long distance signalling systems could be used at sea. However, uniqueness does not of itself automatically overcome inertia – industrial conservatism and commercial penny-pinching, for example. All that had happened in this case was that these had been effectively overwhelmed by the quick and universal naval adoption of wireless and its dramatic importance to safety at sea. Such factors, though, were seen soon enough when Marconi sought to exploit the technology as an alternative to wired telegraphy.

It was the possibility of using radio as an alternative to wired telegraphy that attracted the GPO's William Preece to Marconi in 1896. The General Post Office, unlike its opposite number in the United States, had managed to extend its postal monopoly over the telegraph and, to all intents and purposes, over the telephone as well; but it had never enjoyed a monopoly of submarine cables. Obviously, wireless telegraphy could at least put the GPO in competition for this transoceanic business with the commercial firms that were exploiting cables. Not only that: by helping Marconi, the GPO was giving itself a commanding patent position world-wide. Preece himself was already interested in wireless waves and had endeav-oured to use induction currents to signal across the Solent in 1882 and the Firth of Lorne to Mull in 1895. After putting Marconi in touch with the military, he arranged for a first public demonstration in London which took place in Decem-ber. It was these events which finally galvanised Lodge to apply for a patent.

In April, Marconi was approached by an entrepreneur to set up a company to further develop and exploit his technology. He felt bound to Preece but Preece failed to convince the government that Marconi should be bought out. In June, 'tired of kicking his heels on the inhospitable doorstep of the British Treasury', Marconi took the entrepreneur's money. There follows the by now usual story of patent conflicts, ill-will and slowed diffusion – and not just in the UK. The 'law' of the suppression of radical potential can be noted in the sequel to Marconi's first widely publicised experimental shore-to-shore transatlantic transmission from St Johns, Newfoundland to Poldhu, Cornwall, on 12 December 1901. The Anglo-American Telegraph Company held the telegraphic monopoly from the (then separate colonial) government of Newfoundland and exercised its rights in having the Marconi people thrown off the island. (The government of Canada found another haven for the experimenters.)

By 1911, the usual solution was arrived at. Marconi's bought the Lodge patent, promised to give business to Lodge's company and hired the man himself as an adviser. Given that it was also soon discovered that wireless was seriously subject to atmospheric disturbance, these deals were enough to contain the challenge to the transoceanic cables. Furthermore, there was also the question of privacy where the wires across the landscape seem to have an advantage. Sending a signal to all hearers, if you were not a sinking ship, was an aberrant, even revolutionary act. (This was literally so in the case of the Irish who proclaimed the existence of an independent Ireland in a morse message broadcast from the roof of the Dublin Post Office during the Easter Rising of 1916. The Germans, too, had produced a news bulletin in morse designed to be heard by neutral countries the previous year (Karuppiahya 1996: 9).)

For all these reasons, the wireless telegraph was less disruptive to existing telecommunications industries than was at first, and all too typically, envisaged. Following Marconi's demonstration of 1896, it was commonly believed, as a contemporary lecturer put it, that: 'There is no doubt the day will come . . . when copper wires, gutta-percha covering and iron sheathings will be relegated to the museum of antiquities' (Marvin 1988: 157). Many of these materials are indeed in the museum, but their modern-day equivalents are still providing us with wired communication. The law of suppression, this time aided by atmospheric physics and a widespread blindness as to the possibilities of what came to be called 'broadcasting', once again worked.

## 'INVENTION': FROM WIRELESS TELEGRAPHY TO RADIO

Before the First War World there were a bewildering array of coherers, but most, as the historian of these devices points out, 'were intended simply to indicate the presence or absence of signals in the receiving aerial'. Among them, however, were thermal detectors, which had an added advantage. Because they 'depended on the fact that a current in a wire produces heat, they were also able to provide a quantitative measurement of the received signal' (Phillips 1980: 150). Measuring the heat measured the power of the signal. This and other phenomena connecting electricity and heat had been observed for some time. For example, it had been noted in 1873 that an electroscope would discharge in the presence of a heated metal ball. This was the underlying principle of what came to be known as 'the Edison effect'.

Edison himself, after his contributions to telegraphy and telephony and his production of the phonograph, was now the 'Wizard of Menlo Park', proprietor of a fully fledged industrial laboratory – the 'Invention Factory'. He next turned to the problem of the electric light which had been a largely unrealised possibility ever since 1808 when Humphrey Davy had demonstrated the ways in which electricity could be made to produce illumination (Friedel and Israel 1986: 7). Electric lights in the form of arcs were understood but as Edison himself put it: 'The intense light had not been subdivided so that it could be brought into private houses' (ibid.: 8) For that he needed an incandescent system where the electricity is used to heat a substance until it glows rather than a naked arc of electric energy. Incandescence had also been demonstrated by Davy but the question was how to control the destruction of the heated substance and make it sufficiently long-lived to be useful. As he ploughed through a reported 6000 substances, Edison realised that the solution lay less with these materials than with the environment in which they burned. Perhaps they would destroy themselves more slowly in a vacuum? By February, the lab had acquired a vacuum pump and Edison's phonograph associates, Kruesi and Batchelor, sketched the first lamp with a vacuum bulb-shaped glass envelope (ibid.: 51). By October 1879, the team had put a carbon tread into the bulb. Over the next two decades Edison would sell 24,000,000 of these 'sewing thread' lamps. [3]

Melding this development (which involved passing an electric current through filaments in vacuums) with the experiments in wireless wave detection (which had already produced the wireless telegraph) moved the whole radio-wave detection and manipulation research agenda forward. In 1904, a professor of electrical engineering at University College, London, Ambrose Fleming, built a variation on the light bulb; that is, a vacuum tube which, by specifically exploiting the Edison effect, turned an alternating current radio signal into a direct current capable of activating a meter or telephone. Fleming had been working on these phenomena at least since he was employed as an electrician by the Edison Light Company in 1884 (Beck 1967: 101). The patent for this diode tube rested with the British Marconi Company to whom Fleming was consultant.

Two years later, in Palo Alto, Lee de Forest added a third electrode in the form of a grid between the cathode and anode of the Fleming valve to increase its sensitivity. This was not simply another advance useful for the art of wireless telegraphy and physics experiments. Other researchers, among them Armstrong, at Columbia University, and von Lieben in Germany, realised de Forest's tube would amplify weak radio signals and enable longer distances to be covered. However, it was Reginald Fessenden, a Canadian experimenter who had created an important thermal detector in 1902, who quickly understood that de Forest had given him a new tool. In December 1906, using triode tubes (or valves), he broadcast music and speech from a wireless telegraphy company's station in Massachusetts. 'On Christmas Eve 1906, ship wireless operators over a wide area of the Atlantic, sitting with earphones to head, alert to the crackling of distant dots and dashes, were startled to hear a woman singing' (Barnouw 1975: 13).

Significantly, Fessenden was at a site belonging not to market leaders, Marconi's, but to the Electrical Signal Company. Although Marconi's owned the Fleming valve, it was interested in its application for wireless telegraphy as a detector and amplifier only. Similarly, the telephone companies, although they were interested in transoceanic applications, were more immediately taken with the triode because of its usefulness as an amplifier in land long-line repeaters, not as a way of getting rid of the wires. By 1907 Fessenden was transmitting speech over distances of 200 miles. He had 'invented' the radio (as opposed to wireless telegraphy) but, ships' wireless operators apart, nobody was listening.

## IDEATION AND NECESSITY: THE IDEA OF BROADCASTING

Getting beyond the idea of point-to-point communication was the real inhibitor suppressing the potential of wireless communication until after the First World War. Radio, broadcast radio, essentially involved not knowing in advance where signals would be received. In other words, further exploitation depended on seeing that a major perceived fault of the technology, that anybody could listen, was actually its *raison d'être*. One did not have to be in danger of sinking or in the midst of a revolution or a war to make use of this possibility; yet that possibility did not quite add up to a supervening social necessity.

David Sarnoff, thanks to the *Titanic* a person of some consequence in the new world of wireless, saw how it might. In this, though, he was not alone and not as early as his myth suggests; nevertheless he can stand as an emblematic figure in the ideation transformation leading to radio. During the First World War, Westinghouse had made the comparatively complex but compact SCR 69 and SCR 70 radio receivers for the US Army Signal Corps. In 1920, Sarnoff and a colleague visited an independent radio engineer who had perfected a uni-control radio that was simpler to operate than the SRC 70. Sarnoff claimed he immediately saw that: 'This is the radio music box of which I've dreamed' (Biting 1965: 1017). Enlightened municipalities, he had been arguing by the early 1920s, provided public entertainment – for example, bandstands in parks, where any passer-by could listen. Sarnoff thought this might be a model for broadcast radio but not in the local park; rather he envisaged this as a 'music box' in every home. He had written to his general manager at Marconi's, anticipating sales of one million 'radio music boxes' at $75 the set within three years of the commencement of manufacture – $75 million (Benjamin 1994: 325–35). Although there is some doubt as to exactly when he did this, there is no question that he understood that within the culture music was listened to collectively and radio would have to allow for that if it were to become a mass medium.

There is also no question about the significance of military machines such as the SRC 70 and the servicemen who had learned to use them. They constituted the '100,000', the corps of the amateurs whose continued interest created the world of radio between the Armistice and 1920. They tended to use yet another type of early receiver which relied on the principle of rectification and required considerable finesse to tune. Rectifiers had a surprisingly long history. Frederick Braun, at the University of Marburg in 1874, had demonstrated that a metal wire when placed in contact with lead sulphide produced a device, a rectifier, that would conduct electricity in only one direction. With this was 'invented' a tuned circuit which could be adjusted to pick up the radio waves of a single frequency (Braun and Macdonald 1982: 11–12). Eventually a wide variety of combinations of substances was to be employed and patented for this purpose. One crystal rectifier, marketed before the First World War as the *Perikon*, consisted of 'a brass point resting on the surface (either rough or polished) of a piece of silicon' (Blake 1928: 89). Silica is common in nature, being the second most abundant element in the earth's crust, for instance, as the principal ingredient of sand. Silicon itself was being produced before 1911.

Many understood the technology and more than one worked out that sending one-way signals to an unknown number of receivers might constitute a new use for it. For example, contrary to general understanding, the Marconi station in Montreal, Canada was given a licence as XWA/CFCF and began a regular schedule of transmissions in 1919. Across the border, Frank Conrad, who worked for Westinghouse in Pittsburgh and had been the supervisor of the assembly line which made the war time SCRs, began sending signals out, replaying phonograph records from his garage near Pittsburgh on a regular basis to anybody who might have a receiver within range. By 1920 Conrad's boss became aware of the success of this activity and removed him from the electrical switches production line on which he had been put. He was instructed instead both to increase the power and scope of his transmissions and to revive the SRC 70 assembly line. In November, KDKA became America's first radio station. By 1922, the elegant eighteenth-century term for sowing seeds, 'broadcasting', was being applied for the first time to this new application. (It was also initially applied, somewhat confusingly, to wireless telegraphy and radio telephony as well; but this was to cease.)

The underlying supervening necessities behind various technologies, from the creation of the mass-circulation press through the refinement of the organisation of the popular stage to the appearance of the cinema, can be located in the needs of an industrialised mass society. Across the 150 years of the rise of mass culture, there has been concentration and standardisation of output and product (with a strong assumption on the part of many observers that this has produced an homogenisation of the consumers' experience). Mass circulation newspapers brought each and every reader the same *ümwelt* and, supposedly, the same thrill; centralised booking and theatre ownership systems brought each member of the audience the same act, the same spectatorial experience. The cinema mechanised this spectacle (Winston 1996: 32–7). The radio brought home this overall process of homogenisation. The rising dominance of the nuclear (as opposed to the extended) family and the provision of ever more comfortable accommodation for that family, reaching even into the working class, had in effect created a further movement to take these homogenised entertainments (except for people seeking mates) into the domestic sphere.

Sarnoff became an executive of the Radio Corporation of America (RCA) which had originally been the British Marconi Company in the United States. The new entity was created in 1919, by government fiat, by expropriating the British owners. It was felt that, as a measure of national importance, radio ought to be locally controlled. In fact, the 1912 Radio Act reserved takeover powers to the US government in the event of war. At the behest of the navy, all Marconi radio coastal stations were nationalised the day after declaring war on Germany on 7 April 1917. The navy tried to get this emergency arrangement transformed by law into a permanent system of public ownership – a 'Post Office arrangement' once again – but did not succeed. Instead, the government created an independent commercial company, RCA, to exploit the technology. Westinghouse, on the basis of Conrad's work, was invited to join in the ownership of RCA with General Electric, AT&T and United Fruit. RCA, by the third year of the radio boom, had sold $83 millions'-worth of sets, $8 millions'-worth more than Sarnoff had apparently predicted. Radio, by 1922, was already a $60-million a year business (Barnouw 1975: 27–8).

## SUPPRESSION AND DIFFUSION: VALVES/TUBES, FM AND CARTELS

This flood does not offend against the model's notion that new technologies are always to a certain extent suppressed. It must not be forgotten that, when the receiver market got off the ground, radio had been delayed for at least a decade, given that the technology was available by 1907 and the first 'broadcasts' did not take place until 1919. Only four of these years can be accounted for by the war. Of more significance was the patent war over the valve, such conflicts always being a sure sign that the 'law' of suppression was at work. In this instance, the row about who had 'invented' the valve produced a series of legal wrangles as protracted as those which had surrounded the introduction of the telephone.

De Forest's valve had worked so brilliantly that 'Fleming never forgave him. It led to very much bitterness and endless litigation' (Sturmey 1958: 33). The reason was that they were very similar devices, so that Marconi, even with the Fleming patent, could not make a real amplifying valve without de Forest's patent as well. On the other hand, de Forest could not himself build a triode without infringing on Fleming and, later, Armstrong. The entire industry was subject to considerable uncertainty because of the conflict between the diode and triode tube until Fleming's patent expired, significantly, in 1922. That year, radio telephony experiments were resumed, leading finally to the provision of a service primarily by the telephone interests. Even then, the valve patent case continued until 1943 when, finally, the United States' Supreme Court decided that, despite the essential contribution of Fleming (and Armstrong), de Forest had sole claim to the triode tube. The latter declared himself 'the father of radio'.

The radio system that swept the world in the early 1920s was capable of considerable improvement and the failure to introduce refinements can be considered another element of suppression. Edwin Armstrong, who had contributed to the development of the valve as amplifier and had licensed his advances to Westinghouse in 1911, now developed a relationship with Sarnoff's RCA. After selling RCA some further radio patents in 1922, Armstrong, as a result independently wealthy, set about obeying a wish of the great man that a radio system less subject to interference, noise, be created. Armstrong continued to work at

Columbia University until, in 1933, he produced a signal of preternatural clarity, at least to contemporary ears, by using a totally new system of modulation.

If an analogue of the original, without digital sampling, is to be impressed on a carrier wave, there are in essence only two ways in which it can be done. Either the signal is modulated in strength or in frequency – AM or FM. (Digitalisation raises different and more complex options.) The first radio system relied on amplitude modulation. Armstrong produced a signal created by frequency modulation but, at RCA, the great man's needs had changed. The noisy AM radios of the early 1920s now worked well enough for Sarnoff to be running a major enterprise. At the height of the depression, RCA shed less than 20 per cent of its employees and, in all the years of economic disaster, it made losses only in 1932 and 1933. Armstrong's device was no longer needed and, worse, it now posed a considerable threat. Sarnoff said FM was not just an invention but a revolution. In the event it was a revolution that RCA did not want. Armstrong was asked to remove his equipment from the Empire State Building (Barnouw 1975: 40–1). The battle for FM radio became, because of frequency allocation issues, inexorably intertwined with the arguments about the development of television. One result of that battle is that FM is used as the standard for television sound. Armstrong sued RCA for royalties and spent a full year in the witness box being grilled by corporation lawyers for his trouble. He gave in and authorised a settlement. All his life, since 1911, he had been embattled, first with de Forest and then with RCA. It proved too much for him. The money, $1 million, was paid to his estate, for he had stepped out of his apartment window before a deal was finalised (Barnouw 1975: 78–9). FM radio had still not entirely vanquished AM in the last decade of the twentieth century.

On the other hand, if the patent row and the FM fiasco indicate suppression, the same patent row plus a dollop of national interests also forced the major players into close agreements which facilitated the diffusion of radio in these early years. We have seen how the American government, primarily at the behest of the United States Navy, in effect nationalised the British Marconi Company and then handed the exploitation of radio over to RCA. With the patent pool which was also signed, a cartel-like arrangement emerged ensuring a stable market for sets. There remained, however, the question of how to absorb the cost of providing programming. In the 1920s most commercial US operators

> were hardly professional broadcasters in the modern sense of the term. The majority were owned and operated by newspapers, department stores, power companies, and other private concerns, and their *raison d'être* was to generate favourable publicity for the owner's primary

enterprise. Indeed, as late as 1929, few if any private broadcasters were thought to be earning profits from the business of broadcasting.

(McChesney 1990: 30)

This is how Sarnoff's great rival, William Paley, started in radio – by advertising his family's cigar business. Advertising had been introduced by AT&T who, in seeking to treat the radio as just another sort of telephone, had come up with the concept of leased time for commercial messages.

Paradoxically, the telephone company was in radio to protect its core telephony interests. Protecting telephony was the essential rationale that lay behind the establishment of the Bell Labs at this time. One of AT&T's central functions within the emerging Bell system had been to continue a serious programme of research and development, a tradition that led to the merging of AT&T's research arm with Western Electric's in 1907. AT&T had, more or less, destroyed or absorbed the domestic telegraph companies, including the giant Western Union by the First World War. It was not going to let any other organisation, brandishing a new technology, do the same to it – hence the Bell Telephone Laboratories, founded in 1925. The Labs, for all their central contributions to the development of mass communications, were not designed to be an engine of innovation, except in a public relations sense, but rather an expression of constraint, of the operation of the suppression of radical potential. Bell Labs' primary interest in all new technologies has been to secure the phone company by controlling at least some of the patents in any new area. The patent system gave the telephone company a series of major bargaining chips to be used, during the first century of its existence, in its evolving relationship with the society it serves.

But the Labs were only part of Bell's response to radio. It owned part of RCA and by 1923 was hungrily eyeing the development of radio stations:

> We have been very careful [said the vice-president charged with radio responsibilities], up to the present time, not to state in public in any way, through the press or in any of our talks that the Bell system desires to monopolise broadcasting, but the fact remains that it is a telephone job, that we are telephone people, that we can do it better than anybody else, and it seems to me that the clear, logical, conclusion that must be reached sooner or later in one form or another, is we have got to do this job.
>
> (Waldrop and Borkin 1938: 172)

This upbeat approach led in that year to the 'invention' of commercial sponsorship – toll broadcasting – at WEAF, the AT&T station in New York, because selling airtime seemed exactly like selling telephone time (Hilmes 1990: 18). However, programming proved to be a real bother – not a job for telephone people at all. For example, it sacked one of its own early radio stars at the prompting of the Secretary of State because the broadcaster had dared to criticise the politician. As one AT&T executive wrote at the time, in conformity with Vail's traditional placatory and diplomatic approach, the phone company believed in a 'fundamental policy of constant and complete co-operation with every government institution that was concerned with communications' (Sola Pool 1983: 121–2), and even, as the incident reveals, a few that were not. All this was a long way from a culture of mass media freedom of expression.

More than that, AT&T's plan to treat radio channels like telephone lines was seen by almost all other parties as yet another attempt to create a monopoly. 'Monopoly' and the threat thereof became, in the debate about broadcasting that raged in America in the 1920s, a code expression for the phone company and its schemes. It was only by threatening to exploit the cross-licensing agreements and to set Western Union up as a rival radio network that the other members of the radio manufacturing pool got AT&T to back off. By 1926 AT&T was prepared to give up this approach to radio. It sold the New York station to RCA, at the same time relinquishing its RCA stock.

Also influencing the situation was the chaos of station wavelength allocation. The Secretary of Commerce, Herbert Hoover, had been doing this, against a background of a series of conferences he had summoned of all interested parties, but in 1926 a Federal judge had declared such action illegal. Many stations then started to broadcast around the 100m wavelength since that was the most effective part of the spectrum for contemporary receivers and 200 unlicensed broadcasters came on air. Legislation was hurriedly prepared and passed as the 1927 Radio Act. It created the Federal Radio Commission (FRC) as the licensing authority but for one year only. This was renewed in 1928 and became a permanent arrangement in 1929.

Commercialisation was not the inevitable result of all this. Sarnoff himself had thought of programming as a municipal responsibility and there were by this time more than 200 educational broadcasters mainly attached to universities, the 'true pioneers of US broadcasting' (McChesney 1990: 30), demonstrating the viability of a public service alternative. The FRC was endlessly admonished to protect them as it set about sorting out the wavelength allocation mess, but it was dominated by commercial interests and did no such thing (ibid.: 32). 'The commercial broadcasters actively cultivated the notion. . . that the status quo was innately democratic and American and that even the consideration of alternatives was absurd, if not dangerous' (McChesney 1991: 109). By 1934, when the FRC was replaced by the Federal Communication Commission (FCC), a Rooseveltian agency to control all aspects of telecommunication, the commercial nature of American broadcasting was irrevocably established. The period of suppression was over and, once again, the American government had shown itself to be unwilling to intervene in a communications system which had demonstrated an ability to make profits for private interests.

Elsewhere, as with telegraphy and telephony, a different approach developed. In Britain the government tackled both set manufacturing and programme provision at the same time. Radio in the UK was in much the same basic legal situation as in America. In place of the US 1912 Radio Act, the British had ratified the two Berlin Conventions and, in 1909, had passed a Wireless Telegraphy Act requiring wireless telegraphy stations to be licensed. The Act in effect nationalised all the Marconi's and Lloyd's stations by passing them to the GPO. The precedent of the mails, which had held for the telegraph and the telephone, was now applied to the wireless telegraph. In practice, wireless telegraphy proved to be close enough to telegraphy for the same solutions to be applied, namely an extension of the Post Office communications monopoly except internationally where the Post Office was prepared, of necessity, to be one player among many. Marconi's was left with the long distance, transoceanic business (Sturmey 1958: 58–9).

Broadcast radio conformed less to this model. Nevertheless, when Marconi's built and began operating an experimental radio station at Chelmsford in 1920, there was no question that, as with all wireless telegraphy stations, this enterprise would be licensed by the GPO. As had happened with telephony, though, the GPO's involvement ensured caution and delay. Broadcasters were already active in a number of European countries; but still the GPO hesitated to approve Marconi's as a radio monopoly. After all it had just spent two decades struggling to prevent it from becoming a wireless telegraphy monopoly. At one point, the GPO even offered to license a society of radio enthusiasts instead. By late 1921, though, delay was no longer possible. A number of other radio equipment manufacturers were applying for licenses. The Post Office responded by insisting that no more than two entities would be allowed to broadcast to the general public and the manufacturers therefore lined up either behind Marconi's or Metropolitan Vickers which was in partnership with Western Electric and had Westinghouse connections. Post Office hostility to a perceived Marconi monopoly was dictating a complex solution but in the course of negotiations with the radio manufacturers it was eventually determined that one corporation collectively owned (RCA-style) by the 300 or so firms then in the business would work just as well as two (*BBC Yearbook* 1928: 37).

The fundamental point of the exercise was quite clear. In the interests of limiting disruption to the established wireless telegraphy market, all players in that market were to become privileged players in the new radio market. Not only that; the potential conflict of ownership over the new application of the technology was contained by ensuring that wireless telegraph and telephone entities were involved. Receivers would be licensed just as transmitters were and a fee would be charged for this. By manipulating the basis upon which these revenues would be distributed, Marconi's was forced into a real partnership with its rivals. A Marconi monopoly was thereby avoided while at the same time a system of structured development was imposed on the single licensee. The British Broadcasting Company, which had already begun broadcasting from London, Manchester, Birmingham and Newcastle in late 1922, received its licence on 18 January 1923 (Sturmey 1958: 137, 145). It was to run for two years. These arrangements for the BBCo were confirmed by the recommendations of British broadcasting's first committee of inquiry, led by Sir Frederick Sykes in 1923. Sykes was asked, somewhat belatedly, what form radio should take in the UK. It chose to confirm the BBCo as a *fait accompli*.

But in Britain, the question of private ownership still loomed large and the renewal of the BBCo's licence afforded further opportunity for argument about this issue. Again a little belatedly, a second committee, chaired by Lord Crawford, was convened in 1925. Received opinion holds that when the Crawford Committee visited the USA, it was the cacophony of commercial stations which confirmed it in the opinion that a unified public service offered a better solution. But this is somewhat simplified. On the one hand, it must be remembered that no American commercial broadcaster was obviously making money from programming in 1925 and, conversely, the universities had established a precedent for non-commercial educational broadcasting. On the other hand, the tradition in the UK, prior to Crawford, was that communications systems would not be run for private profit. Moreover, as Graham Murdock points out, several other factors were also in play – echoes of a pre-war American debate as to the civic failings of the commercial press, the idea that radio was a cultural amenity like libraries or adult education provision (as Sarnoff believed), and the wartime model of running essential services as public corporations (Murdock 1992: 24, 26). Crawford once again confirmed the main outline of the GPO's dirigiste solution but proposed converting the BBCo into a Commission authorised by Royal Charter. On 1 January 1927 the BBCo became the BBC, exactly as Crawford and John Reith, BBCo's chief executive wanted, except that the 'C' stood not for 'Commission' but for 'Corporation', albeit in a medieval rather than modern commercial sense. The manufacturers who were BBCo's shareholders were paid off and a second model for the organisation of an independent broadcasting system was placed before the world.

These somewhat protracted developments allowed radio to take its place beside other forms of recreation, notably records, the cinema (which was still mute although not silent), the theatre (with its popular forms of variety, etc.) and the newspapers. This happened albeit not without a certain amount of friction as these various elements adjusted to the newcomer. These rubs can be seen as a species of further negotiations designed to suppress radio's potential for disruption.

## LIVING WITH RADIO

Radio had used recorded sound from the very beginning. Copyright in mechanical recording had been, after a certain amount of difficulty, established by a Berne Convention meeting in Berlin in 1908. Copyright Acts in the US in 1909 and in Britain in 1911 established the royalty principle for recordings and a system of compulsory licensing which allowed artistes to record whatever material they liked providing they paid the royalty. In 1914, the American Society of Composers and Publishers (ASCAP) was formed to collect these various revenues (Chanan 1995: 35). The system for licensing radio use of recorded material was therefore in place when, more or less a decade later, the radio industry was finally under way. At the second of Secretary Hoover's radio conferences held on 20 March 1923, ASCAP insisted that royalties be paid for the broadcast of music in any form (Hilmes 1990: 16).

The relationship between records and radio was complex. On the one hand, just as the radio was giving away programming to sell sets, so the record industry was more interested in selling players and saw discs as a way of helping this. This was the sort of mind set that led Victor to do a deal in 1925 with WEAF whereby the record company provided an hour of free music while AT&T waived the advertising fee. Radio could sell records as effectively as it could sell anything else (Chanan 1995: 55, 61). There was also a measure of protection for the record industry because audiences came to expect radio to be live and objected to 'canned' or 'bottled' programming (Winston 1993: 182). This was reinforced by a predilection on the part of the regulators, when they came into being, to privilege live broadcasting. The FRC in 1928, for example, announced it would favour licensees who provided live entertainment rather than phonograph records (Hilmes 1990: 27). The radio very rapidly became a major patron of music and musicians, again easing the economic impact of its coming on those most directly concerned. The BBC, for example, founded and sustained a wide range of popular and classical orchestras to ensure a supply of live performance.

On the other hand, the radio gave better reproduction because it was electric and after a disastrous fall in sales in 1924, the record industry rushed to introduce electronic recordings and electrical players. But this merely halted the decline for a few years. The radio was a far more economic way to access music and the bottom fell out of the record market as economic conditions worsened. Record sales fell in America from a 1926 peak of 128 million to a mere 6 million in 1932. By 1929, Victor was taken over by RCA (Chanan 1995: 65–6). Radio in the US did play a clear role in this decline and, moreover, the record industry was in no condition to resist, in effect to suppress the development of radio. In the UK, though, there were early attempts to use copyright to limit the broadcaster's access to material, words as well as music, especially before the BBC proper was founded. Thus Kipling could not be used, nor Gilbert and Sullivan before 1926. 'The BBC met with opposition in many places where [its] path ran near land already inhabited' (*BBC Yearbook* 1930: 160). However, these objections crumbled as the broadcasting system was extended.

The American film industry, and the popular theatre which had been battered by it for twenty-five years, did not regard the new medium as a direct competitor. Hollywood felt no need to participate in the radio conferences (Hilmes 1990: 26). On the other hand, there is now a broad measure of agreement among film scholars that Warner's sound film initiative was deeply influenced by its connect-ions to the radio business. Sam Warner set up KFWB in Los Angeles in March 1925 specifically to promote Warner's movies and stars. WBPI followed in New York in 1926. Warner was merely copying the pioneering efforts of Samuel 'Roxy' Rothapfel, movie theatre manager, who used the AT&T station in New York to broadcast the acts appearing in his pre-film vaudeville show. As with records, the radio could be used to sell anything, even movie tickets (ibid.: 33–5). By 1927 such tie-ins were commonplace and led to full-scale experimentations such as one occasion when 'an entire motion picture' was 'broadcast in detail' with a com-mentator describing the film as it unreeled 'before his eyes' (ibid.: 43, 45).

Finally, it can be noted that various moves by the studios to buy their way into the emerging radio networking business came to nothing. Despite this, the film industry, in effect, achieved a mutually beneficial accommodation with the radio industry: 'The major studios found themselves standing on the outside of radio networking and ownership, but holding some valuable assets on the programming side of the radio game' (ibid.: 53). Elsewhere in the world, the indigenous film and theatre industries were simply not strong enough to impact on the radio in any meaningful way; although, once again, the UK variety industry endeavoured to ignore the BBCo by attempting a minor boycott of the studios throughout the mid 1920s (*BBC Yearbook* 1930: 159–60).

If Hollywood learned to live with radio without owning much of it, the converse is true of the American newspaper industry. Here, despite a measure of radio-station ownership, there were serious attempts to control and suppress at least the journalistic aspects of the new medium. Newspaper owners were quick to see radio as potential investment as much as a threat and they rapidly came to constitute an extremely significant group of players in the new industry. By 1932, for example, one-third of CBS stations were owned by them. Yet this did not mean that they were prepared to allow the radio to exploit its potential as a news medium against their other interests. On the contrary.

Reading the news had been part of the earliest phase of radio experimentation. A pioneering radio station was doing it in San Jose in 1909 (Greb 1958–9: 3). The first US election returns were broadcast in 1916 and the Harding–Cox election of 1920 is said to mark the start of regular news broadcasting in the US (Bohn 1968:

268). As radio became a mass medium in the 1920s, the American Newspaper Publishers Association (ANPA) sought to restrict its access to news. As they owned the wire services, they could simply close off the easiest source. While they did not so much mind using their own local news operations to provide a measure of local news, structured to help sell their newspapers, they objected to the use of national and international news by the emerging networks (p. 261). As network affiliates they would have some say over this.

The extensive coverage of the 1932 election and the Lindbergh baby kidnapping brought matters to a head. The ANPA told its members to stop running radio programme listings, even if they owned the stations concerned. The broadcasters started independent news gathering operations for the first time, but in December 1933, they gave in and signed the Biltmore Agreement. This meant that, in return for having the papers once more publish the listings, the broadcasters agreed to restrict their news operations (McChesney 1991: 46–7). But the logic of cross ownership and the limited reality of the threat radio actually posed to newspapers meant that this was not the end of the story. Two things dissolved the ANPA's hostility. First, they discovered that the new medium did not wipe out the old. People who listened to news broadcasts on the radio would still buy a newspaper. Second, they were divided among themselves, that is those who had radio interests against those who did not. By 1937, the ANPA resolved that co-operation was necessary and entirely possible. In time for the major events of the later 1930s and the war, the parties gave up their hostile posturings. However, it may be noted that this structured suppression had prevented the development of radio as a fully fledged news medium for the better part of two decades.

In Britain, the cartel did not allow for any measure of cross ownership and newspaper hostility was even more pronounced. The original BBCo licence prohibited the broadcast of any news bulletin prior to 7 p.m., the time of the last edition of the evening papers. After that time only bulletins provided by one out of four approved news agencies could be used (*BBC Yearbook* 1930: 159). These restrictions disappeared for the first time during the 1926 General Strike:

> When most other forms of communication were almost at a standstill, and newspapers in the ordinary sense, non-existent, the BBC carried on, in addition to its normal activities, an all-day service of news and general information. . . .The copyright usually reserved by the News Agencies was for the period of the emergency waived.
>
> (ibid.: 179)

As in America, the newspaper publishers' worries were seen to be increasingly unfounded and as the pace of events increased in the 1930s, these attempts to limit radio as a news medium died in Britain as well. By 1932, the BBC had established its own news operation.

In both the United States and the UK, this conscious suppression by the newspaper publishers did have the effect of encouraging the development of complex forms of radio reporting and, especially in Britain, a distinction between news bulletins and other sorts of factual programming (e.g. 'talks' or 'document-aries') which worked to create an ideologically powerful culture of objectivity and neutrality in the former.

Beyond the conflict over news, one can see in the first responses of these other 'inhabited lands' a natural hostility and even, with the minor use of boycott and copyright, some futile attempts to limit the growth of radio. But radio had been quite slow to arrive and its growth in the 1920s was more directly suppressed by the regulatory environment than by the action of these contiguous industries. By 1930 it had successfully become a mass home medium over almost all the developed world, the first.

# 5

# MECHANICALLY SCANNED TELEVISION

## SCIENTIFIC COMPETENCE: LIGHT AND ELECTRICITY

Investigations into the nature of light constitute a venerable tradition. By the eighteenth century, various explanations, none broadly agreed, had existed to explain the phenomenon. (This was, in Kuhnian terms, a preparadigm phase.) Newton's theory that light came in discrete bits, corpuscles, was pitted against the contradictory idea of Huygens that it was continuous. Dr Thomas Young, the father of physioptics, whom we have already met in connection with acoustic machines and as an influence on Faraday, here made his most fertile contribution to the scientific competencies underpinning modern communications systems by proving Huygens right. The proof was to stand for the next 104 years.

In 1801, Young was studying the patterns thrown on a screen when light from a monochromatic source, sodium, passed through a narrow slit. Areas lit through one slit darkened when a second slit, illuminated by the same sodium light source, opened. This phenomenon – interference – Young explained by assuming that light consists of continuous waves and suggesting that interference was caused when the crests of the waves from one slit were cancelled by the troughs emanating from the second. He was able to measure the wavelengths of different coloured lights, getting close to modern results. The importance of the concept of interference cannot be overstated since it is still current and lies at the heart of holography; but for television Young's experiment was suggestive because, eventually, it allowed researchers to think of systems which treated light waves as telephony treated sound waves.

Television depends in essence on the photovoltaic (or photoemissive) effect, that is the characteristic possessed by some substances of releasing electrons when struck by light. The observation of this phenomenon is credited to a 19-year-old, Edmond Bequerel, in 1839, but it seems that his father, the savant Antoine Cesar, may have helped him to prepare his account for L'Academie des Sciences. Their experiment demonstrated that a current passes between the two electrodes of a voltaic cell when a beam of light falls on the apparatus.

A Swedish chemist, Baron Berzelius, had isolated selenium, a non-metallic element of the sulphur group, in 1818, without noticing (in advance of Bequerel) that it was photoemissive. Selenium was initially of practical interest because it had a very high resistance to electricity. Willoughby Smith, a supervisory telegraph engineer involved in the laying of the first successful transatlantic cable, was directed to it because of this property.

> While in charge of the electrical department of the laying of the cable from Valentia to Heart's Content in 1866 I introduced a new system by which ship and shore could communicate freely with each other without interfering with the necessary electrical tests. To work this system it was necessary that a resistance of about one hundred megohms should be attached to the shore end of the cable. . . .While searching for a suitable material the high resistance of selenium was brought to my notice but at the same time I was informed that it was doubtful whether it would answer my purpose as it was not constant in its resistance.
>
> (Garratt and Mumford 1952: 26)

May, an operator of Willoughby Smith's, noticed the correlation between the erratic behaviour of the selenium resistor and sunlight. Willoughby Smith investigated and made his results known in 1873.

> When the bars were fixed in a box with a sliding cover, so as to exclude all light, their resistance was at its highest, and remained very constant. . .but immediately the cover of the box was removed, the conductivity increased from 15 to 100 per cent, according to the intensity of the light falling on the bar. . . .To ensure that temperature was in no way affecting the experiments, one of the bars was placed in a trough of water so that there was about an inch of water for the light to pass through, but the results were the same; and when a narrow band of magnesium was held about nine inches above the water the resistance immediately fell more than two thirds, returning to its normal condition immediately the light was extinguished.
>
> I am sorry that I shall not be able to attend the meeting of the Society of Telegraph Engineers to-morrow evening. If, however, you think this communication of sufficient interest, perhaps you will bring it before the meeting.
>
> (ibid.: 25)

It was deemed of 'sufficient interest' and a long process of investigation began.

Some of these enquiries led to devices, using first sodium and then potassium which proved to be more sensitive than selenium, specifically designed to produce photoelectricity. The contrivances never left the lab since, for theoretical physics, photoelectricity became a central area of investigation. Only the light meter (in fact, a practical and sensitive photocell) emerged, reaching the point of commercial production by 1913.

J.J. Thomson's demonstration in 1897 that such photoelectric phenomena depended upon particles and not on waves was the first indication of the existence of sub-atomic particles. He called them, using a term suggested by Johnston Stoney, 'electrons' and suggested that what was happening in photoelectric emission was the liberation of electrons from the atoms of the substance through the action of the light. Thus was the belief in the indivisibility of atoms shattered and the dedicated, and fateful, investigation of the sub-atomic world begun. Crucial to this work was the electron beam tube or, as it came to be commonly called, cathode ray tube (CRT). Cathode rays had been described by Sir William Crookes in 1878 and the tube, which made the streams of electrons visible to the eye, was introduced in 1897, the year of the electron. The CRT, like all these devices except the light meter, remained within the lab, a tool of advanced physics and nothing more.

Eight years later Einstein explained the mathematisation of photoelectric emission (photoemissive) phenomena, in effect using it as a proof and extension of Max Planck's quantum hypothesis of 1900 that 'radiant heat. . .must be defined as a discontinuous mass made up of units (quanta) all of which are similar to each other' (Handel 1967: 39). Maxwell's wave paradigm began to follow Franklin's one-fluid theory into history since the experimental proof of Einstein's 'photons' demonstrated that the higher the frequency of the light the greater the speed of the emitted electrons – which would not be the case if light were continuous. Newton was right after all, but so was Huygens; our current picture of light is a paradoxical synthesis of both descriptions.

The ground of scientific competence for television also contains other elements. In 1602 a Bolognese cobbler and part-time alchemist, Cascariolo, found a mineral – a sulphide of barium known as 'Bologna Stone' – which would glow brightly after being exposed to light. This phosphor was of excellent value for the performance of tricks but it was so rare that a search was initiated for an alternative, that is for a stable phosphor which could be manufactured. In 1886 this was achieved. Fluorescence was a similar phenomenon whose investigation is of equal duration. That certain substances will emit luminous coloured light was noticed in antiquity and much described in the eighteenth century. Sir George Stokes, however, was the first to offer, in 1852, a reasonable explanation of the effect and to name it (after the mineral fluorspar).

All these strands together constitute the ground of scientific competence in relation to which the technological development of television takes place. Phosphors were understood. Fluorescent paint was being manufactured. The long-distance electrical transmission of images by means of the facsimile telegraph had been a reality since the middle of the nineteenth century. The cathode ray tube existed. Research into electro-optical effects led, by 1905, to the direct modulation of an electric arc through the action of a light beam and in 1907 the emission of light from a crystal rectifier had been reported (Phillips 1980: 207). Knowledge of thermionic amplification had produced, by 1907, the practical basis for radio and radio-telephony systems. Photoelectric effects had been utilised in the production of light-sensitive cells by 1913. By the First World War, the dream of television was over thirty years old.

## IDEATION: FAXES AND 'FUGITIVE PICTURES'

Following the announcement of the peculiar properties of selenium and the excitement generated by the introduction of the telephone, numerous notions for 'telescopy' were put forward. The television receiver was first imagined by a Punch cartoonist as a two-way interactive device whereby those at home could talk to those on the screen by telephone. The telephonoscope's screen stretched the entire width of the mantelpiece. It is unlikely that the artist, in 1879, would have had much grasp of how such a device might work. Yet the basic principles which were to lead to television were already understood by the scientific community.

Senlecq, a French lawyer, was the first to suggest how selenium might be used in a scanning system. He was, like most of these early thinkers, primarily concerned with a reprographic apparatus that would work telegraphically – telephotography or facsimile telegraphy, in effect. Senlecq envisaged television, as did most of his peers, not as the instantaneous transmission of images on to a screen but rather as the transfer of a single image, perhaps a series of images, on to paper. He published a brief account of a telectroscope in *An English Mechanic* of 1878. The device would reproduce at a distance the images obtained in the camera obscura. The scanning notion was expressed as follows:

> An ordinary camera obscura containing at the focus an unpolished glass (screen) and any system of automatic telegraphic transmission; the tracing point of the transmitter intended to traverse the surface of the unpolished glass will be formed of a small piece of selenium held by two springs acting as pincers, insulated and connected, one with a pile and the other with the line.
>
> (Garratt and Mumford 1952: 26)

Senlecq's receiver was simply a pencil operating on the same principle as the vibrating diaphragm in a telephone receiver, tracing its responses to the irregularity in the current (generated by the light hitting the selenium) on to paper. Senlecq refined the transmitter in a proposal two years later. Instead of a single moving block of selenium traversing the screen of the camera obscura he now suggested a mosaic of selenium cells, each to transmit by separate wires to a similar mosaic in the receiver.

Senlecq reported: 'The picture is, therefore, reproduced almost instantaneously; . . .we can obtain a picture, of a fugitive nature, it is true, but yet so vivid that the impression on the retina does not fade' (ibid.: 26). It is unlikely that Senlecq's electrically driven pencil would have created the halftones necessary to duplicate a photographic effect; nor was he concerned with movement as he was simply refining the telegraphic facsimile. He had, however, suggested a scanning system, involving moving the selenium across the groundglass screen of a camera obscura.

His talk of 'fugitive pictures' stirred the imagination of others on both sides of the Atlantic. Suggestions along these lines involved increasingly complex mosaics of selenium and spinning mirrors. Some were even built. For example, in 1881, Bidwell demonstrated a contrivance where, for the first time, transmitter and receiver were synchronised. A single selenium cell was mounted in a box with a pin-hole aperture which was arranged within a frame so it could be cranked to rise and fall relative to a screen upon which the image to be transmitted was projected. At the receiving end a drum was rotated to match this motion and created a negative image on paper soaked in potassium iodide. The image was built up of a series of closely spaced brown lines. He showed the system to a number of learned societies (ibid.: 27–8).

The Bidwell machine can be classified in two ways. As a type of facsimile telegraph, it was redundant because these had existed for more than thirty years already (p. 28). In television terms, though, it can be considered as the most partial of prototypes because, although it successfully used photoemission as a means of creating an image, as a transmitter of single images, only in the crudest sense can it be considered as television at all. Bidwell deposited the apparatus in the Science Museum in London and did nothing further for a quarter of a century.

In January 1884, Paul Nipkow, a Berlin science student, filed patents for an 'electric telescope'. He had, over that previous Christmas, placed a small disk perforated with a spiral of holes between a lens and an element of selenium which was inserted into an electrical circuit. He knew that selenium, when exposed to light, would vary any electrical current passed through it in response to the intensity of the light. When the disk spun the image was scanned, breaking it down into a series of varying light impulses. These, as they hit the selenium plate, created variable resistance in the circuit. At the other end of the circuit, the process could be reversed. The electric current could be reconstituted into a series of light waves which, when passed through an exactly synchronous spinning disk, would reconstruct the picture. This could then be viewed through an eyepiece. After another year's work Nipkow filed a master patent for television. Although he had established a viable system of 'scanning' with the disk, he then, like Bidwell, did nothing more. Bidwell was 'inventing' the fax which was already in existence and Nipkow was 'inventing' an *'Elektrisches Teleskop'* which again, as the name he gave it reveals, was a substitute for a device which had existed for centuries.

Although the fantasy, albeit grounded in the principles of telephony, of seeing distant moving pictures with sound was in the air, nevertheless a confusion seems to have existed in the minds of many of these early television thinkers. They dreamed of the reproduction of movement, dreamed of it in advance of the cinema; but they addressed themselves to the transmission of stills, a species of almost redundant effort since (as we have seen) other systems already existed for such purposes. The advent of moving pictures did nothing to increase the need they were addressing with these experiments. This general blindness, though, certainly did not afflict one senior British 'electrician', Campbell Swinton, the man who had introduced Marconi to the Post Office.

In a letter published in *Nature*, on 16 June 1908, he outlined the most significant of all the early schemes for television. This description of a totally electronic system appears to have been prompted by a public promise made by M. Armenguard, the president of the French Society of Aerial Navigation, that 'within a year, as a consequence of the advance already made by his apparatus, we shall be watching one another across distances hundreds of miles apart'. Shelford Bidwell, one of the few to have actually built a selenium device, knew the limitations as well as anybody. Not conceiving of any alternative to mechanical scanning, he was prompted by the Armenguard announcement to remind the world in print of his forgotten demonstrations which had taken place over a quarter of a century earlier. Then, in part in support of Bidwell, Campbell Swinton was moved to lay down the basic principles of modern television. He was dismissive of all mechanical scanning and multiple wire systems and suggested instead that the problem could:

> probably be solved by the employment of two beams of kathode [sic] rays (one at the transmitting and one at the receiving station) synchronously deflected by the varying fields of two electromagnets . . . indeed so far as the receiving apparatus is concerned the moving kathode beam has only to be arranged to impinge on a sufficiently sensitive fluorescent screen, and given suitable variations in its intensity, to obtain the desired result.
>
> (ibid.: 31)

Three years later in his presidential address to the Rontgen Society he elaborated his ideas on the receiver by suggesting a special cathode ray tube which would have, at its front, a mosaic screen of photoelectrical dots but added, 'it is an idea only and the apparatus has never been constructed'. In moving the vote of thanks Silvanus Thompson described the idea as 'a most interesting, beautiful and ingenious speculation' (Thompson 1912: 15). In a way that can perhaps be categorised as rather typically British, Campbell Swinton carefully assessed the difficulties of an all-electric television system and determined it was not worth trying to build because of what he claimed would be the vast expense involved.

Before it became known as television, it was called telephotography, telescopy or teleautography. As late as 1911, a British patent official opened a new file on the matter as a branch of facsimile telegraphy, even though he called it television, a term first coined independently by Persky in 1900. By far the most interesting depositions in the new file were British Patents Nos 27570/07 and 5486/11 outlining 'A Method of Transmitting Images Over A Distance' using a velocity modulation cathode ray receiver awarded to Boris Rozing.

## PROTOTYPES: MECHANICAL SCANNING

Paul Nipkow, who died in Berlin in 1940, worked all his life for a railway signal manufacturing company. In his seventies, in 1934, he assumed the presidency of the German Television Society. For the fifty years between the patent and the presidency he did nothing with television; nevertheless, his patent was a potent stimulus to a large number of others worldwide (Hubbell 1942: 65). In fact, his ideas were much more stimulating, if only because they were apparently more practical than were Campbell Swinton's and Rozing's. The first decades of the twentieth century were the golden age of the Nipkow disk and its variants.

Mechanical scanning systems were now being built and selenium lag was no longer the major problem. More responsive substances had been isolated and various sophisticated arrangements of spinning mirrors and the like had increased the sensitivity of the photoelectrical elements yet further. Although the number of scanned lines generated remained few, the essential problem was perceived to lie more in the difficulties of maintaining exact synchronicity between the disks at either end of the system rather than with definition. From Hungary to the United States, where C.F. Jenkins, who had contributed significantly to the development of the movie projector, demonstrated an elegant apparatus, many 'inventors' were busily spinning disks. From 1923 Herbert Ives and others at Bell Labs were conducting television experiments. In 1927 they demonstrated, over 250 miles by wire and 22 miles by radio, a system identical in principle to these others. Two forms of apparatus were used, one giving a picture $2 \times 2\frac{1}{2}$ inches and the other 2

$\times$ $2\frac{1}{2}$ feet, a multi-element water-cooled neon lamp as the screen (Fagen 1975: 790; Ives 1927: 551). They also used the apparatus to scan film taken either at the transmitter or receiver end, so that a better illuminated picture could be achieved. Over the next few years Ives and his fellow workers increased the lines to seventy-two and introduced colour. By the early 1930s they had a two-way interactive system working in Manhattan. The videophone (that most beloved of all Inform-ation Revolution hardware) is thus decades old (Ives *et al.* 1930: *passim*). Its 'inventor', this same Dr Ives, told a British visitor:

> frankly he has not the remotest idea whether the public want to see the fellow at the other end of the telephone line badly enough to pay a high price for the privilege. But when the AT&T started to develop the transatlantic telephone years ago, they did not know whether sufficient people would pay the necessarily high price to make a service profitable. But the transatlantic telephone does pay.
>
> (Dinsdale 1932: 139)

More seriously, the facsimile implications of these developments remained import-ant, hence at least one strand of the telephone company's interest in the matter. AT&T could, though, at the time of these experiments, do far better with existing equipment than with television. It was using a fax standard well beyond the capacity of any mechanical scanning system – a 5 $\times$ 7-inch image divided into 350,000 elements taking 7 minutes to transmit. Ives calculated that a television band to achieve similar detail would require the then rather unimaginable band-width of 3 million cycles per second, 7000 times the one being used.

By 1928, General Electric's E. F. W. Alexanderson had gone so far with the disks that fairly regular experimental transmissions from the GE radio station in Schenectady could begin. GE also mounted a demonstration using a screen 7 feet square, erected in a local theatre (Biting 1965: 1017). By 1929, the FRC had licensed twenty-two radio stations to transmit pictures. The game with W1XAV, Boston, was for a group of MIT students to go to the station while another group, in the college, gathered round the scanning-disk receiver and tried to guess which of their friends in the studio they were looking at (Fink 1945: 146). But in general, despite the proliferation of different firms and mechanical systems, the American public was uninvolved in these experiments.

Among the many on the other side of the Atlantic who toyed with such devices was the Scottish entrepreneur, John Logie Baird, who spent the decade after 1925 devising increasingly complex scanning systems. By 1928 his Baird Television Development Company (BTDC), working on a thirty-line picture scanning at $12\frac{1}{2}$ frames a second, was nevertheless building televisors (or receivers) for public domestic sale. However, nobody in either BTDC or the Post Office was under any illusion as to the BBC's interest in these developments. Baird, who had been at technical college with BBC Director-General John Reith, founded his Television Company the year before the Corporation received its charter, but the BBC treated Baird's enterprise as that of an unwarranted upstart. Reith's chief engineer, Peter Eckersley, was scathing about it:

> The advisers of the Baird Television Company believe that this apparatus is sufficiently well developed to have a public service value. They contend that the attitude of the BBC is obstructive and irrational. The advisers of the BBC believe on the other hand that the Baird apparatus not only does not deserve a public trial, but also has reached the limit of its development owing to the basic technical limitations of the method employed.
>
> (Briggs 1961: 530 n.3)

The BBC has never found it difficult to adopt such a tone (at least prior to the organisational upheavals of the late 1980s and 1990s). In this instance it was fully justified. The fact remained that Baird's was a partial prototype and it represented the end of the line, just as the BBC claimed.

Nevertheless, through a shotgun marriage once again arranged by the Post Office, the BBC did begin experimenting with television and evolved a working relationship with BTDC which was at times positively cordial. By 1930, 'televisors' were being sold at 25 guineas the set, and in April sound joined pictures in the transmissions. The system still produced an oblong picture of only thirty lines definition, although it had by now improved sufficiently for actual programming to be undertaken. The BBC began serious exploration of the new medium, transmitting, in July of that year, the world's first 'upscale' television play, Pirandello's *The Man with the Flower in His Mouth* in co-operation with Baird (Norman 1984: 61). General Electric had broadcast the somewhat less esoteric melodrama *The Queen's Messenger* from its Schenectady station two years before. The difference in style and ambition that characterised British public service and American commercial television culture can therefore be said to antedate the introduction of the all-electric system.

Whatever the excessive claims of the British press at the time, and the curious persistence of Baird's reputation in British consciousness up to the present, the most extensive application of the Nipkow patent took place, unsurprisingly, in Germany. From 1902, when Otto von Bronk patented the Bidwell principle that the picture should be constructed out of a series of lines, through the demonstration of that technique by Ernst Ruhmer in 1909, the Germans recovered the insightful edge that Nipkow had given them and then abandoned (Hempel 1990: 124). But progress was stifled because the German authorities could see no supervening necessity for the technology. The same imperial arms race, which necessitated the development of the marine wireless, suppressed work on television because no military application could be envisaged. It was not until 1926 that any serious experimentation recommenced. In 1927 an instruction manual for 'building a picture receiver' was published and television demonstrations were the hit of the Berlin Broadcasting Exhibitions of 1928 and 1929 (Elsner *et al.* 1990: 196). By this time the military were at last (and somewhat erroneously) thinking television might be of some use to aeronautics as well. On the other hand, some visionaries on the left were calling for the 'Volksfernseher', or 'People's Television Set' (Hempel 1990: 128).

Goebbels had expressed an interest in radio technology, including television, even before he became Nazi propaganda director whereupon experiments were spurred ahead by what Bill Uricchio has called 'utopian visions and national security interests' (1990: 115). After the Nazis were elected in 1933, television at last became an important item on the Reich's research agenda. Regular transmissions started in Berlin in 1935 using apparatus built by Fernseh A-G, a subsidiary of Zeiss Ikon and Bosch formed to exploit Baird's patents, which achieved, for film transmission, 180 lines and twenty-five frames per second. 'The success of this machine', a colleague of Baird's wrote in the 1950s, 'was to no little measure due to the micrometer precision engineering tools which the Germans had available for disk construction' (Percy 1952: 14). This precision was taken a step further in that the disk was placed in a vacuum to reduce both interference and drive-power. Subsequently the Germans managed a mechanically created variation on interlaced scanning, thus achieving stability very close to the all-electrical (electronic) systems (Gibas 1936: 741). This machine represents the mechanical scanning partial prototype in its final form.

Since this system, like Jenkins', worked best when dealing with film rather than in the studio, Fernseh constructed a film camera with an attached developing tank, building on the proposal made by Ives in 1927. It produced a photographic image in under a minute which was then mechanically scanned – the Intermediate Film (IF) system. The Germans also used an electronic system based on the patents of the American Philo Farnsworth, for which they had signed an agreement in 1935. Farnsworth had produced an alternative electric tube (more on this below) that also worked best when transmitting film; so the IF system was ideally suited for this configuration as well. The Germans began an experiment to test this system against an electronic one based on patents held by RCA's German allies, Telefunken. Because the results were accessible to the public, this was however declared an actual 'service', the world's first. It was used to cover the Berlin Olympics in the summer of 1936. The network embraced five German cities and the service was not halted by the start of war. Moreover, in 1938 the Germans built a videophone link between Berlin and Nuremberg using an outdated mechanical solution to produce a 180-line standard.

Baird's engineers, like their German opposite numbers, were also locked in battle with an all-electrical system (essentially the same as Telefunken's and RCA's) developed by Marconi's and EMI in concert. In 1934, the Postmaster General appointed a committee under the chairmanship of Lord Selsdon to consider the development of television and to 'advise on the general merits of the several systems' then available (Garratt and Mumford 1952: 38). The BBC was entrusted with the experiment. Baird's company had by now refined mechanical scanning to give 240 lines and, to consolidate its strengths, it too adopted the German IF system which was available to it because of its patent alliances. BTDC now duplicated the earlier German mechanical feat and, in 1936, achieved their ultimate in mechanical scanning, 240 lines at one-twenty-fifth of a second. But it was a dead end. Despite Baird's dictum of 1931 that 'There is no hope for television by means of cathode ray tubes', the receivers for these 'high definition' mechanical systems, both in Germany and the UK, were by now all-electric tubes with no trace of spinning disks (Briggs 1961: 553). It was only a question of time before the disks disappeared from the transmission end of the system, too.

Baird withdrew entirely from the activities of the company that bore his name and spent the next three years experimenting with a large-screen, mechanically scanned (at 6000 rpm) colour television system with stereophonic sound! By then, Baird's colleagues were using a mechanical scanner with IF for studio work and a purely BTDC film scanning (telecine) device, which observers felt was better than anything EMI had, for transmitting film. As in Germany, at the government's behest, a final judgement was to be made between electrical and mechanical. The BBC organised BTDC and EMI for this test – a sort of experimental run-off, as Asa Briggs points out, like nothing so much as a nineteenth-century competition between rival steam locomotives (Briggs 1961: 583). Sir Archibald Gill, a member of the 1934 committee, recalled that the case was not quite open-and-shut. The Baird system did indeed, even with the line and frame disadvantage, produce a slightly better picture than the EMI system when transmitting film (Garratt and Mumford 1952: 28). As film transmission was held by all experts in every country to be vital as a major source of television images, this was no small advantage.

In the name of crude firstism, the British somewhat perversely have always dated the start of television 'service' from this clearly experimental exercise inaugurated in studios at Alexandra Palace, London on 2 November 1936 using both systems. It was, anyway, second to the equally unstandardised German 'service'. The game between BTDC/Fernseh and EMI/Telefunken had been fixed by physics as Peter Eckersley had somewhat brutally indicated nine years before. Each mechanical element had given way to an electronic equivalent. Electrical scanners inexorably drew away in terms of performance, ease of operation, reliability and general 'elegance'. Only when transmitting film was there any question of competition and even then the electronic potential was clear. In the words of one of the BBC pioneers required to produce programs, turn-and-turn-about, using both systems: 'Working in the Baird Studio was a bit like using Morse Code when you knew that next door [in the EMI studio] you could telephone' (Norman 1984: 129). By 1936 the question was not 'mechanical vs. electronic?' but rather 'which electronic?'

# 6

# ELECTRONICALLY
# SCANNED TELEVISION

## INVENTION I: ELECTRONIC SCANNING

A full year before Campbell Swinton's 1908 letter to *Nature*, a Russian, Boris L'vovitch Rozing, had patented, in London as well as in Berlin and St Petersburg, an all-electric television cathode ray tube receiver. In the year of Campbell Swinton's presidential address, this same Russian actually transmitted a signal to his receiver.

The cold war casts a curious shadow across the history of television. The earliest published accounts of its technological emergence were written from the mid-1930s to the mid-1950s during which decades the accident of Rozing's birthplace had assumed a significance it otherwise would not have had. British writers in the 1930s claimed that Campbell Swinton's analysis of the basic problem was, despite the fact that he did not work on his proposed solution, superior to Rozing's more pragmatic approach. An American account dating from the 1950s described Campbell Swinton's 1911 proposal as 'a still more startling *invention*' than Rozing's work (Jensen 1954: 175; emphasis added).

The Soviet treatment of technological history was the butt of much Western humour, although Russian 'firstism' about aeronautics was substantially boosted by Sputnik (Winston 1993: 193). Everything from spiral mechanical scanning to a sequential colour system was supposedly patented in Russia before 1900. Nevertheless, such Stalinist claims that Russians had invented both radio (Popov) and television (Rozing) are no less – and no more – substantial and, at least as far as television is concerned, compared well with British pretensions in these matters. Certainly Rozing's experiment is of a quite different magnitude from Campbell Swinton's musings, for all that the latter envisaged the more completely modern scheme that was to prevail three decades later. But Rozing's is an achievement that neither the chauvinism of others nor the rodomontade of official Soviet accounts should be allowed to taint although, since his contributions all predate the revolution, the rhetoric of the latter was faintly comic.

Boris Rozing was born in St Petersburg in 1867, took his degrees at its University and taught, from 1893, at its Technical Institute. He was interested in the electric telescope (as he was still calling it in the 1920s) and, noticing that the electron beam in the common cathode ray laboratory oscilloscope left complex luminescent patterns on the front of the tube, decided that this was his 'ideal mechanism' (Gorokhov 1961: 75). In 1907 he patented such a circuit using electron beam deflection to modulate the intensity of the beam, by altering its velocity, in the receiver. Rozing's idea, innovative and important though it was, had its precedents. His transmitter was built along the lines that were being commonly suggested before the turn of the century, that is, an electro-mechanical system using a mirrored drum of a known design. His more revolutionary receiver had been anticipated, too. A German patent of 1906 had already suggested the use of a cathode tube specifically for 'the transmission of written material and line drawings'. This apparatus was designed and built by Dieckmann, and, like Bidwell's, it survives. It used a standard Nipkow disk transmitter but here for the first time the image scanned was received on a cathode ray tube. Paradoxically, this breakthrough was counterproductive, for Dieckmann's intended purpose was facsimile transmission and the lack of a hard copy was seen as a major disadvantage – just as some thought the radio telephone's lack of privacy was a real drawback (Jensen 1954: 174). In both cases the drawback turned out to be the *raison d'être* of the technologies.

Given the general state of tube technology in this period, Rozing's proposed solution was at the very cutting edge of what was possible. What also distinguishes him is that he did not give up at the patent stage but actually built a series of partial prototypes and on 9 May 1911 he transmitted by wireless over a distance 'a distinct image . . . consisting of four luminous bands'; but the rudimentary state of the cathode ray tube and electronic amplification meant that the line of development was not taken up by others. Even in Russia it seemed as if the problem would be better solved by mechanical scanning using substances of greater sensitivity than selenium, so Campbell Swinton's suggestion and Rozing's experiments were not pursued during and immediately after the First World War. The truth, which Rozing and Campbell Swinton saw but which most researchers ignored, was that while mechanical scanning and cathode ray devices were partial prototypes both working poorly at this point (and the tube was worse than the disk), the all-electrical system had the far greater potential.

Vladimir Zworykin emigrated to the United States twice after the Russian Revolution, the first time failing to find work. On the second occasion in 1920 he managed to secure a research post with Westinghouse (Waldrop and Borkin 1938: 213). He had studied with Rozing at the Institute in St Petersburg and in 1912 he had gone to the College de France to do graduate research in theoretical physics and X-rays. During the First World War in Russia he built tubes and aviation devices for the Signal Corps. In 1923 Zworykin patented a complete electrical television system including a pick-up tube, that is to say an electronic camera, along the lines suggested by Campbell Swinton. The camera was, as was Rozing's receiver, adapted from the standard cathode ray tube but of a very different design. The electrons were now directed at an internal screen or signal plate which they were forced, by magnets mounted outside the tube, to scan in a zigzag pattern. The scanning system produced by the zigzagging dot was one which created the image sequentially, line by line, just as Nipkow's spinning disk had done. At the home end the process was reversed. The internal signal plate of the camera became the phosphor-treated front end of the tube, the screen. The electron beam, again generated by a cathode and controlled by electromagnets, was modulated by the incoming wave. These variations were translated by the scanning electron dot into variations in intensity which became, through the phosphors, perceptible to the human eye.

Rozing had suggested that the speed of the stream of electrons could be varied in accordance with the intensity of the light, but Zworykin followed Campbell Swinton in varying the intensity of the beam itself to reconstitute the lights and darks of the scene before the lens. He also followed a Swedish researcher Ekstrom, who, in a patent of 1910, suggested that scanning could be achieved with a light spot. Zworykin's camera tube, the iconoscope, used a sensitive plate of mica coated with caesium. It proved to be more photoemissive than potassium and certainly much more so than selenium. In the tube which Zworykin built, the photoelectrons are emitted the entire time the screen is illuminated by the spot but the charge is stored until the spot returns to build up the next frame. Then the electrons are discharged. In all the competing systems, whether mechanical or electrical, the stream of electrons was created by a fragment of light striking the cell and being discharged immediately. The iconoscope's 'charge storage' system created an enormous increase in sensitivity.

Zworykin, writing in 1929 after his move to RCA, acknowledged other workers, French and Japanese, who had been following Rozing's use of the cathode ray tube (Zworykin 1929: 38). In Germany that same year, Baron Manfred von Ardenne had demonstrated an all-electrical system with sixty-line definition. He was the first to perfect the flying spot technique for scanning film and slides electronically and a CRT receiver for the home – the *Volksfernseher*. This was demonstrated at the Berlin Radio Exposition of 1931 and widely publicised abroad (Hempel 1990: 129–31).

By 1932, Zworykin had a camera that worked more effectively, at least using reflected light in a studio, than any other available. It produced 240 lines, matching the most advanced mechanical systems, and it was demonstrated by a wireless transmission from New York to the RCA laboratory in Camden 80 miles away. This was still not quite an all-electric system since the synchronising pulses to stabilise the image were provided not by circuitry but by a spinning disk. Over the next two years electronically generated synch pulses were added. At the same time Zworykin designed the interlaced raster which scanned every other line in any one frame so that the frame time was halved to one-sixtieth and picture stability further improved. This was because a sufficiently fast rate of change (sixty a second in effect) was created from frame to frame for the physiological requirements of critical fusion frequency (CFF), the point at which the eye ceases to see discrete pictures, to operate. Achieving this sort of speed was necessary because a single scan in one-thirtieth of a second gave a flickering impression.

Early in 1934 Zworykin wrote:

> The present sensitivity of the iconoscope is approximately equal to that of a photographic film operating at the speed of a motion picture camera, with the same optical system. . . . Some of the actually constructed tubes are good up to 500 lines with a good margin for future improvement.
>
> (Zworykin 1934: 19–20)

Zworykin was fudging a little by not specifying a 16mm motion picture camera; for the ambition of all the television pioneers, mechanical and electrical was to match the quality of the contemporary amateur, i.e. 16mm, picture. For some, Jenkins for example, the home delivery of movies was the prime television research objective. The film industry defines film stocks in terms of lines per millimetre of film surface. The limiting resolutions of emulsions can be determined when the emulsion is used to photograph a chart upon which standardised blocks or lines of black have been printed. The film industry's norm was a 35mm film which could photograph between thirty to forty of these lines per millimetre. To achieve the same density of visual information electronically, something like 1,200 lines on a cathode ray tube would be needed. This same normal film stock formatted for 16mm would, of course, also photograph the same number of lines per millimetre but to far cruder effect, since each line occupies more of the frame area. To match the resolving capacity of the 35mm norm a 16mm stock would need to photograph around twice as many lines (i.e. ninety per millimetre). Conversely, the normal 16mm standard of thirty to forty lines per millimetre can be matched on 35mm by twelve lines. It was at that standard that the television researchers aimed since its electronic equivalent required only around 400 to 480 lines.

In short, by the early 1930s, the whole thrust of the research was directed towards creating a 400-line picture, the equivalent of the contemporary 16mm film image (Schlafly 1951: 50). This became 'high definition' television, the standard eventually adopted, in its 525/625-line guise, by most of the world. (As we shall see, sixty years later 'high definition' was redefined, as the world's television engineering community considered a 1200-line HDTV system (p. 140). Such a new standard simply matches the resolving characteristics of 35mm film.)

The British contribution to the search for an electronic equivalent of 16mm film was much facilitated by corporate musical chairs in the late 1920s. RCA took over Victor Phonograph Inc which in turn owned the British Gramophone Company. Thus RCA, born out of the ashes of British interests in the American radio market, came to own a slice of the British record industry. In 1931, the Gramophone Company was an element in the founding of EMI. In this way RCA now had a share of an English research laboratory. Moreover, the director of research there was Isadore Schoenburg who, like Zworykin, was another of Rozing's ex-students.

Schoenburg, in 1934, decided that his research agenda should be for a 405-line electronic standard:

> It was the most dramatic moment in the whole of television develop-ment. He (Schoenburg) said, 'What we are going to do, in this competi-tion, we're going to offer 405 lines, twin interlace. And we're going for Emitron. We're going to give up mirror drum scanning, we're going along the lines of the electronic camera.'
>
> (Norman 1984: 107)

Sir Frank McGee, perhaps the most distinguished of the team, calls this 'the most courageous decision in the whole of his (Schoenburg's) career', which it might well be; but these British pioneers also insist that they were working independ-ently of their sister lab at RCA which is more difficult to credit. It is hard to believe that Schoenburg decided for the electronic solution without cognisance of what Zworykin had *publicly* announced, in January 1934, to be possible, never mind what private communication might have passed between the two labs. Zworykin, for example, recalled that two of Schoenburg's engineers visited his lab late in the winter of 1933/4 for three months before the 405-line decision was made (ibid.: 105). Yet despite all this, one of these very engineers was claiming, in 1984, that 'McGee and EMI owe nothing to RCA and only in 1936 did the two companies sign an agreement for a complete exchange of patents and information' (ibid.: 49). Nothing?

The record clearly suggests that the essence of both cameras' design was laid down in a patent of Zworykin's dated 1923. Zworykin worked for RCA. RCA owned a slice of EMI. EMI's research director shared a teacher in Russia with Zworykin. The teacher was a television pioneer. EMI engineers did visit RCA. The Emitron looked, not like Zworykin's patent of 1923, but like his development of that patent, the iconoscope of the early 1930s. It was, in McGee's own words, 'fundamentally the same as the iconoscope' (McGee 1950: 598) except that, because of British electrical supply characteristics, the pattern or raster scanned the picture lines every twenty-fifth of a second. By 1934, 343 lines had been demonstrated on the RCA iconoscope, not quite sufficient to match the definition of 16mm amateur movies. Zworykin, as his January 1934 paper reveals, was confident that this could be achieved. Further, the majority opinion in the US was that 441 lines was the maximum that could be accommodated in the six megacycle channels the FCC had mandated for experiments. All this was the context for British 405-line decision. Yet it would be wrong to suggest that the British therefore made no significant contribution to the development of the RCA system.

The American iconoscope, in the early 1930s, was barely usable, being very noisy; that is, it had too high a ratio of interference to signal. Indeed, the tube produced more noise than picture and was a lot less impressive than the high definition mechanical scanning systems then coming on line, which is why Schoenburg was being 'courageous' when he opted for it. The reasons for this poor performance were properly analysed and ultimately corrected first at EMI. In 1933, a member of the EMI team perfected a technique to stabilise the DC component of the signal, thereby solving a clearly understood problem. More significantly, the then mysterious process whereby the electronic signal was derived from the tube was elucidated by McGee. Secondary emission of electrons, within the tube, were found to be crucial (McGee 1950: 599–600).

Indeed secondary emission was a third way, in addition to photo and thermionic emission, to obtain, within a component, free electrons. As a consequence of this understanding, the team of Blumlein, Browne and White (the first two of whom were to die testing experimental radar equipment in flight in 1942) set about suppressing the unwanted signals (Preston 1953: 119). The patented circuits which did this were passed back to Zworykin and incorporated into the RCA camera and became the basis for the 1936 RCA/EMI agreement. McGee and Blumlein, in the emitron, made the iconoscope fully practical; but the emitron was, all protests aside, nevertheless essentially a variant of the iconoscope. RCA, it may be noted, never signed patent agreements, always buying what it needed outright. The EMI deal was one of only two occasions in the 1930s when this company policy was violated, obviously because of the closeness of the two organisations.

In Germany, RCA's correspondent was Telefunken. Its engineers had abandoned mechanical scanning at exactly the same time as Schoenburg took his 'dramatic' decision to do the same thing and for much the same reason. Like EMI, Telefunken was working, with RCA agreement, on a design derived from Zworykin. It yielded the Ikonoskop-kamera. As in Britain, electronics (essentially the RCA interest represented by Telefunken) was pitted against mechanical scanning (essentially Baird represented by Fernseh). There a similar, if considerably more protracted run-off had begun during the Olympic Games. In the years that followed, the systems were allowed to coexist. In 1938, Fernseh covered the Nazi *Parteitag*

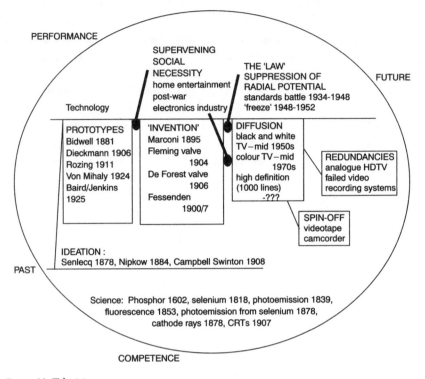

*Figure 11* Television

rally in Nuremberg. In 1939, Telefunken introduced its super-ikonoskop which produced 441 lines and worked well in the most adverse lighting conditions. By the outbreak of the War Telefunken had Fernseh on the ropes. Like BTDC, the latter had only television with which to support itself. Telefunken, like EMI, was a major electronics firm, with or without television. Telefunken slowly demonstrated the superiority of its system and with the Nazis' decision to use the super-ikonoskop for coverage of the 1940 Winter Games, Fernseh finally lost out.[1] The Germans had taken more than five years to reach the conclusion the British had come to in four months (Udelson 1982: 110).

The greatest claim to the invention of television is undoubtedly Zworykin's, and it was in all essentials first built under the aegis of four large electrical manufacturers, for every basic aspect of modern television systems conforms to Zworykin's original patent description of 1923 and the devices he built to refine and develop those ideas in the 1930s. However, in another crucial sense, the invention was still in doubt at the end of that decade because the device was not widely diffused (Figure 11).

## INVENTION II: ALTERNATIVE ELECTRONIC
## SCANNING

What hindsight reveals is that by 1936 the mechanical scanning systems were reaching their limits while the electronics systems were still at the outset of development. It is, though, tempting to ignore this and take a more contemporary view. At the time, the failure of mechanical scanning was seen as a rather good example of how in the twentieth century the lonely inventor (e.g. Baird) with his simple solutions (e.g. spinning disks) stood no chance against the great corporation's team of researchers with their cutting edge technology (e.g. EMI and the CRT).

This rhetoric was implicitly deployed by Campbell Swinton in a lecture before the Radio Society of Great Britain in 1924:

> If we could only get one of the big research laboratories, like that of the G.E.C. or of the Western Electric Company – one of those people who have large skilled staffs and any amount of money to engage on the business – I believe they would solve a thing like this in six months and make a reasonable job of it.
>
> (Jensen 1954: 176)

In the event, with something less than the whole-hearted backing Campbell Swinton envisaged, it took the industrial researchers longer than six months to 'invent' television. The idea, though, that they generally worked in a way different from the old-style individual innovator nevertheless obtains an important boost in the received history. The technical development of television becomes a prime example of the industrialisation of innovation which is generally deemed to be such a prominent feature of modern life.

The position Baird occupies is crucial, for nothing is as powerful as the notion that he, an old-style private inventor, was limited to mechanical systems because he was unable to compete with the industrial lab in the more sophisticated area of the cathode ray tubes. In fact, Baird seems to have just had a thing about tubes and an obsession that his first thought was the best. Vic Mills, his earliest collaborator, alerted Baird to CRTs in 1924:

> I said you can't play about with those spinning discs and think you're going to get television. I told him to go ahead with cathode-ray tubes. I'd read about it in a book printed in 1919 and it made me want to take the long jump and avoid all this mechanical business. But if I knew only a little about the cathode-ray tubes, Baird, apparently, knew nothing. He was simply not interested. He could comprehend the mechanical system

but the idea of doing it all electronically appeared to be out of the question.

(Norman 1984: 30)

These traits could just as well have manifested themselves under the aegis of a great corporation; and conversely, a lone inventor could have seized on the potential of the electronic system.

This last contention is proved by the career of Philo T. Farnsworth, the boy-wonder electrical genius who occupies Baird's place in the popular American understanding of television history. Farnsworth, every bit as much an outsider as Baird was, nevertheless produced a serious, sophisticated electronic system to rival the dominant RCA/EMI/Telefunken one. His contribution was equal in sophistication to those made by McGee and the other workers in the great laboratories. Baird failed not because he was alone, but rather because he was simply wrong and the history of television is not as ready a prop for the industrialisation of innovation thesis as is commonly supposed.

Philo Farnsworth was a rural mid-Westerner who came from a Mormon home which acquired electricity only when he was 14. He learned his science from popular magazines and read up on mechanical television. At age 15 he confounded his chemistry teacher at high school by describing, on the blackboard, an all-electric device which he thought might work better. He left school and had no further formal education (Waldrop and Borkin 1938: 211; Everson 1949: 15–16). In 1927, aged 19, he patented an electrical pick-up tube (the heart of a camera) which operated on significantly different principles from Zworykin's. Called an image dissector, it had the advantages of offering a more stable picture than the iconoscope. It used neither a scanning spot nor the storage principle but worked by translating the image into a pattern of electrons which were then passed across an aperture.

Something of a stand-off developed. The pictures produced by the dissector tube were of better definition and sharper contrast than those produced by the iconoscope. The Zworykin camera was a superior instrument for use in studios and outdoor pickup where lighting was a problem but in the late 1920s and early 1930s it did not work so well that it was self-evidently the clear winner. With the intense direct illumination found in a telecine device, the comparative (but rather theoretical) disadvantage of the dissector was wiped out. Apart from the fact that film transmission had been central to the research agenda from the beginning, this was why Farnsworth made a partner of Fernseh with its IF (instant film) system.

Farnsworth's achievement was that, by one means or another, his was the more effective electronic camera in the earliest developmental phase. He was on to the secondary emission at the same time as EMI and indeed in 1937, made, what was to be his greatest contribution to electronics in general by designing an electron photomultiplier specifically to exploit it. The multiplier allowed the weak electron output of the dissector tube's aperture to be exponentially increased. It enabled Farnsworth to do this without using the charge storage principle patented to RCA. He was close enough, in fact, to worry RCA considerably. Both Sarnoff and Zworykin visited his laboratory and their professions of uninterest in his advances were not backed by their corporate moves against him. RCA mounted an interference action which Farnsworth successfully defended (with the help of his chemistry teacher and at a cost of $30,000).

By then Farnsworth was no longer a man alone. Unlike many individual engineers, he conducted himself as well in the boardroom as he did in his laboratory. He had joined the Philadelphia Battery Company. Philco, now a major rival of RCA, had begun by selling large domestic batteries to houses not on the electricity grid. As electrification killed this business, the company moved to radio manufacturing, first establishing itself by specialising, from 1927, in car radios. When Farnsworth joined, it was outselling RCA at nearly three-to-one and had over one-third of the market. Rivalry between the two firms climaxed, with Philco bringing an action against RCA for industrial spying, specifically charging that RCA operatives took some of Philco's female employees to Philadelphia where (in the words of the affidavit) they 'did provide them with intoxicating liquors, did seek to involve them in compromising situations, and thereupon and thereby did endeavour to entice, to bribe and induce said employees to furnish them. . .confidential information and confidential designs' (Waldrop and Borkin 1938: 219).

Protected by Philco's broad back, Farnsworth was now able successfully to resist all RCA attempts to dislodge his 1927 patents. The dissector was sufficiently different from the iconoscope for him to maintain his rights, but his receiver was close enough for him to pick up Zworykin's pictures on his apparatus. In 1935, after a three-year proceeding, Farnsworth successfully won his own interference action against Zworykin and RCA. Farnsworth's device scanned an electronic image – in the words of his 1927 patent application, he had designed 'an apparatus for television which comprises means for forming an electrical image' (Udelson 1982: 105). Zworykin, in his 1923 patent, the patent official held, had suggested scanning an optical image – a significant difference (ibid.: 112). Farnsworth left Philco (amicably) and in the early 1930s forged his international links, assigning his patents to Baird in the UK and Fernseh in Germany. In 1937, upon the introduction of the photomultiplier, he reached cross-patenting agreements with both AT&T and CBS, two more of RCA's great rivals (ibid.: 107).

Farnsworth was too good a scientist not to realise that Zworykin's charge storage principle, despite the photomultiplier, was superior – was indeed television, while his concept had produced, by however small a margin, a more partial prototype; but he was also too shrewd a businessman not to fully exploit the very real contributions he had made. He and his partners poached RCA's head of licensing to be the president of the Farnsworth manufacturing company which he created in 1939. The iconoscope was by now superior to the dissector even in telecines but the improvements that had allowed the iconoscope to overtake the Farnsworth camera had been purchased by incorporating Farnsworth's concepts (as well as EMI's). Indeed Zworykin acknowledged this by now designating his machine the 'image-iconoscope' exactly because it scanned an electronic analogue of the image, clearly infringing Farnsworth's 1927 dissector patent. After five months of negotiations RCA was forced into a licensing agreement with him – an event whose only precedent was the EMI secondary emission deal. In September a general agreement was reached with Farnsworth and Zworykin published the details of his latest camera (Iams et al. 1939: 541). Farnsworth's biographer claims that the RCA vice-president who signed the contract wept (Everson 1949: 246).

Both Zworykin and Farnsworth had opted for modulating their signals by strength – intensity – as the underlying principle of their television systems, although they dealt with the electron stream very differently. But at the outset Rozing had proposed, albeit very vaguely, a sort of frequency modulation system, whereby the greater the light the faster the stream of electrons. Frequency modulation of the audio signal had been perfected by Edwin Armstrong, another extremely sophisticated lone investigator. During this period Armstrong turned his attention to modulating the video signal in this way and his interest and presence further muddied the corporate and patent waters.

This phase of technological performance – 'invention' – can take place either synchronously with or subsequent to the crucial supervening necessity which ensures diffusion. In the case of television, the invention phase is synchronous with some underlying supervening necessities. These would include the general drives conditioning the development of popular entertainment which underpinned the development of cinema and radio – the addiction to realism in the culture, the supremacy of the nuclear family and its home, the industrialisation of the entertainment business. But there are other specific elements in the supervening necessity underpinning television which had not yet manifested themselves – spare industrial capacity at the end of the Second World War, for example, and the push to consumerism. Thus this invention phase is responsive to only some of the underlying social necessities sustaining the development and the eventual diffusion of television.

This partial operation of the full range of social necessities also accounts for the fact that 'invention' in this case proceeds synchronously with the second phase of prototype performance, allowing the British and Germans to hold run-offs between a partial mechanical prototype and the invention proper. But more than this, the lack of a clear supervening social necessity delays the diffusion of television and becomes meshed with certain elements of suppression which also begin to emerge as television becomes ever more practical. Let us deal with the accelerators first.

## NECESSITY AND SUPPRESSION: ENTERTAINMENT

Television, electronically scanned television, was a partially demonstrated but soundly grounded theoretical option by 1911. It was a mass medium by the mid-1950s. These forty-plus years yield one catalytic external supervening necessity, which is of greater moment than any single technological advance in the same period. It occurred after the conclusion of the Second World War.

The crucial enabling factor which transformed television from toy to mass medium was the spare capacity of the electronics industry in 1945/6. In the two years from April 1942 (according to the premier issue of *Television* magazine), defence spending had expanded the radio industry of America by between 1200 and 1500 per cent. More than 300,000 workers were involved. As the magazine put it: 'The question now arises what to do with these facilities after the War, for the demands of aural radio alone will not be sufficient to keep many of them going. Only *television* offers the promise of sufficient business' (Boddy 1990: 45; emphasis in the original). James Fly, then chair of the FCC, wrote: 'I think it quite likely that during the post-war period television will be one of the first industries arising to serve as a cushion against unemployment and depression' (Hubbell 1942: xi).

As with radio in 1918, so with television in 1945. In America it was still 'experimental'. RCA had built a plant for the Navy at Lancaster, Pennsylvania, which had mass-produced cathode ray tubes. Immediately after the war RCA bought the plant back and within a year was manufacturing a 10-inch table-top television, the '630 TS'. It sold for $385, which compares well with Sarnoff's proposed 1916 price of $75 for a radio.

Even beyond the not inconsiderable commercial consequences of marketing the sets, RCA and others were strenuously arguing that the post-war economy needed enhanced levels of consumer demand in general which could be fuelled only by an effective new advertising medium. These considerations were finally to break the deadlock in the development of American television. As we shall shortly see, the social brake – suppression – was already being applied by various interests since at least the start of German and British public services (using, to all intents and purposes, RCA systems) in 1936. In the intervening decade the United States had been at war for only three years. The war cannot be claimed as the delaying factor in all the years of peace up to 1939 (or 1942). On the contrary, it was this war which provided, by creating a vast electronics industry, the final supervening necessity for television.

This necessity, though, would have been insufficient of itself had it not been for the other long-standing drives at work in the society, drives which created and sustained the research interest in television. As in Tolstoy's tale of the giant turnip, the efforts of the mouse are required at the end of the farmer's line of stronger helpers to get the monstrous vegetable out of the ground and into the house. The slowing cathode ray tube assembly lines are the mouse. The farmer, his wife and all the others are to be found, as it were, in those tendencies within society, previously discussed, that create entertainment and information forms for the urban masses. Television then follows the path beaten by radio to the home. It also trades, as does cinema, on those deep social addictions to realistic modes of production and narrative. All the background supervening necessities — addictions to realism and narrative — reinforced these industrial and economic perceptions of need (Winston 1996: 22–6).

This then can help explain the stalls and delays to be seen in the history of television's development. These general cultural traits constitute powerful underlying supervening necessities for television, but they are not of themselves strong enough in the period from 1936 (at the latest) to get a television system widely introduced to the public, either in the US, where such a possibility is denied by the government, or in the UK and Germany where, as I have explained above, it is encouraged. They sustained the R&D but they could not overcome the forces working to protect the status quo against the disruptive effects of the new technology.

This uneasy balance suffuses both the German and British experience of television in these years. Despite the clear articulated propaganda policy of the regime, the Germans never had more than between 200 and 1000 sets in the entire country, although admittedly almost all were sited in halls seating between forty and 400 (Uricchio 1990: 115).[2] The technical developments outlined above and the boost given by the coverage of the Berlin Olympics in 1936 'failed to meet public expectation'. By the time the Nazis decided to allow the *Volkfernsehen* (and risk people being rude about the regime in the privacy of their own homes) it was 1939 and the war intervened.

The technology was no more popular in the UK. The British, ignoring the supposed beneficence of the marketplace, inaugurated by government fiat a full-scale public experimental service in November 1936 using the two systems. In February 1937 the London Television Standard of 405 lines at 1/25th of a second, interlaced, was adopted and Marconi/EMI was allowed to broadcast alone. It was thus no longer 'experimental' but the public take-up of the service proves that it was nevertheless premature. Barely 2000 sets were sold in the initial year of operation, and this despite a reduction of about 30 per cent in their cost and the wonders of the first televised coronation. By the outbreak of war only about 20,000 sets had been sold.

There were a number of problems. Although viewers' responses, audience research and the press were all largely favourable, the level of repeats drew criticism (Norman 1984: 210–11). More serious public concerns among non-adopters of the new medium included the limited hours, worries about obsolescence because of the conflicting systems and an unawareness that the highly publicised low definition Baird picture was a thing of the past (Briggs 1961: 611–12). These problems would have vanished if the market had been talked up, if the demand had been there; but the demand was not being stimulated as it was to be in the 1950s. Without the new 'high definition' electronic system being given the same level of public exposure Baird had generated for his almost unwatchable low definition experiments, television was by the outbreak of war in 1939 an over-hyped technology – in fact the first we have encountered. It will not be the last.

The making of extravagant claims ungrounded in performance realities is a new factor in the operation of the 'law' of suppression. Disappointed early adopters and media reporting of that disappointment become a deterrent. In the case of television, this allowed the BBC in the late 1930s to avoid having to make the sorts of decisions confronting it in the late 1940s, i.e. how to begin diverting resources to the new medium from the old, radio. And this draws attention to another obvious reason for the slightly lukewarm approach to television from the BBC in the late 1930s; radio was not then an old medium.

Giving established players in one technology the task of exploiting a new cognate, and therefore threatening technology is a not unusual way of ensuring that the 'law' of the suppression of radical potential will operate. Radio (and with it, the BBC) had barely come of age; and talking pictures were even younger than that. Both were prospering despite the Depression. Public attention, and with it the public's purse, were therefore elsewhere. Whereas the public might tell researchers it wanted television, the entertainment industry stood ready to ignore the demand. In the US, the FCC saw its regulatory role in terms of ensuring corporate stability. That was the public interest it was defending. It took no notice of any evidence of public demand such as a 1939 poll which estimated that four million Americans were eager to purchase television sets (Udelson 1982: 96). Instead, the commission still insisted on 'experimentation'. Via its good offices, the radio and movie industries, because of the investments they had entailed, constrained television development.

The British experience shows that American hesitancies were probably justified because public demand, whatever people told the pollsters, was not really there. Asking people if they would like more entertainment and would pay for it is different from actually offering it to them and demanding money; but this is exactly what the BBC, having been forced into television, was doing in the years before the Second World War. However, no mass audience was created so no manufacturing base emerged and, as we have seen, by 1939 there were almost no television sets in British homes.

Television was invented in the straits between the Scylla of established industry and the Charybdis of innovation; between the brake of established markets and the need to create, through innovation, new markets. The broad social supervening necessities, requiring highly iconic home-delivered entertainment systems, sustained technological performance so that research on the device continued through all this, but slowly. It would take the particular necessity of maintaining wartime levels of electronic manufacture to make the television receiver – in Britain and the US, as well as in the rest of the world – 'the shining centre of every home'. Without that final push, the brakes were more powerful than the accelerator.

## SUPPRESSING TELEVISION: 1935–48

The received explanation of what happened, in America, after television had been 'invented' is as follows:

The Radio Manufacturers Association (RMA), a trade group dominated by, but not wholly a creature of, RCA, had set up a television committee which, by 1935, was ready to set about establishing appropriate standards. RCA by this year had reached 343 lines in an interlaced raster scanning at one-thirtieth of a second, although Zworykin had made some tubes that could produce more than 400 lines.

In the following year, the FCC began the difficult business of making frequency allocations for television in what was then still called the 'ether spectrum'. The RMA attempted to expand this agenda by offering ideas on standards as well. It suggested that the FCC should establish, within the spectrum allocated, that all 'experiments' use a 441-line picture on a band six megacycles wide (the lines being thought the maximum accommodatable in that bandwidth). Other matters, – the polarity of the signal, the aspect ratio of the picture, the synchronisation standard – were agreed within the RMA and also presented to the FCC. No mechanical scanning systems were envisaged.

The FCC more or less accepted the bandwidth proposal as outlined by the manufacturers but otherwise did not respond. The commission felt that further 'experimentation' was in order not to test mechanical against electrical scanning, as was the case in Europe, but essentially because it was unable to arbitrate effectively between RCA and its rivals, Zenith, Philco and Dumont. RCA's increasingly commanding patent position created fears of monopoly, especially since the company's style was to seek technological exclusivity. In 1930 the direct pressure of consent decrees had pushed General Electric and Westinghouse out of RCA. (AT&T had presciently given up its interests four years earlier.) The Justice Department had found it increasingly uncomfortable to have the other companies, at the manufacturing level, in supposed competition with themselves. RCA was no longer a creature of the industry but was now a corporation like any other. It did not dominate radio manufacture nor did it dominate programming, but none of its rivals in either of these spheres could match its total range of operation. Its corporate culture was a consequence of this. It owned a telegraph company and in 1937 was seen to be trying to extend its business in this area by buying up Western Union. It was a strapping and overweening bully-boy when it came to television. There Sarnoff was even prepared to take on the phone company by harking back to the earliest phase of the television research agenda: 'The ideal way of sending messages (he said) is to hold up a printed sheet that will be immediately reproduced at the other end; facsimile transmission and television are about ready [for that]' (Waldrop and Borkin 1938: 127–8).[3] Such behaviour provoked the thought in some minds that the Justice Department might have been deliberately encouraging the creation of a giant capable of taking on AT&T.

AT&T, with its history of constant conflict with the US government, tended to conduct itself with more restraint. It was far more amenable to cross-licensing agreements and the like, seeing the patent system as providing less complete protection than bargaining positions. Unlike RCA, AT&T's corporate culture, formed in the Vail era, dictated controlled technological exploitation, careful market positioning and diplomatic engagement with the American regulatory regime. Since the threat was always against its telephone monopoly, it was prepared to share everything else to protect that core enterprise; that is to say, it always wanted a patent position in areas cognate to telephony. A good example of this can be seen in the way it chose to handle film sound. It did not directly take over Hollywood which its command of that technology would have easily allowed but which would have been anathema to the Justice Department. Instead, it made sound as widely available as possible.

It also sought to maintain a position with television. For example, when signing up every major film studio to its Westrex sound system, bar RKO which was owned by RCA, it insisted from the outset in 1927 – well before any seriously viable all-electrical television system was in the offing – that all sound films shot using its equipment (the majority) were not licensed 'for any uses in or in connection with a telephone, telegraph or radio system or in connection with any apparatus operating by radio frequency or carrier currents' (Waldrop and Borkin 1938: 128) – that is, television. In its usual farsighted way it was seeking a position in a developing technology which might metamorphose into a threat to one of its established businesses, i.e. the ERPE film sound company which marketed Westrex. Using ploys like this, AT&T hedged its bets. In the next decade, it maintained its interest in the videophone and concluded a deal for the Farnsworth patents which in turn gave it a lever over RCA. It was then forced to play the Westrex card by dropping all restrictions and limitations in the contracts and royalty agreements for sound film as soon as RCA brought a legal threat to bear. But this concession allowed AT&T to force RCA into a general cross-patenting agreement (Greenwald 1952: 185). At the end of the day, AT&T only had one real interest in this matter. It was determined to position itself in television as it had done in radio by building the network (p. 262).

Unfortunately, from the FCC's point of view the other television players were less well placed and the commission could see them being swamped by RCA. The ostensible technical agenda of the American debate between 1936 and 1941 was comparatively meaningless. The hidden agenda was to hold down RCA by refusing to agree standards and permit a full-scale public service. The irony is that within weeks of this negative decision of the FCC in 1936, the Germans began broadcasting their version of the RCA system and within months the British variant was established as the London Television Standard. Defining the term 'experiment' as opposed to 'service' was becoming more a matter of policy than an assessment of the efficacy of the systems involved.

Thus RCA's 1939 demonstration at the World's Fair was designated as a 'television service', but by the company not by the commission. The RMA resubmitted barely altered suggestions for the standard but to no effect. A year later the FCC was still insisting that:

> no attempt be made by the industry or its members to issue standards in this field for the time being. In view of the possibilities for research, the objectives to be obtained, and the dangers involved, it is the judgement of the commission that the effects of such an industry agreement should be scrupulously avoided for the time being. Agreement upon the standards is presently less important than the scientific development of the highest standards within reach of the industry's experts.
>
> (Fink 1943: 11)

Had the war in Europe not suspended transmissions, the British would have been preparing to celebrate a fifth birthday at the time of this decision. The London Television Standard, with only 405 lines, worked well enough for there to be more complaints about repeats than about technical quality. The German broadcasts were not halted by war and their service continued. In America, the pattern established in 1927 to issue only experimental licences continued with anything between twenty and forty licensees being active, but without a standardised service. The FCC continued to insist that 'As soon as engineering opinion of the industry is prepared to approve any one of the competing systems of broadcasting as the standard system, the commission will consider the authorisation of full commercialisation' (Fink 1943: 12).

In this stand-off situation within the industry and between the industry and the commission, the FCC and the RMA finally agreed to the formation of a National Television System Committee, which would include all qualified engineering opinions whether within the RMA or not. In short order, at least by comparison with the previous pace of events, 168 people produced 600,000 words in minutes and reports, met for 4000 man-hours and spent a further 4000 hours gathering on-site evidence and watching twenty-five demonstrations. All this was done within six months. From the time of the initial agreement to proceed in this way to the acceptance, by the FCC, of the final report of the NTSC a mere fourteen months had elapsed.

This was a rather less startling display of efficiency than appears at first glance. After all, virtually everything of substance had already been previously decided. The lines were increased to 525 because it was now known that this rather than 441 was nearer the effective maximum for the six megacycle band. FM audio was chosen. The VHF spectrum was secured. But for the rest the NTSC endorsed the RMA proposed standards of 1939 which were a rerun of the 1936 suggestions. On 27 January 1941, the chairperson of the FCC, James Fly, said: 'This is another example of the best that is in our democratic system, with the best in the industry turning to a long and difficult job in an effort to help the government bodies in the discharge of their function so that a result may be achieved for the common good of all' (Fink 1943: 3).

What had been gained technically in television during the period of the 1936–41 delay was marginal: 525 lines were better than 441 lines but both were in the same range, the quality of the 16mm home movie image. At 525 lines that was still all that was achieved. As for the imposition of FM sound, it can be argued that the VHF band, being less subject to the sort of interference FM was designed to combat, did not require it – certainly, it required it less than did radio where the imperative was created by the poor quality of the AM bands. More than all this, at the end of the day in 1941, the two major technical options which really did need serious consideration were ignored. The possibility of moving to the UHF band, which the FCC had begun to license for experiment in 1937, was left hanging over the future of television and FM radio (which would have occupied the vacated VHF TV channels). And, prior to the NTSC agreement, CBS had demonstrated a viable colour system which was also ignored. Indeed the uncertainties of the art in 1941, when the bullet was bitten, were if anything greater than in 1936.

The introduction of a television service in the United States was delayed because the 'law' of the suppression of radical potential was at work. The disruptions feared were many. Television had to be made to fit into a media system already accommodating live events of all kinds, print, films and radio. And the diversity of manufacturing and programming interests had to be continued so that the balances achieved across the entire mass communication industry would not be upset. Central to this were concerns over RCA's approach. The British, grappling with the same problems, were quite specific as to what had to be guarded against. As the Selsdon Report which mandated the 1936 race between the television systems put it – 'any monopolistic control of the manufacturing of receiving sets'. The report goes on:

> The ideal solution, if it were feasible, would be that as a preliminary to the establishment of a public service, a Patent Pool should be formed. . . .We have seriously considered whether we should advise you [The Postmaster General] to refuse to authorise the establishment of a public service of high definition Television until a comprehensive Patent Pool has been formed.
>
> (Selsdon 1935: 16)

Although it had happened with radio, Lord Selsdon and his committee decided this was impracticable this time, perhaps because of the widespread range of techniques being suggested for television, and so gave the nod to the service anyway. In America the commission remained fearful of an RCA monopoly. However, the delaying tactic worked. RCA was contained. When television finally happened after the war, the firm was not alone. There were rival networks, many manufacturers, diverse programme suppliers. Its containment does not imply that it did not profit mightily from its television investment; as William Boddy says: 'RCA. . .won the war' (Boddy 1990: 34). Nevertheless, it did not profit as mightily as AT&T had done from the telephone – that is, with a virtual monopoly.

The marketplace itself was not enough to ensure that result. On the contrary, since no 'inventor' came up with a system as viable as that of RCA's 'inventors', the unfettered company would have cleaned up; or, as with early American telephony, chaos would have ensued with many minor competing systems needing to be absorbed. Hence the interventionist role of the FCC, unconcerned about the public but working most effectively to keep the industry stable through a period of threatened upheavals. The 'law' of the suppression of radical potential ensured that all the major radio industry players and AT&T should remain in the new game, and they did.

In this the commission was further aided by the war. The FCC had authorised the commercial (as opposed to the experimental) operation of television stations in accordance with the twenty-two NTSC standards on 1 July 1941. On 7 December the United States entered the war. The war prevented the creation of the mass medium of television but it also allowed the manufacturers to regroup for the new product with a minimum of disturbance. They ceased making domestic radios, more or less, and worked on material for the armed forces. When that stopped, they were ready to take up television. Indeed, their need to make television receivers was the final supervening necessity.

However, if the end of the war found AT&T and the radio industry agreed about television, AT&T's movie clients on the West Coast were not yet accommodated into the emerging order.

Received opinion has been that the film industry was caught napping by television and the Hollywood studio system was destroyed, but it is now generally agreed that the consent decree of 1948 forcing the studios to divest themselves of their cinema chains is of far greater moment than the arrival of American television's first big year. At best, television was a third blow to Hollywood, which was not only suffering under this enforced reorganisation but also enduring the beginnings of McCarthyism.

The movie moguls knew all about television. After all the very first public television demonstration in America, by Jenkins, was specifically designed for the home delivery of movies. By the late 1920s AT&T was contractually limiting the studios by forbidding them the right to sell sound films which used its Westrex system to television even before the technology was in the marketplace. H.E. Alexanderson had used film for early GE television demonstrations in 1927 (Hilmes 1990: 118). The Academy of Motion Picture Arts and Sciences in its report on television, in 1936, stated: 'there appears to be no danger that television will burst upon an unprepared motion picture industry' (Waldrop and Borkin 1938: 126). By then radio shows, either with stars or edited soundtracks or both, had been produced in Hollywood for years and the movie community's understanding of that world influenced its basic attitude to television. It was neither ignorant nor disdainful but rather imperialist. The moguls tried to usurp electronic distribution of video signals. They failed, but for all that their forces were distracted during a crucial period of television's development, the 'law' of the suppression of radical potential saved them anyway.

Television became the dominant medium and it was owned by the radio interests yet, despite that, Hollywood (albeit changed and regrouped) nevertheless became its major production centre. Exactly how that was achieved constitutes the last phase of the operation of the 'law' of the suppression of radical potential in television history – from the end of the war to the mid-1950s. The maintenance of stability among the radio production interests during this same period is another element.


## SUPPRESSING TELEVISION: 1948 TO THE MID-1950s

By 1948 television was finally poised to cover the nation. It had not been making much money but there were four networks, fifty-two stations and nearly a million sets in twenty-nine cities. In those communities, at least according to popular press reports, all other entertainments were suffering. Then, in September, the FCC ceased to process licences. The official account justifies this action because stations, at 150 miles minimum distance, were found to be interfering with each other.

Originally, in 1945, the commission had determined that stations using the same channel should be 200 miles apart. This meant that whereas Chicago was assigned five channels, New York got only four and Washington and Philadelphia three each. The industry protested and the FCC dropped the distance to 150 miles against the advice of the engineers. The engineers were right. The confusion that followed caused a four-year freeze on new stations. A further 400 applications were simply held up.

Since it is clear that a competent radio engineer with a good contour map could have solved this problem in something less than the forty-three months it took the FCC, interference is scarcely a convincing explanation for the length of the delay. Adding the Korean War (which halted nothing else in America but which is cited as contributing) hardly helps to explain the length of 'the freeze'.

The period between 1948 and 1952 saw the refinement of the *de facto* deal made in 1941 within the radio industry. The main threat to the stabilised diffusion period, which the 1941 agreement on standards had made possible, was caused by colour. By 1949, RCA engineers had produced what Sarnoff had demanded of them in 1946, a colour system compatible with the NTSC 1941 standards; that is to say, the colour signal would appear in black-and-white on a precolour mono-chrome receiver. Abandoning a semi-mechanical system, the RCA Laboratory concentrated on a method which used green, blue and red filters to sensitise three separate pick-up tubes within the camera. When the three resultant signals were superimposed on each other, via a system of mirrors, a full colour signal was created.

To receive it, RCA followed up on a concept of a German engineer, W. Flechsig, who had thought of a colour cathode ray tube in 1938, in which triads of colour phosphor dots, red, green and blue, were to be activated by a mesh of fine wires. Flechsig's concept was simply an electronic version of the Lumières' autochrome colour photography system of 1907 which also used this Pointillist sort of approach. Keeping the triads of phosphor dots, RCA engineers had modified Flechsig's otherwise difficult, if not impossible, proposal by suggesting that instead of wires, electron beams could be used passing through a mask drilled with holes – hence 'shadow mask tube'. When Sarnoff demanded a compatible colour system, this was the prototype to which H.B. Law of the Lab turned.

CBS had a rival system. It had been experimentally broadcasting in colour, under the direction of Peter Goldmark, since 1940, transmitting 343 lines. The CBS machine appears to be the very last in the line that starts with Nipkow in 1884, for Goldmark used a spinning disk, both in transmission and at the home end; but, as the disk was used to create colour rather than for scanning, it really owed more to the earliest colour film projectors with their spinning trichromatic filters (Anon 1940: 32–3). Goldmark was in a considerable tradition, even leaving the pre-twentieth-century Russian proposals aside. Baird, using trichromatic filters in a disk, had transmitted a colour picture in July of 1928 (Norman 1984: 50). After his retirement from the race of 1936 he went back to this work. Also, in 1929, Dr Ives, of the Bell Labs' videophone, although presumably no more certain as to the utility of the device than he had been two years earlier, nevertheless revealed a colour version (Ives 1929). It used sodium photo-emissive cells that were sensitive to the full range of visible colours.

In 1941, the NTSC had ignored both this tradition and the CBS experiments when making its recommendations; but, as it did not believe colour developments would necessarily result in compatibility with the monochrome standards it was establishing, this was logical. In a questionnaire issued at that time, the NTSC advisory panels concerned with this matter voted twenty-eight to seven against a compatibility requirement (Fink 1943: 41). Anyway, contrary to the received history, by the late 1940s the CBS system was compatible with RCA monochrome receivers, if they had tubes smaller than $12\frac{1}{2}$ inches and a simple tuning bracket had been added to the set. In the light of this the FCC, determined to thwart any further extension of RCA's dominance of television technology, adopted the CBS system in the middle of the freeze, in September 1950. The ploy did not work and the system was never introduced to the public. The manufacturers, tied to RCA for their black-and-white business, refused to accommodate the CBS bracket or make spinning disk receivers. A lawyer, involved in a congressional investigation of the FCC's apparent failure to implement its stated anti-monopolistic policies, wrote: 'We do not know whether any pressure was brought on them [the manufacturers] by their licenser [RCA]; but we do know that their refusals effectively 'killed' the CBS colour system which the FCC had adopted' (Schwartz 1959: 789).

A Senate report of 1950 evaluated the CBS/RCA systems (and a third system in a yet more experimental state) finding, across some eighteen measures of utility, efficiency and effectiveness, that the RCA system had eight better performance characteristics than CBS, four as good and six worse. In all, CBS's colour fidelity was deemed to be better, but its sets could not, because of the spinning disk, produce pictures bigger than about 1 foot across (Senate 1950).

It might perhaps be thought that this hidden battle about colour, rather than the public débâcle over station distances, was the reason for the freeze. In one sense this is true, since the colour issue was part of the whole question of the continuing stability of the radio industry during the period of television's initial diffusion. But colour in a more direct sense cannot be the reason. It came to the fore after the freeze had begun and was resolved, in favour of RCA, after it was over – at the end of 1953. Anyway, rather like the British introduction of monochrome service in 1937, colour was premature. Americans no more rushed to buy colour sets than had the British to buy black-and-white televisions in the late 1930s. Sales did not really take off until the early 1970s and the result of American pioneering in the early 1950s was the adoption of an RCA system markedly inferior in quality to the systems developed slightly later for European broadcasters.[4]

The Commission, in opting for RCA colour in 1953, abandoned the rhetoric it had used to constrain television in the late 1930s and early 1940s; that is, an argument that delay was necessary because technical improvements could be expected. Further, the RCA decision was made despite the policy of resisting monopoly in all aspects and at all levels of American broadcasting. FCC lawyers warned of the serious consequences of proceeding with the RCA system without considering the patent situation. However, the commission had seen that the dangers of RCA's monopoly were less disruptive to the industry than an insistence on the CBS system for the ideological sake of diversity (Schwartz 1959: 788). Some went so far as to suggest that the colour inquiry was reopened, after the wavelength assignments had been cleared up, specifically to consolidate further the protection the major players had already received (Boddy 1990: 51).

Beyond the fracas about colour and signal interference, the truth about the freeze was that the industry was not 'frozen' by it at all. In 1946 there were 5000 sets. By 1950 there were just under ten million. Two years later, the number of sets had increased to fifteen million and more than one-third of the population had them. Television was bringing in 70 per cent of broadcasting advertising revenues by 1952. The 'freeze' worked to suppress television as an area of exploitation for new interests. NBC, after all, had been encouraging its affiliates to obtain television licences for years. It and its main rival, CBS, transferred their hegemony to television. The owners of the first 108 stations, in effect the radio industry, were able to bed down and sew up the new structure as an echo of the old (Boddy 1990: 50). The shape of American television behind this protective wall was established with the minimum of disturbance, despite the internecine disputes. Advertising revenues, programs and personnel were transferred from radio to television with comparative ease.

The freeze concluded with the issue of the FCC's *Sixth Report and Order* which institutionalised these results. By 1952, in utter obedience to the 'law' of the suppression of radical potential, the broadcasting industry had metamorphosed from radio to television and nearly every audio-caterpillar had successfully become a video-butterfly.

Something else, less remarked upon, also happened during the 'freeze'. In 1948 the top programme in the television schedule was Milton Berle's *The Texaco Star Theater* on NBC, a variety show. It was soon joined by Ed Sullivan's *Toast of the Town* on CBS. Both of these were live productions from New York. In 1952 the top show was filmed in Hollywood, *I Love Lucy*. This is not to say that in these four years production moved from the East to the West Coast. It is simply to point out that the television industry's structure, which looked at the outset of this period to be essentially live and in New York, looked at the end of it also to have a place for film and Hollywood. The implications of this move would take most of the 1950s to work out, but by the end of the decade, the era of the live New York productions in the prime-time schedule was largely past and people were already referring to it as 'the Golden Age of American television'.

Hollywood's first idea about television was to incorporate it. All the early pioneers had shown large screen as well as small formats and the possibilities of theatre television looked as real as domestic options. At the Swiss Federal Institute of Technology Professor Fischer shared Hollywood's general view of television's potential as a theatrical entertainment form and, in 1939, he developed the Eidophor which was to become the standard device for large screen television projection (Dummer 1983: 119). In 1941 RCA demonstrated a 15 × 20-foot screen which was installed in a few theatres (Hilmes 1990: 121–2). By 1948, Paramount's own system was installed in their Times Square showcase and the heavyweight boxing bout was established as a staple of the distribution system. By 1952 a network of more than a hundred cinemas was equipped with electronic systems yet within a year, theatrical television's promise had been blunted (ibid.: 123). AT&T used the coaxial rate card to price the movie interests out of the market while the FCC denied them the right to use parts of the UHF spectrum instead. This block occurred exactly at the moment the freeze ended and the boom in domestic television finally took off. Even as this market opened out for its product, the film industry also decided to roll out a number of technological responses, as alternatives, as it were, to the Eidophor – Cinemascope, 3-D and other spectacles (ibid.: 123–4). Theatrical television, except as an occasional technique for big boxing matches, was totally suppressed. The large screen equipment, especially the Eidophors, survived as back projection devices only inside television studios until colour allowed for electronic image matting – Colour Separation Overlay (CSO) – instead.

A further option was explored during the 'freeze' and took a longer time to die, if indeed it is dead yet. Subscription television, for which (by the late 1940s) there was an ample range of hardware, began in Chicago on a trial basis in 1949 (Hilmes 1990: 126). In 1953, Paramount's test in Palm Springs was closed in response to a threatened legal action. The charge was that as the producer of the films it was showing on its system, it was once more, and illegally, engaged in exhibition. In 1953 it bought itself into ABC and became a major part of the raucous campaign against pay television which, for a time at least, united the cinema owners and the broadcasters. The FCC regulated these tests, but made it clear that it thought its duties lay in protecting the existing system from unexpected competition. Pay TV, where individual programs rather than whole channels or services are bought, also languished.

Hollywood's way forward into the television age did not lie with alternative television distribution systems but with the radio broadcasters. The freeze had shown two things: first, that short-form Hollywood series could be as popular as anything produced elsewhere, and, second, that old movies had appeal. The studios were quicker to respond to the former possibility. They had difficulty in establishing telefilm operations because to do so would have upset their theatrical clients – just as, in the 1980s, the American networks could not offer popular programme services to the cable industry without upsetting their broadcasting affiliates. But despite this, RKO did set up a subsidiary for telefilms as early as 1944. Slowly the deals were done; ABC with Hal Roach Jr; the first Disney special; *Warner Brothers Presents*.

After the freeze the trickle of Hollywood prime-time product became a flood. By 1955, telefilm raw stock consumption was ten times greater than that of the feature side of the industry. Of course, there were many new production entities involved in this but, despite the rise of some smaller entrepreneurs, it was essentially old Hollywood. A few of the players had regrouped under new banners but most were still manning the same stores.

After the freeze, with this beachhead in the schedules firmly held, beginning with RKO in 1956, the majors sold their libraries. By that time, New York had come to call, with both CBS and NBC building major production facilities in Hollywood, consolidating the tradition begun with radio. New York was left with news, sport, documentaries, variety and the daytime soaps, and Hollywood got the dramatic staple of the schedule. In 1949 none of this was clear. By 1952, the mould of American broadcast television was setting fast. After the freeze, the number of stations jumped to 573 broadcasting to nearly thirty-three million receivers. Between 1955 and 1960 another eighty stations and 36.5 million sets finally made America into the earth's first televisual nation (Owen 1962: 820).

The 'law' of the suppression of radical potential worked against the supervening necessities to hold television in limbo just outside widespread diffusion throughout the 1930s and 1940s. After the supervening necessity of spare electronic industry capacity made its introduction inevitable, the 'law' worked to contain its disruptive forces. This is true not just of the United States where the regulatory process existed in such an uneasy harness with the potential excesses of the free market – in the sense that, without the FCC, America could well have had more than one system on more than one standard, as had been the case with telephony in the years between the lapse of the Bell master patent and the imposition of order by the US government. In the UK, where government fiat had encouraged the premature television service, post-war progress matched that of the United States, although it was conducted somewhat more rationally. Here, and throughout most of the rest of the world, the 'law' of the suppression of radical potential worked straightforwardly through austerity.

By the end of 1952 there were still less than three million receivers in the UK. When, by 1952 (the year when America finally got the go-ahead for national television), the BBC completed its network of major transmitters to reach 78 per cent of the population, it had less to do with the shakedown of warring elements within the industry than with basic economics. Yet there were such elements, and, as had been the case with radio, the BBC was allowed to develop a new technology without competition from commercial broadcasters. Only when the system was established and the BBC had successfully transformed itself from a radio into a bi-media entity did the advertising lobby in Britain finally get in on the act, winning, in 1954, the right to broadcast commercials and also, necessarily, the programs to put round them.

Elsewhere, with improving economic conditions, 1952/3 marks the true start of television diffusion. Italy began a five-year plan to cover the nation. North Germany's network was completed. The French added Lille to Paris and started work on three other transmitters. In Canada, CBC began programming. By the early 1950s, and only then, could it be said that television had finally arrived. Further, in every nation, the arrival did not displace whatever interested parties pre-existed the 'invention'. Everywhere, radio manufacturers and producing entities switched to television. There were no casualties. There were few new faces.

# 7

# TELEVISION SPIN-OFFS
# AND REDUNDANCIES

SPIN-OFFS AND REDUNDANCIES: VCRs, CDs *et al.*

This book is not focused on how manufacturing and production sectors progress after a given technology reaches a launch platform for diffusion. The industrial and cultural formations which grew up around the expansion of television, the production phase in the model, are largely outside our scope; on the other hand, spin-offs, which in the case of television could, for example, include certain non-broadcast uses of the cathode ray tube, television recording methods and new standards for the television signal, are not. The most important non-broadcast uses of the tube have been in connection with computing and this will therefore be dealt with in Part III. Here let us deal with a spin-off which has come to be called, in distinction to television, 'video'; that is, videotape and all the domestic devices, the competitive technologies and the further spin-offs it has spawned.

Of all the new media technologies now available the home videocassette recorder has proved to be the most significant. Overshadowed by the enormous public relations exercise mounted first by the world's cable and satellite interests and then by proponents of home computing and the Internet, VCR growth has gone, by comparison, almost unnoticed; yet between 1980 and 1995 the number of VCRs increased, in the US, from 1.8 million to 86 million. Ninety per cent of all households with television had one by 1995. Each of these homes was renting a video nearly every week, over 4000 million transactions per annum in a $10,000 million market (Veronhis Suhler 1996: 172, 176). No device has been adopted more quickly even though it took five years, from 1974 when VCRs were first freely available until 1979, for sales to become significant. That year, as in 1962 for the colour televisions, nearly half a million units were sold. By 1981, the 1.3 million VCR sales matched the 1.3 million television set sales of 1964. Again, in 1983, more than 4 million VCRs marched with the nearly 5 million colour sets sold in 1966. In 1984 nearly 8 million units went into American homes – far more than the number of television sets sold in 1967, colour having peaked as a consumer item since by then more than three-quarters of all homes had one. By the 1980s, the VCR was penetrating the US home at more than twice the rate the PC was to achieve a few years later.

In Britain, where diffusion of the device was aided by the television set rental business, penetration was even faster than in the US with 60 per cent of British homes having a VCR by 1988. By 1994, 76 per cent of all homes had one and there were 66 million rentals worth nearly £700 million. Across the rest of Western Europe more than one household in three had the device by the late 1980s with rates in Germany and France being closer to two in three (Lange and Renaud 1989: 81). In some other parts of the world, penetration was even faster; 85 per cent of all Saudi Arabian homes, for example, had a machine by 1985 (Tracy 1985: 23). Curiously, though, there has been almost no hyperbolic reaction to this development despite this being by far the most widely diffused of the new media technologies.

As with radio and television itself, this is a technology that 'fits' culturally; that is to say, the VCR meshes with abstractions such as the ongoing drive to put entertainment in the home as well as practicalities such as the fact that it displays its signal on the cathode ray tube of the domestic television receiver. It is even packaged like the hi-fidelity audio systems that preceded it as part of the growing 'home entertainment centre'. Second, it offers a real add-on advantage to television since it breaks the tyranny of the programme scheduler, allowing for time shifting and personalised archiving. Third, after initial purchase, even including regular rental fees, it is inexpensive. It affords opportunities to enjoy theatrical films at a fraction of the present cost of a cinema visit. Whereas 10 per cent of American VCR owners hired pre-recorded material in 1979, 70 per cent did so in 1983. By 1995, the average American VCR household was buying about four videos a year outright in addition to their weekly rental. Hollywood was taking three dollars from video sales and rentals for every dollar it took at the cinema box-office (Veronhis Suhler 1996: 186). Finally, video is competitive with the cable and satellite home movie channels which have, like broadcasting, fixed schedules and, unlike broadcasting, a fixed monthly charge. (Cassetted movies are also more pornographic, at least in America, than those shown on cable.)

Despite all this, the diffusion of the VCR still took some decades. Critical to its acceptance was the decision of October 1981 on copyright, when a US court held that no infringement was involved in home taping of broadcast signals. Sony had successfully resisted this action which had been brought by United Artists and Disney. The rest of Hollywood, even then, was not overly concerned. Since that time sales and rentals from pre-recorded cassettes have become a major source of revenue. As for American cinema owners, they perceived, largely correctly, that the cassette user was quite distinct from their audience and otherwise lost to the movies. In other countries there were more overt attempts at suppression. In

France, for instance, cinema owners managed legally to restrict the speed with which distributors could release cassettes of films still popular in the theatres. In Britain and Germany cassettes were blamed for a diminution in broadcast television's audience in the early 1980s. Yet the impact on all these areas, film exhibition, broadcast scheduling, copyright, has been quite gradual and certainly uncataclysmic.

Radio and television had already transformed the cinema audience. Video was but one of a variety of new competitors and not the one which attracted the most attention. For television, balancing the potential threat of pre-recorded cassettes was the advantage of increasing audience through time-shifting. Copyright holders, after the initial worry, have been placated by the growth of an extensive and controllable distribution industry in the form of local video-stores, many grouped into large chains. Unlike the situation with recorded music, there is little copying of video cassettes. Even if homes boast two VCRs they are unlikely to be in the same room and attached to just one television. Illegal commercial duplication remains a problem but not one which destroys the basis of the distribution system as a whole.

The domestic video cassette-player is a spin-off of a recording technology developed for broadcasters, specifically for network operations (p. 266). It was available for this purpose by the mid-1950s but from the very beginning of this line of development, some had seen its potential as a home entertainment system. As early as 1953 General Sarnoff had pronounced: 'Magnetic tape recording of video signals should make possible simple means by which a set owner can make recordings of television pictures in the home. And they can be "performed" over and over through the television receiver just as a phonograph record is played at will' (Sarnoff n.d.: 891). By the late 1960s the expectation was growing that videotape would be able to provide 'home libraries of films and television programs' (Falk 1968: 322).

To this end, Sony put 1-inch tape into a cassette in April 1969. The tape width was reduced to $\frac{3}{4}$ inch seven months later and the speed to 3.15 inches per second. That same month Panasonic introduced a machine using a $\frac{1}{2}$-inch tape cassette which Philips had developed and which ran at $7\frac{1}{2}$ inches per second. Philips revised this design the following summer, keeping the $\frac{1}{2}$-inch tape but reducing the speed to 5.6 inches per second (Abramson 1973: 195). One other addition to this proliferation of mutually incompatible boxes appeared in 1969: JVC introduced a square cassette using $\frac{1}{2}$-inch tape. 'Video cassette' was noted as a neologism at this time.

Eventually the $\frac{1}{2}$-inch tape size, but in a number of revised formats, was to prevail. There was a considerable battle between the Beta and VHS configurations of Sony and JVC, which concluded in the 1980s with the former being beaten back from the home while maintaining the edge as the last non-digital professional standard, while the latter came to dominate the domestic home market. Although

Beta was superior in quality and available earlier, in its earliest form it could only record for one hour, not enough for a feature film. Building film libraries from off-air recordings turned out to be a major application and the capacity of VHS to record for more than an hour gave it what became a complete advantage. Despite introducing cassettes with greater capacity, Beta never recovered.

These various video cassette systems penetrated society more quickly than any other technology considered here. Nevertheless they appeared nearly two decades after their industrial reel-to-reel cousins were introduced. It was to take about five years for them to create space for themselves on retailers' shelves and the better part of another decade for them to achieve the status of a major consumer durable. This is the fastest aspect of the 'revolution', as society has experienced it so far.

The VCR also occasioned a considerable number of redundant technologies. Redundancy is, in part, a matter of timing, although it in part relates to function. It occurs, like spin-offs, when technological performance continues beyond the point of invention. With redundant performance, all that is produced are devices that duplicate the essential functions of the invention or its spin-offs. Their efficiency (as with prototypes in the second phase of the model) is not the crucial factor. Redundant devices can work as well as those they seek to replace or sometimes they can work less well. Such levels of performance will not disturb the diffusion of the previous technology. Even superior performance will not be sufficient, necessarily, to sweep away established inventions and spin-offs. In fact, superiority can be nothing but a snare and a delusion for a redundant device is, in essence, nothing but a retarded spin-off. Timing is everything.

Polaroid's response to instant video, for example, was to produce an instant film for the 8mm market. This failed to provide video's off-air recording capability, produced no library of material such as theatrical films and did not match, in price or quality, 8mm film. It was thus redundant not only in terms of tape but also of amateur film and was rapidly withdrawn.

A number of firms tried to avoid becoming Sony or JVC licensees by introducing alternative video cassettes but they made no headway. Nor did those who tried to avoid tape altogether. There were repeated attempts to impress or capture the wave-form of the video signal on to various non-electronic media, a concept that went back to de Forest in 1931 and Edison's British lab in 1934. As alternatives to videotape, General Electric in 1959, Eastman in 1961, RCA in 1964 and 3M in 1965 all produced systems which recorded on to film the television picture after its conversion into an electron beam. The most strenuous attempt to get this technology into the market was mounted by CBS which developed a technique marketed as EVR in the late 1960s. The acronym stood for Electronic Video Recording, a considerable misnomer since it was actually an electron beam process using 8mm film in cassettes.

Then there were videodisks. The problem here was that the audio disk analogy did not seem to work for video. Perhaps this was because, unlike radio, where the first retrieval technology, disks, did not allow for home recording, with video the first retrievable home system, VCR, did. Time-shifting and personal off-air archiving rendered the sustained attempt to market pre-recorded videodisks almost as futile as the efforts to diffuse EVR. It must be said, though, that CBS's commitment to EVR was terminated with a great deal more dispatch and foresight than for example, RCA exhibited pushing its version of the videodisk ten years later.

Of itself, the videodisk offers two advantages over videotape. It can be randomly accessed to display instantly any frame; and, if utilising laser-based technology, it is the most durable means available for recording audiovisual signals. It was the first of these capabilities that led to the earliest developments. By 1960, Philips, and various other players, major (like Sony) and minor (like the MVR Corporation of Palo Alto), produced disk devices which stored instantly accessible single picture frames. Typically the disk held only a few hundred pictures, a few seconds of movement. The supervening necessity that brought these hand-built machines into the television studios was the sports programs' need for careful, considered, not to say academic, analysis of plays. (Supervening necessities must not be subjected to value judgements along utilitarian lines of the greatest good for the greatest number. They can be found in the small as well as the big. For producers and watchers of sports shows, the need for 'instant replays' was obviously real and pressing enough for these devices to be built and sold.) In August 1965, an MVR unit was used in a CBS football game transmission. The world witnessed the wonders of an 'action replay' for the first time. Two years later MVR produced a slow motion machine.

RCA introduced a domestic variant of this device which used a physical system, a stylus, to read the signal on the disk. The method had first been demonstrated by Telefunken/Decca in 1970 and was, with considerable hullabaloo, marketed in 1981. By this time, RCA had around $200 million tied up in this CED videodisk (Graham 1986: 26). It only had one good sales point: it gave a picture of sharper resolution than VCR. However, since this was still bound by the line standard of the domestic television, such improvement was not enough to make the device a necessity. Otherwise, the disk did not even initially deliver stereophonic sound. That the disk could randomly access frames and alter running speeds, etc. was also of little interest since, within the culture, that is not, by and large, how audio-visual messages are viewed.[1] Other advantages proved just as illusory. Disks were cheaper than pre-recorded cassettes, but the majority of VCR users, especially during the period the RCA disk was initially marketed, did not buy pre-recorded cassettes. They rented them or used the VCR's recording ability to copy off-air, either ploy making cassettes cheaper than disks. (The rapid rise of the rental business, especially in pornography, in the early 1980s apparently came as a totally unexpected shock to RCA's executives (ibid: 214).) RCA persisted with the marketing of its videodisk, despite a long involvement with videotape, a domestic version of which they had introduced as a consumer standard in 1969. Finally in the spring of 1984, having endangered the entire corporation (network operations at NBC also at this time performing poorly in ratings and profits), and with at most half a million players sold, RCA gave up.

That RCA should have bet the company by pitting its outmoded physical system against videotape (and, as we shall now see, the laser disk) is curious. The only explanation is that, as we have seen, unlike AT&T, RCA did not have a history of patent sharing. On the contrary, from the moment of its founding it seemed only to be comfortable if it had a commanding technological position. NTSC colour television was the last occasion when this had been achieved and it was as if the corporate mind saw the CED disk as the best hope for regaining such a position; but the world had changed.

RCA's CED disk must not be confused with the rival laser disks. These are virtually indestructible – a life of six centuries without any special storage is claimed – and are clearly needed if the world's audiovisual archive is to be preserved. They also have uses as computer data storage devices for the same reason. Despite this, laser videodisks were initially marketed like the CED disks; that is, as redundant alternatives to videotape. Pioneer beat RCA to the stores, having a laser disk system on sale in the US in time for Christmas 1980. However, neither the CED nor the laser disk sold. The laser disk, though, was then reborn as the compact disk or CD, an alternative to the audio long-playing (LP) record and audio-cassette, as well as a personal computer programme storage device, the CD-ROM. Philips, working with laser technology as a source of possible computer data storage applications, had been the first to produce a practical laser-based audiovisual image storage device when, in 1972, they unveiled the VLP disk. On this the information was stored in a series of micrometer pits arranged in a spiral pattern which were read by a laser-generated spot. The disk held up to forty-five minutes' worth of material (Dummer 1983: 198).

The ground of scientific competence that leads to the laser goes back once more to Dr Young. The experiment establishing the wave hypothesis of light also demonstrated that certain light sources were coherent – with waves in phase both temporally and spatially – while others, natural light say, were not. In 1913 Niels Bohr made an assumption about the nature of atoms which was to impinge most fruitfully on Young's observation of coherent light. Atoms exist in a ground – low-energy – state or can be excited into higher-energy states. They do this by absorbing one of Einstein's light particles – photons – of exactly the frequency required to reach the excited state. Conversely the atom can decay from the excited state into the ground state by emitting a photon of this frequency. Atoms do this spontaneously. In 1917 Einstein demonstrated that atoms could be induced to release photons by the external presence of a photon of the right frequency. The external photon and the one released by its stimulation would be exactly in phase, coherent in terms of Young's experiment. Once begun, the stimulated emission of photons would be like an avalanche. But a problem arose. As the emitting atoms decayed they reabsorbed some of the emitted photons and the avalanche petered out. To prevent this, a 'population inversion' is required whereby a greater number of atoms must be in the excited state than there are atoms in the ground state.

The search for a substance and technique in which this would happen constitutes the ground of scientific competence for the LASER, Light Amplification by Simulated Emission of Radiation. The ideation transformation occurs in a seminal paper, written by Charles Townes and A.L. Schawlow (of Bell Labs) in 1958, which outlined the general principles and suggested potassium vapour as the substance (Dummer 1983: 157). Townes already knew how to achieve avalanches of emission but with microwaves, comparatively long invisible wavelengths. In 1951 he and his colleagues at Columbia built a MASER – Microwave Amplification by Simulated Emission of Radiation – using ammonia. The same year a Russian, Fabrikan, had the same idea.

All this activity clearly indicates a strong supervening necessity. Masers were of interest to the telecommunications industry as a means of amplifying very weak signals, such as those coming from space or passing through a transoceanic cable and were at the heart of the generation of cables which came on stream in competition with communication satellites (p. 288). Lasers would be of similar value in a number of applications. The idea of using light as a carrier, after all, goes back to Bell's photophone (upon which he was working as he designed the grapho-phone) and the experiments of Alexanderson at GE. Sputnik, by inaugurating the space race, reinforced the general supervening necessity for all aspects of high technology created by the cold war and specifically helped lasers – which, like masers, were potentially useful in space side communications.

Lasers are a device, like the transistor, whose development is said to offer a contrast between the supposedly serendipitous nature of pre-twentieth-century innovation and what today's technologists do. Yet here again the historical record does not quite sustain this picture. The pace of development up to the point of ideation was leisurely. Science fiction dreams of death-rays did not speed them up even during the Second World War and, before the cold war took on its extraterrestrial aspects, the concept languished. Now, in the 'invention phase', looking for a substance that would allow for laser transition led to a search, albeit limited by a sophisticated understanding of the atomic structures of the substances examined, but not too unlike the procedures of the nineteenth-century 'amateur inventors'. The gold at the end of this rainbow turned out to be a ruby and it was identified in 1960 by Theodore Maiman of the Hughes Aircraft Company. (Hughes was at the heart of the developing race to produce a satellite communications system (p. 284).) Bell Labs understood the potential of rubies for lasers but had abandoned them as being too poor to give any hope of success and had concentrated instead on gases. Maiman had persevered with the stone, or rather a synthetic version of it, and in 1960 had achieved laser action. Once this was done a helium/neon laser was made and in the years that followed hundreds of different laser transitions were demonstrated. Four decades had passed since the theoretical possibility of the device had been determined and the ground of scientific competence laid. Rubies, of course, had been around a lot longer.

Laser videodisk technology was first released in 1978, by Philips, as a variant for computer data storage. The disks' interactive capability was exploited by the US military for education and training purposes (just as 16mm film had been used forty years before) and then, widely, as CD-ROMs. At the same time, the disks were being marketed as an entertainment medium, but, as we have seen, to no great effect. In 1984, the year RCA abandoned its CED videodisk, Pioneer, its laser disk rivals, ran an advertising campaign to sell the players which featured, uniquely in a commercial for a visual device, the blind musicians Ray Charles and George Shearing, stressing the wonderful sound the system produced. The failure to find a mass market for the laser videodisk as a consumer durable in some sense has endangered its survival as an archival tool. Archive requirements are not, of themselves, a supervening necessity despite the growing awareness, at least in industrial and academic circles, that the stock of audiovisual images held around the world is in danger of deteriorating beyond the point where information can be retrieved. Colour films especially are subject to degradation and it is already the case that much early imagery has been lost.

The most widely diffused application of the technology has turned out not to be visual at all. In 1983, Philips, in agreement with Sony (always a suspicious event), marketed a 5-inch laser videodisk upon which nothing was recorded except sound. The plan was to have the population which was addicted, in various degrees, to a mode of musical reproduction, called stereo, jettison this in favour of the new system, compact disks (CDs),within ten to fifteen years. It worked.

CDs use digital sampling techniques. Beyond analogue amplitude and frequency modulation, there are a variety of other systems for modulating signals digitally. These involve converting an analogue signal into a stream of digital data bits. The resultant pulses can be transmitted by modulating their strength (PAM – Pulse Amplitude Modulation), their frequency (PIM – Pulse Interval Modulation) or their length (PDM – Pulse Duration Modulation). The most important of these systems, however, is Pulse Code Modulation (PCM), developed in the Paris office of IT&T and patented, in 1938, by A.H. Reeves. In this system the analogue wave-form is sampled and each discrete level of amplitude is assigned a digital value. This stream of values represents a digital encoding of the original signal. The rate at which the analogue signal has to be sampled depends, of course, on its complexity; but the mathematical formulae allowing Reeves and his successors to build actual systems to do this were published in 1928 by Nyquist. All of these various digital modulation methods have considerable advantages for telephony by enhancing the integrity and robustness of the signal. Some also allow for the economically efficient bundling of data-streams to increase the capacity of a system to carry calls. On the other hand, there was a problem with them: PCM, for example, required thirty times the bandwidth needed by analogue telephony and this profligacy made it initially uneconomic until, in the last quarter of the century, effective techniques for compressing digital signals evolved.

A general point needs to be made in this connection: the digitisation of analogue electrical signals is at the heart of the concept of 'convergence', the idea that all the machinery of communications is coming together, especially the television and computer, with profound effects. Convergence is an important element in Information Age hype. I simply want to point out that the basis of convergence lies in a body of maths which goes back to the 1920s and was an established technique which dates from the late 1930s – and therefore antedates the building of the first digital computers. Again, it might well be the case that digitisation will have the profound social effects the technicists claim for it – or not. Either way, the pace of its introduction has scarcely been revolutionary, although it has had significant impact in specific areas.

For example, the digital CD has been exploited to destroy the analogue LP. The technology of the long-playing record (LP) dates back to pre-First World War sound film systems which synchronised gramophones and projectors. However, comfortable with a business that sold music segmented in $3\frac{1}{2}$- or 5-minute chunks recorded on easily breakable shellac, the industry did nothing to bring more durable disks of longer duration to the market. (After all, they had only adopted electric recording when faced with the competition of radio.) Eventually, in 1948, CBS broke ranks and introduced the $33\frac{1}{3}$ LP. GE followed a year later with the Extended Play, EP, or 45 rpm. Both these formats depended on the use of a new plastic, vinyl, which had been developed by CBS in 1944 after the Japanese had interrupted shellac supplies by invading the Malay peninsular. Vinyl was comparatively unbreakable but still easily damaged by scratches. It permitted finer grooves to be pressed thereby increasing the amount of music which could be recorded on a disk. There is nothing to suggest that this advance was based on new scientific knowledge.

The record industry was just as slow about stereo. Stereophonic effects had, apparently, first been demonstrated with telephone loudspeakers in Paris in 1881. The first stereo movies date from 1940, Disney's *Fantasia* following two years later (Limbacher 1968: 225). Stereo disks were pioneered by Alan Blumlein of the EMI television research team (Chanan 1995: 133). It took the industry a further decade after the introduction of the LP before it offered the public stereo using Blumlein's recording technique (ibid: 93,134).

This conservatism persisted when Sony and Philips immediately eschewed one advantage that would accrue from using the developed digital VLP for audio purposes, to wit the complete recordings of long musical works on a single platter. Apparently the record industry believes that it and its need for profit, and not, say, Wagner, should dictate the 'natural' package of a piece. The 12 inches of the LP became the 12 centimetres of the CD and, armed with this device, the industry set about killing off the LP. In 1984, 800,000 CDs were shipped in America as opposed to 200 million LPs and 131 million vinyl singles. This was not surprising: initial sales of CD players, despite the superior sound reproduction they provided as well as the greater indestructibility of disks, were slow. Projections were not being met and by 1984 there were fewer than a million worldwide. In the UK fewer than 30,000 CD players were sold in the first year. However, cheaper players began to appear in 1985 and sales started to pick up. The disks' robustness made the technology attractive to boat and car owners and the adventurous affluent began to bite the bait. However, to effect (or force) the change from LPs and singles on the public, the recorded music industry showed itself to be quite willing to reduce its production of vinyl, despite this slow take-up. Vinyl was anyway already giving way to cassettes. In the first three years of the 1980s US production of LPs had fallen from 322 million to 209 million while cassettes had increased from 110 to 236 million. In that sense, the CD simply augments the change-over from vinyl already in hand. The difference is that the rise of the cassette was on the back of the solid success of the player, culminating in the Sony Walkman, a personal portable stereo which dramatically altered the practice of listening to recorded music.

The Walkman was a last logical step in a process which had been developing for the previous two decades and more. The record industry had objected to tape, which had been introduced in Germany in the early 1930s and was finally adopted by broadcasters in the early 1950s (p. 266). The delay was attributable to their well-founded fears about home duplication. On the other hand, a market was opened up, significantly by an outsider, the aircraft manufacturer Lear, for portable systems to play pre-recorded material in cars – the eight-track cassette. This eventually broke through these solid objections to tape and Sony and Philips agreed a format for the audiocassette, thereby wiping out the intrusive eight-track. Sony then encouraged this liking for mobile recorded music in cars with the Walkman, which could be used anywhere; but it did not need to use industry pre-recorded cassettes. Because of this, the industry saw its worst fears of tape being realised. Audiocassette recorders were being manufactured which not only recorded vinyl on to tape but also had a second head for copying cassettes.

Some industrial opinion held that each record sold was being copied no less than five times. In Britain the audio disk business had peaked in 1978. By 1983 sales of singles had fallen by 13 per cent, and LPs by 27 per cent. Significantly, pre-recorded cassette sales were up by 75 per cent but this increase of 15 million units was not enough to balance the loss of nearly 32 million LPs and 15 million singles. In this half-decade, all sectors of the British record industry, which employed some 12,000 people in manufacture, distribution and retail, lost 1000 jobs a year (Anon 1984: 7).

In this situation, the CD, unrecordable in its original form by analogue cassette machines, represented nothing less than the long-term salvation of the industry and that was the supervening necessity underlying its development and introduction. The only problem was that the CD player, by contrast with the Walkman and despite its superior quality, was selling slowly. By 1990 still only one US house in five had one. The answer for the industry, cushioned to a certain extent by pre-recorded audiocassette sales, was to ignore comparative failure and simply switch from vinyl. Already by 1987 this starving of the LP market was underway as almost as many CDs as LPs were shipped – 102 million to 107 million. By 1995, the change-over had been accomplished. A mere 2.2 million LPs were pressed but no less than 727 million CDs were sent to the American market. And cassettes, which had peaked at 450 million units in 1988, were back to their pre-CD level of some 250 million plus units (Veronhis Suhler 1996: 198). Almost no attention has been paid to this curious history which, on its face, would appear to be a completely effective manipulation of the market by a few international communication conglomerates.

A further proof of this manipulation can be found in the curious history of the suppression of domestic digital audiotape-recording systems in the period following the introduction of the CD. Almost as soon as CDs were being marketed, the industry readied itself for another advance, digital audio tape (DAT). There were no conceptual difficulties in applying digital sampling techniques to either the audio or video signal and a number of organisations explored the possibility from the 1960s on. As a recording technique PCM would permit not only improved reproduction of the original analogue sounds but also their cloning, rather than copying, once they had been recorded. The Japanese State Broadcaster, NHK, demonstrated a prototype PCM audiomagnetic tape-recording machine in 1967. The BBC built one in 1976. In that year though, Sony linked a digital audio processor to a domestic VCR to create the first home DAT machine. This was marketed in 1977.

By the turn of the decade there were two separate standards being offered by Sony and JVC in what many in Japan saw as a potentially harmful rerun of the Beta vs. VHS war. In June 1983, no less than eighty-four Japanese and foreign companies formed a 'DAT Conference' specifically to avoid this by agreeing a standard designed to 'replace the mainstream of present audio recording' (Nakajima and Kosaka 1986: 407). Agreement was reached in favour of the Sony concept and machines were supposed to be on the market by 1987 at the latest. However, the CD strategy had not been considered; so: 'The conferees . . . decided to delay the introduction of DAT so that the CD market could mature' (Gow 1989: 10). The crucial point of DAT was that it would allow for perfect duplicates – in fact, clones – of CDs to be made. The laborious advantage gained by forcing the market to move away from analogue sound systems, LPs and cassettes, would be lost.

The delay to DAT was due to the two firms in the world who had the greatest spread of interests as both hardware equipment and software CD manufacturers, Philips and Sony. Key was Philips: 'Philips had impressed the Japanese companies with its ability to persuade the European Economic Community (EEC) to impose a 19 per cent tariff on all foreign CD players sold in Europe after 1984' (Gow 1989: 11). The threat to do the same or worse to DAT machines was enough to halt the introduction of domestic DAT everywhere, except in the professional recording studio. There *M*odular *D*igital *M*ultitrack (MDM) recorders using videotape formats and tapeless *D*igital *A*udi *W*orkstations (DAWs) were becoming the audio production norm. Yet, by the mid-1990s, domestic DAT was still to be effectively marketed. To all intents and purposes, the 'DAT Conference' failed in its announced purpose and, although a Sony vs. JVC battle was avoided, Philips eventually broke ranks and introduced its own rival system to Sony. On the other hand, the CD market had indeed 'matured'. Seldom has there been a clearer exercise of the 'law' of suppression.

Digitisation is also having an effect on the most successful spin-off of the video cassette spin-off, the camcorder. At the outset, many manufacturers were seduced into developing and marketing 'redundant' videotape formats, looking to overturn the hegemony established by Sony and JVC. Finding the electronic substitute for the amateur 8mm movie camera was an especially attractive option. In the 1970s, Akai marketed a $\frac{1}{4}$-inch monochrome system to this end which did not survive. Much more successful was 8mm video introduced by Sony in 1980. In part Sony's development of DAT fed into this new format, since PCM required an extremely high-density recording medium and 8mm recycled this digital audiotape for analogue video purposes. Thus 8mm, with all its comforting backward-looking connotations, emerged from an international industry-wide agreement – as the DAT story again reveals, always a suspicious event – not so much as a rival for VHS or an attempt on Sony's part to compensate for Beta's defeat but more as a format for new applications. As we have seen, 8mm as DAT did not fare too well, but 8mm as a substitute for 8mm amateur film was a success. Around it, Sony engineers built a small, battery-driven combined camera and cassette recorder of a size suitable for home movie use – the camcorder. But, again, this represents the end of a twenty-year development period.

From the mid-1960s on the electronics industry began to recycle, as it were, old black-and-white camera technology for 'video' as opposed to 'television' purposes. Transistors and integrated circuits made possible the production of comparatively crude cameras which started to appear as surveillance devices in the mid-1960s. For example, by 1967, Sperry Rand was selling a sophisticated closed circuit system which would sound an alarm if anything moved within a given observed area.

In addition to these small cameras, reel-to-reel black-and-white videotape recorders, VTRs, had been made smaller by the introduction of helical scanning systems. First produced by Toshiba in 1959, these slowed tape transport speed by spinning the recording head as well as recording the information diagonally across the tape rather than laterally. The picture could be constantly displayed in fast motion, forwards and backwards or as a still frame. The tape speed and size could also be reduced. The first non-broadcast helical machines of Ampex and JVC, introduced in 1962, used 1-inch tape but this was followed by $\frac{1}{2}$-inch versions. Helical scanning became essential to the non-broadcast diffusion of videotape by corporate users and, a little later, by educationalists first in reel-to-reel machines like the Sony Portapak, and then, eventually, in the domestic VCRs (Brush and Brush 1981: 15). Small-scale black-and-white studios using crude cameras, basic video-switching boxes and helical-scan VTR video started to appear in the training departments of sophisticated commercial organisations as well as in universities and some schools.

As this was happening, the American cable industry was maturing and a new radical concept of access to broadcasting was being articulated (Engleman 1990: 2–3). One aspect of this was to lead to the public access television movement which sought both slots on public television and dedicated cable channels. For the latter, the same sort of equipment as was already to hand in these non-broadcast corporate and educational television studios could be used. Then, in 1968 Sony introduced the 'Portapak', a portable battery-driven reel-to-reel $\frac{1}{2}$-inch helical scan VTR which weighed about 20 lbs. and to which was attached a black-and-white camera equipped with a zoom lens. This device fertilised the video access movement and expanded the video market enormously to embrace a far wider range of institutions, especially schools. It was, in fact, sufficiently successful to engender a line of ever smaller camera and recorder units. These quickly came to utilise the cassette principle, Sony again being the pioneers by introducing a $\frac{3}{4}$-inch U-MATIC machine for non-broadcast video application.

However, reel-to-reel machines and even portable U-MATICS were still too bulky and expensive for home use; hence the development of 8mm video. By 1984, Sony had established the tiny Betamovie camcorder as a viable consumer durable. In that year a large number of manufacturers marketed camcorders and JVC responded by both building a VHS version of the device and producing a down-sized VHS cassette to make such machines smaller and therefore more competitive. This time, despite the fact that the VHS cassette could be played directly into the home VHS/VCR, Sony maintained its market position. People did not mind plugging the camcorder into the domestic television for playback and the fetish of smallness overcame the VHS/VCR advantage. (Amateurs are apparently unaware that cameras need a certain heft if they are not to be too easily waved about.) By the mid-1990s, nearly half a million camcorders a year were being sold in the States but the capture on camcorder of the beating of Rodney King by Los Angeles police a few years earlier in 1991 really marks the machine's coming of age as a fully diffused device. Television shows cheaply recycling homevideos enjoyed a minor vogue, while the BBC's experiments in the same area produced a more significant strand of supposedly non-professional programme making in *Video Diaries*.

The next development in the 1990s was to market still video cameras. These take advantage of a specialised electronic receptor chip, the Charge Couple Device (CCD), a substitute for the old photo-emissive metallic pick-up. CCDs were already being introduced into analogue television cameras when the first prototypes of the professional electronic still camera were seen at the Los Angeles Olympics in 1984. By 1990 Sony had an amateur version which displayed its photographs on domestic television. It would seem that professional uses, where digital image transmission to speed photographs to the press was anyway coming on stream, would be the likeliest market. Outside the newspaper industry, though, the digital still camera was making less progress. In the mid-1990s, it was as yet unable to approach the highest resolutions of traditional 'wet-photography'. Nevertheless, despite this patchy pattern of professional diffusion, such cameras were reformatted for amateurs playing back their images through personal computers, including the more advanced games consoles. This piggy-backing use of the PC seemed to work. In 1993, after only three months, sales of 100,000 'Photo-CD' units were being claimed (Horner 1993: 16). By 1996, the price in the UK had fallen from £300 to £100 but the 'fit' remains dubious. In the culture, photographs exist as hard copies on heavy paper stocks for frames and wallets. Computer print outs still did not quite match the old photographic norms. Providing dedicated hard-copy devices is cumbersome and expensive. The digital still camera had by no means vanquished the old photographic process which, despite depending on expensive silver nitrates, still had potential for amateurs.

As for the broader implications of digitising images, it may be noted that as with digital audio, there is now considerable potential for manipulation to the point where the value of the photograph as evidence might well come to be questioned. Professionals had dedicated computer systems, such as Scitex, specifically designed for such work (Winston 1995: 5).

Finally, uninhibited by the commercial considerations such as those which held back DAT, the digitising of the electronic moving image had been advancing inexorably. Camcorders, also equipped with CCDs, as was all professional television and video equipment, were going digital. Digital camcorders, as small as the amateur ones but producing an image to complete professional standards, were coming on stream in the second half of the 1990s. Although expensive by high street shop standards, as professional devices they were very cheap. These machines generated a great deal of professional hyperbole with much talk (not for the first time) of greatly reduced production costs. Such debate ignored, as usual, the other factors in play – notably in this instance the threat and promise of a new high definition television standard which would be anything but cheap.

## REDUNDANCY: 1125-LINE ANALOGUE TELEVISION

The digitisation of broadcast television has two main aspects. On the one hand it can vastly increase the number of available terrestrial and satellite channels because of compression techniques which overcome the profligacy of PCM; on the other hand, it can be made the basis for an enhanced and expanded television standard, yielding a wider picture with the equivalent of double the range of lines produced by the original standards but a reduced increase in the number of channels. These two outcomes have been confused with each other and with a rival proposal for a new analogue standard, a true redundancy.

World television standards were fixed, as we have seen, by the mid-1950s and, although some later variants in line numbers and colour systems have been introduced since then, in essence almost all countries have either 525 or 625 lines and one of three colour systems, American, German or French. Just as the Americans found that 6.5 megahertz would accommodate more than the 400-plus lines originally envisaged, the Europeans further discovered that another 100 lines, and more in fact, would fit in too. Hence 625. Other standards, the revived London one of 405 lines, for example, were abandoned with the coming of colour.

All of these changes, however, were compatible so that the majority of the audience continued to be served on their old receivers. The earliest diffused colour system had established this precedent. American engineering opinion in 1941, perhaps influenced by the incompatibility of FM radio to AM, had not thought that colour/black-and-white compatibility would be possible, but this proved to be wrong. With the introduction of the NTSC colour standard, an expectation was established that all advances would be compatible. Compatibility became a political and cultural necessity. Of itself, this worked as a very strong brake and for thirty years there was no serious discussion about fundamental revisions of the standards. Other alterations, for example, the move in Britain from the original London Standard to 625, were accomplished by long change-over periods with dual transmission and double-standard sets.

But then in the 1980s there was a push from Japan to move from 525/625 lines, initially the electronic analogue of the 16mm film image, to 1125 lines which would duplicate 35mm. Those arguing for this change wanted it both to become a world standard for television and also to replace 35mm in the film studios. They managed to achieve neither ambition. Although offering a clearly superior picture to the contemporary television signal, the failure of this spin-off technology to establish itself makes it, in terms of the model, a redundancy.

The high definition television system (HDTV) proposed in the early 1980s was, electronically speaking, much like everyday North American or Japanese NTSC television. The major and significant differences lay in the number of lines scanned to make the picture and the shape, the aspect ratio, of the screen. Instead of the current US standard of 525 lines and a 4:3 screen, the Japanese demonstrated a system with 1125 lines and a Cinemascope-style screen of 5:3 ratio. The R&D for this proposal had began in 1968 and had been funded by Japanese television licence payers. The Japanese state broadcaster, NHK, wanted to develop a television signal which would match the image resolution of 35mm film, i.e. 1000 lines or one million pixels (Fink 1955: 283, Table II). Creating a picture with this number of lines required little ideation and less invention. All the pioneers understood the relationship between image resolution, lines and bandwidth, and, from time to time, prototypes had been built or proposed which strived for 35mm quality and therefore produced 1000 lines or so. There are references to 1000-line systems from 1944 on (Boddy 1990: 42; Anon 1945: 56) and in 1952 Philips produced a black-and-white camera capable of this level of resolution. For closed circuit, largely medical imaging applications the SMPTE had agreed a 1023-line standard in 1969.

But all engineers understood that delivering a signal of this complexity to the home would require a great deal of bandwidth – which was unavailable because the spectrum was already assigned. Not only that, it would not be possible to double the lines, inevitably increasing the band width, and maintain compatibility between the old and the new signals. So these options, while well understood, were not pursued for transmission purposes (Sandbank and Moffat 1983: 552). Anyway, who was complaining about the quality of the picture? Certainly far fewer people than those objecting to the programme content. The supervening necessity driving NHK was a tradition of using technological advances such as colour and alphanumeric screen-writing (teletext) as bargaining chips in its periodic re-negotiations of the domestic television licence fee level with the Japanese government. In this context, novelty was more important than compatibility.

In 1979, NHK tested the system in a home delivery mode using the Gigahertz (GHz) band, which accommodates thousands rather than hundreds of millions of cycles per second. The signals were transmitted via an experimental satellite sending to a 1.6 meter receiving dish (Ishida et al. 1982: 165–71). This was the analogue HDTV 'invention'.[2] Two years later, Sony (which with other companies had been co-opted into the NHK R&D programme) was ready to market the system as a new production method offering 35mm quality at 16mm prices but its efforts were not helped by NHK's emerging desire to go beyond the original research mandate and offer the technology as a *transmission* standard for the whole world. This was because such a proposal provoked considerable overt resistance on compatibility grounds. To have implemented the NHK scheme would have meant, in the face of no public demand, total upheaval and huge expense, primarily benefiting the Japanese patent holders.

At the obscure international meetings where such things are decided, a concerted campaign against NHK's 1125-line HDTV developed. At first *Neuerungsfreundigkeit,* that love of new things which is a crucial mark of Western culture, appeared to triumph. 1125–HDTV pictures were after all a breathtaking improvement on the current technology. But the law of suppression was at work. The pictures were not so breathtaking as to be instantly adopted and, by 1986, the proposal was put on permanent hold. Beyond the compatibility problem, the final factor suppressing this technology involved stressing alternatives; in fact, proposing a quite different 'invention' – digital high definition. As we have seen, digitisation had been understood as an option for the modulation of electronic signals from the 1920s and for many television engineers the prospect of digital signal sampling suggested that the NHK analogue research agenda was very much beside the point.

Already in the 1970s work was underway to agree sampling standards and digital techniques were having their effects, especially special effects. After the NHK intervention, the possibilities of digital became even more attractive because, although digital high definition also required large bandwidths, such signals could be more easily compressed than could analogue ones. Furthermore, digital offered easier options for progressive scanning, a sharper alternative to Zworykin's interlaced raster (Wilmotte 1976: 73–80). A dedicated chip, a frame store, could hold a frame, wait for the next and display both together. This would create a progressive scanned picture of 1050 lines at no bandwidth cost. A number of variations of this were proposed and developed. Another idea was to adapt an existing satellite transmission system, *M*ultiplexed *A*nalogue *C*omponent (MAC), for high definition purposes. In this system, the current analogue signal is broken down into its component elements, compressed and transmitted in bursts – a bit of chrominance, a bit of sound, a bit of luminance, a bit of chrominance and so on. A 'smart' set reassembles the picture (Arlen et al. 1987: 25–8). Again a number of variations were outlined. Beyond all this, there were, and are, further suggestions involving signal folding, other types of computer-aided processing and filtering (Jurgen 1989: 26–30).

Prototypes along many of these lines followed. Indeed, they so effectively killed off 1125/60 30 MHz NTSC that the very service it was designed for, which NHK began experimentally in 1989, itself used a variant on MAC technology. But the world as a whole was still without a widely diffused high definition system despite the fact that many versions of the 'invention' now existed and many obey the prime requirement for compatibility. This speaks not just the power of the 'law' of suppression but also to the need for a supervening social necessity. Those who in the early 1980s pronounced that the NHK system 'had brought high-definition television within the grasp of the consumer by 1986' have been simply proved wrong (Anon 1981: 29). The NHK team, in many of their technical papers, wrote about 'the needs of a post industrial society',[3] a concept they nowhere elaborated. In fact, there were no such needs when the work started and they have yet to manifest themselves clearly. Even in Japan in 1995, four years after the experimental service became a permanent one marketed as 'Hi-Vision', only 20,000 sets at $7500 each had been sold – exactly the same level of penetration as that achieved by 1930s' 'high definition' television in Britain up to 1939. Meanwhile, in a classic example of making the best of a bad job, Sony started marketing widescreen domestic television receivers. These were a species of faked HDTV in that there were ordinary analogue sets using a chip to expand and crop the image. By 1995 they had sold three million in Japan. The company's attempt to substitute 1125–HDTV video for 35mm film foundered (although the film industry increasingly used conventional video and computing electronics especially in post-production).

There can be little doubt that the basic television standard will change in the coming decades. I am certain that when the change-over begins to happen in earnest, the hype at that time will suggest that it is the result of rapid, uncontrolled technological developments; yet, as we have seen, the process began in 1969 and its disruptive power has been, and is being, contained. It is likely that, as usual, this transformation of 'the shining centre of every home' will take about half a century to work through. And when it happens, the new standard will be digital not analogue (p. 301).

# PART III

# INVENTIONS FOR CASTING UP SUMS VERY PRETTY*

<hr>

* 'but not very useful': *Samuel Pepys Diary*, 14 March 1668.

# 8

# MECHANISING
# CALCULATION

## SCIENTIFIC COMPETENCE I: 'THINKING MACHINES'

The idea that 'inventions' are actually more matters of system engineering than of eureka breakthroughs and of slow adoption rather than sudden ubiquitousness has been a central contention of this book; but, at first sight, it seems singularly inappropriate to the history of the most radical, the most revolutionary of all the technologies here considered – the computer. How can the pattern of available technology, delay and constraint established above, be meshed with the sudden arrival of computing in every corner of our lives? The answer is that the misperception which saw television as an explosive newcomer in the 1950s has been at work again with the computer. The received history of the computer selectively downplays the lateness of its development and the comparative slowness of its diffusion.

> As is now realised, we had the technical capability to build relay, electro-mechanical, and even electronic calculating devices long before they came into being. I think one can conjecture when looking through Babbage's papers, or even at the Jacquard loom, that we had the technical ability to do calculations with some motive power like steam. The realisation of this capability was not dependent on technology as much as it was on the existing pressures (or lack of them), and an environment in which these needs could be sympathetically brought to some level of realisation.
>
> (Tropp 1980: 119)

Thus Henry Tropp, the Smithsonian's historian of the computer pioneers, seeks what in this book is termed a supervening necessity. Moreover, the conformity of the computer's beginnings to the model are repeated in the pattern of its diffusion. The 'law' of the suppression of radical potential operated to delay various stages of development for significant periods, exactly as the schema would suggest and, above all, diverted research effort away from the small desktop device that represents the full radical potential of the computer.

The computer – *machina ratiocinatrix* – is, in terms of the philosophical underpinnings of our culture for these last three centuries, an unthinkable instrument. It offends, fundamentally, the Cartesian duopoly of mind and matter. Boyle speaks for all the West when he claims 'engines endowed with wills' are men and cannot be anything else – not even, in those years, other animals (Burtt 1967 113–4). Although from the first, objections were raised to this dichotomy and although much of Descartes' view (that the pineal gland was the seat of the mind, for instance) has long since collapsed, it is still to a large extent true that '*Nulla nunc celebrior clamorosiorque secta quam Cartesinorum*' (Hazard 1964: 157). Certainly the arguments around artificial intelligence are cast in terms which Descartes and his 'school' would have no trouble in comprehending.

These same seventeenth-century savants were also intent on enshrining mathematics as the 'queen' of all sciences and the clearest evidence available of the glory of God's creation. The dominance of the empiric scientific method which began in this period stressed observation and measure and thereby, to a degree, encouraged the production of calculating devices both mental and physical. This work was enormously aided by the appearance of printed tables, freed from the inevitability of scribal error and capable, through repeated editions, of incorporating corrections (Eisenstein 1983: 22). All this led to a tradition of contradictory attitudes to machines that 'think': Western scientism, it can be claimed, requires on the one hand calculators while, on the other, philosophically denying the possibility of what are today described as computers.

Crucial, then, in developing the ground of scientific competence for the computer is the removal of the mental roadblock against the *machina ratiocinatrix* erected during the seventeenth century. This, despite some earlier musing and theorising, finally occurred in pure mathematics in 1936.

Alan Turing was a scion of empire, the son of an Imperial civil servant and, as such, doomed to a Kiplingesque round of English foster homes, somewhat reduced in term by his father's early retirement. (He numbered Stoney of the 'electron' among his forebears.) After Sherborne, he went up to King's College, Cambridge where he studied under Max Newman. Following a brilliant undergraduate career, Turing was elected fellow, at the age of 22, in 1935. In 1936 he published a paper 'On Computable Numbers, with an application to the *Entscheidungsproblem*' which dealt, elegantly, with the Cartesian obstruction (Turing, 1936/1937: 230–65/544–6).

The agenda Turing addressed was at the heart of advanced pure mathematics. By the late nineteenth century, in the wake of the creation of non-Euclidean geometries (among other developments), mathematicians were becoming, for the first time since the Greeks, increasingly concerned about the consistency of the axiomatic systems they used.

> [T]he creation of non-Euclidean geometry had forced the realisation that mathematics is man-made and describes only approximately what happens in the world. The description is remarkably successful, but it is not the truth in the sense of representing the inherent structure of the universe and therefore not necessarily consistent. . . .Every axiom system contains undefined terms whose properties are specified only by the axioms. The meaning of these terms is not fixed, even though intuitively we have numbers or points or lines in mind.
>
> (Kline 1980: 192)

It was against this background that Bertrand Russell coined his famous epigram: 'Pure mathematics is the subject in which we do not know what we are talking about, or whether what we are saying is true' (Nagel and Newman 1958: 13).

Despite this there were those, led by David Hilbert, the greatest mathematician of his generation, who in the early decades of the twentieth century insisted on the primacy of the axiomatic method. But against their assertions stood, ever more starkly in relief, a set of highly technical problems which can perhaps be most simply instanced by drawing 'the cork out of an old conundrum' namely the ancient 'liar paradox'. This paradox can be classically expressed in the sentence, 'This sentence is false'. For twentieth-century mathematics, dealing with mathematical equivalents of the 'liar paradox' meant confronting the problem of consistency across an increasing range of topics. At first, although at the cost of developing a variety of methods and schools, many of the paradoxes or antinomies (strictly – contradictions in law) were resolved; as, for example, in the system proposed in Whitehead and Russell's *Principia Mathematica*. Because of this work, well into the 1920s, Hilbert continued to assert: 'that every mathematical problem can be solved. We are all convinced of that' (Kline 1980: 261).

In 1931, his time-honoured approach sustained the most telling attack yet. It was contained in a paper by the Kurt Godel – 'On Formally Undecidable Propositions of *Principia Mathematica* and other systems'. In this Godel demonstrated that it was impossible to give proof of the consistency of a mathematical system 'comprehensive enough to contain the whole of arithmetic':

> Godel's second main conclusion is even more surprising and revolutionary, because it demonstrates a fundamental limitation in the power of the axiomatic method. Godel showed that *Principia*, or any other system within which arithmetic can be developed, is *essentially incomplete*. In other words, given *any* consistent set of arithmetical axioms, there are

true arithmetical statements that cannot be derived from the set.
(Nagel and Newman 1958: 58; emphasis italics in original)

Godel's incompleteness theorem highlighted a number of subsidiary problems, chief among them, from our point of view, the question of decidability. If there were now mathematical assertions that could be neither proved nor disproved, how can one determine effective procedures in such cases? This was the decidability or decision problem – *das Entscheidungsproblem*. Just as Hilbert had declared that mathematical systems had to be consistent and complete, so too had he insisted upon the discovery of effective procedure as a necessary part of mathematics. Godel's attack on consistency and completeness rendered the decidability problem moot.

It was Turing, five years later, who dealt with *das Entscheidungsproblem*. Turing had been struck by a phrase in a lecture of Newman's where Hilbert's suggestion that any mathematical problem must be solvable by a fixed and definitive process was glossed by Newman as 'a purely mechanical process'. Turing, in his paper, found a problem that could not be so decided, i.e. solved – in Turing's language 'computed'. It involved an artificial construct known as the Cantor diagonal argument whereby 'irrational numbers' could be created. (Cantor was one of those nineteenth-century mathematicians whose work set the stage for the crisis in axiomatic methods.) To dispose of the decidability problem, Turing constructed a mental picture of a machine, a conceit, and demonstrated that it could not compute certain numbers. Therefore there were mathematical problems which were not decidable; but, Turing wrote, 'It is possible to invent a machine which can be used to compute any *computable* sequence' (Turing 1936: 241; emphasis added).

Because of this conceit of a machine, 'On Computable Numbers' had, beyond its immediate significance in pure maths, broader implications. Turing's proof involved imagining a machine which read, wrote, scanned and 'remembered' binary numbers inscribed on a unidimensional tape. It might not be able to compute the irrational numbers of Cantor's trick but it could, in theory, deal with a vast range of other computations. The very disposal of Hilbert's problem required no less. Turing had conceived of a tremendously powerful tool. He was not overstating the case when he christened it (in homage to the nineteenth-century pioneer Babbage) a 'universal engine'. Of course, he had no intention of building such a machine. Later it would be said of him – perhaps unfairly in the light of his wartime experience as a practical electronics engineer – that although 'He was intrigued by devices of every kind, whether abstract or concrete – his friends thought it would be better if he kept to the abstract devices' (Randell 1980: 78). In Cambridge in 1936 he was still concerned only with the abstract.

When he wrote 'computer', he meant, as did all his contemporaries, a person who performs computations:

> The behaviour of the computer at any moment is determined by the symbols which he is observing, and his 'state of mind' at that moment. We may suppose that there is a bound $B$ to the number of symbols or squares which the computer can observe at any one moment. If he wishes to observe more, he must use successive observations. . .Let us imagine operations performed by the computer to be split up into 'simple operations' which are so elementary that it is not easy to imagine them further divided. Every such operation consists of some change in the physical system consisting of the computer and his tape.
>
> (Turing 1936: 250)

The human computer and his tape were to become the machine computer and its program. 'To each state of mind of the computer corresponds a. . .configuration of the machine' (Turing 1936: 250). It was to be a *machina ratiocinatrix*:

> His argument held out the possibility of building an actual machine to do all the work that can be done by any human computer; and he extended the same model to provide a new analytic account of states of mind and mental operations. At their intellectual or rational core (which was a central preoccupation of René Descartes' arguments) all such states and operations rested on the kinds of procedures that his universal machine could in principle perform; and, from this insight. . .very general conclusions followed. First, the idea of a 'thinking machine', which the seventeenth-century philosophers had regarded as a contradiction in terms, was now after all an admissible idea.
>
> (Toumlin 1984: 3)

Of course, with mathematicians all over the world attempting the *Entscheidungsproblem*, it was almost inevitable that Turing would have competitors. In mid-April 1936 he presented his paper to Newman in Cambridge. On 15 April, Alonzo Church of Princeton sent away his demonstration of a different unsolvable proposition for publication. Church's solution was close enough to require Newman's intervention on Turing's behalf to ensure that the younger man's work could be published. Turing equated Church's idea of 'effective calculability' with his own notion of 'computability' and offered, in an Appendix to 'On Computable Numbers', a proof of their equivalency, admitting Church had reached 'similar conclusions' about the *Entscheidungsproblem* (Turing 1936: 231).

In October 1936, Emil Post, a mathematician at the City University of New

York, submitted a paper to Church suggesting a mechanical device – a 'worker' – for demonstrating Church's proposition along lines close to, but less ambitious than Turing's 'universal machine' (Post 1936: 103–4). Post nowhere mentioned 'states of mind'. Church, in a footnote to Post's paper, wrote: 'The reader should compare an article by A.M. Turing, *On computable numbers*, shortly forthcoming in the *Proceedings of the London Mathematical Society*.' In a subsequent comment he went further, acknowledging the power of Turing's approach by coining the phrase 'Turing machine' (or now, 'turing machine') as a synonym for 'universal machine'.

These men stand in a line of mathematical logicians traceable back to the self-taught nineteenth-century English savant, George Boole. In 1854, Boole faulted the Cartesian foundation by demonstrating that logics can be expressed algebraically. Boole's investigation was designed to explicate

> the fundamental laws of those operations of the mind by which reason is performed; to give expression to them in the symbolic language of a Calculus, and upon this foundation to establish the science of Logic. . . . There is not only a close analogy between the operations of the mind in general reasoning and its operations in the particular science of Algebra, but there is to a considerable extent an exact agreement in the laws by which the two classes of operations are conducted.
>
> (Goldstine 1972: 32)

Turing, as a child at prep school, complained that his first arithmetic master gave 'quite a false impression of what is meant by $x$', presumably because he did not sufficiently indicate Boolean possibilities (Hodges 1983: 11). For most of us the $x$s and $y$s of elementary algebra 'stand for' unknown numbers, which was after all what François Vieta, the seventeenth-century mathematician who introduced them, intended; for the pure mathematician, though, these letters can be manipulated to symbolise the entire world of mind and matter. 'Pure mathematics were discovered', states Russell, 'by George Boole in his work published in 1854'.

The most powerful of Boole's concepts, so far as the scientific competency needed for the computer is concerned, is a 'special law to which the symbols of quantity are not subject': 'this law in effect is that $x^2 = x$ for every $x$ in his [Boole's] system. Now in numerical terms this equation or law has as its only solution 0 and 1. This is why the binary system plays so vital a part in modern computers: their logical parts are in effect carrying out binary operations' (Goldstine 1972: 37). Boole's law turns on the use of a binary system of notation which, although arguably the most primitive conceivable such system, dates in its modern mathematical form to Bacon and to Leibniz, the latter using it for – among other things – the creation of a mathematical proof of the existence of God. Boolean algebra, by reducing certain types of thought to a series of on/off states, is the means by which a Turing machine can be said to 'think', make judgements and learn. That Boole and all the other pure mathematicians, including Turing before the end of the Second World War, built no such machines does not detract from their centrality in preparing the ground of scientific competence which could be transformed by technology into the computer.

In the third decade of the twentieth century there was much going on in mathematics which would help to translate activities popularly considered as uniquely human into forms that would be 'machine readable', if any such machines had existed. In 1938 Claude Shannon, whom Turing was to meet during a wartime visit to the United States, published his MIT master's thesis, 'A Symbolic Analysis of Relay and Switching Circuits' in which the insights of Boolean algebra were applied to telephone exchange circuit analysis (Shannon 1938: 713–34). This produced a mathematisation of information which not only had immediate practical applications for his future employers, Bell Labs, but also plumbed another part of modern computer science's foundations. Information Theory, as Shannon's work is called, defines information as the informational content of signals abstracted from all specific human information. It concerns not the question, 'what sort of information?' but rather, 'how much information?' (Cherry 1961: 168). 'The word information, in this theory, is used in a special sense that must not be confused with its ordinary usage. In particular, information must not be confused with meaning' (Weaver and Shannon 1949: 11).

In a telephone exchange, design requirements dictate that there be less concern about the content of messages than with the accuracy with which the system will relay them. Information becomes reified, quantifiable so that it can be treated as a measure of the probability or uncertainty of a symbol or set of symbols. By how much does the transmitter's message reduce uncertainty in the receiver? By that much can the informational content of the message be measured and capacity of the channel of communication be determined. Say we were awaiting the result of a race between four horses which would be signalled to us by flag – the code, as is necessary in any information system, having been previously agreed between transmitter and receiver. The waving of two different-coloured flags would suffice to convey the information. (Horse 1, red/red; horse 2, red/blue, etc.) In an eight-horse race the same two flags could be used but each horse would require three waves. (Horse 1, red/red/red; horse 2, red/red/blue, etc.) Each wave of the flag is a binary digit, a bit - red being, let us say, the equivalent of '1' or 'on' and blue being '0' or 'off'. The four-horse race requires a channel with a two-bit capacity, the eight-horse race requires three bits. Sixteen horses would require four waves or bits and so on. Each wave, each transmission of a bit, reduces our uncertainty as to the outcome of the race. The 'bound B to the number of symbols or squares which the computer can observe at any moment' (of which Turing wrote) can be expressed as the capacity of the computer, human or mechanical, to address a discrete number of bits.

The quantification of information in Information Theory parallels and perhaps determines the reification of information which is so crucial a part of the 'Information Revolution'; that is to say, the rhetorical thrust which has the production of information in so-called 'post-industrial societies' substituting for the production of physical goods depends upon such reification. It allows people to be comfortable with the somewhat curious notion that we can survive by making 'information' instead of producing things.

The implication of all this work in the 1930s at the outer edges of advanced mathematics was not immediately apparent even to those most able to grasp it, the mathematical community. Pure mathematical logic was so pure that few human activities could be considered further from putting the bread on anybody's table. But many were to get rich at Turing's feast, once they understood him:

> To illustrate the difficulty of deciding when something is really under-stood, consider that many mathematicians have the experience of know-ing a theorem and a proof for several years and then suddenly 'understanding' the theorem in a new way. . .
>
> The example I shall take to illustrate the difficulty of measuring when an idea was first understood is the idea of the computer as a symbol manipulator rather than as a number cruncher. This was in a sense one of the decisive steps in the history of computing. . . .One could claim that Turing, when he proved that the universal computing machine could do anything any computer could do, must have understood the idea that computers are symbol-manipulating machines.
>
> (Hamming 1980: 7)

Here then is the importance of 'On computable numbers'. By moving from number-cruncher to symbol-manipulator, Turing threw the first plank across the Cartesian chasm between human being and machine. The thinking of those who were to design the first computers broadened and strengthened this bridge.

John von Neumann, a student of Hilbert's and mentor of Turing's, was one of the fathers of the American computer and a mathematician of enormous range – from game theory to nuclear devices – who dominated the field in the first decade after the war. He wrote, in 'First Draft of A Report on the EDVAC', the document that contains the original master-plan for the modern computer: 'Every digital computing device contains certain relay-like elements, with discrete equili-bria. . . .It is worth mentioning, that the neurons of the higher animals are definitely elements in the above sense. They have all-or-none character, that is two states: Quiescent and excited' (Neumann 1945: 359–60). The seductiveness of the analogy between human neural activity and digital symbol manipulators has proved irresistible. Drawing such parallels, though, is not new. It has been a characteristic of Western thought throughout the modern period, beginning with Lamettrie's *L'Homme Machine* in 1750. Seeing humanity in the image of which ever machine most dominates contemporary life is what might be called *mechanemorphism*. With Lamettrie it was the clock. The combustion engine followed. Freud thought electromagnets were a good metaphor for the brain. Today this tendency finds its most extreme expression with the computer, especially among the proponents of 'strong' artificial intelligence. Mechanemorphism has conditioned not only our overall attitude to computers but also the very terminology which has arisen around them. To take one example: what crucially distinguishes the computer from the calculators that precede it is its capacity to store data and instructions. Calling this capacity 'memory' and the codes that control its overall operation 'language' facilitates contemporary mechanemorphism.

But from the beginning there were those who resisted the attractions of the mechanemorphic view. For instance, both Douglas Hartree and Sir Charles G. Darwin, those in charge of computer development (and Turing) at the British National Physical Lab (NPL), immediately saw fit to decry it even as the earliest large machines were being publicised: 'The term "electronic brain" is misleading. I hope this term will be avoided in the future', wrote Hartree (Wulforst 1982: 111). His hope has not been fulfilled. By the end of the century the original computers and four further generations of machines have been developed displaying the prerogatives of choice and judgement but still appearing to be manifestly inhuman to the average interrogator. As M.V. Wilkes, the man who, contrary to received history, after the Second World War built the first full-size electronic computer to work on a real mathematical problem, wrote in 1956: 'I see a bright future for machines in executive capacities, but I do not see them behaving like human beings' (Wilkes 1956: 293).

All this has little or nothing to do with Turing's grasp of the difference between a number-cruncher and a symbol-manipulator. Symbol-manipulation was to be of ever-increasing significance over the twenty years from 1936 and, although not clearly perceived at first, it was inexorably to transform schemes for building number-crunchers into the first computer designs.

## SCIENTIFIC COMPETENCE II: BABBAGE

There was also an element in the ground of scientific competence which has to do with the basic architecture of what a Turing machine might look like. When Turing himself thought to call his conceit a universal engine in honour of Charles Babbage he was referencing this element.

By 1833, the English mathematician Charles Babbage was abandoning work on a complex calculator which had occupied him for the previous decade. Instead he now envisaged a device which could tackle, mechanically, any mathematical problem. This universal analytic engine (memorialised in Turing's 'universal engine') was never built, but the design embodied a series of concepts which were to be realised a century or more later. The machine was to be programmed by the use of two sets of punched cards, one set containing instructions and the other the data to be processed. The input data and any intermediate results were to be held in a 'store' and the actual computation was to be achieved in a part of the machine Babbage designated 'the mill'. It would have been able to perform conditional branching operations, basic logical steps, by hopping backwards and forwards between the mill and the store. It was to print out its results automatically.

This is so close to the modern computer – the mill as the CPU, the operational cards as the ROM and the store as the RAM, etc. – that Babbage has been hailed as its father. Wilkes stated: 'Babbage was moving in a world of logical design and system architecture, and was familiar with and had solutions for problems that were not to be discussed in the literature for another 100 years' (Randell 1973: 11). Nevertheless, the possibility that the analytic engine could alter its pro-gramme in the light of its computations remained an 'indistinct conception' in a late notebook and therefore, for all his prescience, his thought remained one crucial step away from the computer proper. For this ability to alter the pro-gramme is what distinguishes the two classes of machines. It is the central difference between number-crunchers and symbol-manipulators. Babbage's pro-posed device was, by this criterion, a calculator of a most advanced type. His contribution, therefore, remains in the ground of scientific competence rather than at the level of ideation.[1]

Babbage's interest in automatic calculation sprang from the common root – boredom. Like Leibniz, Pascal and Napier before him and Mauchly, Zuse and Aitken, three major computer pioneers a century after him, Babbage disliked the computational aspect of mathematical work. In one story he reportedly muttered to a colleague, the astronomer Herschel, 'I wish to God these calculations had been executed by steam.' Herschel is said to have replied: 'It is quite possible.' In another account, Babbage remembers himself 'in a dreamy mood', dozing over a table of logarithms in the rooms of the Analytical Society at Cambridge (of which he was a founder member) and when questioned by another member as to what he was dreaming about, he replied, 'I am thinking that all these Tables (pointing to the logarithms) might be calculated by machinery' (Goldstine 1972; 11: Hyman 1984: 49–50).

By 1823 Babbage had convinced the British government of the viability of his plan to do calculations, if not by steam, then certainly mechanically. The Navy's need for nautical tables – a need dramatised by shipwrecks supposedly caused because of errors in the Nautical Almanacs – was the supervening necessity that set Babbage to work. The creation of error-free mathematical tables thus had important military aspects as well as being an essential part of the work of what Thomas Kuhn has called 'normal science'. From the simple multiplication table of the schoolroom to complex topics such as lists of air densities as a function of altitude at a given time, the table, thanks to the printing press, is a basic tool of scientific culture. However, creating tables is a work of utter drudgery, involving 'intolerable labour and fatiguing monotony' as Babbage wrote in 1822.

Babbage planned and began to build a difference engine. A calculus of differences, the theory of which was to be comprehensively treated by Boole in 1860, created a method for converting multiplication and division into operations of addition and subtraction. A mechanical device, not unlike the ratcheted wheels which record mileage in a car but more complicated, can automatically and without error calculate complex polynomials using such a calculus. Babbage himself, in working on this machine, was in a tradition already two centuries old in his time. Indeed, his exact proposal had been made, unbeknownst to him, by a Hessian Army officer in 1786 (Augarten 1984: 42).

Logarithms were the first modern mathematical aid, introduced by the Scottish mathematician and theologian, John Napier, in 1614. He too was driven by the drudgery of calculations. Three years later, he produced a simple logarithm-based device to perform multiplications. A set of rods with numbers inscribed on them, Napier's Bones, could be manipulated to give instant answers. These led to the development of a variety of contrivances, some of which, like the slide-rule or the mechanical calculators devised by Blaise Pascal (the Pascaline), were to enjoy considerable longevity and wide popularity. Leibniz improved the Pascaline by introducing cogged wheels milled in steps – Leibniz wheels – so that the processes of multiplication and division could be done more directly. All over Europe, throughout the eighteenth century and beyond, scientists worked on such calculators.

This was the background informing Babbage's thinking on the difference engine. It was also, perhaps, the key, beyond his own erratic temperament and lukewarm official support, to why he abandoned the project in the early 1830s (Hyman 1984: 134–5). His proposed difference engine was, in some ways, a step back from Leibniz's machine and its derivatives. Although it was much more powerful, it was also more limited. Leibniz's calculator could aid a human computer in any mathematical task. The difference engine needed far less human input, but produced results across a more limited mathematical field. Thus Babbage conceived of the universal or analytic engine as having the broad capacities of a Leibniz calculator but requiring as little human input as the difference engine: 'If intelligently directed and saved from wasteful use, such a machine might mark an era in the history of computation, as decided as the introduction of logarithms in the seventeenth century did in trigonometrical and astronomical arithmetic' (Randell 1973: 61). But it was not to be. Like the abandoned difference engine, the analytic engine was never finished. At the time that the report I have just quoted was written Babbage had been dead for seven years. His son, the Major General, was seeking funds to continue the work but, in the event, he too, like his father, failed to complete the machine.

## SCIENTIFIC COMPETENCE III: CALCULATORS – MECHANICAL TO ELECTRICAL

It was left to Georg Scheutz, Swedish lawyer, newspaper publisher and litterateur to build Babbage's difference engine. Scheutz's machine was based on an account he had read of Babbage's work in an *Edinburgh Review* of 1834. When finished, the Scheutz machine, which had 'four differences and fourteen places of figures', punched its results on to sheet lead or papier mâché from which printing stereotypes could be made. The machine was operable by 1844 and refined, to the point where duplicates were possible, by 1855. But this was 'after many years' indefatigable labour, and almost ruinous expenses, aided by grants from his government, by the constant assistance of his son, and by the support of many enlightened members of the Swedish Academy' (Goldstine 1972: 15). Thus did Babbage, with rare generosity of spirit, introduce to his countrymen the work of the man who had succeeded where he had failed.

Scheutz even made an engine for the British Registrar General's office and it worked, calculating actuarial tables, between 1859 and 1864. In my model for technological development, this device can be thought of as fulfilling two functions. It can stand in the line of machines from the slide-rule and the Pascaline and, in advance of both a supervening necessity (beyond the avoidance of drudgery) and a clear enunciation of the idea of programmability, it is thus part of the general scientific understanding of the mechanisation of calculation – part of the ground of scientific competence. On the other hand, in the history of calculators, it is a species of accepted prototype.

The Scheutz engine was built in advance of any real supervening necessity and, despite a few such applications of the actuarial type, the avoidance of drudgery was scarcely a motivating force in Victorian life and therefore no pressure existed to relieve the tedium of low-paid clerks, or even economically marginal pure scientists. The calculator remained, more or less, at the technological level achieved by Pascal. Although not rare, it was scarcely a ubiquitous item outside the savant's study or the labs of the emerging technological universities. But by the 1860s and 1870s, as I have noted in the history of telephony, forces of change were at work creating, in their train, a supervening necessity for a number of devices fundamental to contemporary life. In short, these were decades which saw the emergence, in law, of the modern limited company. The new corporations necessitated the modern office and, as I have pointed out (above p. 51), with it the telephone, the geared hydraulic elevator, the typewriter in its modern shift-key form, and the modern mechanical calculator with the spring-loaded pin wheel – the Baldwin (1875). This new wheel was the first serious modification of the mechanical calculator since Leibniz (Augarten 1984: 79).

Commercial desktop calculators were in immediate production and the office equipment industry was born. The first key-driven calculator was demonstrated in 1887. Five years later, William Burroughs added an elegant roll-paper printing mechanism. Other machines were more desk-like than desktop. The Millionaire, for example, had built-in (i.e. stored) multiplication tables and was manufactured continuously from 1899 until 1935.

The new motive power, electricity, was also used. In 1876, at the very same Centennial Exposition in Philadelphia where Bell made such a stir, an engineer, George Grant, showed an electrically driven piano-size difference engine. For the 1890 American census, Herman Hollerith designed a device of even greater significance both in its use of electricity and for the fortune it made his company, eventually to become IBM. The decennial census was proving ever more difficult to complete. By 1887, the Census Office (it became a Bureau in 1920) realised that it would still be processing the 1880 data even as the 1890 returns were being collected. In a public competition held to find a solution to this problem, Hollerith proposed an electro-mechanical apparatus. He resurrected the punched cards that Babbage had intended as the input for the analytic engine. Babbage had, in turn, borrowed these from the French silk weaver Joseph-Marie Jacquard who, in 1804, pioneered them as loom-controlling devices whereby different cards could cause the loom to produce different patterns of cloth (Noble 1984: 147).[2]

Hollerith's cards contained the census data as a series of punched holes. The operator placed the card into a large reading device and pulled a lever. This moved a series of pins against the card. Where the pins encountered a hole, they passed through the card and into a bowl of mercury, thereby making an electrical circuit which activated the hands of a dial. In the test which won him the contract, Hollerith's machine was about ten times faster than its nearest rival. Six weeks after the census, the Office announced that the population stood at 62,622,250. Hollerith declared himself to be 'the world's first statistical engineer'. The census was completed in a quarter of the time its predecessor had taken and the Tabulating Machine Company was founded. Hollerith's enterprise became part of the Computing Tabulating and Recording Company (C-T-R) which in turn became IBM in 1924. By then he had some rivals in the field of business machines, for example, James Powers. Powers had been put in charge of the manufacturing division which the Census Bureau established after falling out with Hollerith, a notoriously difficult man. The company Powers founded upon leaving the Bureau would eventually become Sperry Rand, IBM's great computer competitor in the years after the Second World War.

All these devices can be thought of as descending from the Pascaline and the Leibniz wheel, but there is also another line of analogue machines whose ancestors include Napier's Bones and even older artefacts – from Stonehenge (if the view is taken that it is an astronomical calculator) to ancient bronze calendrical calculators and the astrological and astronomical contrivances of al-Kashi, chief of the observatory at Samarkand in the fifteenth century. The slide-rule which converts numbers into distances is also an analogue device. Working in this tradition, Maxwell had built an analogue device – an integrator – for measuring the area of an irregular plane. Some years later, Lord Kelvin, following this lead as well as designs made by his brother, sought 'to substitute brass for brain in the great mechanical labour of calculating the elementary constituents of the whole tidal rise and fall' by building an elegant calculator – disk-globe-and-cylinder integrator – to tabulate the times and heights of high tides at different points around the coast. In 1876, he proposed a general purpose analogue device, a differential or harmonic analyser, which essentially required that a number of these integrators be arranged in sequence so that the output of one inputted the next. Such an arrangement would allow complex linear differential equations to be calculated, such as 'vibrations of a non-uniform stretched cord, of a hanging chain, of water in a canal of non-uniform breadth and depth' (Goldstine 1972: 47–8). However, since the integrator's output was measured by the small rotations of a shaft, there was insufficient torque to continue the process from integrator to integrator. The machine could not be built and there was no progress for the better part of half a century.

Vannevar Bush, like von Neumann a most distinguished scientist, was Shannon's professor at MIT and an important enabling figure in computer development through his work directing the US Office of Scientific Research and Planning in the Second World War. (He was also one of the first to envisage the web (p. 322).) The team he established in the 1920s at MIT first built a device which had at its heart a meter of the sort that measures on-site consumption for the electric company. It could only cope with first-order differential equations, which drastically limited its use, most problems facing physical and electrical engineers being second order. In 1927, Bush produced a revision of this 'Continuous Intergraph' which could solve a single second-order problem by putting the output of the meter into an integrator. But in that same year a torque amplifier, something like a ship's capstan in principle, was introduced. This could so increase the movements of the integrator's shaft that another integrator could be thereby powered. When this device came to Bush's attention, he used it to build a complex differential analyser in which no less than six integrators were placed in sequence. It looked much like an enormous Meccano toy; and, indeed, Douglas Hartree built a small replica of part of it out of Meccano.

Hartree saw the original during a visit to America in 1933 and, on his return, raised the funds to build a full-scale duplicate for Manchester University. Another was built in Cambridge, UK. By 1940 there were seven or eight worldwide, including one built for the Russians by General Electric, as well as the two involved in ballistics research at the Moore School (University of Pennsylvania) and the Aberdeen Proving Ground, the American Army's main test site. The Aberdeen machine took a commercial company two years to build and had ten integrators. At the same time, the Moore School machine with fourteen integrators was built by the Civil Works Administration as part of its programme to put skilled technicians, unemployed during the Depression, back to work. These analysers worked well, but they were slow and 'programming' them required days of effort with wrenches and hammers. These tools were needed to keep the machines going as well. Nevertheless, as with any accepted prototype, they did satisfy at least part of the appetite which scientists had for advanced calculators and, in this, they matched the machines then being produced by IBM and others for business.

So well accepted were the products of the office equipment industry by this time that business's requirements for automated machinery were completely satisfied. Indeed so satisfied were they that, it can be argued, a market for more advanced calculators, calculators that could alter their programs and thus be classed as computers, was non-existent. IBM, to take the industry leader, had been making sorters, tabulators and punched card equipment since 1914. It introduced a printing tabulator in 1920, a horizontal sorter in 1925, an electrical calculator that could add, subtract and multiply (the first of the 600 series) in 1931 and an eighty-column card as well as a subtracting accounting machine in 1938 (Hurd 1980: 397). The IBM 601 was a crossfoot multiplier which used cards and was leased for payroll calculations and other tasks. It contained a plug-board which allowed it a degree of versatility. There was little reason to seek more efficient solutions for most big commercial computational tasks, although competition meant that a steady programme of research and development was undertaken. For example, Vannevar Bush himself moved on from mechanical analogue machines after 1936 to RAMP (Rapid Arithmetical Machine Project) which was supported by the National Cash Register Company (NCR), a major IBM rival. A parallel project, funded by NCR and Kodak, was for a device automatically to retrieve and photographically copy data held on reels of 35mm film, but, by the time America joined the Second World War, this work had produced only partial prototypes and the team was broken up as more pressing duties were assigned its members (Randell 1980: 81). However, the point remains: the most advanced business machines of the 1930s were of a sophistication now forgotten. Commercial needs were not creating a supervening social necessity to produce a research agenda which might have led to a computer.

## PROTOTYPES: ELECTRO-MECHANICAL CALCULATORS

The possibilities of building an electro-mechanical digital calculator along the general lines proposed by Babbage had been first outlined by the Spanish scientist Leonardo Torres y Quevedo in the *Essais sur L'Automatique* published in 1915.

> An analytic machine, such as I am alluding to here, should execute any calculation, no matter how complicated, without help from anyone. It will be *given* a formula and one or more specific values for the independent variables, and it should then calculate and record all the values of the corresponding functions defined explicitly or implicitly by the formula. It should work in a manner similar to that of a human calculator, i.e. executing the indicated operations in the necessary sequence, taking the results of each as factors or arguments of the subsequent operation, until the final results are obtained.
>
> (Torres y Quevedo 1915: 91; emphasis in original)

Torres y Quevedo suggested the way to do this was with switches, 'i.e. *in the place of an index which runs over a graduated scale, we shall have a brush which moves over a line of contacts and makes contact with each of them successively*' (Torres y Quevedo 1915: 89). In 1920, Torres y Quevedo built a prototype to illustrate the feasibility of his suggestion, the first machine to have a typewriter as the input/output device. But his basic idea of a switch sounded like nothing so much as the then current mechanism used in telephone exchanges, the Strowger uniselector.

'By 1925 the designers of switching systems had become most adept in devising complex logic circuits using general-purpose electromagnetic relays of telephone quality' (Schindler 1982: 2). Although Bell Labs began to think about the Torres y Quevedo line of enquiry in this same year, it was not until the late 1930s that any devices appeared in the metal. The Model K (for kitchen table) Bell 'computer' was made of old bits of telephone exchange mounted on a breadboard, one weekend in 1937, by George Stibitz. Stibitz, a staff mathematician at the Labs, was convinced he could wire a simple logic circuit to produce binary additions because the ordinary telephone relay switch was a binary - an on/off – device, and over the weekend that is exactly what he did. There was little immediate enthusiasm for the breadboard calculator but a pilot project was funded and the first complex calculator was built.

The internal supervening necessity was the endless calculations necessary in the developing theory of filters and transmission lines. The complex calculator (aka Model l) was finished by 1940 and did the job the Labs required. Apart from building the first binary machine, at a meeting of the American Mathematical Society, Stibitz also performed the first remote control calculation by hooking up the teletype input keyboard in a lecture hall at Dartmouth and communicating via the telephone wire (of course) with the Model 1 in New York. (Here is the earliest application of telegraph technology to computing. This would eventually lead to the Internet.) Stibitz now looked to make a more complex device, but the cost, $20,000, 'frightened the Lab administration and no further computers [sic] were built for several years' (Stibitz 1980: 481). When the USA joined the war in 1941, Stibitz's expertise did find a proper outlet, in building a series of specialised electro-mechanical complex calculators. The Model 2 had a changeable paper-tape programme and was self-checking. It was designed specifically to test anti-aircraft detectors. The Model 3, designed for anti-aircraft ballistic calculations, made, like its predecessor, for unattended operation, rang a bell in the staff sergeant's quarters if for any reason the computation was halted. By now Stibitz had left the Labs for the University of Vermont but two Model 5s were built after his departure. One of these versions was placed at the Aberdeen Testing Grounds. The building of these machines was abandoned, in 1950, for a second and final time (ibid.).

Stibitz's experience during these years parallels, albeit rather less dramatically, that of Konrad Zuse, who was also drawn to automata because of boredom. 'In 1934 I was a student in civil engineering in Berlin. Berlin is a nice town and there were many opportunities for a student to spend his time in an agreeable manner, for instance with the nice girls. But instead we had to perform big and awful calculations' (Zuse 1980: 611). In 1936, Zuse gave up his job at Henschel Flugzeugwerken in Berlin and began building electro-mechanical binary calculators out of relays, machines which were to occupy most of the living room of his parents' apartment. The Z1 and Z2 were test models. He had failed to interest the German office machine industry in his project except for some partial support from one manufacturer (Randell 1973: 155; Wulforst 1982: 93–4). In 1939, work on the Z2 was halted as Zuse was inducted into the Wehrmacht. As Zuse explained to his American interrogator in 1946, the *Deutschen Versuchsanhalt für Luftfahrt* (the Aerodynamics Research Institute) was interested in his Z2, and so he was relieved and went to back to Henschel which was now building V2s. By 1941, still finishing the Z3 in his spare time, he began building the special purpose S1 to increase missile production by speeding computation. It worked so well that in the later part of 1943 Zuse, supported by the Air Ministry, established his own small firm, Zuse Apparatbau (Goldstine 1972: 250–1 and n.). The Z3 was, like the contemporary models in America, programmable, but by holes punched in 35mm film rather than paper tape. (The idea of using paper tape had been published in 1909.[3] The Z3 was a floating-point binary machine with a sixty-four-digit store and was the first of its general purpose class to work, by December 1941 (Randell 1973: 156). At the war's end Zuse was working on a Z4. As the Allies closed in on Berlin he was given one truck on which he loaded the Z4 and headed south. By the surrender he was holed up in the village of Hinterstein in the Bavarian Alps close to the Austrian border, the Z4 hidden in a cellar.[4]

Howard Aitken, the builder of the third major line of electromagnetic machines, came to computers, like many others in this history, while slogging through the calculations he needed for his thesis. By 1937 he had a proposal ready for mechanising the process. He showed it to the military but he also took it to a calculating machine company which decided the device was impractical, against the opinion of its chief engineer. The engineer then directed Aitken, via the IBM connection with Columbia University, to IBM itself. Using contacts at the Astronomical Computing Bureau at Columbia, which had IBM equipment, and the good offices of a business professor at Harvard, Aitken got to Thomas Watson Sr, the then president of IBM (Aitken 1964: 197).

IBM's Watson was a somewhat bizarre executive but a salesman of genius (Rodgers 1969). In 1929, as part of his public relations, he had donated a full collection of machines to establish the Columbia University Statistical Bureau, which used them for educational testing. He then funded the development of an up-to-date version of the Scheutz engine. The University began to experiment with the machinery in performing astronomical calculations and after further gifts of equipment the operation, suitably enlarged, was renamed the Thomas J. Watson Astronomical Computing Bureau (Goldstine 1972: 109). However, far from illuminating the corporate mind as to the potential of advanced calculators, all this simply reinforced what had become IBM's traditional indifference to them as a business proposition. These uses, in effect, obscured the potential for computers and the fancy applications the machines were put to in Columbia confirmed the view that profit lay in the simpler needs of commerce. When Aitken arrived this perception had changed slightly, for the imminence of war sharpened Watson's appetite for new markets – he had been after military contracts for some years – and Aitken brought with him a potential naval connection (Rodgers 1969: 136).

In 1939, Aitken was contracted to build his electromagnetic machine at IBM's Endicott Lab, the money to come from the US Navy and a million-dollar gift from Watson. Aitken was still salaried through his Harvard professorship and was given the reserve rank of Naval Commander. His staff was navy, too. IBM furnished the space and the equipment, mainly, as with Stibitz and Zuse, relay switches, but it also provided a team of engineers. Within four years the machine, the Mark 1, was working. It was transferred to Harvard, as a present from IBM. Watson insisted it be clothed in gleaming, aerodynamically moulded steel, an IBM vision of 1940s high tech. Aitken thought it should be left naked in the interests of science. Watson won, but Harvard virtually excluded him, and IBM, from the dedication ceremony. IBM called the machine the ASCC (Automatic Sequence Controlled Calculator); Aitken called it the Harvard Mark I. Watson did not get the expected honorary degree and IBM ignored the Mark I as a prototype for a business machine yet nevertheless set about building a bigger and better one; but the world got, in the publicity brouhaha, its first glimpse of a 'robot brain' (Rodgers 1969: 171–2). Aitken's young naval help organised a routine which made the machine produce strings of meaningless numbers to the accompaniment of much clicking from the relays and many flashing lights. Visiting admirals were impressed (Wulforst 1982: 39–41) Like the Z3 and the Bell Model 2, the Mark 1 was externally programmable, using paper tape. In its general scope and speed it was also of a piece with these other devices.

Given that IBM was not in the computer business but rather engaged in some high level public relations work, it is not surprising that 'Aitken did not always appreciate Thomas J. Watson Sr., and all the co-operation he got from IBM' (Birkoff 1980: 22). (Aitken had seen the subservience demanded of the faculty in the Columbia facility Watson had endowed.) Yet IBM could have been in the advanced electro-mechanical calculator business had it so desired, for Stibitz, Zuse and Aitken had invented nothing. Their machines were built out of readily available parts and this was to be the case with the all-electric calculators which came next. These accepted prototypes speak directly to the lack of a real supervening necessity. Occasional tasks, like Bell Labs' need to crack filter theory, might produce a machine. Inspired amateurs, like Zuse, might do so too. And in certain corners of the military needs were perceived and met, but basically the world worked well enough with these various prototypes. A universal analytic engine was simply not needed. It was to take two wars, one hot and one cold, to change that perception.

# 9

# THE FIRST COMPUTERS

## ELECTRONIC PROTOTYPES I: ENIAC AND 'THE FIRING TABLE CRISIS'

The art of ballistics, until the total mechanisation of warfare in the twentieth century, had been, one might say, a hit and miss affair. In a series of experiments between 1864 and 1880 the Reverend Francis Bashforth related air drag to velocity and produced the first firing tables to be consulted on the battlefield as a guide to the ranging of artillery pieces. These tables were refined by a French military commission working in Grave but, at the onset of the First World War, there was still a lot of guesswork involved. Many factors were simply not calculated. Since, without firing tables, any artillery weapon is much reduced in utility, the Americans took ballistics very seriously and established a tradition of research in the aftermath of that war. At the Aberdeen Proving Ground a succession of highly educated ballistics officers appeared during the 1920s and 1930s and it was these officials who moved to acquire a Bush differential analyser as detailed above.

Nevertheless, despite these preparations, the ballistics work generated by the Second World War was overwhelming. Each firing table for every new weapon required the tabulation of dozens of factors across thousands of possible trajectories, any one of which represented half a day's work for a human computer with a desk calculator. By the summer of 1944 the computing branch of the Ballistics Research Laboratory was producing fifteen tables a week, but the need was for forty (Wulforst 1982: 60). This, the so-called 'firing table crisis', was the supervening necessity for a fully electronic complex difference analyser, the machine which became known as ENIAC. Professor John Brainerd, the Moore School's official ordnance liaison officer, wrote: 'The proposed electronic difference analyser would, if successfully developed, not only eliminate such delays but would permit far more extensive ballistic calculations than are now possible with existing equipment' (ibid.).

It is also possible, though, that too much has been made of the 'firing tables crisis'. The Harvard mathematician Garret Birkoff often visited Aberdeen at this time and is of the opinion that the whole issue had been overblown. 'This is because it [the war] was not fixed position trench warfare, it was mostly point-blank fire, often at a moving tank' (Birkoff 1980: 24). In support of this view is the fact that victory was secured before ENIAC came on stream, despite the 'crisis'. Yet, on the other hand, tanks were not the only target; planes, for example, posed a real difficulty, one which Norbert Wiener spent considerable effort addressing. Either way, there can be no doubt that the Ordnance Department gave high priority to the creation of firing tables and was not averse to mechanising their computation.

John Atanasoff, an associate professor of physics at what was then the State College of Iowa, had coined the term 'analogue computer' to describe Bush's complex differential analyser but was engaged in building a quite different sort of machine, a binary digital device having about 300 valves (tubes), in fact the first prototype of the all-electronic calculator. In a 1940 paper, really a grant proposal, Atanasoff stated: 'substantial progress has been made in the construction of the machine' (Atanasoff 1980: 329). Its purpose was to solve linear algebraic equations and Atanasoff, in addition to path-breaking valves in his logic circuits, used capacitors arranged in drums as the store and a built-in pulse by which the machine could internally time its own operations. The device, which Atanasoff designated in honour of himself and his assistant the ABC (the Atanasoff-Berry Computer) was the size of a large desk. A photograph of it appeared in the local paper, dated January 1941, with a story saying the machine would be ready in about a year. It was, at a cost of about $6500. As an electronic and binary calculator, it was, on the one hand, extremely sophisticated; but, on the other, malfunctions on a peripheral electro-mechanical binary-card puncher prevented it from fulfilling its design purpose. Further, it was to do multiplication and division, like the seventeenth-century Pascaline, as a series of additions and subtractions; and, like Babbage's difference engine, it was a single-purpose machine. Nevertheless it was indisputably the first prototype electronic calculator to use valves (Goldstine 1972: 123–5; Augarten 1984: 114–20).

In December 1940 Atanasoff read a paper on his work at a conference in Washington attended by John Mauchly. In the 1930s, Mauchly had been eager to avoid the slog of hand computations. Indeed, he had been driven away from one investigation, an analysis of meteorological data, because of the mechanical enormity of the task. He was to claim he had built some experimental circuits at that time using valves (Mauchly 1980: 545), but some doubt this. What is indisputable is that he was intrigued enough with the ABC to drive all the way to Ames, in the summer of 1941, for a period variously described as between three days and a week (Augarten 1984: 113–14; Wulforst 1982: 28–9). Atanasoff was to claim that he discussed in great detail with Mauchly plans for a general purpose electronic calculator, obviously utilising valves. Mauchly, on the other hand, claimed that he advised Atanasoff against certain aspects of his design, notably the capacitors. After this trip, Mauchly went on a defence training course at the Moore School and subsequently obtained a faculty post there. From this position, he invited Atanasoff to join the Moore School team. Instead Atanasoff, who did not get round to patenting the ABC which was eventually broken up, went to the Naval Ordnance Lab on the outbreak of war and never returned to computing machinery (Randell 1973: 288). A judge in 1974 was to hold that Mauchly got all his ideas from Atanasoff, yet, confusingly, at the same time found that Mauchly had nevertheless 'invented' ENIAC (Mauchly 1980: 544).

The basis of this opinion was that in August 1942 Mauchly had written a paper, 'The Use of High Speed Vacuum Tube Devices for Calculating', which led directly to the ENIAC project. Beyond speed of calculation, he suggested greater accuracy, enhanced checkability, a certain degree of programmability, easy faultfinding and labour saving would result from the use of valves (tubes) but the idea had scarcely ignited imaginations and the paper itself was buried until Herman Goldstine, eight months later, went looking for it (Mauchly 1942: 329). Lieutenant Goldstine, who was in the Moore School as the naval officer commanding the Ballistics Research Laboratory's Philadelphia substation, was charged with the responsibility of producing firing tables on the complex differential analyser (Atanasoff's 'analogue computer') housed in the basement. An ex-student of Mauchly's, Joe Chaplin, had been hired to keep the machine running – no small job – and one day, with Goldstine standing over him while he tried to maintain it, he suggested that Mauchly might have a better way. Goldstine, who had been getting further and further behind in the work, was eager to explore Mauchly's proposal.

Goldstine discovered that not only had Mauchly's original paper not been acted upon, it had been lost. It was now the spring of 1943. The proposal was reconstructed out of the secretary's old shorthand book and Goldstine used it to smooth the way at Aberdeen and with his own brass. Oswald Veblen, the chief scientist of the Ballistics Research Laboratory, fell off his chair during the presentation – presumably with excitement – and upon recovering simply said, 'Give Goldstine the money'; and so, by early April, after a bout of furious work, Goldstine and Mauchly presented detailed proposals and costings. The 'Report on an Electronic Diff.* [sic] Analyser' was produced by 2 April 1943 (Burks 1980: 314). 'Diff.*' stood for both differential, i.e. the mechanical device in the basement, and the difference between that machine and the one proposed, i.e. that the latter would be all-electric. There was another difference. The machine was to be sixty times larger than the only valve calculator then in existence, the ABC, and was budgeted to cost twenty-three times as much. On 31 May , a request for

$150,000 having been approved, work began. In June the machine was redesignated 'Electronic Numerical Integrator and Computer' (ENIAC).

J. Presper Eckert Jr had grown up a mile away from Farnsworth's Philadelphia television laboratory, to which he was a constant boyhood visitor. He came to the Moore School in 1937 and, by his graduation in 1941, had shown himself to be a most promising electrical engineer. He was the graduate assistant on the course that brought Mauchly to the School. They had spent time talking about calculators and the relationship continued after Mauchly was appointed to the faculty at the course's end. Mauchly immediately involved Eckert in the ENIAC project not least because Eckert was prepared to defy conventional wisdom as to the reliability of valves. He understood that, if valves were left on constantly, the failure rate was much reduced. His hunch was that it would be low enough to allow Mauchly's plan to work. The importance of the decision to use valves for ENIAC cannot be overstated. (If Eckert were to be proved right – and he was – ENIAC would also demonstrate that there was no technological reason for an electronic calculator not to have been built much earlier.) The big gamble in ENIAC's design, then, was in the number of valves required. The original plan called for 17,000 tubes operating at 100,000 pulses a second. It had (theoretically) 1.7 billion opportunities to break down every second it was switched on (Wulforst 1982: 54). In addition, it had an IBM 601-style plug-board suggesting that some degree of operational flexibility was planned.

Eckert and Mauchly began work on the ENIAC a week before the final contracts between the University and the Ballistics Research Laboratory were signed in June 1943. From then until the official hand-over, ENIAC was to take three years of laborious and painstaking effort. The reasons for this slow pace were manifold. The work itself was tricky but accomplishable. Getting the parts off the shelf, in the face of wartime shortages, was more difficult by far. It is likely that, had the Ballistics Research Laboratory set out to have an ENIAC built in the late 1930s, it would have been finished rather more quickly than it was in the mid-1940s. Weeks were wasted, months even, waiting for electrical supplies. The racks were made by a kitchen cabinet manufacturer in New Jersey who was going out of business for lack of steel. ENIAC had just sufficient urgency to prevent this from happening. Sometimes the supplies were of inadequate quality. Despite low priority (or perhaps because most of the money had already been spent), when the war ended, the work still went forward.

By November 1945, ENIAC's debugging procedure started and, at von Neumann's suggestion, a team from the Manhattan project at Los Alamos came to Philadelphia with a problem for ENIAC to calculate. (Von Neumann, to whom Goldstine had introduced himself on a railway station, had kept himself abreast of progress at the Moore School since the summer of 1944 and, in turn, had informed Los Alamos.) Early in the New Year, the Moore School and the Army elaborately prepared to unveil ENIAC to the world. It had eventually cost $500,000 (but then so too had the latest Bell Mark 5 electro-mechanical device) and, although the war was over, ENIAC did what it was designed to do:

> [W]e chose a trajectory of a shell that took 30 seconds to go from the gun to the target. Remember that girls [sic] could compute this in three days, and the differential analyser could do it in 30 minutes. The ENIAC calculated this 30-second trajectory in just 20 seconds, faster than the shell itself could fly.
>
> (Augarten 1984: 99)

There was already a degree of awareness, from the 'Robot Brain' ceremonies for the unveiling of Aitken's Harvard Mark 1, that a new generation of super devices was emerging, and on 15 February 1946, upon the public demonstration of ENIAC's powers, the *New York Times* quoted 'leaders' as 'heralding it as a tool with which to rebuild scientific affairs on a new footing' (Wulforst 1982: 72).

## ELECTRONIC PROTOTYPES II: COLOSSUS vs. ENIGMA

The brouhaha surrounding ENIAC stands in stark contrast to the treatment given by the British to their equivalent device, Colossus. For more than four decades after the end of the war, Colossus remained only partially declassified. There is a contrast too between the gravity of the British and American supervening necessities which lay behind the building of ENIAC and Colossus. While there can be some argument as to the seriousness of the firing table crisis, in Britiain's case there is less room for debate. Advanced electronic calculators were needed for cryptanalysis especially to overcome German submarine dominance in the Battle of the Atlantic. The work of the British teams, which developed the machines to do this in the secret war, appears to have been essential to overall victory.

From the outset of hostilities in 1939 until the middle of 1941, the British government's Code and Cipher School (GC & CS) struggled to break open the encoding of German messages. Alan Turing, who came to Bletchley Park, the wartime site of GC & CS, the day after war broke out, led one of the groups working on this problem. They had a certain head-start. They knew the Germans were using an encoding machine, the Enigma; they had a fair idea of the principles involved in it and its design. It was based on a commercial device developed by an American, Hebern, for use by banks and anybody else who needed to transmit secret messages. Inside were a series of 'hebern' wheels which substituted letters for the originals of the message. How it did so depended on the number of wheels involved, the way the machine was wired through its electrical rotors and the use of a predetermined but easily changed 'key'.

Thanks to the efforts of Polish intelligence, a lot of detail was known about the German version of this machine. The Poles became aware of encrypted German radio traffic in 1928 but failed to make much headway with its decipherment. From 1932 on, they kept a more serious watch (Rejewski 1981: 90–1) and by 1935 had started to construct machines, cyclometers, in an attempt to mechanise the search for the daily keys. Eventually the Poles produced a contrivance called the Bombas (or Bombe in the Western European literature) which worked as Enigma's *alter ego*. Put crudely, it reversed Enigma. Encoded messages were fed into it and it ran through all possible combinations until it produced German. The Polish Bombe had been rendered obsolete when, in 1938, the Germans increased the rotors again. Inside the naval Enigma, for instance, there were now eight rotors, so that the machine had 336 rather than the six settings possible with the original three-rotor model. As war increasingly threatened, the Poles shared their work with British and French Intelligence and on 25 July 1939 one of GC & CS' top cryptographers flew to Warsaw to consult. After the outbreak of hostilities some five weeks later, the leading Polish cryptologists were removed to France.

Turing was in charge of Hut 8 at Bletchley Park, his official address Room 47, Foreign Office, Whitehall, London. Eventually he was to have a dozen mathematicians, four linguists and about a hundred other people, all women apparently, to do mechanical clerical work, and a number of eight-foot high bronze Bombes. British Intelligence had some breakthroughs on the German codes but it was Hut 8 that cracked the problem by building an improved Bombe. Using a 'probable word' system, the new Bombe had a diagonal board which allowed the increased complexity of Enigma's variable wiring patterns to be duplicated. By August 1940, this device was being used to speed the work of GC & CS. As a specialised electro-mechanical machine it was, if anything, a rather straightforward, indeed simpler, cousin to the Zuse and Bell machines and the Harvard Mark I then being built. In its particular design objectives it was not unlike the primitive electro-mechanical apparatus – a number sieve – created to discover whether, for instance, any given number is a prime or a composite (Goldstine 1972: 271). Such research tools had existed since 1932. There was also a British tradition of pure research calculators upon which to draw. In 1931 an electronic binary counter had been built for nuclear research at the Cavendish Laboratory by Dr C.E. Wynn-Williams. By 1935, this apparatus had been developed to provide binary-decimal conversion and printout (Randell 1980: 57).

Hut 8, building on these traditions, had, however, not cracked the Naval Enigma, a more complicated machine than the one used by the other German forces. In February 1941 a special raid into Norway brought the Naval version back to Turing. In response, the Bombes became more complicated, involving punch-cards and an army of clerks. By May 1941, British Intelligence was able to read all U-boat messages within a day (Hodges 1983: 199). Jack Good, a member of Turing's team at Bletchley Park, remarked – it would seem without hyperbole – that: 'It was only after the war that we learned he [Turing] was a homosexual. It was lucky the security people didn't know about it early on, because if they had known, he might not have obtained his clearance and we might have lost the war' (Good 1980: 34). Although unaware that Enigma was opened, the Germans introduced another refinement to it in January 1942 and secrecy was again attained. Once more the U-Boat fleet was hidden from sight and losses in the Atlantic began to climb precipitously. It is true that other factors can be cited apart from intelligence blackout – German successes in cracking Allied codes or the United States' diverting ships to the Pacific – but failure to decode was paramount. So much tonnage was sunk that by March 1942 Churchill was telling Washington: 'The situation is so serious that drastic action of some kind is necessary. . . .The only other alternatives are. . .to stop temporarily the sailing of tankers, which would gravely jeopardise our operational supplies' (Churchill 1951: 104–5).

However, in December 1941, before the veil of secrecy fell, a U-Boat radio operator had sent a message using a hitherto neutral wheel in the Enigma. He had corrected it, but the error, when recalled, revealed to the British and Americans that the problem was caused by the enemy's use of this new extra wheel. Not only were more Bombes needed but a whole new class of calculator was also required. All these solutions were put in hand. The Turing team built a better Bombe; the Americans built a vast number of Bombes and by the autumn, Max Newman, Turing's Cambridge teacher, had created the first of a series of prototypes for the machine that would be designated Colossus. Newman had come to Bletchley Park as a civilian volunteer in the summer of 1942, the height of the second Enigma blackout. He and his team, in F Hut, known as the Newmanry, created a series of machines whose closest antecedents were to be found in the work just then being abandoned by Vannevar Bush at MIT. Three machines were built, the original being named with some justice the Heath Robinson; for these were temperamental in the extreme. Designed for Boolean operations and built (in part) by Wynn-Williams (who arrived at Bletchley Park a few months before Newman) they used relays, photoelectric paper-tape readers and a teleprinter output as well as between forty and eighty valves. On occasion the whole apparatus threatened to burst into flames. The Heath Robinson and its variants were built in part by Post Office engineers working in the GPO's Research Station at Dollis Hill, London. The machines were constructed out of available components in fairly short order, the first being on stream, insofar as it ever was, by April 1943. Because of the Robinsons, the latest German encoding devices known as *Geheimschreiberen*, secret writers (Deavours 1981: 232), were neutralised. Once more the U-Boat fleet could be accurately tracked via its messages, but Bletchley Park continued to search for more reliable devices.

T.H. Flowers of the GPO was the main engineer involved in the work of the Newmanry. He had been in charge of the switching group at Dollis Hill and had spent the 1930s grappling with the problems involved in substituting electrical for mechanical parts in telephone exchanges, exactly the move now required in automating calculations. He had seen the Manchester University analogue differential analyser in 1937 and had been in contact with an X-ray crystallographer who was interested, like Stibitz, in building a specialised differential calculator from telephone exchange relays. At the outset of the war he was working on an electromagnetic digital device for ranging anti-aircraft guns. In all of this, one thing distinguished Flowers – he shared Eckert's faith in valves. Flowers' long-term solution to the requirements of Bletchley Park Hut F, an assignment for which Turing apparently suggested him, was to avoid one of the major problems of the Robinsons, the physical synchronisation of the two tape inputs, one containing instructions – the patterns the machine was to look for – and the other, the data – the German messages. He proposed doing this by cutting out one paper input and storing the patterns internally, on valves. This would mean the machine would have a huge number of valves, 1500 in its first version.

Bletchley Park was not convinced. Nevertheless, with Newman's backing and supported by a general top-priority instruction from Churchill for whatever GC & CS needed, the Colossus project was given top priority. When the team, working at Dollis Hill, asked for electric typewriters, these were immediately flown over from the States. When another thousand valves were demanded from the Ministry of Supply, they were forthcoming, albeit with the comment, 'What the bloody hell are you doing with these things, shooting them at the Jerries?' (Randell 1980: 77). In eleven months, by December 1943, it was finished. Jack Good and others found they could manipulate the machine while it was running, acting, as it were, something like a human version of the stored programme, albeit a limited one designed simply to seek out, at each stage of choice, the solution closest to German. Immediately work was begun on a Mark II to automate this function in the machine. The Mark II, with 2400 valves and an operating speed five times as fast, i.e. 25,000 characters per second by a combination of parallel operations and short-term memory, was working by 2 June 1944. It had taken a mere three months to build. At least five copies followed (Randell 1973: 328).

The original Colossus, by recognising and counting, was able to produce the best match of a given piece of pattern with the text. The new Colossus, by automating the process of varying the piece of the pattern, was able to work out which was the best one to try. This meant that it performed simple acts of decision which went much further than the 'yes' or 'no' of a Bombe. The result of one counting process would determine what the Colossus would do next. The Bombe was merely supplied with a 'menu'; the Colossus was provided with a set of instructions.

(Hodges 1983: 277)

Nobody on the British side knew that at the same time precisely the same solution, serried ranks of valves, was being proposed in the Moore School in Philadelphia. Indeed Eckert's faith in valves perforce outstripped Flowers' since ENIAC was not a binary machine and it needed to have 18,000 of them. As with ENIAC, so with Colossus; the valve decision was central.

ENIAC and Colossus were the first all-electronic calculators to be built. In the development of the computer, therefore, they stand as the last, most powerful of the accepted prototypes, lacking only the stored programme capacity of the computer. This lack, though, was not at all clear-cut and the degree by which these two machines missed being computers is a matter of debate, especially the Colossus Mark II. It was entirely electronic, fully automatic, programmed by a punch paper-tape system (read photoelectronically) and it contained conditional branching logic facilities. The machine, like the ABC, generated its own pulse. It could count, do binary arithmetic and perform Boolean logical operations. Almost certainly nothing but cryptanalytic problems were ever put to it so in that sense it is, technically, a special purpose machine. In the opinion of some who worked with it, 'The use of Colossus to do other things unconnected with the purpose for which it was built, although possible, would have been strained and artificial'. Others disagree: 'It was general just because it dealt with binary symbols but it wasn't designed to be an ordinary number cruncher' (Randell 1980: 74). 'There were in fact many ways in which Colossus could be used, exploiting the flexibility offered by its variable instruction table' (Hodges 1983: 277). There is even some evidence that the Mark II Colossus was, if only by a hair's breadth, a little more sophisticated than ENIAC; it could even be 'almost set up to perform numerical multiplication' (Hodges 1983: 301).

It was on the brink of being a computer.

## IDEATION: 'THE STORE'

Nevertheless, the ENIAC team's vision was, without question, more advanced and there is nowhere in the record anything comparable to the conceptualisation of the electronically stored programme and extensive memory they came up with during this period. (The pioneering British computer scientists, unlike their pre-war television counterparts, have never denied their direct reliance on the Americans.)

The confusion in the popular account between the earliest computers and these powerful electronic calculators which immediately preceded them is because the line between number-crunchers and symbol-manipulators was, in the 1940s, a thin one. A symbol-manipulator, as opposed to a number-cruncher, must have an in-built set of instructions which can be varied by the operation of the machine itself as a result of its actual calculations; and it must therefore have an extensive data-store. In practice, meeting these requirements most likely means that the symbol manipulator must be entirely electronic. This is a computer; everything else, even if entirely electronic and massively fast, is a calculator. The problem is that the very same people were involved with both sorts of machine. These teams, created by many wartime combatants to assemble the ultimate calculators, used that experience to launch themselves into the designs of full-scale computers; as they built the one they began to draw the other. The two classes of machines looked very similar, performed similar functions and were, largely, assembled from the same parts.

Moreover, programmability and 'memory' factors can be surprisingly difficult to determine, for is a machine unprogrammable if it can be rewired, however laboriously, to perform different tasks? And since the biggest electronic calculators did store and retrieve some numbers in the course of their operations, how much 'memory' constitutes an effective data-store?[1] For example, under pressure of patent cases years later, Mauchly was to claim that the ENIAC design incorporated branching and looping requiring 'electronic stepping switches and counters that contained program information which was altered by the program itself'. Later still, he even went so far as to state: 'Clearly, we were already providing "stored program" in the most important phases of control' (Mauchly 1980: 547). But this 'control', if it could be so called, was of a very limited and physical kind, really no closer to a true stored program than was the human interventions into the operation of Colossus 1. In terms of ENIAC such claims are tendentious. In terms of what the team was thinking of doing next, they are not.

ENIAC's progress, as we have seen, was very slow and Eckert and Mauchly began to generate ideas for improvements. However, these new ideas could not be incorporated into the ongoing machine, for that would have slowed the pace even more. By August 1944, Goldstine began lobbying for a new machine to utilise the advances being suggested. In September he put on paper the superior lines of enquiry he thought ought to be followed:

> there are two further directions in which we should pursue our researches. The switches and controls of ENIAC [which are] now arranged to be operated manually, can be positioned by mechanical relays and electromagnetic telephone switches which are instructed by a Tele-type tape. . .[With this arrangement] tapes could be cut for many

problems and reused when needed. . . .The second direction to be pursued is providing a more economical electronic device for storing data than the accumulator. Eckert has some excellent ideas on a cheap device for this purpose.

(Wulforst 1982: 60–1)

This note contains suggestions for both programmability (the Teletype tape) and 'memory' (a 'device for storing data'). The 'memory' suggestion is well formed for all that the program suggestion is still crude. It gives no indication that the machine might alter its own functions in the light of its actual operations – that is, have the read-write capacity which is the final distinguishing mark of the symbol-manipulator. As I have said, this is the heart of the matter.

As Mauchly put it:

[L]et us consider some of the fundamental characteristics of this type of machine, in particular those points which differ significantly from present machine design [i.e. ENIAC-type calculators]. Of these, three have a definite bearing on the handling of problems: (1) an extensive internal memory; (2) elementary instructions, few in number, to which the machine will respond; and (3) ability to store instructions as well as numerical quantities in the internal memory, and *modify instructions so stored in accordance with other instructions.*

By extensive internal memory is meant a memory accessible at electronic speeds, of the order of a thousand numbers, each of perhaps ten digits.

(Mauchly 1948: 365; emphasis added)

Although the program is still here being envisaged as 'elementary instructions', nevertheless these are clearly to be stored in the memory and to be modifiable – in other words, the machine was, by virtue of its data-store, also to be programmable. And it was Eckert's 'excellent idea' for the memory system which exactly went beyond Goldstine's tickertape to read-write at electronic speeds.

William Shockley, a Bell Labs scientist, had developed an elegant device which could achieve this. It allowed electronic pulses to be converted into a physical form and then reconverted into electrons. By January 1944 (apparently), using this development, Eckert had outlined a 'memory' system for the calculator in which mercury-filled tubes, $4\frac{1}{2}$ feet long, would be arranged so that the pulses (representing the digits in the calculator) would activate a quartz crystal at one end of the tube. This would create an ultrasonic wave in the mercury. The wave would travel infinitely more slowly than the pulse. The slow-down would act like a memory, storing the pulse. At the tube's far end, another crystal would convert the ultrasonic wave back into a pulse. Place the mercury tube in a loop and a stream of pulses, digits, could be made to circulate continuously until needed by the computer. The machine would 'remember' the digits.

This proposal for a read-write storage system constitutes the moment of ideation but, as is not unusual, who had the idea is somewhat shrouded by time. Certainly the evidence is that, sometime before Goldstine's August 1944 paper, the implications for programming in the mercury-tube 'memory' solution had already been understood. For instance, Richard Clippinger, of the Ballistics Research Laboratory, had suggested that programming instructions might be encoded into the mercury as well as the data that needed to be stored. Presper Eckert had written a paper early in 1944, 'Disclosure of a Magnetic Calculating Machine', suggesting that: 'An important feature of this device was that the operating instructions and function tables would be stored in exactly the same sort of memory device as that used for numbers' (Metropolis and Worlton 1972: 687). This paper also explored various storage systems, including magnetic disks or drums and made subsidiary suggestions such as neon gas display panels. The attribution problem arises because Presper Eckert wrote this paper in January 1944 but it was not typed up until February 1945 and even then it still remained secret (Eckert 1980: 537–8). By September 1945, the nascent world of computing would know of the stored program idea from another source.

Von Neumann was, as I have already indicated, a major figure who had begun visiting the ENIAC team in 1944. At a series of meetings he and the team explored the problems of logical control that the storage lines would create. Von Neumann organised the memoranda of these meetings into a report, issued on 30 June 1945, 'First Draft of A Report on The EDVAC'. EDVAC stands for Electronic Discrete Variable Automatic Computer, where the crucial term is Variable. The 'First Report' was issued by the University; but, since it fails to credit the others, it has been suggested by his partisans, this was done without von Neumann's approval. Be that as it may, this paper publicised the stored program concept and was the earliest comprehensive written outline for the modern computer. Its publication also marks the beginning of what was to be an increasingly acrimonious relationship between von Neumann and Goldstine on the one hand and Eckert and Mauchly on the other (Burks 1980: 339). Leaving all the claims and counterclaims aside, it was the 'First Draft', whatever its degree of originality, which received wide circulation.

For example, Turing used it to be read 'in conjunction' with his own proposal made at the National Physical Laboratory to which he had gone in October 1945 specifically to build the ACE computer. All the other teams – at Manchester University, at Cambridge, at Princeton and at the Moore School – were deeply influenced by the 'First Draft'. It was as if, in the early 1890s, somebody had specified, in some detail, the fundamental design elements of an automobile – and that this document acted prescriptively to limit the range of options available to engineers in the decades following. Von Neumann's influence cannot be overstated. Positioned at the heart of the military-industrial complex, he planned a generation of enormously complex machines primarily useful to government-funded applications. All other potential exploitations of the stored program idea, including most significantly the implications of the small size of the very first working computer, the Manchester Baby Mark I, remained unexplored.


## SUPERVENING SOCIAL NECESSITY: THE H-BOMB

The war constituted the supervening necessity for the advanced electronic calculator and, at its end, all the teams involved in such work were in danger of being returned to other projects. Neither the firing table crisis nor cryptanalytic needs were sufficient to maintain them; and general scientific or business requirements were no more visible in 1945/6 than they had been throughout the 1930s. However, the idea of the stored program machine – the true computer – was not lost because a new supervening necessity came into play during the first years of the peace.

ENIAC was finally working by November 1945. As indicated above, Nicholas Metropolis and some colleagues from Los Alamos had already the previous summer, at John von Neumann's suggestion, come to Philadelphia to explore how the machine might aid the computation of some problems in thermonuclear ignition. In November, Metropolis returned and ran the calculation. Scientists from Los Alamos were so early on the machine that their problems were used to debug the device (Goldstine 1972: 225). The results appeared on punch-cards containing no 'indication of what they were or what they were intended to represent' (ibid.). 'The study of the implosion problem gave one of the great impulses to the development of fast computers. . .because it had to solve these problems Los Alamos, consciously or not, made a great and fundamental contribution to the development of computing' (Ulam 1980: 96).

One war was over, but another, with a nuclear arms race at its heart, was starting. There was a hiccup in computer development as the implications of this were imperfectly realised; after all, the Russians would not explode an A-Bomb for four years. Aside from the academy, elsewhere in America, computer plans were being abandoned. Mauchly and Eckert, having left the Moore School and gone into business for themselves, nearly went bankrupt trying to sell computers (p. 190). Even at Los Alamos there was a hiatus. Nicholas Metropolis had left for the University of Chicago in 1946. But then, two years later, he was called back and began to build his computer along lines laid down by von Neumann, himself now back at Princeton. Whirlwind, the path-breaking real-time machine that Jay

Forrester of MIT was building for the Office of Naval Research to study aircraft stability design, was on the point of closure when it was realised it would serve to meet the perceived threat of Soviet air attack. Whirlwind affords the best illustration of the hiccup caused by the disappearance of one supervening necessity – the hot war – and the emergence of another – the cold.

In August 1949, the Russians exploded an atomic bomb and the spectre of a Soviet nuclear strike over the North Pole suddenly loomed. A Whirlwind team member recalled:

> A major threat came from low-flying [Soviet] aircraft. At low altitude, radar range is very short, and information from many radars had to be netted to cover large areas. George Valley at MIT was concerned about radar coverage. He met Jay and it turned out that what he needed was a [real time] digital computer and what we needed was air defence. So Air Force financial support appeared in the nick of time.
>
> (Robertson 1980: 375)

In June 1950 the Korean War began. By November instead of being abandoned Whirlwind had acquired airforce backing and 175 personnel.

The first hydrogen bombs were exploded in November 1952 (US) and August 1953 (USSR). The perceived threat of Russian nuclear capability cleared the hiccups. IBM's proto-computer, the Card-Programmed electronic Calculator (CPC), built in essence out of available IBM bits (a 603 calculating punch and a 405 alphabetical accounting machine), was commissioned by Northrop as part of guided missile development and was delivered in six weeks. Thomas Watson was, at last, in the defence business. He telegraphed President Truman offering IBM's full services to the government. The first IBM computer proper, the 701, a development of the CPC, was originally designated a 'defence calculator' and the first customer for it was, again, Los Alamos. Of the next seventeen 701s, nine went to aircraft companies, two to the Navy, one to the Livermore Atomic Research Laboratory, one to the Weather Bureau and one to the National Security Agency (Hurd 1980: 399–404).

Even within the purest bastions of the academy, at the Institute for Advanced Studies (IAS) at Princeton, where von Neumann was building a machine specifically for the purposes of advancing computer science itself, the cold war intruded. Giving evidence in the matter of J. Robert Oppenheimer, von Neumann testified:

> We did plan and develop and build and get in operation and subsequently operate a very fast computer which during the period of its development was in the very fast class. . . .
> Q: When was it finally built?

Von Neumann: It was built between 1946 and 1952.

Q: And when was it complete and ready for use?

Von Neumann: It was complete in 1951 and it was in a condition where you could really get production out of it in 1952.

Q: And was it used in the hydrogen bomb program?

Von Neumann: Yes. As far as the Institute is concerned. . .this computer came into operation in 1952 after which the first large problem that was done on it, and which was quite large and took even under these conditions half a year, was for the thermonuclear program. Previous to that I had spent a lot of time on calculations on other computers for the thermonuclear program.

(Goldstine 1972: 318)

This is not to say that non-military uses for computers were not essayed in the early days after the war. Everybody, from the pari-mutuel betting company in America to the Joseph Lyons Tea-rooms in the UK looked into its potential. Few, though, were prepared to write cheques. Against this, it is certainly the case that within meteorological circles as well as the Census Bureau the device was quickly regarded as a *sine qua non*; as it was also within certain parts of the Academy. But the fact is that all of these latter requirements antedate the war and they were not then, in the 1930s, of sufficient import to get computers built, despite the readily available parts. The new factor, maintaining the impetus created by the Second World War, was neither old scientific needs nor the spotty interest of business. It was the cold war.

Perhaps the ultimate proof of this can be seen in the British experience. The British rapidly picked up on the thinking done by the ENIAC team and, still propelled forward on the wave of expertise created during the hostilities, built the first undeniable electronic-stored program computer actually to compute. Yet this lead was lost by the early 1950s, for why would a post-Imperial Britain need to be in the forefront of such developments?

At the war's end, then, the computer stood ready to be invented. The concept was to hand and much of the hardware had been effectively demonstrated by ENIAC and Colossus Mark II. The only technological question mark over the nascent computer was the form of its memory, which was crucial since this was the device's distinguishing characteristic; but the mercury lines were built and were found to work as planned. Alternatives to them also appeared at this same time, before any computer was operational. Nevertheless, it was to take a number of years before a stored program machine was to work. This immediate post-war period, from 1946 until the first years of the 1950s, was subject to an iron rule called in America the 'von Neumann Constant'. In Britain the same law applied, only under the title the 'Hartree Constant'.

Some people have mentioned it as being part of von Neumann's machine, but as I remember Johnny developed it as a universal constant — that constant number of months from now until everyone's machine is expected to be completed. After the ENIAC, many computers had been started, but at that time [1948] none had reached the promised land.

(Slutz 1980: 472)

This constant, a species of the 'law' of the suppression of radical potential, was essentially the result of the slow and uneven emergence of the cold war as a supervening necessity. Some projects were thwarted by the obstruction of science bureaucrats and, as we shall see in Chapter 10, the short-sightedness of potential commercial buyers; but overall, because the supervening necessity of the cold war had not fully operated to make the machines indispensable, the whole trajectory of development rocked uneasily between this lack of need and the forward impetus generated by the wartime work.

There is an appositeness in the fact that the International Research Conference on the history of computing, the published record of which has been much used in these pages, should have convened, in 1976, at the Los Alamos Scientific Laboratory in New Mexico rather than at IBM in Endicott, New York or the Institute for Advanced Studies at Princeton, or the Moore School in Philadelphia, or at Manchester University in Britain. The computer survived the Second World War *in utero* to be born as a child of the nuclear age.

## 'INVENTION': INCUNABULA

The British did not know of the EDVAC plans until 1945. Then a flurry of visits — Douglas Hartree and T. H. Flowers among others — apprised them of the latest developments, making them aware of the stored program concept and the mercury delay line solution. The pioneers who had worked on ENIAC and designed EDVAC, in contrast to their increasingly strained internal relations, presented to the outside, albeit minuscule, world of fellow computer scientists a face that was open and friendly in the extreme. A summer school was held at the University of Pennsylvania in 1946. Among those stimulated was another ex-TRE scientist, F. C. Williams, whose alternative to the mercury lines, the 'Williams electrostatic memory', was to be the most important single British contribution to the 'invention' of the computer during the years of the 'Hartree/von Neumann Constant' — the incunabula period (as it might be termed).

Williams, who had accepted a chair at Manchester, patented his data-storage device, 'in which numbers are represented by distributions of electric charge on a surface inside a vacuum tube', in this case a cathode ray tube, in December 1947 (Wilkes 1956: 160). This solution to the memory store problem used a suitably modulated beam of electrons to 'write' the information on the surface in the following way:

> [T]he 'mud puddle' analogy is useful. Imagine a flat area of thick mud (analogous to the phosphor coating of a cathode-ray tube) and above it, a source of drops of water (analogous to the electron beam). If water is dropped at a particular location a crater is created (analogous to a potential well in the phosphor) and a binary '0' is stored. If the water source is moved slightly (technically known as a 'twitch') and more water is dropped, the original crater is partially refilled, and a binary '1' is stored. Sensing of the stored information is achieved by returning the water source to the original location. When water is dropped, more mud will be displaced for the stored '1' following the twitch than for the stored '0' without the twitch.
>
> (Robertson 1980: 356–7)

The system was far from perfect but it did use a readily available and quite cheap component and it was many times quicker to access than a delay line. It was to be a popular solution, computer operators even learning to read some aspects of the machine's operations from the patterns displayed on the CRTs.

In order to demonstrate the efficacy of his memory system, Williams and another colleague from TRE, Tom Kilburn, set about building a computer. In contradistinction to von Neumann's monster plan, their design philosophy was to make the machine as small as possible, but this was not because they had escaped the influence of 'The First Report'. Rather it was so that a machine, which was not really thought of as a computer because it did not match American specifications as to size and power, could be built quickly and electrostatic storage effectively demonstrated. With this more limited ambition, progress was swift. They circulated a paper, 'A Storage System for Use with Binary Digital Computing Machinery' which was written by Kilburn and dated 1 December 1947. Six months later, on 21 June 1948 the machine, designated the Baby Mark I, ran a 52-minute program (Lavington 1980: 18–19, 36).

The Baby Mark I was the first fully electronic stored program device to work anywhere in the world – in fact, the invented computer. And it was also to be the first and last baby machine for thirty years (except for two built for the similar purpose of demonstrating a potential component – one, the magnetic core memory in the early 1950s (p. 187) and the other integrated circuits, in the mid-1960s (p. 231)). But the Baby's creators declared: 'The machine is purely experimental and is on too small a scale to be of mathematical value', and proceeded to subject the apparatus to 'intense engineering development' over the course of the next twelve months so that it was big enough to warrant the name computer (Williams and Kilburn 1948: 387). This is why the 'First Report' and the nuclear supervening necessity were so important. Von Neumann made it clear that computers were not to be 'babies'. Thermonuclear ignition problems demanded a certain size of machine. The Manchester pioneers therefore set aside the 'invention', the Baby Mark I, in favour of a 'large machine design' (Hodges 1983: 406). Although in British fashion not quite so gigantic as the machines the Americans were proposing, the Manchester University Mark I or the Manchester Automatic Digital Machine (the MADM) proper, which was working experimentally by April 1949, was what everybody expected a computer to be – a room full of valves.

Among those attending the 1946 Moore summer school was M.V. Wilkes. In the 1930s, he had worked on the Cambridge differential analyser and was now director of the Cambridge University Mathematical Laboratory. He resolved, upon his return from America, to build a computer along the lines suggested in the 'First Report' – a British version of EDVAC. He obtained a measure of official scientific support, and some money from J. Lyons & Co, a commercial exception to prove the general rule of business uninterest (p. 190). Thirty months after he had begun, in May 1949 EDSAC was fully operational. (The MADM only became available for 'regular' problems that autumn.) Wilkes' designation described the device, Electronic Delay Storage Automatic Calculator, that is, an electronic calculator with the capacity to store data and programming instructions in its delay lines – a computer. EDSAC, with its thirty-two mercury lines, was the first full-scale electronic computer to incorporate Eckert's memory system and to be used for proper mathematical work. Wilkes had produced elegant new systems for control and arithmetic hardware design using closed sub-routines, micro-programming, which made it 'much easier to find one's way about' (Wilkes 1980: 501). In the literature which acknowledges the significance of the stored program – that is, the literature which refuses ENIAC the title of first electronic computer – EDSAC is accorded that honour. (The Baby Mark I is not even considered.)

All this activity in England can be traced to a quite brief period during which Britain, in victory still a great Imperial power, continued independent nuclear development. She needed the computers because she had been cut off, momentarily, from her main source of information and primary research, the USA, by an Act of Congress in 1946. The decision to proceed without this information was made in the first months of 1947. Thus the British created for themselves the same supervening necessity that the Americans had. Official British thinking, though, had been laid down in the first year after the war and was not altered by these changed circumstances. All the nation's computing needs were deemed to require if not only one machine then certainly not more than one centre and that the National Physical Laboratory was to be the place. This continued the wartime plan which, in advance of the electronic machines, envisaged that the NPL's Mathematical Division would be able to concentrate all military calculating needs under one roof. The work at Manchester and Cambridge was thus 'unplanned'.

Turing had been recruited from Bletchley Park to the NPL. He took the view that this invitation was a sort of repayment for his wartime efforts. Now, in return, the British government would fund a universal Turing machine which he therefore began designing (Hodges 1983: 305–7). Turing's device at the NPL was to be the computer, the only one. The NPL took an imperialist view. Wilkes was involved, at these early stages, as a potential builder of the Turing blueprint yet he responded somewhat gingerly to these overtures. On the one hand, he wrote to the NPL that 'I am beginning to do a little work on electronic calculating machines and that I am anxious to co-operate with you' (Hodges 1983: 351); but, on the other hand, his anxieties were not translated into actual co-operation. The 'little work' became a rival project which yielded the EDSAC. Similar attempts were made to interest Williams in the NPL project and some abortive meetings were held (Lavington 1980: 26–9). Max Newman, who had taken the chair of pure mathematics at Manchester, after spending a semester with von Neumann at Princeton, obtained the support of the Royal Society to establish a 'Calculating Machine Laboratory' in part in support of Williams. However, as he wrote to von Neumann in 1946: 'Once the NPL project was started, it became questionable whether a further unit was wanted' (Hodges 1983: 341). Newman only got his funding by arguing (after the fashion of von Neumann himself) that, in contrast to the NPL plan, the Manchester machine would be used for theoretical problems in pure mathematics, and with considerable prescience he mentioned 'testing out the four-colour theorem' which would only be proved, with the help of enormous computing power, thirty years later.

What saved the Cambridge and Manchester initiatives was the inefficiencies of some of the scientific bureaucrats at the NPL – the 'Hartree Constant'. Before the end of 1945, Turing, also influenced by the EDVAC outline, had produced on paper designs for a stored program computer to be designated ACE (Automatic Computing Engine – 'Engine' in honour of Babbage). His proposals for ACE envisaged a very ambitious machine involving 200 mercury delay lines and a capacity some six times greater than the biggest of its planned rivals – 6400 thirty-two bit words. Many more refined blueprints of the ACE were developed in the course of the next two years but getting the thing into the metal proved ever more difficult. An obscurantist head of a new Electronics Section of the Radio Division of the NPL had been charged with developing industrial devices to help rebuild Britain and decided that ACE would be of no use in this task. Turing, frustrated, then accepted Newman's offer to go to Manchester. The Royal Society agreed that his salary could come from its grant and he was made deputy director of the lab where he arrived in September 1948, too late to influence the shape of the MADM but in time to write its manual. This, Turing's last move was to prove fatal because it was in Manchester, during the aftermath of an investigation for burglary at his house, that the police began proceedings against him for homosexuality. His suicide followed shortly thereafter (Toumlin 1984: 3). Eventually, back at the NPL, a smaller machine, Pilot Ace, was built to illustrate Turing's architecture. It ran for the first time, in a preliminary way, in May 1950 and it worked well enough to do years of service at the lab, one advantage of its limited physical size being that it could be moved, unlike its competitors. Pilot Ace was also the effective mould for a commercial version built by English Electric and marketed as Deuce.

In America the role of the NPL was being played by the National Bureau of Standards (NBS). The NBS, according to American official thinking which was along the same lines as the British, was to be the organisation co-ordinating the entire computational needs of every branch of the government. Consequently the bureau, in conjunction with its most obvious governmental client, the Census Bureau, simply commissioned outsiders, in this case Eckert and Mauchly, to provide it with a computer. The 'von Neumann Constant' operated to such draconian effect in the newly formed enterprise which Eckert and Mauchly had founded that no machine appeared. Under pressure from the Air Force (whose needs were more significant than the Census Bureau's), the NBS therefore revised its strategy and began to build an 'interim' computer in-house, again using the basic design outlined in the 'First Report', to plug the gap. With such elements as a magnetic wire cartridge from a commercial dictating machine, as well as Williams tubes and magnetic tape, it became fully operational in May 1950 – as did Pilot Ace. So this Standard Eastern Automatic Computer (SEAC) was the first true computer to work in the USA. Of course, 'It was not many weeks before Nick Metropolis. . .showed up with a problem from Los Alamos' (Slutz 1980: 457).

SEAC was also the first computer to use solid state components – diodes – for its logic circuits, reserving valves for amplifying functions. Eschewing the latest type because of the uncertainty of their operation, SEAC used instead 1N34 'whisker' diodes, 10,000 of them, as well as 750 valves. It was, then, a 'cat's whisker' computer but, despite this, it remained operational well into the age of the transistor, finally being closed down in 1964. Aside from this innovation, in its architecture SEAC otherwise remained true to the 'First Report'. The Moore School, which had announced that it was building EDVAC in the spring of 1947, overcame the 'von Neumann Constant' to finish the machine, in conjunction with the Ballistics Research Lab, by 1951 (Randell 1973: 351).

Meanwhile, von Neumann had decided to build his own machine for purely scientific purposes, although, given his connections with both IBM and Los Alamos, there was clearly some overlap with the 'real world'. To accomplish this scheme at Princeton, where the Institute of Advanced Studies (IAS) had set its face against anything but theorising, von Neumann took advantage of his status as one of the men of the atomic hour and orchestrated a campaign of offers from MIT, Harvard and Chicago. Princeton surrendered. He got his funding ($1.4 million from Princeton, RCA and, mainly, the military) and his machine, which he assured the university would not be used to solve any problems in any field of study; rather it was the machine itself which was to be the scholarly object. Taking Goldstine as well as a number of others from the Moore School with him, von Neumann was in business – the business of pure science, but with the atomic connection looming very large. By 1946, the Atomic Energy Commission was also giving support and von Neumann, at government insistence, had involved Los Alamos, the national laboratories at Oak Ridge and Argonne as well as the Rand Corporation and the University of Illinois to help speed up the work. First a new building to house the project was erected. It then took two years to assemble the computer and a further year to test. Needless to say, among the earliest users, in the spring of 1951, were scientists from Los Alamos. Contrary to von Neumann's promise, they were less interested in the machine itself and more in what it could do for them. They ran one nuclear problem for sixty days without cessation, twenty-four hours a day. The IAS computer with its store of 1024 words of forty bits and 2,600 tubes, was in use until 1960 when it was given to the Smithsonian (Bigelow 1980: *passim*).

The distribution of information insisted on by the US government meant that other copies were produced within the same time frame. First, by March 1952, was the Los Alamos version. Metropolis, irked by the acronymic christening then fashionable for these machines, called his MANIAC (*M*athematical *A*nalyser *N*umerical *I*ntegrator and *C*ounter) in a futile attempt to kill the fad (Metropolis 1980: 460–1). The University of Illinois was part of the IAS network so that it could build two machines for the Ballistics Research Laboratory. Although the team relied on the preliminary design specification of von Neumann's group, the resultant computers, ORDVAC and ILLIAC, contained much that was contributed locally. Both were handed over in 1952. AVIDAC, *A*rgonnes *V*ersion of the *I*nstitute's *D*igital *A*utomatic *C*omputer and ORACLE, *O*ak *R*idge *A*utomatic *C*omputer and *L*ogical *E*ngine, were in operation by 1953. The Rand version was named for von Neumann, the JOHNNIAC.

Von Neumann had been eager to engage Eckert as his chief engineer but had failed to secure his services. Perhaps because of this, given the centrality of Eckert's idea of the mercury delay tubes for the store, the IAS team was eager to find another method for data storage. In the summer of 1947 the team was experimenting with a magnetic wire recording system which, in its physical design, relied heavily on bicycle wheels. But the possibility of an electrostatic solution was well understood from the beginning, which was why von Neumann had involved RCA in the Princeton project specifically to develop a cathode ray tube for memory purposes (Burkes *et al.* 1973: 375). The magnetic wire devices were a stop-gap while waiting for Jan Rajchman at the RCA lab to produce the Selectron, a digital, as opposed to the normal analogue, cathode ray tube. It took four years to bring this to the point of manufacture, during which time Williams had demonstrated how to use readily available ordinary CRTs. By January of 1950 a full-scale 'Williams Memory' was built into the IAS computer. ORDVAC and ILLIAC reconfigured the Williams tubes to provide for the random access of data. In the event only the JOHNNIAC used the RCA Selectrons. No others were ever sold (Rajchman 1980: 468).

CRTs, delay tubes and wire recording devices were not the only options; computer engineers were also well aware of the emergence, from the rubble of Nazi Germany, of recording tape. Indeed, the Dirks, Doctor G. and Engineer G., had registered a number of German patents for the use of magnetic tape in calculators as early as 1943 (Randell 1973: 186). Eckert's 'Disclosure' document of 1945 discussed magnetic recording techniques as one of a number of possible data stores and devoted time during this period to designing superior methods of accessing. Turing had examined a captured German Magnetophon audiotape machine before leaving Bletchley Park but, envisaging the extent to which the tape in 'On Computable Numbers' would have to move, he rejected it as a medium. Others, given the available tape movement mechanisms, agreed and avoided tape not just because its access time was slow but also because of its variable quality (Wilkes 1956: 185). 'We had the same problems with magnetic tape as everybody else. The tape had blemishes, bits of dust or other flaws that would push the tape away from the head as it went by and cause a dropout' (Everett 1980: 372). Nevertheless, ORACLE essayed a 2-inch magnetic tape system as a back-up to its 'Williams memory' (Chu 1980: 346).

The full-scale MADM used a variant on tape, a magnetic revolving drum store, as a back-up to its 'Williams memory'. Drums, introduced in 1947, were made of brass or bronze and either nickel plated or sprayed with iron oxide and, although still slow, were more accessible and reliable than linear tape. Eventually Jay Forrester of MIT — who was working on the most significant of these early machines, Whirlwind — would produce, in the final stages in co-operation with IBM, a core memory drum which by the mid-1960s became the industry standard. For Whirlwind's memory he first used a special magnetic material marketed as Deltamax and then ceramic ferrite which he made into a sort of chain-mail. He had one of his team, Kenneth Olsen, direct the building of a small computer to test this magnetic core memory system — the second abandoned baby computer. The core memory system was working in the main Whirlwind machine by the summer of 1953 (Augarten 1984: 201–2). (MANIAC also used a 10,000-word magnetic drum.)

Whirlwind had begun as an analogue real-time calculator to build a sort of flight simulator – an aeroplane stability analyser – for the Special Devices Centre of the Navy. It was to be a cockpit and a computer and it would 'fly like an airplane not yet built' (Everett 1980: 365). The computer part of the device went digital in 1945 when its designers, led by Forrester, became aware of ENIAC and the other planned digital machines; but it was otherwise quite different from the EDVAC and IAS design. By 1947, the year Forrester began developing the core memory, the design was ready. It was working about four years later – the first device to use a visual display system and (by 1953) the first to use the magnetic random access core memory drum system. Eventually it metamorphosed into the central control for the Cape Cod air defence system. This was the initial machine in the entire Semiautomatic Ground Environment (SAGE) Air Defence system (Robertson 1980: 377). Whirlwind in its developed form was the basis of an IBM series later in the 1950s and, although it was the biggest of the early machines, it was, in its overall architecture and design as well as in use, the closest of them to the present generation of mini and micro or personal computers.

Nineteen fifty-two was the last year of the computer's period of *invention,* the age of the incunabula, of one-off machines. In November the USA exploded an H-Bomb. In the UK the world's first two commercial computers were already in production. In January 1953 IBM was to ship its first production-line computer, based on the IAS design and designated the 701, to Los Alamos. More significant for the supposed revolution than these almost secret applications was Eckert and Mauchly's commercially produced UNIVAC, which had been used on television, with an enormous flurry of publicity, to predict the outcome of the 1952 presidential election. In the public mind, the computer age was in full swing. In fact, the better part of nine years had already passed since Clippinger and the ENIAC team had clearly articulated the stored program idea and there were as yet barely two dozen machines worldwide. The incunabula period closed off many options for a generation. The machines were all massive and unbelievably expensive, designed for extremely complex work at the heart of the cold war, each, as one of the IAS's builders remarked, 'an exceedingly complicated thing' (Wulforst 1982: 142). The need for secrecy alone meant nobody had any real interest in the possibilities of accessible, smaller and cheaper devices. The 'law' of the suppression of radical potential was already at work.

# 10

# SUPPRESSING THE MAIN FRAMES

## NO BUYERS

Outside the heart of the military-industrial complex, the operation of the 'law' of the suppression of radical potential was fuelled by three factors. The first was the indifference:

> Indeed, at this stage of the field's development most industrialists viewed computers mainly as tools for small numbers of university or government scientists, and the chief applications were thought to be highly scientific in nature. It was only later that the commercial implications of the computer began to be appreciated.
>
> (Robertson 1980: 377)

Von Neumann's decision to be in the business of science was therefore far sounder than the desire of Eckert and Mauchly to be in the business of business. Although UNIVAC, as their commercial version of EDVAC was called, worked at about the same time as its IAS computer, its developmental path was very much rockier. And even though UNIVAC was designed for commerce, it was actually as much a government device as any of the other incunabula machines.

Even as ENIAC was unveiled to a startled world, Eckert was finding life at the Moore School increasingly difficult. A new policy requiring that all patent rights be vested with the school was particularly galling. He was considering the von Neumann offer to go to Princeton but decided instead to throw in his lot with Mauchly. They resigned on 31 March 1946 to form the Electronic Control Company (ECC), and began to seek backers in the financial community. They were unsuccessful. Only the NBS and the Census Bureau responded at all positively but they were uncertain about passing the large sums of money necessary for computer development to a fledgling private firm. ECC had no procurement record so no government agency was willing to be the first to fund it. The most sustained commercial interest shown in their plans came from Bryan Field, a racetrack manager in Delaware, eager to dislodge American Totalisator which had a monopoly on pari-mutuel betting equipment. After reading of ENIAC in the *New York Times*, he presented himself to the tyro entrepreneurs as the one businessperson anxious to put at least racetrack affairs 'on a new footing'; but Eckert and Mauchly were unwilling to build the specialised machine Field needed and so this supervening necessity was left unfulfilled. This was despite the fact that Howard Aitken had advised them, somewhat mysteriously, that there was a lot of money to be made at racetracks (Wulforst 1982: 82–3).

At this point in 1946, the Moore School was about to hold its seminal summer course, von Neumann was staffing the Electronic Computer Project at the IAS and Turing's ACE had just been approved as a working scheme by the NPL. World-wide, three computers were funded and under way, and another – the Manchester Baby Mark I – was being put together without full-scale official sanction.

Apart from ECC, there was just one other commercial organisation in the US dedicated to computer work – Electronic Research Associates, founded by ex-naval cryptanalysts who had been attached to 'seesaw', i.e. CSAW, Communications Supplementary Activities, Washington – an American equivalent of Bletchley Park. ERA exploited its naval connection. Investment came from John Parker, owner of the Northwestern Aeronautical Corporation, who was desperate for projects to replace his wartime glider-making activities. Unlike ECC, ERA was not committed to building a general purpose computer, although a commission for such a device – Atlas (named for a comic strip character) – did come from the Navy in the summer of 1947. ERA's willingness to build specific bits of equipment, however, meant that this was to be its thirteenth job. By the time it was started, the firm had received more than $3 million from the Navy, still its only customer, and was employing over 400 people (Tomash 1980: 486). This growth was aided by the excellent procurement record of ERA's glider-making parent. (That this had little to do with electronics did not seem to matter.)

Eckert and Mauchly, with their more focused plans for a general purpose machine, failed to find an investor. There was a further problem: the NBS had sent the EEC general computer proposal to George Stibitz, Bell Labs' electro-mechanical calculator expert, for review. Stibitz knew all about ENIAC and was not impressed. As a Bell man he believed that switches (which Bell made and which he had put into complex calculators) were just as good as valves (which Bell did not make). He had written: 'I see no reason for supposing that [a Bell Labs machine] is less broad in scope than ENIAC. . . .I am very sure that the development time for the electronic equipment would be four to six times as long as that of relay equipment.' This last, while true, somewhat missed the point – similarly, circa 1810 say, the development time for an improved horse-drawn wagon was shorter than that for a new steam locomotive. Stibitz confirmed that as far as the Eckert-Mauchly proposal was concerned: 'There are so many things undecided that I do not think a contract should be let for the whole job' (Wulforst 1982: 96). The NBS also consulted Aitken, another switch-man, who told them: 'There will never be enough problems, enough work for more than one or two of these computers. . .stop this foolishness with Eckert and Mauchly' (Augarten 1984: 156). (Perhaps this is why Aitken told them to make their money at the racetrack.)

Thus armed with the best available opinion, the NBS did not let the contract for the entire computer, referred to as the EDVAC 2, although that is what Eckert and Mauchly needed. Instead they gave ECC a development grant of $75,000 to have models of the delay-line system built and, as we have seen, set about building a machine – SEAC – in-house. A dangerous pattern was being established. The money was insufficient to maintain the establishment necessary to do the work for which it was provided so further prospects had to be found; but these either distracted Mauchly or, in some ways even worse, came through in the same partial way, causing more work and more expense. The A.C. Nielsen company, a consumer research organisation now famous for its assessments of the broadcasting industry's audience, declined Mauchly's offer to build them a computer for $100,000. They questioned the fundamental value of the device and the basic financial stability of ECC; but they too provided partial funding, a monthly stipend to aid research. Mauchly also failed to convince the Prudential Insurance Company that they needed a full-scale machine although they did contract for a magnetic tape input device. Again, it was the cold war supervening necessity which finally intervened in the affairs of ECC to save it from disaster. In October 1947, two months after ERA had obtained its contract for Atlas, Northrop Aircraft Corporation contracted ECC, in return for $100,000, to build a specialised binary computer for its guided missile project (Wulforst 1982: 100,114).

Bankruptcy thus averted, the company now faced the major problem of overcoming the 'von Neumann Constant' and building, with dispatch, BINAC. Northrop, driven by this real supervening necessity, meant real business. It put its own man into ECC who immediately proposed that the company incorporate as a way of finding much-needed investors. In December 1947, Year Three of the computer 'revolution', the ECC gave way to the Eckert-Mauchly Computer Corporation. Henry Straus, the owner of American Totalisator, had not been unaware of his rival Bryan Field's approach to Eckert and Mauchly the previous year and was most interested in it. Investing in the Eckert-Mauchly Computer Corporation represented a sure bet on each horse in a two-horse race; either the company would fail, and a potential competitor would be removed, or else it would succeed and he would still be in a monopoly position in the betting industry, as well as making a further fortune from computers. He put in $400,000 and got 40 per cent of Eckert-Mauchly and seats on its board. Eckert and Mauchly could not avoid the track. These incidents in effect suppress the diffusion of the device because, by and large, industry, as in the 1930s, still failed to identify a supervening necessity for a large computer. (It is worth reflecting that the fad in UK government circles in the 1980s and 1990s to subject scientific research bids to rigours of business assessment would, if applied at this time, have almost totally prevented the development of any computers at all.)

BINAC, contracted to be completed by May 1948, was not actually delivered until September 1949; but, despite the thrice-extended deadlines, it did not suffer too badly from the von Neumann Constant. Eckert and Mauchly had built the world's sixth computer, specialised though it was. However, a $178,000 overspend had to be absorbed and other projects were seriously delayed. As we have seen, NBS had SEAC on-line even before BINAC was delivered. The bureau now began another machine on the West Coast. Nevertheless, with the Straus investment, Eckert and Mauchly were hopeful that the NBS computer, EDVAC II, could now be built. They renamed it UNIVAC (*Universal Automatic Computer*) as the Moore School had announced it was building the original EDVAC. UNIVAC was designed as a decimal machine to attract commercial interest, despite the market, such as it was, being governmental and scientific and preferring binary devices. Nevertheless, the *New York Times* was impressed, reporting that UNIVAC would be 'capable of making the Army's world famous ENIAC look like a dunce' (Wulforst 1982: 97).

The NBS was less so and contracted the Raytheon Corporation – a valve manufacturer which had become the US computer industry's third firm – to build a machine for the Air Force. The bureau was still waiting for this device and UNIVAC. Eckert-Mauchly was now focused on UNIVAC's development but, a month after BINAC was completed, Straus was killed in a light aircraft crash. Without him, the American Totalisator Company panicked and plunged the computer firm into a fresh round of uncertainty by seeking to bail out. The company once more veered towards bankruptcy. Bendix Aviation, International Telephone and Telegraph, Hazeltine Electronics, Westinghouse, Federal Telephone, Burroughs Adding Machine, Mergenthaler Linotype and Hughes Aircraft were added to the list of those corporations which saw no future in building computers and owning Eckert-Mauchly.

Remington Rand (RemRand) was an integrated office equipment company which had grown by absorbing a whole slough of specialised firms making things, anything, for the office. Among the firms RemRand had acquired long before was the Tabulating Company which Hollerith's rival Powers had established. James Rand, who had succeeded his father as RemRand's chief executive, was not only conditioned by this pattern of growth via acquisition; he was also virtually alone among American business people with interests in areas congruent to computing to show any awareness of the supposed new age. In 1946, he had established a small research laboratory and had secured the services of General Leslie Groves, late of Los Alamos, to run it. Rand teased American Totalisator but eventually bought them out in March 1950. So when, a year later, the first UNIVAC was at last delivered to the Census Bureau (having taken the better part of six years to build), it bore the name of IBM's great rival.

As with the Air Force rescue of Whirlwind, Rand's takeover of Eckert-Mauchly came at the same propitious moment, between the first Soviet A-Bomb test and the North Korean strike across the 38th parallel. The 'law' of suppression operating through commercial indifference was set aside by the supervening necessity of a hotting up cold war. RemRand rescued Eckert-Mauchley from the racetrack. The price was to place them firmly in the military sphere where its rivals, commercial, governmental and academic, had been all along. This had one other paradoxical effect on the firm's founders. The same cold war which secured a future for Mauchly's machines prevented the man himself from working on them. The month the first UNIVAC was shipped, he was denied clearance on the grounds that he had been a member of the American Association of Scientific Workers (a supposed red-front organisation); had signed a petition for the civilian control of nuclear power; and, even, that his wife had drowned while taking a midnight swim with him. He was not 'cleared' for six years (Augarten 1984: 289–94). At least, unlike Turing, he lived to tell the tale.

With four more government UNIVACs to build and another four orders on the books, Rand set about consolidating his position against his seemingly slumbering business opposition. ERA was still undercapitalised, although being closer to the heart of the military-industrial complex it had performed far better than Eckert-Mauchly. Nevertheless, 'under the frugal defence funding of the Truman administration before the Korean War', employment at ERA started to drop back from its 1948 high (Tomash 1980: 491). John Parker, the glider maker, was still the chief executive and he, like Mauchly and Eckert, began to look for a buyer. NCR refused (for a second time) as did Raytheon, Honeywell, Burroughs and IBM, but James Rand bought it, concentrating a fair percentage of America's computer talent under one corporate umbrella. Indeed, because security prevented Rand from making an assessment of ERA's potential, the sale price was arrived at by multiplying its 340 engineers by a factor of $5000. ERA's Atlas, the thirteenth task assigned it by the Navy, was put into commercial production as the 1101 (thirteen in binary notation). Machines were sold to the Office of Naval Research (which had almost killed off Whirlwind), the Civil Aeronautics Administration, various airforce bases and one to the John Plain Company of Chicago, the first to be used as an electronic inventory system in a commercial setting.

The apex of Rand's dominance was reached on the night of 4 November 1952 when UNIVAC was programmed to guess the result of the Stevenson/Eisenhower election. Walter Cronkite introduced it thus:

> It's going to predict the outcome of the election, hour by hour, based on returns at the same time periods on election nights in 1944 and 1948. Scientists, whom we used to call long hairs, have been working on correlating the facts for the past two or three months. . . .Actually, we're not depending too much on this machine. It may be just a sideshow . . .and then again it may turn out to be of great value to some people.
>
> (Wulforst 1982: 164)

It was probably best not to depend on the machine in the studio which, given the addiction of the fake that television is heir to, was only a mock-up. The deal that got the mock UNIVAC to CBS, and a real one at the other end of a line in Philadelphia, grew from a simple request by the television network to Remington for the free loan of around a hundred electric typewriters and adding machines which would, in the gently corrupting way these things are arranged, appear on camera during election night coverage; free commercial for free machines. Free computer for free commercial sounded even better. With only three million votes (7 per cent) counted, UNIVAC predicted an Eisenhower landslide, 438 electoral college votes to ninety-three for Stevenson. Nobody in Philadelphia believed it, so the programmers fixed the machine to give a more acceptable result. However, in the event, Eisenhower secured 442 votes to Stevenson's eighty-nine. When the night's story got out, Ed Murrow said, 'The trouble with machines is people' (Augarten 1984: 164). It was a brilliant publicity *coup*. One IBM senior computer executive recalled: 'The name UNIVAC appeared to be on its way to becoming the "Frigidaire" of the data processing industry' (Hurd 1980: 392).

The publicity contributed to public awareness, as had that for Harvard's 'robot brain' and the Army's ENIAC, and, slowly, more machines were being sold. Parker, now chief salesman for RemRand, placed UNIVACs in General Electric, US Steel, Metropolitan Life and Westinghouse (which had refused to buy Eckert-Mauchly a few years previously) – forty-six non-governmental sales in all (Augarten 1984: 164). But RemRand's dominance was not to last. Computers were a rental and maintenance affair, the tradition in the tabulating equipment industry, so the more Parker sold, the more capital Rand needed to stay in business. And RemRand now had a competitor, twice its size and more than three times as profitable. In the very month Parker went to New York to start selling computers, IBM shipped its first production model to Los Alamos.

As we have seen, IBM had spent the 1930s encouraging advanced calculation in the Academy. It had spent the war building an electro-mechanical device for Harvard and the Navy and in the aftermath of the war it had built for itself a hybrid, the SSEC, the world's first and last electro-mechanical (near?) computer. Significantly, computing, within IBM, came to be referred to as the 'magnetic-tape area', highlighting the crucial stored programme capability of the new machines. But the company had a long distance to travel before it could get itself into the business of 'magnetic-tape'.

IBM remained well aware of computing science (as evidenced by the SSEC's measure of stored program capacity), yet it still failed to connect these activities to the mainstream of its business. The SSEC, at $300 an hour, was booked up a solid six months in advance, mainly by the armed forces, throughout the late 1940s – but this made no difference (Rodgers 1969: 177). It served only to reinforce the belief of Watson and IBM that complex calculators had more to do with government and the Academy than the world of commerce. This attitude was also in evidence when IBM lashed up an advanced calculator for Northrop's guided missile programme over six weeks in 1948. The original Card-Programmed Electronic Calculator (CPC) used standard IBM machines – a type 603 calculating punch, no longer in production, in connection with a 405 alphabetical accounting machine. In the summer of 1949 a revised CPC was marketed with an electro-mechanical store capable of sixteen ten-digit words.

> Tracking a guided missile on a test range now is the only way to make sure of its performance. At one Department of Defence facility this is done by planting batteries of cameras or phototheodolites along a 100 mile course. During its flight, the missile position is recorded by each camera at 100 frames per second, together with the camera training angles. Formerly these thousands of pictures from each of many cameras were turned over to a crew of [human] computers, to determine just what happened. It took two weeks to make calculations for a single flight. Now this is done on the International Business Machines Card-Programmed Electronic Calculator in about eight hours and the tests can proceed.
>
> (Sheldon and Tatum 1951: 229)

By 1952, IBM had installed 250 CPCs, in universities, defence establishments (for neutron shielding calculation, jet engine thermodynamics, helicopter vibration analysis) and, in civilian life, for such purposes as utility billings, all at $1500 a month rental. At Northrop an engineer named Reiss 'developed a technique for using the CPC to program some of its own operations' – which is to say, he pushed it from calculator towards computer (Sheldon and Tatum 1951: 253). Still the decision to build a computer was not taken.

IBM did not, despite Watson's PR efforts in the 1930s (or perhaps because of them), look to the academy for talent. It was essentially a company wedded to its late nineteenth-century technology, as refined, which continued to be enormously profitable. Before the war, it was not remotely a high tech operation, as were, say, RCA and AT&T. It had never been technologically threatened and so it had made no real investment in research and development or even in science graduates. Watson, whatever else he was, was one of the century's great salesmen. He, and the company he built, tended to allow the market to establish needs and then ask the engineers to meet those needs as quickly and as cheaply as possible, using as many interchangeable parts as could be accommodated. The resultant patents were as often as not jointly filed by Watson and the engineer (Rodgers 1969: 174).

Given general commercial indifference to computing, it was just this sophistic-ated responsiveness to the market that held IBM back. IBM machines rented for hundreds of dollars a month but, because of the company's pricing policy, a computer along EDVAC lines would have to cost thousands. Although the CPC fetched $1500 a month or more, received opinion within the company was that the market would not stand for EDVAC, a view confirmed by the shaky progress of the firms in the fledgling business. Watson had decreed: 'No reasonable interaction possible between Eckert-Mauchly and IBM' (Rodgers 1969: 199). It was only when the Census Bureau ordered its third RemRand UNIVAC that IBM saw the light. According to one IBM man the whole episode 'frightened. . .the old man, who was convinced he had lost his grip' (ibid.). 'We went into an absolute panic', said Thomas Watson Jr, the executive chosen by his father to meet the threat. 'Here was our traditional competitor, whom we had always been able to handle quite well, and now, before we knew it, it had five of these beasts installed and we had none' (Wulforst 1982: 173).

Not for the last time in its history as a computer manufacturer, IBM began to play catch-up. Internally, PR work for large computers was being done. The success of the CPC was played down, although it was possible to see the future in terms of cheaper (and more fully programmable) CPCs rather than larger, more expensive devices. Most importantly, the Pentagon was visited and a positive response obtained. It must be remembered that Watson had offered the services of the company to Harry Truman in the defence effort occasioned by the Korean War, although his eagerness to help the American government did not extend to allowing IBM apparatus to be attached to other people's equipment – the IAS team was so prevented (Bigelow 1980: 307). By Christmas 1950, Year Six of the 'revolution', Watson Jr called the meeting at which these various strands came together and the decision to build a 'defence calculator' along IAS lines was finally taken.

In January 1951, the engineering calculation that the proposed machine ought to cost $5500 a month was 'rounded off' to $8000 by the financial vice-president. In 1952, von Neumann was contracted to IBM as a consultant for thirty days a year – and the IAS team was allowed to use IBM card handlers. The fully tested specifications of the defence calculator were released to production. In March 1952, the machine, now designated the 701, was demonstrated for the first time, without its drum memory. A month later, at a dedication addressed by the Watsons, Sr and Jr, and by Oppenheimer, the demonstration problem was of neutron scattering, prepared by Los Alamos but of a suitably unclassified nature for such a public occasion. In May the price went up to a maximum $17,600 per month, but nevertheless, seventeen 701s were leased in the years 1953/4, the vast majority by US military agencies and the aircraft industry.

The 701 represents, even more than do the other commercial machines (UNIVAC, ERA's 1101 as well as such British products as the Ferranti Mark I, the English Electric Deuce, HEC, etc.) the end of the incunabula period. The 701 was of modular design in that this designation properly belongs only to the Electronic Analytic Control Unit. The memory, along Williams lines with seventy-two CRTs, was named a 706 Electrostatic Storage Unit; 731 was the Magnetic Drum Reader and Recorder, Power Supply and Distribution Box; and so on. 'It was already intended that there would be a series of improved machines not only in the type 701 central processor itself but in the memory and the peripherals' (Hurd 1980: 392).

The MIT connection was of great importance to IBM. Whirlwind was the first real-time computer, the first with magnetic core memory, the first to multi-process, the first to network, the first to have interactive monitors. IBM was building Whirlwinds for SAGE and acquiring a great deal of expertise. In 1954 it began, for instance, a ten-year development process that eventually provided American Airlines with a cut-down real-time computer for airline reservations (Augarten 1984: 209–10). This flurry of activity continued until, simply, the competition was outrun and IBM was left dominating the field. RemRand, anyway late with UNIVAC II, could not match the capital IBM had available for the building and placement of large numbers of machines. But IBM's success throughout the 1950s was still heavily reliant on the defence needs of America. The computer industry was now a reality, but, despite a trickle of commercial interest, its supervening necessity was still the cold war.

Once again, the British experience proves the point. In Britain the lack of a large defence market curtailed commercial development. Contrast with IBM the experience of Ferranti's who managed to sell nine Mark 1s (based on the Manchester University machine) between 1951 and 1957. Only one went to a weapons establishment, Aldermaston, the only such institution in Britain. Two went to the aero industry and the Ministry of Supply took two – of which one went discreetly to GCHQ, the successor to GC&CS, where Turing had continued as an adviser. Two more went to academic institutions, one in Rome and one, in the University of Toronto, to help design the St Lawrence Seaway; and one went to an industrial lab, Royal Dutch Shell's in Amsterdam (Hodges 1983: 438). Even starker was the fate of the most purely commercial device to emerge in this early period.

The British catering company J. Lyons, which saw the potential of computing for stock and payroll tasks, pioneered such applications by building for itself a commercial machine derived from EDSAC, the Leo, or *Lyons Electric Office*. Under Lyons executive Raymond Thompson, a subsidiary company was formed and the first Leo II, which had mercury delay lines, drums and tape decks, was shipped in 1957. A mere thirteen were sold. By 1960, the British computer industry had sold only 300 machines in toto and was an estimated five years behind the Americans. The Leo III was introduced in 1962 and, eventually, 100 were placed – less than the number of IBM 650s shipped in that model's first year of availability. As a company, Lyons remained the exception that proved the rule. Most businesspeople could not see the point of such expensive devices and the British military was in no position to fill the demand gap this created. Instead of the lavish support which American strategic necessities produced, Thompson's unpublished *Leo Chronicle* gives a vivid indication of the scale of British needs: 'October 1951: Brigadier Hines writes to offer us £300 for carrying out some ballistic computations for the Ministry of Supply' (Lavington 1980: 72). The performance of machines such as the Leo III was not enough to push the industry forward and a pattern of consolidation emerged. English Electric took over Leo Computers in 1963 and then English Electric Leo became English Electric Leo Marconi which absorbed Elliot Automation, only to eventually become ICL (Lavington 1980: 68–77). This was not consolidation arising from strength but contraction growing out of weakness.

This failure cannot be attributed to the quality of British personnel because many wartime computing experts continued to hold commanding positions. For example, not untypical was W. Gordon Welchman, late of Bletchley Park. He worked on Whirlwind and offered the world's first university digital computing course at MIT before returning to Ferranti's (Randell 1973: 57). Ferranti's still tried to compete with the Americans into the first period of the diffusion of these large machines. It built, for instance, a British Atlas to challenge IBM's 7030 (Stretch) in the early 1960s. But in Britain, apart from the scientists and a small progressive minority of industrialists, the new electronic machines were treated with suspicion and the government, as the cold war stabilised, was either ignorant of or indifferent to their other implications (Handel 1967: 147).

I want to suggest that, in some sense, the British responded correctly by ignoring machines not appropriate to their new reduced post-war position in the world. Perhaps because of this fundamental, if unacknowledged, truth Harold Wilson's attempt to revive computer pre-eminence by fiat in 1965 struck a somewhat comic chord, and the rhetoric of the 'white heat of technology' drew forth little significant response except the continued collapsing consolidation of the computing industry in the UK. But this is to run ahead.

Between its ideation in 1944 and the mid-1950s, the computer had increased enormously in capacity and speed and had become a regularly produced industrial item – but it was barely diffused much beyond the government, attendant client-firms of the military, limited parts of the Academy and only the very largest and most far-sighted of civilian businesses. The media-fed confusion as to its supposedly innate capacities, coupled with its actual increasing scope, produced the fertile soil in which the idea of a 'revolution' was planted. But the increasing scope, although impressive, involved no breakthrough to new technological areas – any more than the machine itself had done; and it was achieved against a faltering sense of demand, at least outside of the needs created by the supervening necessity of the cold war. This is not to demean the computer's significance, for the market it created was no small thing and companies within the business, especially IBM, grew vigorously. Yet, despite these successes and the endless background hype, the result was that, in failing to make its case to the world at large, the computer's announced capacity for radical change was effectively contained by the comparative uninterest of business. By 1955, Year Eleven of the 'revolution', there were still just 250 computers in the world.

This argument is strongly sustained by the historical record but a question is raised: could the machines have been less complicated, cheaper, more accessible than in fact they were, earlier than they were? Did the machines need to be so inaccessible, so 'user-unfriendly'? My contention is that they could indeed have been and that the failure to produce such devices demonstrates how the 'law' of suppression applies to computing.

## NO LANGUAGES

Take accessibility. By 1953 it was possible to state:

> The difficulty of programming has become the main difficulty in the use of machines. Aitken has expressed the opinion that the solution of this difficulty may be sought by building a coding machine. . . .However it has been remarked that there is no need to build a special machine for coding, since the computer itself, being general purpose, should be used.
> (Knuth and Pardo 1980: 228)

The debate about programming in the early 1950s speaks to a crucial constraint in computing development. Specifically the slow emergence of programming languages was definitely an obstacle, and an unnecessary one, to the diffusion of computers. The debate begun in these years still echoes in contemporary design philosophies which continue to favour the machine rather than its user and which therefore constitute a constant element in suppressing the device's radical potential.

In its first appearance, the argument was between those who favoured using some of the expanding capacity of the machines to produce decimal numeration and others, the purists, who felt that, if one could not read binary rows of noughts and ones, one should get out of computing. Of course, this latter group was engaged in the time-honoured pursuit of protecting its mysterium, the secrets of its guild.

> This feeling is noted in an article in the 1954 ONR (Office of Naval Research) symposium: 'Many "professional" machine users strongly opposed the use of decimal numbers. . .to this group, the process of machine instruction was one that could not be turned over to the uninitiated'. This attitude cooled the impetus for sophisticated programming aids. The priesthood wanted and got simple mechanical aids for the clerical drudgery which burdened them, but they regarded with hostility and derision more ambitious plans to make programming accessible to larger populations. . . . Thus they were unalterably opposed to those mad revolutionaries who wanted to make programming so easy that anyone could do it.
>
> (Backus 1980: 128)

Were the mad revolutionaries possessed of anything more than dreams? Indeed they were and had been for some years. The German electro-mechanical calculator engineer, Konrad Zuse, was contracted after the war by IBM and eventually set up in business in West Germany by Rand; but, during his enforced idleness on the top of the mountain at war's end, unable to work in the metal, he could only think. What he thought of was the *Plankalkul,* the program calculus, the first high-level computer programming language. It antedates the first electronic computer by three years.

> Before laying this project aside, Zuse had completed an extensive manuscript containing programs far more complex than anything written before. Among other things there were algorithms for sorting; for testing the connectivity of a graph represented as a list of edges; for integer arithmetic (including square roots) in binary notation; and for floating-point arithmetic. . . .To top things off, he also included forty-nine pages of algorithms for playing chess.
>
> (Knuth and Pardo 1980: 203)

The high-level language is the key to the computer. As Zuse wrote: 'The first principle of the *Plankalkul* is: data processing begins with the bit. . . .Any arbitrary structure may be described in terms of bit strings; and by introducing the idea of levels we can have a systematic code for any structure, however complicated' (Zuse 1980: 621).

Zuse's scheme was scarcely known, even in the German-speaking world, and others developed the concept of the programme language without reference to him. But his is the first annunciation of an idea which was as necessary to the computer's diffusion as was von Neumann's 'First Report' to its *invention*. That it was done so early is evidence that the programming bottleneck of the mid-1950s was artificial. Collectively the fledgling industry was not really interested in discovering how to sell as many computers as possible and devoted almost no attention to programming as a result. The programmers presented themselves as an integral part of the 'exceedingly complicated thing' that was a computer. For many – the majority – engaged in security tasks, the very incomprehensible nature of computer operations was a distinct advantage. Nicholas Metropolis and his Los Alamos colleagues could run highly classified problems in virtually open circumstances on every computer in the country as it came on stream. The continuing interface of computing and the cold war encouraged the persistence of the mysterium.

Of course, in the incunabula period few if any general languages could be written because each machine was different; but the incunabula period was prolonged by the lack of commercial opportunity for computers, in part a function of the lack of languages. Nevertheless, the unread Zuse apart, some progress was made. Wilkes had developed 'assembly routines' to combine numbers of sub-routines and one of Turing's last acts as a computer scientist was to produce for the Ferranti machines a manual explaining how programs were to be written (Hodges 1983: 437). There were early attempts at 'compilers', although none was so broad in scope as Zuse's. Mauchly suggested a Short Code which was implemented in the design of the first BINAC but it was not apparently popular with UNIVAC users (Knuth and Pardo 1980: 215). Arthur Burks, a member of the original IAS team who had moved to the University of Michigan, explored the possibilities of going from 'ordinary business English' descriptions of a computational problem to the 'internal program language' description of a machine-language programme appropriate to that problem. However, the result was still too complex in its symbolism for general business use. For the Manchester MADM, which was distinguished by a 'particularly abstruse' machine language, Alick Glennie, of the Royal Armaments Research Establishment, developed the Autocode. Glennie was working on the British bomb and his language was designed for highly skilled professional users, which is to say it was still very much machine oriented but nevertheless it was 'an important step forward' (ibid.: 228–31).

Most significant of these efforts was that of J. Halcolme Laning Jr of MIT who, with Niel Zierler, after two years' work, ran an Algebraic Compiler on Whirlwind in 1954: 'The system is mechanised by a compilation of closed subroutines entered from blocks of words, each block representing one equation. The sequence of equations is stored on the drum, and each is called in separately every time it is used. The compiled routine is then performed interpretively' (Backus 1980: 129). It used instructions like 'Stop' and 'Print' but it slowed Whirlwind down tenfold. Yet each new computer was so much faster than its predecessor that, even in the short term, this was no real obstacle to the development of programme languages. Moreover, the slowdown, in commercial settings, would still leave the machines infinitely faster than any mechanical, electro-mechanical or human alternative. The real problem continued to be objections from programmers. Programming was a skill just born and already seemingly threatened.

It is an unremarked irony that the first to fear computerised automation were among those whose very work had been necessitated by the computer.

> At that time most programmers wrote symbolic machine instructions exclusively (some even used absolute octal or decimal machine instructions). Almost to a man [sic], they firmly believed that any mechanical coding method would fail to apply that versatile ingenuity which each programmer felt he [sic] possessed and constantly needed in his [sic] work.
>
> (Knuth and Pardo 1980: 241)

Yet this obstructionist tendency was not universal.

Among the most senior of programmers was Grace Hopper, a Vassar mathematics professor who had been on Aitken's naval Harvard Mark I team and who was a strong believer in automatic programming. She was working for RemRand in 1951 when she developed an 'automatic programming' system, a compiler, for UNIVAC which went well beyond Mauchly's Short code (Augarten 1984: 214). As a member of the naval reserve – she was to achieve the rank of captain in 1973 and eventually become an admiral – she set up a critical ONR conference at which, for example, Laning and Zierler unveiled their work. John Backus, then assembling a group within IBM to explore the issue, had gone to this conference with a paper which queried 'Whether such an elaborate automatic programming system is possible or feasible has yet to be determined'. He came away knowing that it was and, after visiting MIT, set about developing what would become FORTRAN I (*Formula Translating* System) against an IBM background where 'our plans and efforts were regarded with a mixture of indifference and scorn' (Backus

1980: 131). Although the most significant, this was not the only result of Professor Hopper's initiative. Boeing developed BACAIC for the 701 and other algebraic compilers appeared.

IBM (as usual, scarcely the innovators) were by now convinced by Backus. He was confident enough to suggest that 'each future IBM calculator should have a system similar to FORTRAN accompanying it' (Knuth and Pardo 1980: 241). It was claimed that, instead of days of hands-on experience, an average programmer after one hour spent learning FORTRAN could understand a programme written in it without further help. It was still to be some years, till the spring of 1957, before the system finally worked though. And even then there was residual resistance. In 1958, a survey of IBM users revealed that only half the time did half of the users take advantage of the language.

It was therefore more than a decade after the Baby Mark I and EDSAC and fifteen years after the *Plankalkul* that the principle of compiling instructions into languages to ease programme writing came into general use and with it perhaps the most essential tool necessary to the wider diffusion of the computer. A computer that used everyday icons as the basis of its instruction mode would not appear – again to the derision of the serious computing enthusiast – until the early 1980s.

Computer history has its share of straightforwardly hostile obstructionists, this first generation of programmers among them. But what must be stressed is that they were in thrall to something other and greater than what is commonly, and most erroneously, called Ludditism (Thompson 1968: 600). The programmers are scarcely believable as representatives of the innate conservatism which supposedly governs all human response to change. They were at the innovative cutting edge of a civilisation which, for over four centuries, has anyway in every aspect rebutted this putative natural obstinacy. Innovations, properly grounded in supervening necessities, are not thwarted by threatened workforces. Workforces in such circumstances are always shaken out, for King Lud's writ seems never to run very far. This group's protection of their jobs succeeded for a number of years because the failure of commercial vision within and without the computer industry inevitably aided and supported them. To the indifference of commerce must therefore be added the failure of language-creation as the second element constraining the computer's diffusion.

## NO BABIES

Both of these elements contributed to the design philosophy, conditioned by wartime approaches, which stressed ever larger and more expensive machines. The military-industrial complex which was the prime market for these devices fed upon advanced technologies of the very largest scale. Thus neither buyers nor sellers of computers had much interest in breaking the circle that had been created. The question remains, though: Were smaller devices possible during this period?

We have already seen how the ABC was transformed into ENIAC and the Baby Mark I became MADM. Further, although the suggestion to build the smallest possible version of Turing's ACE was taken up by English Electric and marketed as the Deuce, even this scale of machine did not prevail. The suggestion that the IBM CPC be made programmable was ignored within the company in favour of other developments such as the 701 giant. The computer lobby within IBM was also looking to replace the CPC with what was called a medium size computer, eventually designated the 650. Following the management's reluctant agreement to the 701, there was further strong internal opposition to this plan as well. The first 650 with an external magnetic drum store was installed in December 1954 and was rented for a cost of between $3000 and $4000 a month. Within a year 120 were placed and by the time the model was phased out fifteen years later,

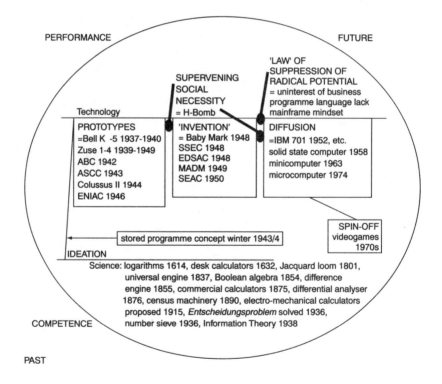

*Figure 12* Computing

1500 had been used (Augarten 1984: 209–10). But the success of the 650, like that of the CPC before it, as well as the existence of Deuce, still did not push IBM or the computer industry in general in the direction of these smaller midsize machines.

Instead IBM built a succession of ever larger computers. A more commercial version of the 701 had been developed in 1953 as the 702, although of the first fourteen of these, four went into the military-industrial complex just the same. However, one was sold to the Bank of America and one to the Prudential. The 704 was announced in 1954 and, since one went to France and another to the British Atomic Research Establishment at Aldermaston, it was with this model that IBM became a multinational computer manufacturer. About one hundred 704s and its successor 705s were placed and into the 1960s the machines just got bigger and bigger. By the time Ferranti produced Atlas, its IBM competitor was a 400,000 instructions-per-second machine designated as the 7030 but, significantly, known as Stretch.

In all this, the potential of the very small experimental devices, the Baby Mark 1 and the machine which was used to test Forrester's magnetic core memory system, remained unexplored.

# 1 1

# THE INTEGRATED CIRCUIT

## SUPPRESSION (CONT.): IGNORING SOLID STATE
## ELECTRONICS

From the beginning of the computer age, there is no question that smaller machines were not built and could have been. But, given available valve technology, of what use could they have been? And, second, were the solid state electronics, essential to the contemporary personal computer, simply not available; indeed, not yet 'invented'?

As to the first of these questions, differently configured supervening necessities – the electronic office and the non-nuclear science lab rather than the cold war – could have produced applications for which developments of the Baby Mark I, for example, would have been perfectly viable. But, more than that, a different research agenda would have yielded solid state devices earlier. My contention that the 'law' of the suppression of radical potential operates in computer history depends finally on denying the supposed 'synergy' of the technologies of computing and solid state electronics, and the idea that the micro-computer had to wait for the microelectronics to come on stream.

Transistors, it must not be forgotten, were 'invented' late in 1947, so every machine we have so far discussed came on stream in the semiconductor age; yet, contrary to received opinion, transistors did not become the norm in computers. In fact, the failure to exploit solid state electronics constitutes a fourth element, apart from indifference, language provision and size, in the operation of the 'law' as it applies to the computer. Received opinion of the relationship between microelectronics and computers simply ignores this:

> It all began with the development thirty years ago of the transistor: a small, low-power amplifier that replaced the large power-hungry vacuum tube. The advent almost simultaneously of the stored program digital computer provided a large potential market for the transistor. The

synergy between a new component and a new application generated an explosive growth in both.

(Noyce 1977: 30)

Thus Robert Noyce, one of the fathers of the integrated circuit and a founder both of Fairchild Semiconductor and Intel – a man who should know (but doesn't).

The received history is that computers ate transistors ravenously. The historical truth is – and herein lies the proof of this fourth element of constraint – that they did no such thing. The transistor was not crucial to the development and growth of the computer. IBM, for example, never marketed a commercially successful fully transistorised computer, and valve-based machines were still being shipped to customers a decade after the transistor was commercially available. The two industries did not come together in a synergetic way until the 1970s.

Indeed, it will be my argument that the transistor was not, of itself, a significant 'invention' at all but rather the signpost to one – the microprocessor. It took twenty-one years to get from the transistor to the microprocessor; twenty-one years in which the computer industry played very little part, except towards the end, and was certainly not a major consumer of solid state devices. To make this case, we must now digress and deal with the entire history and development of the microprocessor.

## SCIENTIFIC COMPETENCE: CAT'S WHISKERS TO TRANSISTOR

The transistor, even more than television or the computer, seems to have burst upon society unannounced. It is without infancy, without past history, born fully formed in Bell Labs on 23 December 1947. The internal Bell 'Memorandum For Record' dated 27 December 1949 commences:

The history of the transistor begins with the decision to study intensively the properties of silicon and germanium. This decision was made in 1946 as a result of series of conferences intended to establish a plan for semiconductor research.

(Millman 1983: 97)

But this is untrue. Collectively, Bell Labs seem unable to remember that this line of work started at least a decade earlier, as I shall detail below. The point is that the impression of instantaneity is created at the cost of an amnesia profounder than that affecting our memories of the development of the other technologies examined in this book. The transistor had not been publicly promised for decades as was television; nor had it been celebrated by the media as was each new 'robot brain'. The world was unprepared for it and, anyway, it was promoted only as an electrical amplifier, a curious sort of valve – not a device to set hearts racing.

The history of the transistor illustrates a basic way in which media and their technologies become misunderstood. Simply, the device's antecedents have been struck, as it were, from the public record. Yet not only did it have antecedents, but an application of the same species of electrical phenomena was among the most widely diffused of all such innovations in the early part of the twentieth century; for at the heart of the cat's whiskers crystal radio was a solid state device, of the same genus as the transistor (Figure 13).

Crystal detectors, all relying on the semiconductivity of various metals, were a staple of early wireless telephony and subsequently of radio enthusiasts eager to build their own receivers. Semiconductors, as the history of selenium reveals, were understood in the nineteenth century as being substances whose conductivity varies according to either thermal (Faraday's 1833 experiment with silver sulphide) or light conditions (Willoughby Smith's experiment with selenium previously described) (p. 89).

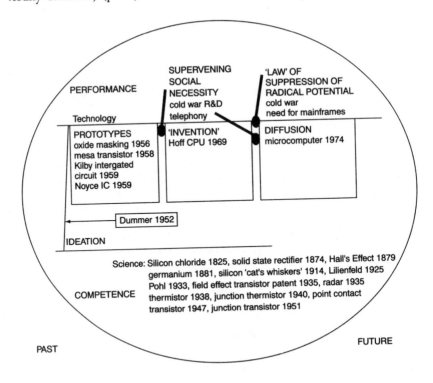

*Figure 13* Solid state devices

The scientific competence for the transistor and its successor devices thus accumulated over a similar time span to that of the other technologies here described. Among the most important developments was the demonstration in 1879 of what came to be called the Hall effect. This showed that, when a wire carrying electricity is placed in a magnetic field, a further electromotive force is produced. The possibilities of using the Hall effect for amplification were first outlined in a series of patents by the physicist Julius Lilienfeld in 1925. Lilienfeld's proposal was for a quite complex sandwich of semiconductor and conductor layers which, whether it would have worked or not, is nevertheless in vague terms the ideation transformation for the transistor.

At Gottingen during this same decade, R.W. Pohl was making a study of the photoelectric properties of solids in the course of which he elaborated a picture of the behaviour of the electrons within crystals. In 1933, supporting Lilienfeld's line of investigation, he suggested that vacuum tubes in radios would give way to small crystals wherein the movement of the electrons could be controlled (Braun and MacDonald 1982: 17).[1] In 1935, another solution to the problem, a field-effect solid state amplifier was patented and actually built but, although an elegant exploitation of the Hall effect, it refused to work. Anyway, in a world of valves, there was no supervening necessity for such amplifiers and semi-conductivity for other purposes was already being used effectively.

As we have seen, proto-solid-state devices were widely diffused as primitive radio receivers – cat's whiskers or crystal radios. Many used sand or silicon as the basis of the detector and this fact was to condition the entire development of solid state electronics well into the last quarter of the century. But also of importance to this line development is the metal germanium, the existence of which had been predicted in 1871 and discovered in 1886. Although rare in nature, it can be obtained by smelting certain zinc ores.

There is a supposed hiatus in the use of solid state devices between the coming of the valve in the years before the First World War and further developments in semiconductors in the late 1930s but the gap is more apparent than real. Crystals had barely disappeared from every scientifically inclined child's repertoire of radio tricks and experiments in the 1930s, only to reappear immediately in the thinking, experiments and devices of physicists and electricians (many of them with a Cat's Whisker radio in their background). Valves, although a staple device, were none the less bulky, comparatively unreliable and generated much heat – all of which made Pohl's opinion as to the viability of crystals most attractive – and needs were being generated, supervening necessities, for applications beyond the capacities of valves.

In telephone exchanges, for instance, great gains would obviously be made if unreliable valves and physical switching systems could be replaced. Steps were being taken in this direction with the development of 'crossbar' central switching equipment. T.H. Flowers, the man who built Colossus for Bletchley Park, had a pre-war interest in solid state telephone switching and managers at Bell Labs also believed that the all-electronic exchange was worth pursuing. The labs were already investigating silicon, but as a detector of short-wave signals. By the end of the decade this interest was important enough to justify a team of chemists being given the task of producing purified silicon. William Shockley began his career at Bell Labs in 1936 in the valve (tube) department working on the electronic exchange problem.

He then involved William Brattain, who had been experimenting with copper-oxide rectifiers. These, which were being manufactured commercially, were used in electrical apparatus where diode valves would neither work nor fit, primarily in situations with low currents and/or tight spaces. Brattain and Shockley began to explore copper oxides, but Brattain was clear that this was somewhat unoriginal: 'Anybody in the art was aware of the analogy between a copper oxide rectifier and a diode vacuum tube and many people had the idea of how do we put in a grid, a third electrode, to make an amplifier' (Braun and MacDonald 1982: 37). Pohl had by this time created a partial prototype for the transistor by demonstrating how a crystal of potassium bromide could be made to imitate the action of a valve and amplify a current. The paper on this was published in 1938, but since the crystal had to be heated to obtain this effect, the point was rather lost. Such devices would eventually be called thermistors. By the eve of the Second World War, Shockley and Brattain had determined that semiconductors, about which in general little was understood, might indeed yield a device which would amplify electrical signals without generating heat; but after only two months, with results still rather poor, they stopped, diverted by the impending war to work on underwater radar for submarine detection (Brooks 1976: 203). All of this is ignored in the 1949 'Memorandum For Record' .

The war halted Bell Labs' interest in semiconductor amplifiers but in other ways it speeded progress in the area. Fessenden, the radio pioneer, had used waves for depth sounding in 1904 and scientists in the mid-1920s determined the height of the ionosphere with reflected radio signals. The similar reflection of radio waves from aircraft had been observed in 1931 and three years later the British began to develop a serious interest in the possibility of using this for detection. By 1935, Robert Watson-Watt, superintendent of the Radio Division of the NPL, was working on a practical system. Five RADAR (*Radio Detection and Ranging*) stations were built (Dummer 1983: 94). To detect very high frequency signals used in radar, though, requires low capacitance in the receiver, lower than that provided by vacuum tubes. In 1939 the Magnetron, an unconventional triode which was five times as powerful as a valve and reached frequencies four times as high, was produced at Birmingham University. It was the basis of airborne radar equipment. Cat's whisker detectors were also used and refined, eventually being of tungsten and silicon.

The importance of semiconductors in microwave applications generated a most extensive research blitz to uncover their secrets. The general need to improve radar, the rarity of germanium and the comparative ineffectiveness of common silicon (when compared to germanium) all contributed to the supervening necessity of this work. These metals were used and investigated heavily because they were known to work – there was no time to worry about whether or not others might be more effective.[2] Improving silicon was the focus of the research and, at the behest of the US government, as many as forty American laboratories were organised by MIT to do it. One lab was at Purdue and it was here discovered that semiconductivity does not depend, as had been thought possible, upon impurities in the materials.

Much had been learned, but there were a number of unexplained phenomena. For instance, in 1940 R.S. Ohl, another worker at the Bell Lab had shown Brattain a silicon slice doctored so that a particularly sharp boundary existed between *n*-type silicon (where the majority of electron carriers are negative) and *p*-type (where they are positive). A light shone at this junction produced an unexpected flow of electricity. Ohl went on to build an unreliable semiconductor amplifier – a thermistor, like Pohl's of 1938 – which he used to power a radio (Shockley 1976: 604).

After the war, two Purdue graduate students, Seymour Benzer and Ralph Bray, continued to investigate the spreading resistance resulting when a point contact wire was placed on germanium. The resistance measured was lower than theory predicted. They publicised their results at a meeting early in 1948 when Brattain was in the audience. He spoke with Bray after his paper.

> Bray finally said, 'You know, I think if we would put down another point on the germanium surface and measure the potential around this point, that we might find out what was going on.' And I couldn't resist saying, 'Yes Bray, I think that would be probably a good experiment.
>
> As Bray said later, 'What's perfectly clear is that if I had put my electrode close to Benzer's electrode . . .we would have gotten transistor action'.
>
> (Braun and MacDonald 1982: 38–9)

This was, in fact, the experiment that Brattain himself had done the previous November, the experiment that for the first time demonstrated the transistor (*trans*fer of electricity across a re*sistor*) effect. It was still a Bell secret at this time. As has been said, 'The amazing thing . . . is why Purdue didn't invent the transistor' (Braun and MacDonald 1982: 39).

One difference, a crucial one it is claimed, between Bell and Purdue was John Bardeen, a senior theoretical physicist who had joined the reconstituted semiconductor group in the summer of 1945. Shockley had returned the group to the investigation of copper-oxide-based field-effect amplifiers despite the poor results obtained before the war. The months went by. Then Bardeen, on 19 March 1946, committed to his notebook [3] a theory to account for the failure of Shockley's field-effect experiments. The problem, he hypothesised, was that electrons were being trapped on the surface of the semiconductors. The experiments were not working because they depended upon the electrons moving as freely on the surface as they did with the body of the substance. But, in reality, this was not what was happening. The attempt to build an amplifier was abandoned for the time being so that surface states could be investigated.

Shockley's analysis of the group's notebooks reveals that it was thirteen months before the next significant step occurred, an insight into the nature of electron and hole densities. (Holes are unfilled vacancies or absences in a valence band – a band of energies in a solid wherein electrons are fixed to atoms and cannot move freely.) The summer and autumn of 1947 passed. Finally, on 17 November 1947, at the suggestion of a chemist on the team, Robert Gibney, Brattain applied voltage to the semiconductor while it was immersed in an electrolyte. A strong field-effect was created, for Brattain had liberated the trapped surface electrons with the help of Gibney's electrolyte. The best substance to facilitate the effect was found to be 'Gu', which was extracted from old batteries, 'electrolyte capacitors by using a vice, a hammer and a nail' (Shockley 1976: 609). (Scientifically, 'Gu' is glycol borate.)

A new series of experiments started. With some difficulty, the electrodes were placed close to each other on the germanium surface and it was found that a small positive charge to one greatly increased its capacity to carry current. Bardeen hypothesised that by even more closely spacing the two electrodes an amplifying effect could be achieved. Brattain – who said he had 'an intuitive feel for what you could do in semiconductors, not a theoretical understanding' – began to mess about with the crystal, the wires and the 'Gu'. On 16 December he found that two wires two-thousandths of an inch apart produced a fortyfold amplification – the transistor effect. On 23 December the team demonstrated the effect to some Bell Lab colleagues and early in the new year, they learned how close the Purdue investigators were getting to duplicating the effect. For the very first internal demonstration of the transistor to AT&T executives, '[t]o emphasise the Transistor's possible-role in radio reception', the Lab showed 'a popular make of portable receiver whose vacuum tubes had been entirely replaced by Transistors. Reception was excellent' (Braun and MacDonald 1982: 196).

In July 1948, Bell unveiled what was described in the rather low-key press release as 'a device called the transistor, which has several applications in radio where a vacuum tube is ordinarily employed' (Brooks 1976: 223). Shockley's contribution was deemed to be too far from the work to warrantise a patent award and the point contact transistor is essentially credited to Bardeen and Brattain alone. The application delay was occasioned because of a need to 'improve the scientific aspects' of what came to be called the point-contact transistor. Its theoretical underpinnings were deemed shaky enough to threaten the patenting process, especially with others so close. Shockley therefore conducted further experiments on the p-type surface layer of the point-contact transistor before the patent application was made (Shockley 1976: 615). Even then, this transistor was not the foundation upon which microelectronics were to rest. Although manufactured in the early 1950s, in its general design it was a throwback to the cat's whisker.

> [I]t never really emerged from the laboratory stage mainly because its construction limited very severely the currents which it could handle. The real importance of the point-contact transistor was that it demonstrated the possibilities of the practical application of electron flow in crystals.
>
> (Handel 1967: 83)

Shockley, even while working on bolstering the point-transistor's patent claims, was nevertheless convinced that a better device must be possible, a belief buttressed by the poor performance of the Brattain/Bardeen solution. The unexpected effect Ohl had shown Brattain years before with the mixed n- and p-type silicon had always been much in Shockley's thoughts, as evidenced by his April 1947 notebook entries. Filled with a 'competitive urge to make some transistor invention on my own', Shockley finally conceived, by an 'accident for which my unsuccessful inventive efforts had prepared my mind' the concept of the junction transistor, a transistor built like a sandwich (Shockley 1976: 614–5). This idea, after all, was in gross general terms along the lines that Lilienfeld had suggested twenty-three years earlier; but, by January 1948, Shockley had formulated the precise way in which such a sandwich transistor might be made to work – by placing a doped n-type semiconductor between two slices of p-type. This was the shape of the future for, if such a junction transistor could be created, it would depend on entirely internal operations of electrons and would have nothing of the cat's whiskers about it. While considerable efforts began to refine the point-contact transistor, Shockley worried about how junction transistors might be made at all. The patent was, nevertheless, applied for on 26 June 1948.

At a practical level, a method of manufacture had slowly to be determined and the junction transistor 'invented'. The technique, as it evolved, required adding doping substances to drops of melted germanium, in three separate stages, to make the *p-n-p* sandwich within the growing crystal. Then the crystal was sliced and the leads attached. It took till 1951 to produce a comparatively reliable transistor along these lines. By 1952 Bell's manufacturing arm, Western Electric, was making just 300 of them a month; it was making twenty-eight times as many point contact devices.

Received history suggests that 'The transistor is one of the supreme examples of an invention truly based on science' (Braun and MacDonald 1982: 182). How Bell 'invented' it is a very clear example of the fundamental twentieth-century change in the way technological innovation occurs:

> Goodyear was not a very impressive mind or talent. But he developed an obsessive idea that it would be nice to do something with rubber. He therefore did a great many different things with rubber, from freezing it to burying it in the ground, until one day an accident provided him with the happy thought, and he popped the substance on the stove - hence vulcanised rubber. The case of Goodyear is a little too close to turning monkeys loose on the typewriter to produce Hamlet as a statistical probability, to be of use, but it does suggest the difference between then and now. . . .The difference between then and now is, to a considerable extent, the difference between the way in which Mr. Goodyear went about things in getting vulcanised rubber and the way in which the Bell Laboratories got to the transistor.
>
> (Morison 1968: 12–3)

But how sustainable is this? I have detailed the development of the transistor specifically to essay an answer to this question because the notion of modern structured innovation is a significant element in the technicists' current rhetoric.

We can note immediately that the synchronicity of nineteenth-century technological developments – what brought Bell and Gray to the patent office on the same day, for example – has not changed. Bell Labs and Purdue were just as close in getting to the transistor. But, more seriously, the suggestion is that the difference between 'then' and 'now' is a question of theoretical understanding underpinning the work rather than intuition. To what extent, then, can the development of either transistor be described as being theory-led?

It is clear that Bardeen's theoretical approach pointed Brattain in the right direction – just as it is clear that Shockley's knowledge of theory and the work of his predecessors prevented any real way forward for the first years after the war. The effect of learning and theory on the team would seem to balance itself out as far as the point-contact transistor is concerned. And Bell Labs kept that innovation under wraps for months while trying to tie down the theory of the effect more securely so that the patent position could be better assured. Beyond Brattain's intuitive approach, Shockley himself refers to the month of November/December 1947 as 'the magic month', echoing, as a Bell historian has pointed out, Thomas Watson's description of an exactly similar period of feverish activity on the part of Alexander Graham Bell as 'that exciting month of June 1875' when 'the first vocal sound ever transmitted by electricity' was heard (Brooks 1976: 223; Watson 1926: 72). In their day-to-day labours, Brattain and Bardeen seem to offer no new model for a revised method of innovation.

Shockley's subsequent procedure in developing the junction transistor makes the more impressive case for theory since he articulated the design principles involved fully three years before the device was successfully produced. He himself privileges this reading by highlighting theoretical considerations in his own 1976 account of his work, stressing, for instance, the influence of Fermi and other theoretical physicists on his thinking while omitting any mention of the experimental tradition; but his junction transistor theory was rejected by a leading scientific journal as being insufficiently rigorous. In other accounts, he can be quite explicit about the gap between the practical plan he had thought of and its theoretical basis: 'The record . . .shows that I was aware of the general considerations needed to develop the theory of the junction transistor. But I did not formulate several key concepts until *after the junction transistor was invented* (Shockley 1976: 599; emphasis added). That is to say, after 23 January 1948, the date Shockley gives for this event. (In my model, this date marks the specific point of ideation for his particular solution to the problem, not the 'invention').

Thus neither the teasing out of a method actually to make a junction transistor nor the development of the point-contact transistor required a full theoretical understanding of the properties of semiconductors. Bray or Brattain, given the fact that germanium was so much to hand, could have stumbled across the effect without understanding it at all. Such ignorance would have been no bar to its exploitation. Gibney's contribution of the 'Gu' in his suggestion of 17 November 1947, which marks the beginning of the breakthrough, was similarly inspired rather than argued. Moreover, the mysterious semiconductors had been in use for a variety of purposes for three-quarters of a century without anybody having much idea as to why these materials behave the way they do. Theory was of importance for Bardeen, of course, but it would be stretching the point to claim it was absolutely crucial to the discovery of the transistor. The transistor effect was demonstrated in a totally unexpected way, after months – if not years – of work looking for an amplifier, while investigating something else – surface states, and using, for no sound theoretical reason, an electrolyte.

In short, then, how can the transistor be 'one of the supreme examples of an invention truly based on science'? The argument that the point-contact transistor represents some perfect example of a new style of innovation is seriously flawed. It can be better attached to Shockley's work – but that is not what is normally meant by talk of 'how Bell got to the transistor'. 'Theirs was not a blind empirical fumbling' (Braun 1980: 73) in the style of Goodyear or Edison. It is typical of such descriptions and refers to Brattain's demonstration of the transistor effect, not Shockley's building of the junction transistor. But what was the team doing, from 1945 on, month after month, year after year, if not empirically fumbling, in however open-eyed a fashion? Technicist claims that a revolution in innovation has occurred cannot rely on this history.


## TRANSISTORS vs. VALVES

Like the cat's whiskers and the point-contact transistor, Shockley's transistor was a signpost to a major innovation, albeit the first to indicate accurately the direction to be followed. It took eighteen years from the introduction of the junction transistor to the invention of the 4004 chip, announced on 15 November 1969. Perhaps because we are so close to these years and certainly because they are systematically misrepresented by the hype of the Information Revolution, the speed and impact of the invention is misunderstood. Obscured by changes of product within the electronics industry, this technological history commonly conflates and telescopes the diffusion of the transistor in the decade to 1960, the decline of the valve to the late 1960s, the development of the integrated circuit (IC) in the two decades from 1952 and the invention of the microprocessor in the 1970s. The resultant historical stew is one of the Information Revolution's main dishes.

It is here proposed to treat each of these ingredients as either marking advances in the development of the ground of scientific competence or as partial prototypes for the microprocessor. The result is that many devices were successively in the field before being vanquished by the microprocessor 'invention'. The transistor vs. valve battle was still unresolved by the time development of the IC begun; and ICs were still gaining acceptance when LSIs (large-scale integrated circuits) were introduced, which in turn were just about being diffused at the time of the invention of the microprocessor. All this confusion did not, however, cause constant upheavals in the electronics industry, nor does it evidence a supposed speed-up in the rate of innovation. On the contrary, the overlaps are the result of the persistence of the previous device, the containment of the radical potential each had to destroy its predecessor. The overall result is, rather, that society gained forty years of preparation wherein to contain the small-scale personal computer and its microprocessing heart.

This process begins within Bell Labs itself where the operation of the 'law' of the suppression of radical potential was immediately apparent. Among others, Gordon Teal, who was to be a crucial contributor to the development of the junction transistor, had each proposal he made for germanium research turned down between February and August of 1948, and, given his credentials, it is unlikely that every last one of his ideas was inadequate. Eventually, he took his expertise to Texas Instruments and was responsible, in 1954, for TI's silicon transistor, the first to be commercially produced. In fact, after the initial success, progress in making junction transistors took place outside Bell altogether.

AT&T, as we have seen, had evolved a complex corporate stance when it came to new technologies. It sought to balance its needs for technological protection (which required if not dominance then at least a significant patent presence in each new field) with its worries that an ever-watchful Justice Department would pounce upon it for technology-based monopolistic practices. In the case of the transistor, this stance accounts for Bell's initial actions to secure the patents and its subsequent willingness to share them with all comers. From 1952 on AT&T began to divulge not only the basic science of the transistor but also the know-how gained in its manufacture. Of course, this was not done as a free gesture. The sum of $25,000 a seat was charged for potential licensees to attend the first Bell Labs symposium on transistors in that year. The money was to be deducted from licence fees should the firm go into production. However, the licensing system was leaky. As a basic protection against accusations of monopoly, AT&T had by now established extensive cross-licensing agreements with RCA. Companies happy to forgo explanations of Bell's know-how could pick up transistor manufacturing information from RCA without paying the entrance fee. Bell was relaxed about this because it bought a measure of protection from the Justice Department. It also allowed the developmental load to be shared, specifically the problems of mass-producing the junction transistor. General Electric and Raytheon produced versions which were easier to manufacture than the Shockley model, and Philco demonstrated the first etching technique.

Transistors had been developed to replace valves, but valves did not need replacing, at least not badly enough to cause an upheaval. The transistor was more expensive and less reliable than the valve, and was to remain so until the early 1960s. 'For that decade or so, from '53 to '63, we had no choice but to go with vacuum tubes because they did a better job, and up until that time they were cheaper' (MacDonald and Braun 1977: 1063). The Bell Labs remit to the Shockley team was to mount a specific search for an solid state amplifier, a valve. The further research and development of the transistor was given over to technologists dedicated to old-style valves who thought of the newcomer as 'the enemy' (ibid.). Valves were themselves still a dynamic technology capable of doing practically everything a transistor could do, including playing the central role in the manufacture of computers. (Raytheon, the US computer industry's third firm, was in that business specifically because it was established in valves.) Even in the US military, where the greatest *aficionados* of new technology were to be found, little practical notice was taken of the transistor. Project Tinkertoy, an electronics miniaturisation programme, was started in 1950 and, ignoring transistors, remained valve-based.

AT&T itself did not begin a wholesale rush to convert, although transistors were placed in long-line switching situations and some experimental telephones by 1953. It is true that transistors were bound up with the computerisation of the central and public branch telephone exchanges and their utilisation within the Bell System marched with the introduction of ever more complex computers; but they marched slowly. There was no 'explosive growth'. The first experimental fully 'electronic central office' did not appear until the end of the 1950s and was tested for two years, until 1962 (Schindler 1982: 199). The transistor was still unreliable enough for AT&T to hesitate about putting it into submarine cables in 1966 and a decade after that it remained possible to state: 'the fully electronic public telephone exchange is still very much a research proposition' (Braun and MacDonald 1982: 196). The supervening necessity for electronic exchanges, which Bell Labs had first articulated in 1936, was, forty years later, still being constrained by the inertial weight of established, expensive and, above all, profitable plant. When this plant finally came to be replaced, the transistor was as much a thing of the past as the valve. The thunderous general silence that had greeted Bell's initial announcement in 1948 was prescient. Only hearing aid manufacturers leapt at the transistor, the first transistorised version being made in late 1952. AT&T, as a gesture to the interest Bell himself had in the deaf, waived the licence fees for this application in 1954 and Raytheon established itself as the primary manufacturer.

It was Texas Instruments, with Teal's cheaper silicon transistor, that began to create a more general market. Texas Instruments was the typical outsider company, having been, up to 1950, an oil industry service firm providing exploration surveys. Moving from an interest in electronics as applied to its own business, no sooner did it have the silicon transistor to hand than it set about putting it into a consumer item – a portable radio. TI's production model was marketed in October 1954. A battery-driven model was introduced the following year by Regency of Indianapolis. The synecdoche which made 'trannie' the British slang for such a radio is not a measure of the ubiquity of transistors, but rather the reverse. 'Trannie' came to mean portable radio exactly because that was the only widely diffused device to contain transistors.

Transistors were of further value, especially to the military, in airborne or high temperature situations. Teal's silicon was more effective than germanium for such uses and, following Sputnik, the Signal Corps doubled its R&D grants for transistor research but only to a paltry annual million dollars. The transistor industry did not benefit, to the same extent as did others, from the enormous increase in military spending during these years. Contrast the nascent computer industry which was virtually a military subsidiary. The military subvention, though, was crucial in furthering the transistor's refinement. Texas Instruments sold more transistors to the armed services than they did to civilian radio manufacturers. Nevertheless the whole market was still small. In the years before Sputnik (1954–1956), transistors were worth $55 million, valves $1000 million and the entire electronic component industry $6500 million (Braun and Mac-Donald 1982: 60).

Sputnik and the publicity attached to the Nobel Prize won by Shockley, Brattain and Bardeen in 1956 helped turn this situation round. By 1959, sales of transistors overtook those of valves for the first time (Braun 1980: 76). The value of military business to the transistor manufacturer between 1955 and 1960 climbed from one-third of the market to nearly half. The space programme alone in 1963 used $33 million of them. For the newcomers, this transistor trade was of major significance. Texas Instruments shares increased in value thirty-eight-fold between 1952 and 1959 (Braun and MacDonald 1982: 80–1).

Yet for the old valve firms the transistor was not the disaster it is always presented as being. All eight major US valve companies were making transistors by 1953 and it was not until the second half of the 1960s that valves were finally phased out. It took television manufacturers, to take one crucial example, this long – fifteen years – to move to solid state electronics, by which time the transistor, as is described below, had given way to the integrated circuit. Of the eight major valve firms, only one (RCA) was still in the business twenty years after the semiconductor industry began and this is commonly read as clear evidence of the industrial equivalent of massacre. But all the firms involved had histories of flexibility in their approaches to new technologies. They had adopted and abandoned a number in the period since the First World War and they had survived. One would need to know less than nothing of American life to assume that, because such entities as General Electric and Westinghouse were no longer in this market in 1975, the new technology had destroyed them. Further, by 1975, the list of semiconductors' top ten manufacturers, although dominated by new-comers, also contained such well-established electronics giants as Motorola and Philips who had not been there twenty years before.

Another view of this history is possible: the slow exploitation of the transistor, including paltry R&D support, gives the valve industry a decade to respond, followed by a further decade of semiconductor diffusion in which to run down. In all, the transistor, far from causing a massacre, is a classic example of what results from the balance between a slow working supervening necessity and the suppression of a device's radical potential, to wit – a fairly stabilised change-over period. Again, here is a chicken-and-egg situation. If transistors had been more urgently needed they would have been developed more quickly.

## IDEATION AND PROTOTYPE: THE INTEGRATED CIRCUIT

In 1952, G.W.A. Dummer, of the Royal Signal and Radar Establishment, Malvern (RRE), delivered a paper at a symposium in Washington:

> At this stage I would like to take a peep into the future. With the advent of the transistor and the work in semiconductors generally, it seems now possible to envisage electronic equipment in a solid block with no connecting wires. The block may consist of layers of insulating, conducting, rectifying and amplifying materials, the electrical functions being connected directly by cutting out areas of the various layers.
>
> (Dummer 1983: 141)

This represented the specific ideation transformation that was to lead to the microprocessor, the 'invention', because Dummer's concept revealed the true potential of semiconductors as the replacements, not of valves, but of entire circuits. He thought of it as commercial transistors were coming on to the market.

The British government was uninterested in inventing microelectronics and Dummer 'never received the backing that his degree of inspiration would have justified' (Braun and MacDonald 1982: 80). Dummer himself understood the lack of supervening, specifically military, necessity in his native land and how without such pressure his idea was not likely to be pursued: 'In the United Kingdom and Europe a war-weariness prevented the exploitation of electronic applications and it was probably not realised how important electronics was to become' (Wolff 1976: 53). In September 1957 at an RRE conference, Plessey displayed a non-working model of what an integrated circuit might look like, Dummer having secured the firm a small research contract the previous April; but even Plessey treated the job as a 'laboratory curiosity'. Americans at the gathering were far more impressed than was the Radar Establishment which did not renew the Plessey agreement. Thus the IC idea crossed the Atlantic a second time.

The received view is to see the IC and its successors as spin-offs from the transistor, not, as is here suggested, to see the transistor and IC as precursors of the microprocessor. The transistor, because its existence prompts the ideation transformation, can be considered as an element arising from the ground of scientific competence leading to the microprocessor; and the IC is a prototype of that device. One major reason why the development of the transistor has been privileged over the microprocessor 'invention' is that the transistor is seen as the science-based artefact *par excellence* whereas the microprocessor is only a further exploitation of the same physics. Jack Kilby of Texas Instruments, who was the first to patent an IC, states: 'In contrast to the invention of the transistor, this was an invention with relatively few scientific implications. . . .Certainly in those years, by and large, you could say it [the IC] contributed very little to scientific thought' (Braun and MacDonald 1982: 90). Yet, as we have seen, the case for the transistor being a science-led innovation is somewhat overstated. In fact, what Kilby says of the IC can be said of any communications technology device, virtually in the nature of the case, i.e. the production of such devices is a performance of a previously established scientific competence.

Kilby had attended the 1952 Bell symposium on behalf of Centralab, a large mid-Western radio and television component firm. In 1958 he joined Texas Instruments, where the person who hired him, Willis Adcock, remembered conversations with Dummer. Kilby (a man who in his own words 'gets a picture and then proceeds doggedly to implement that picture') arrived just as the firm shut down for its annual holiday. 'Since I had just started and had no vacation time, I was left pretty much in a deserted plant. . . .I began to cast around for alternates and the (integrated circuit) concept really occurred during that two week vacation period' (Wolff 1976: 47). In essence he mounted more than one junction transistor together in a solid slab and wired input and output terminals to each miniaturised section. This was exactly what Dummer had been groping for six years earlier. However, like the point-contact transistor, it was cumbersome – a minute block upon which the entire circuit had to be created by hand, and the more complicated the circuit the more vexed the wiring. Nevertheless, by October it worked – 'a body of semiconductor material . . . wherein all the components of the electronic circuit are completely integrated', in the words of Kilby's patent application of 6 February 1959 (Dummer 1983: 158). Within weeks Kurt Lehovec, the research director of a Massachusetts firm, designed an IC in which the components were separated by the p-n junctions themselves (Augarten 1984: 242).

In the meantime, a new production technique had been introduced which was to make the discrete transistor both very cheap and, shortly thereafter, obsolescent. The breakthrough to full-scale planar methods, which also laid the foundation for the economically viable production of IC and LSI chips, resulted from seeking improvements in junction transistor manufacturing. The technique was developed by Fairchild Semiconductor, a firm started by seven refugees from the organisation Shockley himself had formed after winning the Nobel Prize and leaving Bell – The Semiconductor Laboratories. Shockley had returned to his home town of Palo Alto where, encouraged by Stanford University, a number of electronics firms were already located in what was to be nicknamed Silicon Valley, among them, for instance, the company founded by two Stanford graduates, William Hewlett and David Packard. (Shockley's lab was eventually acquired by ITT which closed the Palo Alto plant.[4]) The Fairchild seven had disagreed with Shockley's approach to junction transistor production. In the words of Robert

Noyce, who was brought in to run the breakaway firm: 'Shockley was concentrating on four-layer germanium diodes at a time when there seemed to be a swing in the semiconductor community from germanium to silicon. . . .The people traditionally in the business are so committed to the previous course of action that they don't really get on with the new thing' (Hanson 1982: 91). (This failure of 'people traditionally in the business' to embrace the new can be generalised as yet another formulation of the 'law' of suppression.) Fairchild, though, was well placed to exploit the 'new thing'.

At that time the cutting edge of transistor design involved having the emitter protrude above the silicon base which acted as the collector, the so-called mesa transistor. These were none too robust and in 1958, Jean Hoerni of Fairchild, by utilising advances in photolithography, specifically photo-resist techniques, bypassed the troublesome mesa altogether (Noyce 1977: 32 ). The silicon wafer was sensitised to light so that the pattern of the transistor could be photographed on to it. After the exposed parts were washed away, the base silicon could be etched and the doping substances – to create $n$- and $p$-type material – diffused on to the exposed portions. The advantages of the method are that many copies of the same transistor can be placed on the one wafer which can then be sliced up. By 1959 Fairchild was manufacturing silicon transistors by this planar method and within three years the price of its product fell by a factor of ten. The result was simply a market glut. The real significance of planar techniques was not to be cheaper transistors but, as Robert Noyce began to appreciate in the early months of 1959, ICs.

Noyce saw that the planar process could allow different conduction levels of complex patternings to be placed on the one wafer – an IC which would avoid impossibly expensive hand wiring. By that summer, Noyce had produced a viable IC by the planar process. Both Kilby and Lehovec ICs posed even more of a production nightmare than had the point-contact transistor, and, because of this flaw, Kilby's claim to the integrated circuit has been seriously disputed by Noyce. TI, on Kilby's behalf, filed for patent interference in 1963 but the court found, in certain aspects, for Noyce in 1969. The companies, despite these differences, collectively licensed all comers to exploit ICs (Hanson 1982: 97–8).

The planar process was already causing a transistor glut and the industry was clearly unable to accommodate so fundamental a development as the IC. Like the transistor, then, the IC was initially left confronting a very basic problem – what use was it? The answer was the same in both cases; by December 1963, the first IC hearing aid was marketed. Otherwise there was little immediate demand. The US military were intent on imitating the Bourbons and, having learned nothing from Tinkertoy and the miniature valve, were now involved in the so-called 'micromodular plan' which used transistors but ignored ICs. The army continued to fund that scheme into 1963, spending $26 million on it. Thus to the decade of slow transistor diffusion can now be added a second decade of slow IC diffusion. But the military, still reeling from the implications of Sputnik, were evolving weapons systems, such as the Minuteman intercontinental ballistic missile, which would depend on ICs. Nevertheless, military applications when they were found, because of their limited scale, did not transform the world of electronics. The demand was not great enough and its pace, thanks to procurement procedures, was too slow. By 1963, ICs accounted for only 10 per cent of the circuits sold in the US.

The valve, never mind the transistor, was still very much in evidence in the early 1960s. For instance, it took an act of Congress, the All Channel Law, which required that 1964 television sets be able to receive both UHF and VHF to get valves out of the sets. 'There was an attitude on the part of the television makers that if the integrated circuit was such a hot new product, why hadn't it come from research at RCA, or GE, or even CBS? Fairchild, and Texas Instruments were out West and just not that well known yet.' Fairchild built a solid state television simply to show the manufacturers that such a thing would work and would, indeed, have advantages for UHF, but nobody bought it (Hanson 1982: 106–7).

Nor, initially, was there much of a market for the next development either. By 1967, finally, the cheap metal oxide semiconductor (MOS), which had been patented but failed to work in 1935, was successfully transformed into a field-effect transistor. This was done at General Microelectronics, a company founded by refugees from Fairchild – Fairchildren, as they were now being called. The MOS enabled the emerging IC, because it permits a multitude of high density circuits to be etched on the chip, to become large scale (LSI) and then very large scale (VLSI). General Micro's pioneering of MOSs did not translate into instant commercial success and the firm was bought out by Philco-Ford in 1966. It was not until the widespread popularity of the pocket calculator in the early 1970s that MOS/IC technology became widely diffused.

The first semiconductor calculator had been introduced, with discrete components, i.e. transistors, in 1963 by a British firm. It was the size of a cash register. Texas Instruments brought out one with an MOS chip in 1967 but without much response. However, within four years the pocket electronic calculator, aided by Japanese production methods, arrived. The IC calculator was initially a device, like the Pascaline or the Baldwin, for the office. However, accessible enough to take the labour out of even everyday arithmetic, it attracted far more than those who customarily worked extensively with figures. As sales skyrocketed, the price fell – from some $200 in 1970 to around $15 for the same model by 1975. Elsewhere, within this time frame ICs made their way into a host of devices, all of which had been well established with either conventional electronics or even older technologies. Digital watches, for example, were the other early wonder of the semiconductor age, but here again there is a history which goes back to the first quartz timepiece of 1928. Greenwich Observatory had one in 1939 and by 1968 they were small enough to be battery powered on the wrist – at around $1000 per piece (Landes 1983: 319).

It might be thought that the subsequent flood of cheap electronic watches constitutes one example where the 'law' of the suppression of radical potential did not work. After all, between 1956 and 1980, the number of Swiss watch firms dropped from 2332 to less than 900 and the number of jobs was halved to 26,228 (Landes 1983: 353). But my point is not to argue that such changes can never occur. The 'law' of suppression suggests only that upheavals are contained when they threaten the central arenas of the economy. So, indeed, here is a major shakeout based on a technological innovation, but it crucially depended on the fact that the trade was an export one and there was therefore no constraint internally within any one market – except Switzerland, of course. The innovation eventually, after a decade, began to provide a device markedly better than the traditional one – as the electronic watch developed multiple alarms, internal lights, stopwatch facilities, etc., all of which were found to be of value by users. But then, somewhat curiously, the fad passed and watches once more adopted their traditional form, albeit with solid state works inside the case.[5] Many American semiconductor firms joined in the rush to replace the Swiss, constantly lowered their prices and flooded what was a seasonal market. The 'law' of suppression, which did not operate to protect Swiss exports, did work to help the American watch manufacturers resist such domestic challenges. By 1977, all but the three largest microelectronics firms had bailed out of digital watch manufacture. For instance, Intel, the company Noyce had created when he himself joined the Fairchildren by leaving Fairchild, had lost a fortune on its watches and sold out its interest in the field to Timex (Hanson 1982: 118). It was the Japanese, understanding marketing as well as electronics, rather than the Silicon Valley folk, who took up the slack created by the Swiss decline in the cheaper watch market.

## 'INVENTION': THE MICROPROCESSOR

Computers were to act as the supervening necessity for the microprocessor, the 'invention' in solid state electronics. The technology of the microprocessor was to hand. Indeed, so much was it to hand that the common perception is (as I indicated at the outset of this chapter) that it was already being fully used – but that was not the case. Computer manufacturers had moved slowly to ICs which, as off-the-shelf components, allowed them to design their machines as they liked. Computers were still expensive – even those smaller devices now designated as 'minis' – and the market for them remained, comparatively, small. But the logic of the computer could no longer be denied in the third decade of its development. As Robert Noyce put it (on this matter quite accurately):

> The future is obviously in decentralising computer power. . . .As it turns out many of the problems addressed are not really big problems at all but lots of little, simple problems. The difference between a computer and a microprocessor is like the difference between a jet airplane and an automobile. The airplane carries a hundred times as many people and it carries them ten times as fast, but ninety per cent of the transportation in this country is done by automobile, because it's the simplest way to get from here to there, and the same is true of the microprocessor.
>
> (Hanson 1982: 123)

Thermonuclear ignition problems were not the only things the machines could compute.

The computer industry, from its inception, had been blind to this possibility. Now, as its eyes were opening, it was hostile to the idea: 'Computer engineers often looked at integrated circuits as a way of putting them out of business. . . . This was the era of big powerful computers, and little computers just weren't that interesting' (Hanson 1982: 106,120). Far from being in the symbiotic relationship suggested by hindsight, these two branches of the electronics business were at a distance from each other. The invention of the microprocessor did not initially bridge this gap for, on the contrary, it implied that semiconductor engineers, not computer engineers, were to be the real designers of computers. The microprocessor was not a component; it was, in design terms, the whole heart of the machine. After its introduction, for instance, semiconductor firms had difficulty in hiring programmers to exploit it. Just as valve people believed the transistor was 'the enemy', so computer people responded to the microprocessor in much the same way. Because of this background, the computer's operation as a supervening necessity to the microprocessor occurred in a series of tangential events and parallel tendencies.

The key element concerned the repositioning of some major semiconductor firms in the late 1960s. Noyce's new company, Intel, was created to exploit a large market opportunity which was emerging – only at this late date, it should be noted – in computer memory chips. Moving from the general Fairchild business of electronic components, Intel was to be specialised. The hostility of the computer industry was minimised for, after all, the memory store was only a peripheral. Intel already had a rival, AMS, and others were known to be interested in helping to replace Jay Forester's twenty-year-old drum which was still the standard data-storage device. For the semiconductor manufacturers, having just successfully broken into the television market with ICs, it was clearly time seriously to sell some state-of-the-art electronics to the computer manufacturers.

In 1969, Busicom, a Japanese manufacturer, approached Intel with an ambitious plan to make an IC specifically for a series of commercial desktop calculators, then the industry's hottest prospect, which could, through the installation of different ROMs, perform specialised functions. The preliminary plan called for twelve chips containing from ten to fifteen times as many integrated transistors as were then currently being used in such devices. Marcian (Ted) Hoff, one of the firm's brightest Stanford graduates and a man interested in possible applications of solid state technology to logic circuits, was deputed to examine the Japanese designs. Hoff simply suggested that the calculator's arithmetic and logic circuitry should be put on the same chip. It would be a blank slate, as it were, capable of taking specific instructions from specially written ROMs. Intel would make the chip and Busicom would get the firm to programme its ROMs for the advanced calculators. The result of this design insight was that the Busicom calculators needed only four chips, a ROM, a RAM, an input/output IC and, centrally, a microprocessor. Hoff now needed to invent the only one of these proposed chips not to hand, the microprocessor (Augarten 1984: 261–5).

With Frederico Fagin, he then did just that. They and their design team produced a silicon chip one-sixth by one-eighth of an inch, containing 2250 microminiaturised transistors. The small size and high density are not the essence of the achievement – rather it is that the combination of elements, including the in-built logic circuits, created a programmable general purpose device, the minuscule Central Processing Unit (CPU) of a computer. Not only would it drive the Japanese calculator, but dozens, thousands, of other devices as well. Manufacturers would be able to use the CPU chip off the shelf, Intel simply executing their instructions in making specific ROMs (Bylinsky 1975: 6). Ted Hoff: 'The actual invention of the microprocessor wasn't as important as simply appreciating that there was a market for such a thing' (Hanson 1982: 118). This is something of an understatement, for it masks the essential creative leap that Hoff made. Yet, in one sense, Hoff is obviously correct. The 'invention' was not very notable and failed to ignite the imagination. The result was a series of CPU devices but no immediate microprocessor computer. A main reason for this was that the suppressive factors working against a CPU application of this sort were, contrary to popular belief, particularly strong.

# 1 2

# THE COMING OF THE
# MICROCOMPUTER

## SUPPRESSION REVISITED: THE COMPUTER
## INDUSTRY

During the 1950s, computers were enormously expensive valved machines largely in military service. For all that visionaries might dream of the new computer-based world, for all that some scientists and the entire media might talk of electronic brains, nobody was seriously interested in fully exploiting the device by making it smaller and cheaper. Ten years after its ideation and five years after the first machine had run, there were but 250 computers in the world. 'For the first two decades of the existence of the high speed computer machines were so scarce and so expensive that man approached the computer the way an ancient Greek approached an oracle' (Augarten 1984: 253). As we have seen, all baby machines were strangled at birth or, like the somewhat larger Pilot Ace, never duplicated.

Transistors did not materially affect this. This was not because of ignorance. On the contrary, as early as 3 October 1948, within months of Bell's announcement, Jack Good wrote in a letter to Turing: 'Have you heard of the TRANSISTOR (or Transistor)? It is a small crystal alleged to perform nearly all the functions of a vacuum tube. It might easily be the biggest thing since the war. Is England going to get a look-in?' (Hodges 1983: 391). Nobody got a look-in, or rather looked in. For instance, a completely transistorised miniature device was built in Bell Labs before 1952 which could multiply two sixteen-digit binary numbers in 272 seconds. An obscurely titled 1952 article, 'Regenerative Amplifier for Digital Computer Applications', about this device concluded: 'Transistor performance equal to that of vacuum tubes can be obtained in computer applications without sacrificing any of the obvious transistor advantages' (Felker 1952: 1596); but the machine was not only never developed, it was later totally written out of Bell's computing history (Andrews 1963: 314). In 1953, the Manchester group designed a small transistorised prototype computer and Metropolitan Vickers put it into production for their own use. Only six were made (Lavington 1980: 48). The English were to market a number of smaller machines in the late 1950s and early 1960s, none very effectively. With the merger process of British computer companies completed, this approach was abandoned and SYSTEM 4, a machine as large as IBM's 360, was built instead (ibid: 52, 75).

Main frame transistorised computers fared no better. By the mid-1950s, a one-off, the Bell Naval Ordnance machine, and a number of transistorised prototypes existed at the IBM Military Products Division and MIT. There were a number of proposals on the board such as one-offs from Univac for the Livermore Atomic Radiation Lab and from IBM for Los Alamos. Philco was working on the Transac. However, the military were not interested in reducing the computer size by using the smaller transistor. On the contrary, the effect of the transistor upon these machines was to make them even more enormous. Freed from the physical constraints imposed by valves, IBM's 1961 7030, the Los Alamos one-off significantly nicknamed Stretch, used 150,000 transistors; but despite the fact that it worked for a decade it did not yield the expected production success. Only a few were sold, even after the price was reduced from $13 million to $8 million (Soma 1976: 39). The commonly made assertion that IBM put transistors into a *commercially* available machine years before this comes from a business journal report in 1955 and, although a fine early example of Information Revolution hype, is not true. IBM's new machine for 1955 was the 705 featuring 'Magnetic core storage, increased speed, simultaneous reading and writing of tape, direct memory transfer, a flexible accumulator, a new flexible card reader, and a record storage unit' but no transistors (Hurd 1980: 413). In fact, the few 7030s aside, IBM was never successfully to market a fully transistorised computer.

IBM was in the business of selling, rather than leasing, machines such as the 7030 because of a consent decree in 1956 which held its traditional leasing policies to be restrictive. 'New products destroy this leasing base, and thus, IBM is naturally hesitant to introduce new products until long after other firms have introduced similar products' (Soma 1976: 37,150). Since the loyalty of IBM's lessors was already working to limit the ease with which even the largest firms, with even the most advanced products, could enter the market, the entire industry settled early into a certain technological conservatism. Philco, for example, brought the Transac to market in 1958 as the first fully transistorised computer, the 2000; but it could not withstand IBM. All this is quite contrary to the received story which holds that:

> In the early 1950s, the switches in computers were valves. Each one was hand-made and expensive – around $5 each at today's prices and the world market was dominated by huge American manufacturers. But in 1948 William Shockley invented the transistor, for which he was to get a

Nobel prize. It murdered the valve industry with a rapidity that was brutal.

(Goldwyn 1978: 297)

Well, William Shockley did win the Nobel Prize; but, as for the rest, none of it stands up.

The next device, the integrated circuit (IC), was to be a slightly different matter. Initially though,

> [t]he computer industry was no more eager to use the integrated circuit than it had been to use the transistor. Within IBM, there were projections saying it would take all the sand in the world to supply enough semiconductor memory in order to satisfy IBM's needs so many years out. . . . It was just too great a risk to commit the total corporation to integrated circuits for computer logic.
>
> (Hanson 1982: 104–5)

But even IBM executives were happier, however marginally, thinking about ICs at least for memory purposes. They were forced into a more fundamental engagement with the new technology after the Atomic Energy Commission (AEC) funded Control Data Corporation (CDC) – a company formed when many of the original ERA people broke away from what was now (Univac) Sperry Rand – to build a full-scale IC computer. The result, the CDC 6600, was two-and-a-half times as fast as Stretch, the first 1 million instructions per second – 1 MIPS – machine. IBM was wrong-footed again.

IBM had been persevering with transistors, despite the unfortunate Stretch sales experience. A new series, the System/360, which used a hybrid integrated circuit/transistor design, was introduced in April 1964. (In other words, they were so slow that transistor technology was overtaken by ICs before a successful all-transistor product was marketed.) The 360 series, despite not being entirely IC, was nevertheless innovative. It was the first 'system' which not only allowed users to update all discrete parts, including the CPU, but to do so without needing to junk software and data. Putting it in production cost IBM $5 billion for five new factories and a one-third increase in the workforce (Augarten 1984: 248–251). The adaptability of the machine helped make it a major hit, some 30,000 being sold before 1970, at a rate initially of as many as 1000 a month. With it, IBM saw off both GE's and RCA's forays into computers. However, it was no match for the more up-to-date CDC 6600, the first of which was delivered in September 1964, sixth months after the first 360. To neutralise that threat, IBM announced the 360/91, a competitive 1 MIPS machine.

CDC was to claim successfully that this was a ploy and the subsequently publicised production difficulties of the 360/91 were actually its design period. CDC thereby lost sales while the computer market, hooked on the 360, waited for the comparable (and compatible) machine from IBM. The ploy, when exposed, cost IBM its software house and about $75 million in an out-of-court settlement with CDC. This result encouraged other firms – already given a foothold by the 360 peripherals market – to take on the giant. The restoration of a greater measure of competition in the main frame industry followed (Soma 1976: 23, 37). The increasing range and decreasing price of these competitors essentially depended on the IC to reduce physical size somewhat while maintaining the computing capacities of the previous generation of main frames. By 1965 there were still only 31,000 computers worldwide, perhaps a somewhat inflated figure, and they were all large main frames.

The IC, though, was starting to have a rather more profound effect. A host of firms – excluding IBM which was initially constrained from entering this market by another Justice Department attack – started to build machines which were really smaller both in size and capacity. These became known as 'minicomputers'. Some computer engineers had begun seriously to think about such a possibility even before the new IC technology was available. Ken Olsen, the member of Forrester's Whirlwind team at MIT who had built the baby to demonstrate the magnetic core memory, had then been deputed to control the SAGE production process at IBM's Poughkeepsie plant. Appalled by the inefficiencies of a large organisation, Olsen had become convinced that he could do better by going smaller both in terms of design and organisation. In 1957 he had established the Digital Equipment Corporation and within three years had produced his first machine, the Programmed Data Processor, PDP 1. At $120,000 it was not cheap, but it was a good deal cheaper than the competition. In 1963 Olsen produced the first true minicomputer, the PDP 8, a transistorised machine the size of a large filing cabinet, costing a mere $18,000. It was a commercial hit and between 1965 and 1970 Digital's sales went up nine-fold while its profits soared twenty-fold (Augarten 1984: 256–9). (The inappropriateness of the term 'mini' for these devices is often remarked on as an example of how quickly the computer developed but, on the contrary, 'mini' celebrates the deliberate design philosophy which made a standard of the giant and downgraded everything else.)

The PDP 8 vividly illuminated a real need for smaller computers and by 1969, IC minis were available for as little as $8000. Two years later one count revealed seventy-five different firms making minis, but the main frame industry continued to ignore the logic at work. In 1969, IBM, for instance, having obviously decided that the world was not going to run out of sand, introduced a complete IC memory for the 360 system. This was the sort of computer industry decision that pushed Noyce and Intel into the memory business. Only in the early 1970s did IBM begin to replace the System/360 with the System/370, machines finally having both memory and logic on integrated circuits (Hanson 1982: 124). All this activity at both main frame and mini level meant that a real relationship between semiconductors and computers emerged for the first time in the decade from 1965 on. This encouraged the founding of Intel and its rivals, specialised semiconductor firms which looked primarily to the computer industry for business. Computer production began to increase. As Year 25 of the computer age approached, there were 70,000 machines in the US, and, by 1976, the first really successful year of the next generation, the 'microcomputer', there were 200,000, 40 per cent classified as minis.

No one had envisaged the possibility of the microcomputer, although there can be no doubt that had the full potential of the IC as a logic circuit device as well as a data-store been seized upon earlier, such a small, potentially more radical machine could have been easily built. Twelve years were to pass from the demonstration of the transistor effect (1947) to the introduction of the planar process (1959), the essential technical breakthrough; and then a further ten years from that advance to the invention of the microprocessor (1969); and a further five years (1974) before anybody thought to use a CPU to build a personal machine. It is significant that the 'invention' of the microprocessor then occurs in a firm dedicated to computer memory solid state electronics, not a computer company. It is also significant that the entire process in both semiconductors and computing takes until the mid-1970s to mature, giving society decades to prepare for such impact as the micromachines would make. As TI's chief executive, J.F. Bucy, said in 1980, 'Looking back we probably should have started on micro-computers earlier', not least, perhaps, because his firm had actually built one and then abandoned it (Bylinsky 1975: 8–9). This is basically more an evolutionary than a revolutionary history.

So with the CPU, the pattern established with the transistor and the IC repeated itself:

> Robert Noyce recalls that when Intel introduced the microcomputer [actually the microprocessor] late in 1971, the industry's reaction was 'ho hum'. Semiconductor manufacturers had made so many extravagant promises in the past that the industry seemed to have become immune to claims of real advances. Besides, the big semiconductor companies – Texas Instruments, Motorola, and Fairchild – were preoccupied with their large current business, integrated circuits and calculator chips.
>
> (Bylinsky 1975: 8–9)

Among the first devices to contain a microprocessor was a digital clock which could also be arranged to sound like an electric piano. Ted Hoff:

Some of the other stuff seemed really weird to us at that time. We were surprised when people came to us with ideas for slot machines, and some other people wanted to use our microcomputer *[sic]* to automate cows. They wanted to automatically record how many times the cows drank water, or something like that and correlate it with milk production.

(Hanson 1982: 121)

Meanwhile Intel had fulfilled its *raison d'être* by introducing, in 1970, the 1103 RAM chip, which was to affect the size and expense of minicomputers by substantially reducing the cost of memory. It worked and worked reliably. The original 4004 microprocessor gave way to the eight-bit 8008 in 1972 which was refined as the 8080 in 1974. By this time, the reputation of the microprocessor had improved sufficiently over its predecessor solid state devices for it to be accepted. The computer was finally ready to open its heart to the chip.

## DIFFUSION AND SPIN-OFFS: PC PRODUCTION

The microcomputer's microprocessor heart had been specifically designed for calculators and by the mid-1970s some three-quarters of a million had been sold for that purpose (Hanson 1982: 128). Other even more widespread uses involved such devices as domestic oven timers, industrial control processes and, above all, videogames. Space War, reputedly created by student computer enthusiasts at MIT in the early 1960s, was the Ur-video game, a widely shared cult among those with access to the main frames at America's universities. Nolan Bushnell was one such Space War *aficionado* who combined his electrical engineering studies at the University of Utah with summer work at an amusement park. These twin experiences suggested to Bushnell the possibility of democratising Space War by making it as accessible as an electro-mechanical game in an amusement arcade. In 1972, he founded Atari and launched Pong, a microprocessor-driven toy which could be attached to a domestic television receiver. In 1974, Pong was featured in the catalogues and stores of Sears Roebuck, America's largest retailer. Atari's revenues reached $40 million annually, and Bushnell sold out to Warner Communications for $30 million. By 1980 Atari was retailing $100- million-worth of games and low-level home computers and at the end of 1982 there were videogames in 15 million American homes. It was a spin-off that happened, as it were, in advance of the parent device – for, in that year, less than one in fifteen of those homes also possessed a personal computer.

Intel's eight-bit chips and the flood of Pongs created a general atmosphere in which the microcomputer, like a ripe fruit, was bound to fall off somebody's tree. *Radio-Electronics* magazine had run a story in July 1974 outlining the design of a machine called the Mark 8, billed as 'Your Personal Minicomputer'. The article described a computer based on the Intel 8008 chip and invited readers to send away for a forty-eight-page instruction manual, costing $5.50, on how to build it. For a further $47.50 circuit boards were available, but the buyer had to obtain, from Intel and others, the chips required. All told the machine would cost the hobbyist about $250 to assemble. *Radio-Electronics* sold 10,000 copies of the blueprints and about 2500 orders were received for boards. The first home computer, with almost no memory and no means of storing its programs after use, was probably assembled by between one and two thousand people. It spawned the earliest hobbyist clubs but it still looked more like a prototype than a real machine.

*Popular Electronics, Radio-Electronics'* rival, having declined the Mark 8 blueprint, was now looking for its own computer project. The editors had felt that the Mark 8 was more of a demonstration device than a real machine and so laid down some requirements for their computer kit – it really had to be able to compute and it had to cost less than $400. The wherewithal to meet this challenge was the next Intel chip, the 8080, introduced six months after the Mark 8 plans had been published. It led to a far more effective machine – the Altair 8800. Altair had been selling a sophisticated electronic calculator kit, until 1974, when the semiconductor firms, exploiting CPUs, marketed equally sophisticated, fully assembled but cheaper calculators and so destroyed that business. Altair decided to move from calculator kits to computer kits and the Altair 8800, with a 8080 CPU and sixteen expansion slots, was headlined in the January 1975 edition of *Popular Electronics* as the 'World's First Minicomputer Kit to Rival Commercial Models'. Like the Mark 8, it was not a very accessible device, but it sold well to enthusiasts, people who knew enough about electronics to make the 8800 work, and it spawned a whole new world – more clubs sprang up; the first computer shop opened in Los Angeles in July 1975; the first home computing magazine *Byte* appeared in August; and the first world Altair Computer Conference was held in Albuquerque in March 1976.

The computer industry, even those in the minicomputer business, ignored these developments. Digital and Hewlett-Packard dominated minicomputers, having a 55 per cent market share between them. They had developed a subsidiary educational market worth, by the early 1970s, about $40,000,000. Digital's educational division chief, David Ahl, became convinced that a machine even smaller than the PDP 8 mini would sell well in this area. He moved to the development group and produced plans for a $5000 computer for schools, but Olsen's firm, now the biggest private employer in Massachusetts, had become too big to continue to think small. The company felt that if one needed less computer than a PDP 8 one simply shared its time with other users, exactly the argument used by main frame supporters in resisting the mini a few years earlier. [1]

In 1975 the other major minicomputer player, Hewlett-Packard, took much the same line as Digital when choosing to ignore a crude single board microcomputer built by one of its more junior programmers, Steve Wozniak, in his spare time. It used a new $20 CPU, the MOS Technology 6502, and had 4K of RAM. He called it the Apple I. Wozniak had failed to graduate from college but he had built a transistor radio while in grade school and, age 13, a transistorised calculator which won a Bay Area science fair prize. In 1971 he had made a small logic board out of ICs with a friend and another new acquaintance, Steven Jobs, who was still at the high school in Cupertino which Wozniak had himself attended. Then he began to manufacture a profitable line of illegal sound emitters used to make free calls on telephones. Wozniak and Jobs created a cash flow of several thousand dollars out of these blue boxes. Five years later, Wozniak was working for Hewlett-Packard and still knocking together electronic devices at home. Jobs, who had also dropped out of college and had spent some time in India, was now working for Atari. The two natives of Silicon Valley met up again at 'Homebrew', the local Altair club.

It was Jobs who had prompted Wozniak to build the Apple I for sale to their fellow enthusiasts at the club. They unveiled it there in July 1976. The proprietor of the local Byte Shop was present and subsequently ordered fifty boards. At this point, with Hewlett-Packard refusing support, Jobs sold his minibus and Wozniak his two Hewlett Packard programmable calculators to pay for the manufacture of the orders. Some 175 were made and sold mainly through Bay Area shops or from Jobs' garage at $666 each. Again, though, this post 'invention' device still had the feel of a prototype. It was certainly not accessible enough to be widely diffused – but nevertheless it was a microcomputer and in the small world of enthusiasts for such things it was a hit.

Flushed with this success, Wozniak began to design and build the machine that was to become Apple II while Jobs approached his Atari boss, Nolan Bushnell, for capital. Bushnell declined, but he put him in touch with potential backers and eventually Jobs made contact with Mike Markkula who had been Intel's marketing manager and had just retired from the firm a millionaire. In October 1976 Markkula became convinced that Wozniak's new machine was a potential winner and he added $91,000 to the $5000 which Jobs and Wozniak put up to found the Apple Corporation. Markkula raised a further $660,000 from, inter alia, a Rockefeller company as well as obtaining a $250,000 line of credit from one of America's biggest banks. Wozniak created the first industry standard disk-drive, using a new $5\frac{1}{4}$-inch standard disk in a burst of furious energy over the Christmas vacation of 1977 while riding high on Apple's first successful year (Augarten 1984: 276–81). The crucial difference between the Apple II and all its predecessors was a design philosophy which saw the machine as a tool rather than an end in itself. As with Sarnoff and the radio box rather than the cat's whiskers, so

THE COMING OF THE MICROCOMPUTER

with Jobs and Wozniak. Apple was willing to adopt any and all available interfaces to make the machine more user friendly.

In this they were following, perhaps unknowingly, the thinking of Joseph 'Lick' Licklider, one of the fathers of Cyberspace, who began worrying about human/ computer interfaces in the 1950s. He was in charge of the first human factors group at MIT by 1953, having begun his career as a behavioural psychologist. In 1960 he published a seminal paper 'Man-Computer Symbiosis' and later in that decade he was involved in the Advanced Research Projects Agency (ARPA) at the Pentagon, whence comes the system now known as the Internet (p. 326). Licklider's vision of 'human brains and computer machines . . . coupled . . . tightly' had an obvious appeal to the military. They needed computing power but they needed it directly in the hands of soldiers, not mediated via the mysteries of the high priesthood of computer programmers and operators. Licklider encouraged the development of graphic interface programs (sketch pads) and the 'X-Y position indicator for a display system' (or mouse) which was created by Doug Englebert at the Stanford Research Centre (Hafner and Lyon 1996: 78). The microcomputer research team at the Xerox Palo Alto Research Centre (PARC) which had produced the little aborted 'Alto' was also deeply influenced by this philosophy (Hafner and Lyon 1996: 238–9). What Xerox failed effectively to exploit, Jobs and Wozniak picked up on.

From the first 10,000 to acquire the blueprints for the Mark 8, through the cult created by Altair, to the establishment of Apple, the computer industry took almost no notice of the burgeoning world of micros. The industry was used to machines costing a good deal more than a few hundred dollars and remained basically uninterested in the potential market these pioneers were unearthing. IBM, thinking as small as it could, in 1975 showed a 48k prototype which weighed a mere 50 lb., but the matter was not pursued. Commodore International, though, was an established electronics firm and it introduced the Pet, a true microcomputer, in 1977. A chain of electronic supply shops, Radio Shack, also produced a viable computer, the TRS-80, for as little as $499 (Hanson 1982: 206). By the late 1970s the attractiveness of what was then still called the home computer was self-evident. Apple, on its launch as a public company in December 1980, was valued by the market at $1.2 billion and a number of firms, some from the mainstream of the industry, some – like Atari – from the games end, were finally becoming involved. Eventually IBM itself was to enter the fray with the 5100, which some considered a much more expensive alternative to the Altair and then, more seriously, in 1981 with the PC. It sold 35,000 of them that first year which was also, of course, Year 33 of the 'revolution' (Augarten 1984: 280).

The number of computers in US homes had gone from a few hundred in 1975, the year of their introduction as a factory-assembled item, through to 20,000 a year later. In 1980 the industry passed the billion-dollar sales mark and by 1982 there were just under a million machines. Sober estimates suggested that by 1984 there were 9,000,000 micros worldwide and a further three-quarters of a million mainframes and minis (Elton 1984). Ten years later one third of American homes had microcomputers, 31 million machines; and 4 million further machines were shipped in 1995. Some 40 million US homes also had a videogames console (Veronhis Suhler 1996: 317, 335).

The driving force, in the decade of the home computer, still remained with those, like Wozniak, who appeared to emerge periodically out of a garage (heavily backed by lines of credit) with a new wonder. Constant advances in microprocessor capacities rendered these machines quickly obsolete if not in terms of their actual use, certainly in the minds of potential buyers. Volatility is used by Information Revolutionaries to account for the bankruptcies and disasters the industry has suffered and there is some justification for this. In the bruising struggle to establish the standard machine, mistakes are easily made, especially when one's opponent is IBM with its Svengali grip on customers undiminished in this new area. Nevertheless, despite the plausibility of this explanation for occasional failures, within the boom there was a real problem. The home computer initially had little or no place in the home. This caused considerable instability.

Altair was bankrupt by 1979. Osborne, producer of the first portable machine, was also bankrupted. Texas Instruments pulled out. Atari failed to keep up with the games and could not balance this failure with success at the cheaper end of the computer market. The division might have been generating nine-figure revenues in 1980 but within four years it was losing so much money it had to be sold. The experience of Coleco, a toy manufacturer, with its Adam is a further significant marker. Here was a machine which did everything that devices twice as expensive did and yet it sold so poorly that it had to be relaunched within months of hitting the American market. Instead the company survived selling a rather horrendous line of traditional stuffed dolls which became a fad in the mid-1980s. Most significant was the record of the managers of Apple, post Jobs and Wozniak, in reducing the company, through a series of wrong decisions about almost every aspect of their business, to the status of a minority player.[2]

It rapidly became clear that the appetite to replace one's cookbooks, balance one's cheque-book, keep track of one's stocks or spend happy evenings recalculating one's mortgage over different terms and interest rates was limited – and no amount of hype was going to change that. In the home, the computer's essential value – beyond games – was at first only as a computer; a device, rather like von Neumann's IAS machine, upon which to study – or better, play with – computing. A semantic shuffle was then accomplished. The home computer became the personal computer, which, while it could exist in the home, also had a function as a tool in the workplace. It was only with the coming of accessible word-processing, which turned the home PC into a very effective typewriter, and the arrival of the modem which permitted e-mail and Internet access (p. 330) that meaningful domestic uses were found. The scope of the device settled on a few applications – games platform, typewriter, calculator, spreadsheet, database and graphics with a communications option. The main impetus to sales, however, was educational. As in previous times, when failure to buy the expensive encyclopaedia was translated, for middle-class parents, into a serious dereliction of duty towards the children, so now the same marketing mechanism was used to shift PCs. Twenty million of America's 35 million PC households in 1995 had children and no less than 96.5 per cent of those 20 million had bought units of educational software (Veronhis Suhler 1996: 329).

Yet the efficacy of these programs, and indeed the usefulness of the computer itself as a consumer durable, remained somewhat undetermined. Since the machines have no clear purpose in the home, their design floundered; and arguably continue to do so up to the millennium. The creative onus within the industry now devolved on the software provider. IBM had been forced out of the software business in the mid-1960s as a result of its attempt to scupper the CDC 6600. It was therefore in line with its corporate culture that it should 'buy-in' an operating system for its PC in 1980. This meant, however, that it had now surrendered control over the development of these machines not just to the maker of the CPU but also to the software house. In this case it chose a small firm, Microsoft, to provide the PC's operating system. Within three years of the 1981 launch, 40 per cent of all personal computers were running its programs. In 1986, Microsoft became a public company and Bill Gates, its founder, an instant millionaire. A decade of ruthless product development and marketing later, Gates was reputedly the world's richest man and Microsoft's influence was as great as that of the manufacturer who gave it a start fifteen years earlier.

Against this were balanced the inefficiencies of the personal computer industry's domestic support services which became a byword for arrogance and ineffectiveness. Computer firms of all kinds were by the mid-1990s shifting their products without much discernible effort and, perhaps in consequence, behaving like the automobile industry before Ralph Nader and consumer safety consciousness got to it. The industry's insolence was compounded by the continued patent limitations of the machine's capacity. While it is true that the speed of the central processing unit increased steadily, the price of memory fell, its capacity increased and printers and other peripherals changed and improved, yet the fundamental architecture and functions remained unchanged.

Interactivity became the buzz-word as the software diskette was being almost totally superseded by the CD-ROM, whose capacities were marketed as 'multimedia'. It was widely suggested that, for example, multimedia would revolutionise such fundamental human activities as the consumption of stories. Readers/listeners, or, better, users could tailor their own tales, for example. However, not only was there less than no evidence that this would happen, the CD-ROM itself could not support its own hype. In fact, it was oversold since its 0.64 gigabyte capacity gave it limited capacity for full motion video. Philips and Sony were promising a Digital Video/Versatile Disk (DVD) with six times the CD-ROM's storage for the late 1990s; but the damage to multimedia as a mass medium had been done (Chesher 1996: 33; Markoff 1997: 13–17), much as television was damaged by being similarly oversold in the 1930s. The market for CD-ROMs as 'info-' or 'edu-tainment' outside of basic programs, games and informational texts such as encyclopaedias did not develop. The gap between the hype of revolution and the reality of the underused, complex and extremely expensive consumer durable sitting in millions of middle-class Western homes grew wider. Only the endlessly replenished smoke-screen of hype prevented this from being clearly seen.

The debate about the computer's impact is all but confounded by the rodomontade. One basic element in all this is the seductiveness of graphs. Nothing captures the essence of the hype surrounding computing so well as the dramatic growth curve graph which peppers the pages and video screens of this literature. The graph's parameters are so chosen that the line of 'progress', whatever form it might take, rises with rocket-like precipitousness towards the top of the page as the present or near future is approached. Its trajectory remains steady as it takes off into the future. Most of these graphs are simply absurd – transistor sales from nowhere to millions, with no account taken of the place of such sales in the total electrical component market. This is, perhaps, the *locus classicus* but there are other equally silly examples. 'Moore's Law', invented by one of the founders of Intel, 'estimates' human brain capacity in terms of computing power:

> In Moore's Law it states that every eighteen months we will see a doubling in the density of integrated circuits. In what is sometimes called the law of the microcosm . . . ., we see that every doubling of the density of IC circuits should lead to a doubling of the price performance of the underlying technology. This model shows [] when we think a personal computer will have the same processing power and memory of the human brain. You can see this suggests that we could see a cross-over point in the year 2010.
>
> (Bond 1996: 7)

In the graph this 'truth' is indeed revealed as these meaningless lines cross over each other at the date in question: PCs will be as smart as us by 2010. QED.

Most such diagrammatic verities, not so self-evidently absurd, nevertheless stand revealed as needing what the linguist Labov has called, in another connection, 'the withering interjection', namely 'so what?' So what that the dollars to compute millions of instructions per second have fallen between 1960 and 1995?

So what that in 1950 1000 valves/tubes took up a cubic foot whereas in 1956 10,000 transistors occupied the same space? So what that by 1968 1,000,000 could do the same thing? (Note that the date in each of these latter cases is typically more than a little in front of itself, but let that be.) Indeed, so what that the economically privileged of the First World are currently buying PCs in their millions – why should this be much more significant than their acquisition of dishwashers or microwave ovens?

Another element of hype is the supposed youthfulness of the chief actors in the PC story – Jobs was 22 when he sold the Apple concept to the 32-year-old Markkula. Noyce was 29 when he took over Fairchild. Gates was 19 when he founded Microsoft and so on. But others, Watson Sr, Shockley, Kilby, Mauchly, Olsen, Dummer (to take a few at random), were older. In fact, in the world of computers, as in other worlds, there is a mix. The ages of those writing the cheques and offering the lines of credit to enable exploitation of the whiz-kids' innovations is less than prominently inscribed in the records. One can further question the supposed significance of the fortunes that have been made – so what that Bushnell earned $15 million from Atari or that Jobs was worth $162 million overnight when Apple went public or that Gates acquired, as a symbol of unimaginable wealth, Leonardo Da Vinci's *Notebook* for his personal use? Has not such wealth always been the reward of entrepreneurship – 'this boundless drive for enrichment' – under capitalism? The amazing youthfulness of certain players and the wonderful growth of ROMs, RAMs and dollars is not evidence that the world is in flux; rather revealed is just a bemused obsession with miniaturisation, youth and profits in the minds of the graph makers and other technicist commentators. The question is largely begged as to what is the real impact of the machine on society. It is emblematic that, throughout the literature of the Information Revolution, the suggested inevitable social upheaval seldom makes sufficient difference for the secretary in the new electronic office not to be a woman and her boss a man.

And what of the baseline statistic, the actual number of computers in the world? How does their rise compare with the progress of other technologies? Is such a rate of diffusion really so untoward, so revolutionary? Take the automobile. In the US, passenger vehicles alone went from 8000 to half a million in the first decade of the century and from half a million to 2 million in the second and 2 million to 23 million in the third, 35 years after the invention of the automobile. And with the automobile came a complete remaking of the entire environment: paved streets, petrol/gas stations, car-parks, the decline of urban centres. Thirty-five years after the invention of the computer there were not yet 10 million of them and where was the equivalent broader impact? A basic fact about the micro-computer is that despite its enormous success there are far fewer of them than the industry expected, less than half as many as the 20,000,000 predicted in the mid-1970s for the 1980s (Hanson 1982: 126). The home computer penetration curve is actually quite modest in comparison with other electronic devices, more like that of the home fax than that of the VCR or the television.

> The computer in its modern form was born from the womb of the military. . . . It is probably a fair guess, although no one could possibly know, that a very considerable fraction of computers devoted to a single purpose today are still those dedicated to cheaper, more nearly certain ways to kill ever larger numbers of human beings.
>
> What then can we *expect* from this strange fruit of human genius? We can expect the kind of euphoric forecasting and assessment with which the popular and some of the scientific literature is filled. This has nothing to do with computers *per se* . . . .
>
> We can also expect that the very intellectuals to whom we might reasonably look for lucid analysis and understanding of the impact of the computer on our world, the computer scientists and other scholars who claim to have made themselves authorities in this area, will, on the whole, see the emperor's new clothes more vividly than anybody else.
>
> (Weizenbaum 1980: 586–7)

But only a minority seem able to see the emperor's new clothes – among them the author of this statement, the computer pioneer, Joseph Weizenbaum.

The fact is that the development of the computer is of a piece with the development of other technologies of electronic communications. For fifty years, technicists have constantly told us the machine will revolutionise our lives. It is time for them to look round the world, with its diminished economic expectations, with its persistence of bigotry and strife, its inequalities and stupidities, and tell us exactly where and how the computer has fundamentally impacted on all that.

# Part IV

# THE INTRICATE WEB OF TRAILS, THIS GRAND SYSTEM

# 1 3

# THE BEGINNINGS OF
# NETWORKS

## THE FIRST WIRED NETWORK

The networking of the world's personal computers in the 1990s was heralded as creating a virtual new dimension of human experience. On the face of it seems to be an extraordinary claim, given that most technologies in this history have depended on exactly the establishment of such networks by corporeal or incorporeal means. In order to provide a context for outlining the development of the Internet we need to go back to the beginning, to the start of electronic communications, to show how central the building of networks has been to their success and how much the current networking of computers conforms to these historical patterns. In this last part, then, I will be revisiting all the technologies previously discussed, from telegraphy on, to describe how the concept of the network determined their diffusion and effectiveness.

The idea of interconnectivity, even incorporeal interconnectivity, is far from novel. Bell, despite his contribution to the 'invention' of the telephone being far less than popular understanding imagines (p. 48), nevertheless was one of the few who clearly saw this potential. On his European honeymoon with Mabel he drew up a prospectus for investors in the companies his father-in-law Hubbard was founding:

At the present time we have a perfect network of gas pipes and water pipes throughout our large cities. We have main pipes laid under the streets communicating by side pipes with various dwellings, enabling the members to draw their supplies of gas and water from a common source. In a similar manner, it is conceivable that cables of telephone wires could be laid underground, or suspended overhead, communicating by branch wires with private dwellings, country houses, shops, manufactories, etc., etc., uniting them through the main cable with a central office where the wires could be connected as desired, establishing direct communication

between any two places in the city. Such a plan as this, though impracticable at the present moment, will, I firmly believe, be the outcome of
the introduction of the telephone to the public. Not only so, but I
believe, in the future, wires will unite the head offices of the Telephone
Company in different cities, and a man in one part of the country may
communicate by word of mouth with another in a distant place.

(Fagen 1975: 22–3)

'This grand system', as Bell called it, represents a significant conceptual leap.

Although Bell had before him early examples of gas and water distribution,
Edison's system for electricity was still a few years in the future (Friedel and Israel
1986: 195–200). Anyway, these were all distributive methods involving a central
reservoir, gasworks or power station, somewhat different from the two-way
network Bell envisaged. Furthermore, the existing electrical signalling system,
the telegraph, did not follow this pattern but had been developed as a point-
to-point service with final message delivery being accomplished by hand, on
the model of the post. Nevertheless, in taking this mixed approach, the
telegraph had managed to become ubiquitous by the time Bell conceived of
the telephone network.

From 1845 on, Morse and his partners began to build a network of telegraph
offices both by themselves and by licensing other entrepreneurs, such as O'Reilly,
to construct lines and offices. The rivalry with O'Reilly, with its costly arguments
in the courts and its even more debilitating vandalism of the telegraph wires
themselves, convinced Morse that the telegraph needed to follow the postal model
of a unified monopoly service. The logic of monopoly inherent in all public
communications systems here began to assert itself, even in an environment
committed to the principle of free markets. After the legal situation was resolved
in favour of the Morse interests in 1851, the telegraph industry moved towards
consolidation along these lines. By the end of that decade only three large
telegraph holding companies existed. Finally William Orton, head of United States
Telegraph, merged it into Western Union in 1866. *The Telegrapher* lamented: 'With
the power which this great monopoly puts into the hands of its officers, salaries
will decrease as surely and as naturally as water runs down hill' (Thompson 1947:
426). The last of the major concerns, the American Telegraph Company, followed
Orton's lead into Western Union. The monster had absorbed more than 150 lines
to establish a system extending 37,380 miles with 2250 telegraph offices and
capital of over $41,000,000.

These offices functioned both as origination nodes and as distribution points on
a store-and-forward basis. Forwarding involved either re-sending the message to a
further office or delivering a hard copy by hand to an address in the service area.
Limited through-patching was also being explored. Not everyone was impressed,

though. In 1854, Henry Thoreau wrote: 'We are in great haste to construct a magnetic telegraph from Maine to Texas; but Maine and Texas, it may be, have nothing to communicate' (Czitrom 1982: 11). Professor Morse, on the other hand, wrote that the telegraph interests were now 'very much as . . .I wished them to be at the outset, not cut up in O'Reilly fashion into irresponsible parts but making one great whole like the Post Office system' (Thompson 1947: 426). It had taken the better part of three decades to accomplish this. In Europe, of course, the systems were unified from the outset since it was the postal services which built them following a pattern understood from the semaphores and in conformity with their (recently established) notions of universal delivery service.

The same conceptual principals were applied to the building of an international, transoceanic, telegraphy network. In 1849, Dr O'Shaughnessy (later Sir William O'Shaughnessy Brooke) laid a bare iron rod beneath the waters of the Huldee in India and  sent a telegraphic signal from bank to bank, a distance of 4200 feet (Fahie 1901: 39). In 1854, a New York, Newfoundland and London telegraph (subsequently Atlantic Telegraph) Company was formed by a retired business-person, Cyrus Field. By 1856 the company's line had traversed the Gulf of St Lawrence to reach land's end in Newfoundland, 1000 miles at a cost of about $1000 a mile. The main task of crossing the ocean was then put in hand and in August 1858 the two continents were joined. Queen and president exchanged telegrams – 'It is a triumph more glorious, because far more useful to mankind, than was ever won by conqueror on the field of battle', said President Buchanan (Bright 1893: 49). However, within a month the cable was dead, due to leakage.

Slowly capital was reassembled and the leak problem was solved by using gutta-percha, a natural latex substance which was a virtual British Imperial monopoly since it was found only in what is now Malaysia. Willoughby Smith, who was to establish the importance of selenium to television while laying this very cable, was the chief electrician of the Gutta-Percha Company. I.K. Brunel's enormous and previously ill-fated *Great Eastern*, the world's biggest ship, was commandeered and finally, in July 1866, a permanent link was opened between Heart's Content on the western shore and Valentia in Ireland.

> Gooch, Heart's Content to Glass, Valentia, 27 July, 6 p. m.: Our shore end had just been laid and a most perfect cable, under God's blessing, has completed telegraphic communication between England and the Contin-ent of America.
>
> (Rolt 1970: 397)

Henry Thoreau was as unimpressed as he had been about the domestic telegraphy network: 'We are eager to tunnel under the Atlantic and bring the old world some weeks nearer to the new; but perchance the first news that will leak through into the broad flapping American ear will be that Princess Adelaide has the whooping cough' (Czitrom 1982: 11).

Thoreau underestimated the appetite for transoceanic communications of all kinds: news, commerce and, for the very privileged, personal. By the end of the 1920s there were twenty-one transatlantic cables and 3500 other wires under the world's waters. From 1879 to 1970 the cost of using them dropped from $100 per message between Great Britain and the USA to a maximum of 25 cents a word. In 1957, the year of Sputnik, the British Cable and Wireless Company carried 491 million words of traffic on its worldwide system. The international telegraphy system created a worldwide networking pattern which was deeply to influence and condition all subsequent telecommunications systems. For instance, the issue of national interests in such systems was addressed for the first time.

In January 1856, when a bill to charter Field's transatlantic telegraph, in concert with the British government, was presented to Congress, there were objections to the scheme more political than, if not as profound as, Thoreau's:

> The real animus of the opposition was a fear of giving some advantage to Great Britain . . . there were those who felt that in this submarine cable England was literally crawling under the sea to get some advantage of the United States.
>
> (Bright 1893: 102)

In reply to Senator Hunter of Virginia who asked 'What security are we to have that in time of war we shall have the use of the telegraph?', William Seward, whose bill it was, could only pray that 'after the telegraphic wire is once laid, there will be no more war between the United States and Great Britain'. In Britain, the parallel bill caused Lord Redesdale to ask why, since the cable began in Ireland and terminated in Newfoundland, both colonies, the US had to be involved at all! Both bills, however, passed (Bright 1893: 104–5).

Out of these arguments the concept of vital national interest, by which states mould their international telecommunications policies, emerged. In 1875, while explaining to Congress why a French company had been denied permission to land a cable six years previously, President Grant enunciated what had rapidly become the established position: 'I was unwilling to yield to a foreign state the right to say that its grantees might land on our shores while it denied a similar right to our people to land on its shores' (Oslund 1977: 150). Grant's price of admission to the French was that American telegraph companies be allowed to share in the French cable. This principle of co-ownership and reciprocity, essentially a restrictive practice, became known paradoxically as the 'open shores' policy. Far from being any such thing, the concept effectively updated the notion of inviolate borders for the age of international electronic communications. It has stood as the foundation of the entire policy edifice, up to and including the right of states to limit (or attempt to limit) reception of radio signals and satellite television transmissions.

Seward's transatlantic cable bill not only engendered American international telecommunications policy, it also confirmed the stand previously taken allowing private ownership of the telegraph, although not without argument. Senator Bayard of Delaware queried the appropriateness of a private company being involved:

> It is a mail operation. It is a Post-Office arrangement. It is for the transmission of intelligence, and that is what I understood to be the function of the Post-Office Department. I hold it, therefore, legitimately within the proper powers of Government, as the employing of a stage-coach, or a steam-car, or a ship, to transport the mails, either to foreign countries, or to different portions of our own country.
>
> (Bright 1893: 100)

Congress, however, declined to reverse the position it had taken in refusing to acquire Morse's telegraphic patents because its domestic profitability was in doubt. Since there was no reason to believe the transatlantic wire would be any more of a money-maker, Bayard's was a view out of step with this crucial precedent. Anyway, Congress had already passed, in 1866, the Post Roads Act which limited government involvement in the internal telecommunications system to providing 'aid in the construction of telegraph lines and to secure the government the use of same for postal, military and other purposes' (Oslund 1977: 146). Government aid in creating infrastructure and providing traffic to enable private profit became the 'tradition' which would inform all policy on these technologies up to the Eisenhower and Kennedy communications satellite plans and beyond, although the Bayard or 'Post Office' objection (as it might be termed) was to be raised more than once.

For all that telegraphy remained an internal 'Post-Office arrangement' in other nation states, internationally the precedent of American telegraphy privatisation was to become more and more powerful as technology moved from transoceanic telegraph cables to wireless telegraphy to radio telephony to cabled telephony and satellites. These developments took a century. In these various ways, nationally and internationally, the telegraph demonstrated how new electrical communications systems could begin to duplicate the principle of universal service which the post, with the 'invention' of the postal stamp, was finally cementing into place even as national telegraph systems were being created. And now the telephone presented itself.

## THE TELEPHONE NETWORK

The first Bell Company had been created in 1875. In 1878, with only slow progress being made in the point-to-point business, Hubbard founded the New England Telephone Company to promote the construction of exchanges by local operating licensees. Bell's vision of the network was beginning to affect how people thought about telephony – not paired stations but subscribers networking through a central exchange.

The first exchange technology using simple patchboards was telegraphic and the earliest exchanges tended to be run by Western Union's telephone subsidiary, the American Speaking Telephone Company, which already had the know-how. Thus Western Union had, in addition to its superior Edison telephones, another advantage in its more developed exchanges. But the patchboard technology was basic enough to be quickly exploited by Bell's partners. In September 1878 Emma Nutt was engaged as Bell's first woman central office operator (Brooks 1976: 66). In distinction to telegraphy, there was no assumption that telephone work was too hard for females. Within three years the rightness of the decision was being celebrated by telephone exchange men everywhere: 'I would like to say right here, I've been asked by Mr. Sabin what our experience has been with young ladies' help; the service is very much superior to that of boys and men. They are steadier, do not drink beer and are always on hand' (Fagen 1975: 484). Various adaptations from telegraphic models were made, but it was not until 1889 that a viable automatic exchange was developed, and with it the eventual possibility of the telephone dial. The assignment of numbers to subscribers, though, had first been suggested in 1879.

Almon B. Strowger is another figure in the pantheon of Victorian amateur inventors, a Kansas city undertaker supposedly dreaming up the telephone exchange mechanism that bears his name without any formal scientific or technical understanding. Motivating him, according to the received story, was nothing more than a burning desire to thwart malicious and corrupt central telephone office operators who were denying him business by not connecting clients. In fact, having had the initial idea, Strowger involved a number of engineers who actually perfected a working system for him. The first Strowger mechanism was operating experimentally in La Porte, Indiana, in November 1892. For the first time subscribers could make a call without the aid of the operator. In 1902 Grey's old firm, Western Electric, developed a 10,000-line system based on another set of patents, but the machinery was not installed (Fagen 1975: 345). In 1916, Western Electric acquired the Strowger manufacturing rights. The comparative lateness of this acquisition suggests, correctly, that too much must not be made of the automatic exchange. Before the First World War, the Bell companies, and the telephone industry generally, questioned whether or not the public would accept dialling instead of operator assistance. It was not until 1919 that Bell finally began the extensive installation of automatic exchanges (Fagen 1975: 545–7).[1] Despite this, the non-automated exchange had long since replaced the point-to-point station.

By the end of 1880 the number of stations, or telephones, had doubled to 123,380. A year later there were only nine cities with populations of over 10,000 and only one with more than 15,000 that did not have a telephone exchange (Stehman 1925: 18). Nevertheless, despite this initial bout of enthusiasm and the wide availability of exchanges, in the early 1880s subscribers were slow to come forward. By the mid-decade there were still only 156,000 phones nation-wide and service was still subject to extreme interference from trolley-cars, telegraph wires, and even thunderstorms. Moreover, with the move to exchanges, the economics of the leasing system started to work against Hubbard. It had been potentially a splendid source of regular revenues requiring little prior capital as long as telephones were being rented as discrete pairs. Now telephony not only required capital to establish and service exchanges but it became a somewhat peculiar business since more stations created more value to the user but at more cost to the provider and less profit per every new subscriber. Economies of scale did not quite work.

Legal actions, always a sure mark that radical potential is being thwarted, also drained funds. Hubbard was forced to involve the 'Boston Capitalists' and with their support, National Bell became American Bell in 1880 with six times the capital of its predecessor (Evans 1983: 9). The removal of Hubbard as well as the resignation of Bell himself, both with tidy but not extraordinary fortunes, soon followed. Theodore Vail, however, remained for the moment as general manager. American Bell, although on a sounder financial basis and protected by its patents, was still paying substantial licensee fees to its major telecommunications competitor, Western Union. Growth continued to be slow. Its new management set about bringing all Bell phones under one corporate roof by buying back the licensees under whose aegis the rash of exchanges had been built. These were then amalgamated into local Bell operating companies. This was essential if cities were to be networked via 'longlines', the next step towards realising Bell's vision of the 'grand system'.

In 1884, American Bell demonstrated a viable longline between New York and Boston. The following year it created, in New York, a longline network subsidiary which it called, despite its agreement with Western Union to stay out of telegraphy, the American Telephone and Telegraph Company – AT&T. 'Telegraph' was incorporated into the name by an act of the New York legislature to reflect the company's leased lines business (Fagen 1975: 34). AT&T invested much effort in long-distance circuit technology. It was the main agenda item for its first laboratory where work on 'loading coils' which preserved the vibration and resonance of the original signal in the fashion of a primitive repeater began in 1889. The company also bought the patents for a similar device developed by a professor at Columbia University (ibid.: 243–4).

Meanwhile, in 1888, the court finally decided (by four to three) the consolidated patent case, all the claimants having been lumped together, in favour of Bell. It held that any system of electronic speech transmission was covered by the original patents, a curious decision, given that (as we have seen: p. 46) one did not mention speech at all and the other did so in a subordinate fashion (Brock 1981: 104). Although subscriber take-up was still disappointing, a serious economic depression now being underway, the firm's earnings increased five-fold to over $2,000,000 a year. The court decision, however, only bought a few years' respite for the master patents were about to run out in 1893 and 1894. Vail, although he was to leave the Bell companies before the patents expired, nevertheless began to position them for the confusions that were bound to follow their lapse. He regarded the longline work of AT&T as the best defence in the coming post-patent battle. But despite this understanding, within ten years AT&T's system had reached barely into the Midwest, and ten years later it had progressed no further than Omaha and Denison, Texas (Fagen 1975: 345). It was essentially an East Coast operation for which wiring the more sparsely settled West was not that pressing a project. In all the years of protection, it had placed only one-third of a million telephones and its network had just reached Chicago.

As a result, with the end of the patent, significant opportunities presented themselves in the western areas ignored by Bell. There were also inroads to be made in the East with the promise of cheaper service. A flood of independent telephone companies appeared. American Bell responded aggressively to the new situation, cutting its rates in towns where there was direct competition, refusing to interconnect with rivals but offering interconnection to systems where it had no prior interests. Bell exercised all its considerable muscle in this fight. For instance, there is the curious incident of the People's Telephone Company which claimed it could not establish itself in New York because New York Bell held stock in the subway operations which were required by the city to duct telephone lines. The subway company said its tunnels were unable to accommodate further wires and refused to build for the People's Telephone. Nevertheless, the president of New York Bell swore that 'no steps had ever been taken to prevent competition from entering New York' (Stehman 1925: 81). In the latter part of this era, that is to say from 1907 on, Bell began to buy up the stocks of its competitors. Bell's approach, which had indeed been essentially élitist, positioning the phone as a middle-class accoutrement, changed.

The independents were constrained but not wiped out. In 1894, eighty-seven independent systems had been immediately established. By 1902 more than 3,000 were in existence, not all of them direct competitors since some were in areas Bell did not serve and many were minute rural arrangements linking only a dozen or so scattered farmhouses. Five Midwestern states had over 200 telephone systems each and in general the majority of non-Bell exchanges were in this part of the world, which had been comparatively ignored by Bell. Elsewhere, Bell services were duplicated even as Bell itself expanded. In a relatively short time 45 per cent of all communities with more than 4000 people had acquired two telephone services, two exchanges and, often, two 'stations' in the home. As a consequence of Bell's initial strategy, a class distinction emerged with businesses and the wealthy on the Bell exchange (with its access to AT&T'S longlines) while the rest of the population was left with a more limited universe, and often inferior equipment, on the cheaper independent systems. The Bureau of Census reported in 1902 that the average independent, even after excluding the minute farmers' phone systems of the Midwest, had a mere 705 subscribers (Stehman 1925: 53). The larger Bell rivals had combined into the National Association of Independent Telephone Exchanges in 1897 to build their own longlines and by 1905 the association had 'almost a continuous system from the eastern slope of the Rocky Mountains to the Atlantic Coast', but not one which connected the major business centres (Evans 1983: 16,19; emphasis added).

Because of Bell's high rate strategy during the years of monopoly, the removal of the patent had the predictable pricing effect. Phones did get cheaper:

> The present Columbus subscriber, who finds it either convenient or necessary to keep two such services, pays $54.00 for one and $40.00 for the other, or a total of $94.00 per year, $2.00 less annually for two than one cost him before competition, or, in other words, competition has brought to the alleged burdened businessman who has to keep two telephones, 20,000 more telephones to talk with and has handed him a $2.00 yearly rebate in the bargain.
>
> (Evans 1983: 19)

Yet this simple parable of the 'alleged' advantages of competition, the logic of which was to be used again in the last third of the twentieth century to justify a return to 'competition', is by no means the whole story.

For one thing, the independents, who by 1900 had 28 per cent of the vastly expanded number of subscribers, were not too bothered about standards:

> The Independent Companies, for the most part were concerned not to improve service for the public good, but rather to make money by corporate manipulations . . . their plants were poorly built. They offered service at low rates, made inadequate allowance for maintenance and depreciation, and paid dividends out of capital for a few years, and then

were compelled to raise their rates or go into the hands of receivers.

(Evans 1983: 95)

In Kansas City, for instance, the company was so undercapitalised it could not extend its lines to new subscribers. In Baltimore, Bell's competitor, which had obtained a city franchise on the grounds that it could provide service at $36 per year for residences and $48 per year for businesses, raised its rates to $60 and $72, claiming it was using better equipment than the contract specified. (This sort of argument was repeated elsewhere as a curious sort of precursor to the case which would be used by cable television companies against the same American municipalities three-quarters of a century later. And, just as was to happen in the 1980s, the municipalities were told in 1905 that in law they could not regulate the rates.)

More than this, the supposed advantage of having '20,000 more telephones to talk with' could not disguise the fact that those new phones could not talk to the old Bell exchange. This offence to the logic of the 'grand system' became increasingly irksome in the years before the First World War. As a decision of the Supreme Court of the State of Kansas in 1915 eloquently indicated, people were simply becoming fed up with the inanities of full-scale competition: 'Two telephone systems serving the same constituency place a useless burden upon the community, causing sorrow of heart and vexation of spirit and are altogether undesirable' (Stehman 1925: 241). (With this obvious disadvantage in mind, when 'competition' was reintroduced in the 1980s – heralded by the 1982 US court decision which divested AT&T of its local Bell operations – it took the impure form of being highly regulated with interconnection between service providers being required by law. In contemporary economic thinking this nevertheless apparently means that a 'market' has been created, although, obviously, not in ways that any Victorian entrepreneur would easily understand. It is exactly that an external force is needed to order connections that leads to the presumption of a natural monopoly.)

Moreover, although there is no question that competition in the late 1890s forced Bell to improve its service, drop its haughtiness and cut its rates, it remains a moot question as to whether or not this could be achieved only in this way. Heavy regulation (which by no means vanished even during the late twentieth-century vogue for 'competition') could also achieve the same results as can be seen from the earliest European experience of telephony. All over Europe, from 1879 on, Bell had set up subsidiaries along the lines of local US operators and in each country local competitors, local licensees, municipal or national governments took them over. In all these cases, the removal of the Americans was an essential prerequisite to reasonable rates (Bennett 1895). Only in St Petersburg, Moscow and Warsaw was Bell left in command, with the result that these cities had the highest annual rent ($121) in Europe. This was in line with Bell's domestic practice. In the early 1890s Washington Bell charged $100; in Greater New York anything up to $240; in Philadelphia $250; in Chicago $175.

Contrast Paris, where the state owned the system, and the rate was $18 per annum and Stockholm, where it was owned collectively by its users, $20. There were five times as many telephones per hundred people in Stockholm as there were in Washington and the system boasted the latest metallic circuit underground which most of the US Bell operations did not. AT&T adopted the same high-charge policy for its longline services. A call from Philadelphia to Washington cost $1.25 for five minutes, whereas in England the same duration and distance cost (in dollars) was 48 cents and in France 30 cents (Stehman 1925: 48).

So while it took the end of monopoly in America to bring Bell prices down, it is equally true that elsewhere other monopolies, heavily regulated, were changing less without the bite of competition. During this early period (to the mid-1890s) the European states, either directly or through the operation of franchised entities, were comparatively effective diffusers of the new technology, although overall penetration outside the great cities was far less than in America. This relative success was not of course universal. The suppression of the telephone's potential to disrupt telegraphy was being handled in the States by legal challenges, cross-patent agreements and formal business pacts; but these remedies were not all necessarily available everywhere, especially where telephony and telegraphy were both 'Post Office arrangements'.

In Britain, Bell had personally demonstrated the telephone to Queen Victoria, who gave her approval by accepting a pair. A well-capitalised Telephone Company (Bell Patents) Limited was established, but Edison had prior rights having lodged his patent in the UK earlier than Bell. A rival company was set up for which the young George Bernard Shaw laboured as a 'way leave manager'. He recalled:

> Whilst the Edison Telephone Company lasted it crowded the basement of a huge pile of offices in Queen Victoria Street with American artificers. They adored Mr. Edison as the greatest man of all time in every possible department of science, art, and philosophy, and execrated Mr. Graham Bell, the inventor of the rival telephone, as his satanic adversary.
>
> (Robertson 1947: xx)

This London rivalry was short-lived. Shadowing American agreements, the two firms became the United Telephone Company (UTC) in 1879.

In common with most European states, Britain had rejected the American privatisation precedent in telegraphy. The General Post Office had been given control of the telegraph in a series of Acts starting in the 1860s but the system remained as unprofitable as it had initially been in the US. The GPO viewed the new telephone technology with considerable disapproval as a further threat to its faltering telegraph service (Webb n.d: 27). In 1880 it moved against the UTC. The UTC went into court believing that a straightforward demonstration of the difference between a telephone and a telegraph would suffice to convince Mr Baron Pollock and Mr Justice Stephen that the Telegraphy Acts did not apply to the new technology. It was wrong. The Court found for the Crown. The GPO then imposed a 10 per cent royalty on the UTC and licensed all comers, private companies as well as municipalities, to operate telephone services. But, unlike other parts of Europe, Sweden say, where the government encouraged local co-operative systems and only built the longlines itself, in Britain the GPO also decided to operate at all levels as a competitor to its own licensees.

The result was total uncertainty on the part of the commercial interests and hostile lethargy from the GPO. Unable to make telegraphy pay, it was unwilling to absorb another potential loss maker; but it was equally fearful that others could make the telephone profitable – inevitably at the further expense of the telegraph. The GPO eventually took over the longlines and then granted no local operating licences to run beyond 31 December 1911, which had the same effect as planning blight. What little expansion there was virtually ceased after the turn of the century. The GPO finally took telephony over in 1912, only to find the First World War halting development. It was in fact not until 1919, forty years after the 'invention', that the telephone began to be seriously diffused in the UK. Out of this initial period of suppression, only Kingston upon Hull survived as an independent municipal system.

This perhaps explains why R. S. Culley, GPO Engineer-in-Chief, refused at the outset in 1877 to see Mr Bell's representative, 'stating that his department was in possession of full knowledge of the details of the invention and that the possible use of the telephone was very limited' – in the event a self-fulfilling prophecy (Robertson 1947: 11). The result was a perfect expression of the 'law' of the suppression of radical potential. The UK, as the world's then leading industrial nation, achieved less telephone penetration and higher rates than any other Western European country; but the failure of the GPO offers no simple case for the advantages of competition over regulation. The British could have been as intelligent as, say, the Swedes; they simply were not.

Elsewhere, with differing details, the same result was achieved. State ownership was, by the First World War, the norm; but Europe lagged behind the States in telephone penetration and this had led to a further argument in favour of private ownership. By 1900 the US had about one phone for every sixty people; the nearest European total, Sweden, had one phone for every 115 people, France one for every 1216 people and Russia one for every 6988 people. As a consequence of this, that major article in telephonic faith – that private enterprise worked better – was bolstered. The suggestion was that the low rates imposed by the public entities, while politically popular, failed to provide sufficient capital for a first-class service.

However, such a conclusion is once again hasty. First, effective service was provided in those countries, such as Sweden, where telephony was perceived as a new sort of utility. Second, cultural factors quickly revealed themselves as crucial. Clearly the discrepancy between Russia and America, where in both cases the service was provided either entirely or largely by Bell, was not just due to the organisation of the institution of telephony. Switzerland had a widespread state system which worked very well but the Swiss made on average a mere two calls a day. Likewise, the Bank of England lived without a telephone until 1900 (Brooks 1976: 93). In general, rural Europe clustered its farmsteads together in villages; rural America spread them out over the vast plain. Moreover, apart from these geographic factors, Americans were simply proving to be more socially adaptable than Europeans and increasingly accepted the telephone from the mid-1890s. It was only in the last quarter of the twentieth century that the range of social and business intercourse conducted on American telephones ceased to strike the European observer as extremely extensive by comparison with home.

Finally, there appears to be a general economic factor to consider. In 1962, Jipp pointed out that there was a direct relationship between per capita GNP and telephone penetration – a law which guarantees America's place at the top of the penetration table; but it can still be noted that in the late 1970s, both Switzerland and the USSR were still, albeit slightly, below average in the number of their phones according to Jipp's Law (Chapius 1982: 43). It was not then simply a question of a better service being provided by free-enterprise American companies (for no such better service was necessarily provided) as opposed to the European states' failure to build systems that worked (for many states did build good systems). It was rather that different countries responded differently to the lure of the telephone for a wide range of cultural and economic reasons; but in each and every case, the logic of universal service was at work. This was to lead the United States effectively to abandon competition within two decades of its introduction.

By 1902 Bell had 57 per cent of the stations, and 70 per cent of the wire. Five years later when all systems together, including Bell's, had three times as much wire and twice as many telephones, Bell's share remained much the same (Stehman 1925: 78). Five years after that, in 1912, Bell companies operated 55 per cent of all telephones. In that year, the last before the state took a hand in the telephone industry, Bell sold 11,000 subscribers and bought systems with 136,000 (Brock 1981: 156). The logic of universal service was forcing the independents to do business with Bell and, by 1912, all but 17 per cent of them were also connected to its wires. By 1916, Bell had eliminated competition in 80 per cent of its markets and had acquired a significant stake in Western Union.

The independents had long since begun to call upon the law, in the form of the Sherman Antitrust Act, for protection. As early as 1910 the independents' association was demanding for regulation: 'We do not ask the Government to fight our battles, but we do ask for protection against outrageous methods of warfare which are illegal and detrimental to the public welfare. . . . We are not afraid of supervision; we believe in regulation' (Brock 1981: 159). This was not just a question of preventing take-overs and requiring interconnection. As Vail had anticipated, the most important technological advantage Bell had over its competitors was in the development of longlines. By 1911, using loading coils, the AT&T network reached Denver. To carry it to the Pacific coast, the newly invented vacuum tubes were used as repeaters, Bell acquiring De Forest's patent in 1913. Two years later, carried by 130,000 poles, the telephone line between New York and San Francisco was opened (Fagen 1975: 262). Apart from its longline research, Bell also continued to exploit its other patent advantages – the Berliner patent, for example, had been delayed until November 1891 and was therefore in force to 1905. Even if the independents had adopted a better notion of public service, they would have been hamstrung, especially in the matter of toll lines, by inferior technology.

Long before America's entry into the First World War, it had become clear that Bell would not be allowed to enjoy its emerging victory undisturbed. However much communities wanted just one telephone company, the wave of populist politics, which had found partial expression in the anti-monopolist Sherman Act, also more directly sought out AT&T as an object of attack. Theodore Vail, having made a fortune outside telephony, had returned to the board of AT&T in 1900 and was persuaded to assume presidency of the company in 1907. Now, thirty years after Alexander Bell had enunciated the 'grand system', Vail began to make it a political reality. He continued, if not intensified, the competitive strategies of the company but he also had a remarkably enlightened view of the need for public service. He stated that:

> With a large population with large potentialities, the experience of all industrial and utility enterprises has been that it adds to the permanency and undisturbed enjoyment of a business, as well as to the profits, if the prices are put at such a point as will create a maximum consumption at a small percentage of profits.

> (Stehman 1925: 241)

In 1912, having bought into Western Union and thereby secured a real dominance of the republic's non-postal communication system, Vail enunciated a new path between the various perils of untrammelled monopoly, limited and wasteful competition and government takeover. He declared himself to be in favour of the strict regulation by government of the telephone industry as long as it was 'independent, intelligent, considerate, thorough and just' (Brooks 1976: 132). As Edison said, 'Mr. Vail is a big man. Until his day the telephone was in the hands of men of little business capacity' (Stehman 1925: 126). Vail's was a long way from the view the company had taken in an annual report of the 1880s: 'No state in fairness ought to destroy what the patent system has created. . . . Sound public policy is surely against the regulation of the price of any class of commodities by law' (Brooks 1976: 82); but times had changed. The US Attorney General in 1908 had tried for one last time to break all the then existing AT&T patents and had failed. Now, pressured by the independents, he warned AT&T that further acquisitions would indeed offend the anti-trust laws. In the same month, the Interstate Commerce Commission, under whose jurisdiction telephony now fell, began an investigation of what some claimed was AT&T's attempt to take over the country's entire communication infrastructure.

It should not be forgotten that a wholly commercial telephone system was unique in the West. Even Britain, the last Western European state to have commercial telephony, had handed the private phone companies to the Post Office which was to close them down in 1912. It is no wonder that, against such a background, the then US Postmaster General, Albert Berelson, revisited Senator Bayard's 'Post-Office arrangement' position outlined half a century earlier. Eager to reopen the question of 'postalisation', he told a congressional committee: 'I have never been able to understand why the use of wires should be denied for the transmission of communications, any more than the use of a man on foot, or a boy on a horse or a stage coach, (Brooks 1976: 149). In reply to these multifaceted threats, Vail agreed that: 'All monopolies should be regulated' – but added: 'Government ownership would be unregulated monopoly'. He continued to hew his statesmanlike path. For instance, he had already allowed Western Electric, breaking the original monopoly arrangements, to sell to non-Bell companies. But the forces arrayed against AT&T were not to be so easily distracted. No aspect of the giant's affairs was left in peace.

The Attorney-General now had a new concern, that Bell was directing customers who used the telephone to send a telegram to use Western Union at the expense of its competitors. This charge was the final straw. After some months of negotiation, Bell officials determined that the wisest course of action would be not to address this latest complaint piecemeal but rather to seek the elimination of all conditions and practices 'repugnant to the Federal authorities' (Stehman 1925: 153). On 19 December 1913 an AT&T vice-president, Nathan Kingsbury, wrote the Attorney-General a letter which became known as the Kingsbury Commitment. In it AT&T agreed to disgorge Western Union, to make its toll lines available to independents and to work with the Interstate Commerce Commission in obtaining prior approval before acquiring any more telephone systems. The

Kingsbury Commitment closes off the period inaugurated by the Bell patent of 1876. It outlined the basis upon which the telephone was to become part of American society and it remained in force for the better part of seventy years. It also marks the end of the period when the 'law' of suppression was operating to constrain the diffusion of the telephone in the United States.

The compromise was so effective that it withstood the high point of populist attacks on the company when, five years later during the war, the telephone was briefly nationalised. The same had happened to the radio (p. 77). However, unlike radio, where nationalisation eventually produced the RCA, the effect on AT&T was minimal. All that occurred was the imposition of a government board of control and the nominal management by the Post Office of a system that remained AT&T'S. AT&T's profits for the one year of nationalisation were $40,000,000, $5,000,000 more than it had managed to make for itself in 1916; but this period of government control, occasioned largely by years of populist demand for cheaper telephone rates, saw a rate increase, and with it a total vindication of AT&T and private ownership. Somehow the need for this increase was never linked to the generous terms secured by the company from the Post Office when it was taken over. With the peace, the Kingsbury Commitment was re-established as the *modus operandi* and nationalisation was abandoned. In 1921, the Graham Act enshrined the Commitment in law. AT&T was exempted from the provisions of anti-trust legislation but no longer prohibited from taking over competing services. Yet, with mandated interconnection and so much of the system already in its hands, it conducted itself – albeit with some internal dissonance – with restraint, just as Vail had always counselled.

In 1931 the government, responding to the depression, ordered Bell to cut its rates in Wisconsin and thereafter across the whole system by 5 per cent. 'Sound public policy' had come to embrace the regulation of the price of the telephone commodity, but without damaging the private corporation. 'One system, one policy and universal service' meant that what was good for AT&T was also good for America, even in these economic circumstances. By 1934 the American Bell Telephone Company and its AT&T successor wholly owned eighteen of the twenty-three entities that resulted from the reorganisation following the passage of the Graham Act. They also held a majority interest in three more. Philadelphia, the last city with two competing telephone systems, came into Bell's sole control as late as 1945.

But the real importance of the Graham Act was that AT&T was encouraged to take the view that its privileged position demanded profit margins be determined by its investments in the system; the more it spent, then politically the more it could earn. This, rather than private enterprise *per se,* accounted for its technical superiority as compared with other nations' systems. It also sustained Bell Labs, since those costs counted as investment. In this way, regulation was responsible both for the fact that Bell provided the most sophisticated and up-to-date service in the world for most of the twentieth century and for Bell Labs, the single most important source of technical innovation in mass communications history so far.[2] The result was that America's early lead in the number of telephones per capita was maintained. By 1914 there had been 12.8 million telephones worldwide, 9.5 million of them in the US (Kingsbury 1915: 530). By 1917 there were 12 million telephones in America, one for every ten people. On the eve of the Second World War, Bell was worth $5 billion, the largest firm in history. It controlled 83 per cent of all US telephones, 98 per cent of long-distance toll wires and had a total monopoly in the US of overseas radio telephony (p. 273).

But this success did not mean that the essential contradictions of its position remained unchallenged. The first question was whether or not universal service and a regulated monopoly also necessarily meant vertical integration, that is, ownership of the equipment supply chain as well as the network. This was vigorously questioned by the FCC, the regulatory agency from 1934 on. In 1949, the Justice Department argued that Bell should divest itself of Western Electric, but failed in its attack; although, as part of its response, the telephone company was forced to agree that its role should be limited to that of a common carrier. Justice kept up the attack, forcing Bell in a 1956 consent decree to keep out of the computer business. In 1968, the FCC ordered Bell to allow non-Bell equipment to be attached to its system.

One consequence of this last was that the modern facsimile machine slowly began to be diffused – a very good example of how much more important such socio-political developments are than are advances in technology *per se*. Facsimile was actually a spin-off initially of telegraphy and had been in existence at this point for over a century. As we have seen, it had played a crucial role in the research agenda of television. Proponents of privatisation point to such incidents as examples of how the monopoly held back advances; but, once again, this is too simple. First, a more enlightened regulatory structure could have as easily encouraged the attachment of faxes. Second, there is a considerable time gap between the 1968 change of regulation and the serious diffusion of the device. In the next twenty-one years only 1.2 million faxes were placed in America and widespread diffusion was only accomplished in the 1990s. The regulatory environment was significant but so were the cost-effectiveness of mail delivery and the comparatively slow acceptance of solid state electronics. The point is that none of these constraining elements depended on the existence, much less the development, of any given piece of technology.

In 1971, the FCC allowed a Bell rival to build a microwave link between St Louis and Chicago to go into operation, the first since the period of competition. The history of American telephony before the First World War began to repeat itself. In 1974 Justice returned to the attack, claiming that Bell's behaviour since

1956 was stifling competition and inflating rates. By 1982, AT&T finally consented to divest itself of its local operating companies. The world's biggest firm was reduced by one-third, but was relieved of its promise not to engage in other businesses. It immediately (and ineffectively) set about becoming a major computer manufacturer, while IBM bought itself into the new longlines services.

The most significant net result in America of this new era of competition was simply to 'superserve' the profitable business sector. The other major effect was to encourage the contemporary universal fashion for telephone 'competition' and over the next decades many national public telephone systems were privatised to the considerable benefit of governments, managements, shareholders and large volume users. In the UK, for example, the GPO's telephone department was privatised and initially provided with one competitor, the old international Imperial telegraph monopolist Cable and Wireless. Unlike America where duplication of wires over 'the last mile' into the home was never envisaged by the privatisation process, in the UK cable television operators (themselves for the most part international subsidiaries of the Baby Bell firms spun off in America in 1982) were also allowed to compete in providing services to the home. Despite this, even in the UK at the height of neoliberalism, interconnection was still mandated. The lessons of the US experience before the First World War may not have been consciously to the fore but the logic of universal service could not be ignored. Privatisation ideologues claim that telephone costs have fallen and services have improved – but then telephone costs have fallen and services have constantly improved under a variety of regimes ever since the device was first marketed in 1879. It remains to be seen whether the new dispensation in America (and elsewhere) can deliver a system as efficiently as did the old under the provisions of the Graham Act.[3]

# 14

# NETWORKS AND RECORDING TECHNOLOGIES

## BROADCASTING NETWORKS

The sustained attack on the AT&T monopoly also effected the development of the radio network. This was because, although radio as a medium of mass communications depended on single point distribution, transmission masts, the creation of national radio networks relied on linking these central transmitters in the first instance by wires. In the United States, this once more involved AT&T. As we have seen, AT&T was one of the radio pioneers and had involved itself in running radio stations until 1926. But that same year a new opportunity opened up.

RCA had decided to aid the sale of receivers and studio equipment by providing a central supply of programme material. As with the record industry's view that disks were essentially a sales promotion device useful in marketing record players, so the radio industry determined that programs should be given away (as it were) to encourage receiver sales. RCA therefore established the National Broadcasting Company to do this and set about linking its licensed stations and encouraging others to affiliate with this new service. It would, of course, take advertising although, until the late 1920s, it seems that commercials were only imperfectly perceived as a major potential source of revenue. From 1926 until the turn of the decade, Sarnoff, for example, presented NBC as a public service giving away programming to help sell sets and only using advertisements 'to subsidise high-quality non-commercial fare' (McChesney 1990: 30). On the other hand, this high-mindedness did not stop William Paley, who came to radio primarily as an advertiser, from establishing a rival, the Columbia Broadcasting System (CBS) in 1927. Clearly the logic of commercials suggested the creation of ever larger audiences, i.e. networks; the more people listening to a programme, the cheaper the cost of each household to the sponsors of that programme.

Following the measure of stability brought by the establishment of the FRC, this logic took hold. Networks, although the FRC legislation had not contemplated this, blossomed. Between 1926 and 1931, network affiliates, with both NBC and CBS grew from 6.4 per cent of broadcast stations to 30 per cent. These last accounted for 70 per cent of the audience. By the mid-1930s network advertising was worth $72,000,000 a year. The real losers were the educational pioneering stations which decreased in number by two-thirds between 1927 and 1933 and by 1934 accounted for a mere 2 per cent of radio output (McChesney 1991: 92–93). The apparent losers were the newspapers but the impact of declining print advertising revenues was cushioned by their considerable interests in radio. For example, publishers owned no less than thirty-five of CBS's ninety affiliates in 1932.

Also among the winners was AT&T. Linking stations was far more obviously 'a telephone job' since it required high-quality long, or, better, landlines; moreover it avoided responsibility for content, a stance much more in accord with the phone company's common-carrier status than station ownership. Radio

> seldom provides as suitable or stable a link as a telephone line for carrying broadcast programs of distant origin to a local transmitter. The lack of available wavelengths, the interference caused by other services, atmospherics, and fading, all combine to make the wireless link unsuitable and unreliable for medium and short wavelengths. Hence, in practice, wireless is not used as a link if a suitable line is available.
>
> (*BBC Handbook* 1930: 381)

Because of the Graham Act, laying such sophisticated wires was clearly an AT&T function; moreover, the Labs had given it a real advantage by producing far and away the best technology for this task. This network landline niche was beginning to reveal itself as the company determined to sell its radio stations. More money was to be made out of leasing longlines to the radio industry than could be earned by owning a few radio stations. Not only that; an inevitable conflict with the Justice Department, given that AT&T had already antagonised the other radio interests, could be more readily avoided. In this way AT&T seemingly got out of the radio business, except that networking depended on it completely. (It was to perform a similar 'invisible' role as Hollywood's ultimate tsar via its control of the dominant sound film system (Westrex) in the 1930s.)

Elsewhere, the postal service remained most governments' primary controlling mechanism and the creation of the radio network was more straightforward than in America. Indeed, the usefulness of the radio as a tool for establishing and maintaining national identity was quickly realised and this became a guiding principle. This was in marked contrast to the US where the concept of market choice become dominant and with it a desire to maximise the number of stations, and indeed networks, available in any area. Perhaps the best articulated alternative to such a broadcasting market model was to be found in the UK. For example, the BBC's founding father

> Reith saw broadcasting the chimes of Big Ben as a particularly potent way of creating a symbolic link between centre and periphery by enabling [as he wrote in 1924] 'the clock which beats the time over the Houses of Parliament, in the centre of the Empire, [to be] heard echoing in the loneliest cottage in the land'. The symbolic community of the nation was further cemented by broadcast relays of state ceremonies and the monarch's Christmas address to the people.
>
> (Murdock 1992: 29)

Reith's plan was to ensure that the BBCo had these effects centred on the creation of a 'National Programme', a network which depended on landlines and therefore the GPO. The establishment of such a service was how the BBCo interpreted the recommendation of the 1923 Sykes Committee that the company provide, in addition to its eight 'main' stations enough 'relay' stations to cover all significant centres of population. However, there was nothing in this proposal to suggest that all these stations share common programming, simultaneous broadcasting or SB as it was known at the time. Nevertheless, as the *BBC Handbook* for 1928 put it, Sykes was treated as a mandate for 'the virtual assumption by the BBC of a responsibility that it had hitherto not had, viz. that of providing a *complete national system* accessible to the owner of the cheapest form of set, wherever he might happen to live' (*BBC Handbook* 1928: 40; emphasis in original). By 1928, the network to accomplish this was already well on its way. The landlines stretched from Plymouth to Aberdeen and, via Glasgow, to Belfast. Regional programming opt-outs were suppressed replacing 'local variety and difference by a standard conception of culture and manners' (Scannell and Cardiff 1982: 166). As with Chappe's semaphore, the purpose was to create 'a national space' (Flichy 1991: 22).

It can be argued that, historically at least, complaints about the BBC's centralised metropolitan nature, complaints which have always been heard up to the present, are grounded in a fundamental misunderstanding of its basic function which was, exactly, to be, however subtly, an engine of British nationalism. The British were not alone in taking this approach and it can be noted that by the early 1930s the landline network stretched across Europe from Rennes in the West to Vilnius in the East but this had no appreciable effect on the national programming of the countries traversed (*BBC Handbook* 1930: 385). The lines essentially served the nation state (with some allowance for commerce) in Europe just as they served commerce (with some allowance for culture) in America.

This pattern was to be repeated with television both nationally and internationally. Given the success of its radio strategy and its continued interest in television as part of the ongoing work of Bell Labs, it is not too surprising that AT&T determined that the one essential which television would need, when it finally got started, was longlines with which to build networks and that it would provide them. In 1934 Bell Labs unveiled 'a radically new form of transmission cable' (Brooks 1976: 202). In 1936 the first of these co-axial (co-ax) lines were laid in New York City and a year later AT&T began to build the national network with a link, costing $580,000, between New York and Philadelphia (Fink 1945: 147; Udelson 1982: 92). From the phone company's point of view radio and television were essentially the same pie and AT&T, having made its peace with RCA, was ready for television even if the rest of the players were not. The war then interrupted progress.

After the War, the radio industry's development of television was protected by the regulatory structure. Part of that protection was to prevent rivals from establishing networks. Some, like Paramount Theatres, were directly prohibited by the FCC. (Plans for theatre television on a UHF net were not allowed (p. 123).) The actions of AT&T in using its co-axial cable rates structure, which was agreed by the Commission, further effectively scuppered networking plans by Mutual and Philco. This was done by 1948 in advance of the 'freeze'. (The aborted Mutual network was revived four decades later by Murdoch who made the core Mutual stations the basis of his Fox network.) The third network, the newly independent ABC (having been, until the FCC ordered otherwise, NBC's second network), barely survived. The fourth, DuMont, also part-owned by Paramount Theatres, was dead by 1955 (Boddy 1990: 55–7). The FCC's Sixth Report, which opened up a huge range of UHF stations, most of which were never assigned and all of which (until the coming of cable rebroadcasting) were economically marginal, mopped up the possibility of an extensive fourth network.

From the late 1940s on, everywhere in the developed world, the radio industry prepared to build the television net. There was no conceptual or technological difficulty about this. It simply required the laying of expensive co-axial cables, sometimes augmented by microwave line-of-sight links. The work continued throughout the 1950s and thereafter in the rest of the world.

## DIGRESSION: BROADCASTING NETWORKS AND RECORDING TECHNOLOGIES

Aside from issues of ownership, control and competition, the establishment of national broadcasting networks in either radio or television was quite difficult in America because of the time zones. The main broadcasting periods, which were to become 'prime-time' because of the premium prices commercials transmitted during these hours could command, were, more or less, the same everywhere (for example, mid-evening). In terms of simultaneous transmission, though, these 'prime-times' are as much as three hours apart in reality. The answer was either to repeat the programming live a few hours later for the West Coast, record it, or abandon the concept of the national audience. Since the last was commercially unthinkable and politically undesirable, and really effective recording techniques were unavailable, the live repeats technique was adopted.

Recording techniques were improving. Researching sound film systems, which had been part of the agenda ever since Dickson linked the phonograph to the Kinetoscope in Edison's lab, continued to be a fruitful source of advance (Winston 1996: 70). By 1926 the Vitaphone sound-film system, which was adopted by Warners, was using large diameter 16-inch single-sided disks turning at $33\frac{1}{3}$ revolutions per minute, each record lasting as long as a single 35mm film reel (Limbacher 1968: 208). In 1931, the radio industry picked up this readily available film technology. RCA produced a new format which stored up to 15 minutes a side on metal disks coated in a thermo-plastic lacquer, far more durable than shellac. It was primarily used to distribute commercials rather than to record programming for network repeats (Chanan 1995: 66). This was because of a host of industrial and cultural pressures from union resistance through an apparent public distaste for recorded ('canned' or 'bottled' ) programming to the comparatively poor quality of the disks. There was, of course, no question of selling the long-playing format to the public or even of producing less fragile records for them, until 1948. That year CBS finally marketed the LP. Although this technology changed the record industry it did not impact on the network recording problem, where another solution was found.

The search for an effective sound-film system also produced suggestions to link Poulsen's underused wire-recording technology to projection. Lee de Forest tried this in 1913 and a system was patented in 1915. Further refinements in the late 1920s improved performance by using a fine steel band or tape instead of Poulsen's wire. In some variations metal disks were used (Nmungwun 1989: 38–48). The founder of Elstree Studios in London, Ludwig Blattner, applied this technology to film in the early 1930s but without success. After his bankruptcy in 1933, Marconi took over the licence selling recorders to the BBC who used them to repeat programming for the Empire Service, a network with even greater time zone differences than the Americans had (Lafferty 1983: 16–37). The greater capacity and improved quality of these machines clearly pointed the way to an eventual solution of the networking problem but the difficulty was the unwieldy nature of the recording medium – steel tape. The answer, magnetic tape on a flexible cellulose acetate film-style base, was about to be introduced as Blattner was being forced to give up. It was first produced by BASF (Badische Anilin-und-Soda-Fabrik) in 1934.

Fritz Pfleumer, an independent industrial consultant of considerable creativity, had developed the idea in the late 1920s. He had been asked to help a cigarette manufacturer prevent the gold in the then fashionable gold-tipped cigarettes from coming off on smokers' lips. Pfleumer embedded the metal in plastic rather than in paper and the problem was solved. He also developed a device which could sense, electrically, whether or not all the metallised tips were at the top of the packet. As a music lover dissatisfied with the fidelity of disks then available, he then thought that this technique of embedding metal into a plastic might be used, if the metal were magnetised, to record sound. He patented the idea in 1928. Physical systems of filing the metal produced particles too uneven to give a good recording result, however; so BASF, industrial chemists, became involved. Chemical precipitation of ferric oxide proved to be viable and, in 1934, magnetic recording tape was ready. It was marketed in a format 5 cm wide and available in very long lengths. In 1937 AEG began to use the tape, now made by IG Farben which Pfleumer had joined, in its Poulsen recorders, marketed as Magnetophons. In 1938, the German state radio, the RRG, adopted the machine. In 1939, Walter Weber, an RRG research engineer, using a technique that had first been described in 1918, introduced a circuit which produced a high-fidelity recording by dramatically reducing the Magnetophon's noise (Winston 1996: 73–4).

These developments, though, went largely unnoticed. Pfleumer's tape, as a medium for recorded music, was redundant, superior quality never being enough by itself to topple an established technology. The 'law' of the suppression of radical potential continued to protect the record industry throughout these decades. Tape had lost out too as a film sound technology. It was not until the 1950s that it began to be used as a distribution medium for stereophonic sound-tracks and it was only in 1962 that it was introduced to Hollywood as a production recording medium (Winston 1996: 74, 103). Elsewhere, no wire recorder – not even for office dictation use – was manufactured in America between the collapse of Poulsen's original firm before the First World War and 1937. In that year Bell, ever watchful across the whole field of these technologies, introduced a high-quality steel tape recorder for its recorded telephone weather service (Jewes, et al. 1958: 324–6). This is typical of the limited specialised uses which were found for tape. For example, the Nazi leaders, at Goering's insistence, had their wartime speeches recorded on Magnetophon tape.

None of this overcame the inertia of the radio industry which persisted with live repeats for the West Coast after the end of the War. Enter Bing Crosby. He objected to doing his extremely popular *Kraft Musical Theatre* show twice and wanted it recorded on LP. NBC Radio, following its own normal practice, refused to allow this on quality grounds; but Crosby was powerful enough to defy Sarnoff.

He took his show to ABC, then only in its third year of operations. However, the disk recordings Crosby made were indeed less than perfect and the show's ratings began to suffer. The Crosby organisation laid down as a matter of some urgency the specification it required for a recording medium.

By this time, German advances in tape technology were known to the victorious Allies. Patent rights to the German Magnetophon could be acquired from the US Alien Property Custodian – the official who, despite his title, was actually in charge of transferring Nazi technology to America as a species of war loot. The key enabling figure was John Mullin. As a major in the Signal Corps in 1944, he had been perplexed as to how the RRG was able to apparently keep whole German symphony orchestras broadcasting in the middle of the night. In the first days of the peace, Mullin discovered the Magnetophon and the mystery was solved. He personally liberated some machines and converted them for 16mm film use early in 1946. He gave the first American demonstration on 16 May 1946 to a professional audience in San Francisco and was put in touch with Ampex, a specialised electronics firm looking to replace its wartime radar component business. Ampex acquired the patent from the Custodian and in September 1947 demonstrated for Crosby's technicians a prototype improved American version of the German machine which met their needs. Thus, the American version of the reel-to-reel audiotape recorder was, as it were, 'invented' (Nmumgwun 1989: 69–76). Bing could now do his show once only and, finally, the radio industry fell in behind him. His firm became sole West Coast distributors of the machines (Addeo n.d.: 11–40).

As this was happening, television was coming on stream with exactly the same network problem, this time exacerbated by the vastly increased production costs the new medium entailed and the huge expense of the co-axial network. This economic factor was eventually to mean that television's network needs (and not just in America) constituted a far more pressing and effective supervening necessity than had radio's in the 1930s and 1940s. Nevertheless, in the 1940s, there were those, Lee De Forest among them, who thought the entire idea of a real-time (or virtual real-time) television network ought to be abandoned. His case was simple: 'A coaxial line from New York to Los Angeles represents about $15,000,000. . .but they can have all this in defiance of all time zone difficulties. . . .How? By the very simple and very sensible method of making television films and sending them from city to city in tin can containers' (De Forest 1942: 71). In 1931, he had even demonstrated what proved to be an abortive prototype to allow the waveform of a television image to be impressed on 35mm film coated with pure silver, using a series of needles mounted on a revolving disk. It did not work, but this was why he was passionate about recording systems as opposed to co-ax cables.

In the immediate post-war period, it seemed as if De Forest's view might prevail using conventional film techniques. The 'law' of suppression was constraining the new medium, via the FCC 'freeze', including the building of the network. Without a national system of co-axial cables, programs recorded on celluloid could indeed be, to use today's terminology, 'bicycled' to stations outside the small East Coast AT&T network. Television after all had an intimate relationship with film. At the very outset, Jenkins had been interested in it as a method for delivering films to the home. As early as 1927 Ives made the conceptual jump from television devices which played back existing films to an apparatus which exposed film specifically for television scanning. Bell Labs at that time wanted to improve its poorly defined television image with the direct illumination that a film/television projector/pick-up tube chain could provide. This was taken up by the Germans whose almost instantaneous film recording systems (IF, intermediate film), it will be recalled, had been developed to maximise the effectiveness of the mechanical scanning systems of the later 1930s.[1]

Experiments with filming standard television began in 1938, the major problem being converting the electronic image of thirty frames per second (in the US; twenty-five frames in the UK) to sound-film's twenty-four frames per second. This discrepancy produced frame roll, whereby the camera's shutter action allows the film to record gaps in the electronic picture otherwise unnoticed by the human eye as black bars; but this could be solved with careful synchronisation and complex shutter design. Although there were some further attempts at transferring the cathode ray image to celluloid during the war along these lines, active experimentation by the BBC and others began in 1947. By January 1948 DuMont was ready, in conjunction with NBC and Kodak, to market a 16mm telerecording, or kinetoscope, a camera which used 1200 foot reels, to record a full half-hour and a fairly sophisticated shutter system to produce a comparatively flicker-free image. The first colour recordings were made on 18 August 1949 (Abramson 1955: 251–2).

As the American net was built, in defiance of De Forest, 'bicycling' was abandoned in favour of co-ax cable and the same time zone problem arose as it had with radio. This led to the era of 'hot' or 'quick' *kines*, requiring that the telerecording be produced in under three hours to enable the other coast to see it. Although film worked within such time frames, its quality left something to be desired. Furthermore, since colour film could not be processed so quickly, the 'hot' solution was clearly not going to be possible when colour television arrived. The matter was therefore not closed and a number of other options were revisited. For example, in 1934 another system which, like De Forest's, took the wave-form of the video-signal but in this case to modulate a light, was demonstrated by Edison Bell (UK) Ltd as the 'Visiogram'. Ordinary 35mm film was exposed to a fluctuating light which was responding to the video-signal, just as in the 'sound camera' a light responded to the audio wave-form of the microphone's output. The film could then be fed back into a television receiver system to recreate the original image; but, as with the De Forest device it also did not work well enough for further development to be then warranted. (Such concepts were last used, futilely, to produce alternatives to domestic videotape – EVR – between 1959 and 1964 (p. 129).)

Faced with the difficulties of colour as well as the emerging threat of videotape, Kodak also produced one of these conceptually elegant proposals. In 1955 it revived a 16mm film with lenticular lenses embossed into it which acted as prisms. This was a development of the dyeless colour film system which captured colour as wavelength data first suggested in 1908 by Gabriel Lippmann (Eder 1978: 668–73). Kodak and Paramount had worked on it in the 1930s, failing however to produce an effective 35mm version; but now, faced with the need for 'hot colour kines' the stock was tried once again. NBC used the film from September 1956, but the game was up. Two months after this, CBS transmitted videotape for the first time. NBC persisted with lenticular kinescopes until February 1958 but its decade-long relationship with Eastman in the telerecording field had in effect wrongfooted it. CBS, who was working with Ampex, was backing the winning technology. Antisocial production hours, production costs cheaper than film, networking across time zones – the solution to all these problems lay with videotape.

A television camera is a transducer converting light into an electrical signal. That signal can be stored, just as audio signals were, on disks. The problem is that the video signal is vastly more complex and is carried at far greater frequencies, millions as opposed to thousands of cycles per second, occupying enormously enlarged bandwidths. The ideation transformation for the video disk occurs in a British patent, filed by B. Rtcheouloff in January 1927, suggesting the Poulsen telegraphone could be adapted for television. The device was almost certainly not built (Abramson 1973: 71). Technological performance of the prototype phase begins with Baird who, because he was working with thirty lines at twelve-and-a-half frames per second, was not overwhelmed by bandwidth and created, in September 1927, the Phonovisor using ordinary gramophone industry audio equipment to impress the signal on a wax disk. He tinkered with it for three months, recorded some images, publicised it, and moved on (Norman 1984: 46–7). Despite Baird, high definition television – in the 1930s sense – produced signals beyond the ability of the recording industry of the day. It was not until the coming of tape and American post-war developments of that technology that a recording system emerged that was sufficiently complex to capture a video signal.

This was achieved on 11 November 1951, when the electronics division of Bing Crosby Enterprises demonstrated a monochrome recorder using specially configured tape. This is the date of videotape's 'invention'. To solve the bandwidth problem, the tape could be moved at high speed past the recording/playback heads, which were stationary; or various arrangements could be made whereby the heads spun as the tape passed them, thus reducing its speed. Just over two years after the Bing Crosby demonstration, RCA showed a recorder that used $\frac{1}{4}$-inch tape for monochrome and $\frac{1}{2}$-inch tape for colour. It ran at 30 inches per second, recording 4 minutes of programming at three-megacycles (about half the allocated broadcasting bandwidth).

The Ampex Corporation, which began work on the problem at this time, was to establish, by 1956, the broadcasting industry standard for the next quarter of a century. Its machine used a magnetic tape, 2 inches wide, driven at 30 inches per second past a drum containing four magnetic heads which rotated at 14,400 revolutions per minute. This was the device CBS used on 30 November 1956, to transmit the first videotaped programme (backed up by kinescopes). RCA, having exchanged patents with Ampex, produced a colour recorder along broadly similar lines the following year. In 1960 Ampex created a circuit which allowed the VTR to be locked into external synch signals produced in the studio or elsewhere. Its output could therefore be cut into a programme or dissolved without any disruptions. In 1964, for the BBC's second channel which was eventually to be in colour, Ampex produced a high band recorder which could successfully deal with the new 625 line PAL signal (Abramson 1973: 89–90).

Spinning the heads created problems and in the early years it seemed as if a direct tape path might be a better solution. In 1956, RCA produced another $\frac{1}{2}$-inch colour machine using this longitudinal scan configuration which travelled at a finger-munching 240 inches per second. In 1958, the BBC demonstrated $\frac{1}{2}$-inch VERA (*Vision Electronic Recording Apparatus*) which ran at 200 inches per second and produced a 15-minute tape on a 20-inch reel. These machines, although not as practical for everyday operations as traverse scan devices of the Ampex type, were none the less worth exploring because they accommodated broader bandwidths on narrower tapes. In experimental devices demonstrated in the late 1960s, tape speeds reached 4000 inches per second and the bandwidth capacity of 50MHz, enough for many television signals, even for a couple of contemporary 'high definition' (1000 lines +) ones. The third possibility, helical scanning, was introduced in 1959 and allowed the tape to move more slowly, recording each field in one long path stretching diagonally across the tape. For professional use, before the introduction of electronic videotape editing (in the late 1960s), this tape path created a considerable disadvantage. Traverse scanned tapes could be, with some difficulty, physically cut; helically scanned tape could not.

Tape's diffusion was constrained by industrial conservatism and the threat it posed to the recorded music industry. Nevertheless, broadcasting networks could not have developed without it and it has become ubiquitous as a spin-off from the supervening necessity occasioned by network operations. (As we have seen (p. 126), spun-off again into home devices it was to have a significant impact in both audio and video forms.)

## PRE-SATELLITE INTERNATIONAL RADIO LINKS

While the national radio and television broadcast networks were being built, an international broadcasting system was also being created. This was not really a question of networks since each country simply broadcast its signals from a single transmission mast, although some measure of rebroadcasting, as with the BBC's foreign services, was undertaken. Nor was this sort of international broadcasting the same as using the cross-border landline network which simply provided occasional national programming from a foreign source. Rather, the international broadcasting system was designed to broadcast specially produced programs to foreign audiences. The pioneering effort was Germany's morse news bulletins transmitted during the First World War to neutral countries.

Conventional cross-border radio broadcasting begins at the Moscow station which was established in 1922. Initially, its international broadcasts were nothing but a programming strand put in place when it was realised that the signal could be heard abroad. But, in the later 1920s, Radio Moscow also pioneered programming specifically for cross-border reception, which meant using a foreign language. The Germans established a short-wave station in 1929 and introduced foreign language transmissions a year after the Nazis came to power. By 1936, the centre at Zeesen was the most powerful in the world. The Vatican station started in 1931 and Italy's in 1934. Even the League of Nations became a broadcaster in 1932, after many years of tests. The USA, having no state broadcasting system, was not part of this development, except as a subsidiary commercial activity, until it joined the Allies. The Voice of America commenced in February 1942 (Karuppiahya 1996: 10, 11, 14–17).

The great imperial powers, France, Britain and the Netherlands, all created short-wave services to bind their empires together. The Dutch began broadcasting in 1927 (to the East Indies), the French in 1931 and the BBC a year later. However, a distinction was drawn between using the metropolitan tongue for this purpose and broadcasting in foreign languages. This last was seen, especially by the British, as being too close to 'propaganda', that is, the sort of programming put out by Radio Moscow. It was therefore only in response to such provocations as the Italian Arabic service, that the BBC began its own foreign language broadcasts in 1938. The Second World War, and the cold war which followed, established international short-wave radio, giving it a vibrancy which sustained it throughout the next half-century. By 1996, well into the age of international television satellites, the major broadcasters – the BBC, the Voice of America, Deutsche Welle and Radios Moscow and Peking – were still each transmitting in forty or so languages for an average of about 1000 hours a week (Karuppiahya 1996: 81).

Radio's origins as an alternative to telegraphy as a point-to-point communications system were also not forgotten. Nationally, of course, the telegraph monopolies, in most countries the government postal services, limited the scope of wireless telegraphy. It was anyway not needed both because of the extensive nature of the wired network and the unreliability of radio (which had led even the broadcasters to network via landlines). But internationally it was a different story. Using long-wave, the GPO had started to build a wireless telegraphy system immediately after the First World War. A service to Madrid was established in 1919. However, in this area the British government finally decided to follow American precedents and allow commercial enterprises to expand the system to Europe in the early 1920s and to the Levant towards the end of the decade. Some circuits, for example, to Egypt, were even taken over from the Post Office (Sturmey 1958: 130–1).

Other circuits relied on short waves bouncing from the ionosphere. The signal sent to Marconi in Poldhu, Cornwall, from St Johns, Newfoundland, on 12 December 1901, the first to cross the Atlantic, obeyed his basic law, since a distance of 1800 miles was achieved with kite-born aerials at around 1000 feet. But until he actually did it, there was some considerable doubt as to its possibility. In the late nineteenth century, faced with the knowledge that radio waves travelled in straight lines like light, scientific opinion was uncertain as to their efficacy for signalling along the curve of the earth (Fahie 1884: 260). Marconi's sensational demonstration was, in terms of Maxwell's wave theory, an anomaly. The existence of a region of the upper atmosphere where radio waves might bounce off a layer of free electrons, created by ultraviolet radiation and X-rays from the sun, was not known. To save the Maxwellian paradigm, Oliver Heaviside and, independently, A.E. Kennelly revived a suggestion made in 1882 to explain changes in the earth's magnetic field and hypothesised the existence of a spherical shell of ionised air surrounding the earth which was impermeable by radio waves. The ionosphere would allow both Marconi's distance law and the straight line hypothesis to coexist. The ionosphere was not experimentally verified until 1925, but it was utilised from 1901.

Marconi established a regular service for news and private messages to ships at sea in the Atlantic from 1904. By 1907 the service was open for transatlantic business. In 1918 the US Army transmitted a signal to France and the Marconi Company bounced one around the world from its station in Caernarvon to Sydney. Full-scale commercial transatlantic wireless telegraphy was reintroduced after the War in 1920. The first short-wave service to Buenos Aires was opened by Marconi's in 1925. By the outbreak of the Second World War, there were some hundreds of established circuits and considerable competition from the Americans (RCA had forty-two circuits by 1929) as well as German and French interests.

Effective radio telephony, as opposed to wireless telegraphy, required powerful transmission apparatus but, inhibited by the effectiveness of the wireless telegraph and its implicit limitation on the market, this developed quite slowly. Despite these difficulties, AT&T had established itself as the leading American entity in non-broadcasting international voice communications. In 1915 it had managed to send a voice signal to Paris via its partner, the International Western Electric Company (Beck 1967: 102). Clearly this was an area of expansion where the constant worries about AT&T's monopolist tendencies were reduced if only because its main competitor, Marconi's, had equally worrying monopolistic tendencies itself. After the upheavals of war, forced nationalisation and post-war reprivatisation, AT&T did little, but between 1923 and 1926 it resumed experiments with the UK, using the British branch of Western Union as its partner. The British government then sanctioned a radio telephony agreement between AT&T and the GPO from January 1927. A call to America cost £15 for 3 minutes. The UK equipment was provided by the Americans. Service to Australia followed in 1930 and to South America in 1931. By 1932, it was claimed that a UK telephone subscriber could 'now communicate with about 90% of the telephones of the world' (Sturmey 1958: 127–9).

However, these circuits suffered much from the inherent uncertainty of short-wave radio communications as well as the lack of privacy. Using the radio to establish long-range telephone links proved not to be a long lasting solution. As soon as effective repeaters were available to enable voice transmission by trans-oceanic cable, the radio telephone system was condemned to a secondary role, except eventually at a very local, not to say, personal level as the mobile phone (p. 304).

## INTERNATIONAL WIRED LINKS

In the early 1950s it became possible, with MASER technology, to build voice-carrying cables using repeaters, amplifiers, of such durability and sensitivity that they could be placed under the oceans. Maser is *M*icrowave *A*mplification by *S*imulated *E*mission of *R*adar, a technique developed by Charles Townes in 1951 at Columbia University and the Russian Fabrikan who had the same idea. This was essentially to simulate a substance to produce microwaves which could be used as amplifying carriers. The devices thus created would be durable enough to be left in cables on the ocean bed and powerful enough to amplify extremely weak signals, such as an analogue of the human voice, across thousands of miles. Masers used ammonia. (LASER, a cognate technology using coherent light and, initially, rubies rather than invisible microwaves and ammonia, came out of this same research tradition (p. 131).)

All this activity clearly indicates that radio telephony constituted a strong supervening necessity for this research. By 1952, AT&T had already joined the

GPO and the Canadian government to plan a telephone voice link across the Atlantic. Ninety years after the first Atlantic telegraph cable, twenty-seven years after the inauguration of the Atlantic radio telephone, at a cost of $16 million, with fifty-one repeaters (built in the US and the UK) and a capacity of thirty-six channels, the wire was opened for business in September 1956. Its success fuelled other plans – a second cable from the US to France, a third from the UK to Canada, the first leg in the upgrading to voice of a worldwide Commonwealth system first established for the Empire in the nineteenth century. This upgrading was to continue, for, despite the space race, the cable system persisted as a competitor for satellites.

More, though, was at stake here than a simple competition between these two technologies. The international transoceanic cable telephone network developed along traditional lines. That is to say, ownership of the cables was shared between the nations they connected and they followed the physical pathways which had been established first with the Victorian telegraph. This meant that the traditional hegemony of Britain and, to a lesser extent, France over the international system was being maintained into the era of decolonisation and American international dominance. As Herb Schiller points out:

> The decisive role played by the British world-wide communications net-
> work – both its control of the physical hardware of oceanic cables and its
> administration and business organisation of news and information – which
> held the colonial system together, promoted its advantages, and insulated
> it from external assault, had not escaped attention in the United States.
> (Schiller 1976: 26)

In the 1856 debate on the transatlantic telegraph, Seward, when asked why the cable was needed, allowed that the United States had 'no dominions on the other side of the Atlantic Ocean'. Clearly a worldwide telegraphy system of which the transatlantic wire was the first link would be of greater benefit to Britain and her empire than to the USA. British Imperial interests, which included a monopoly on the gutta-percha produced by trees in British Malaya, ensured her dominance of the system. So strong was the hold that even the transformation to Common-wealth in the 1930s and the loss of empire in the aftermath of the Second World War did not seem to affect it, as this new generation of telephone cables indicated.

In the United States, it was realised that, all technological considerations aside, communications satellites could finally break this spell. It was against these finely spun, structural ties that an American offensive was mounted. Conveniently, the attack could avail itself of the virtuous language and praiseworthy objectives of 'free flow of information' and 'world-wide access to news' (Schiller 1976: 26). The international cable system could be overthrown by a satellite system dominated by the USA. The problem, it transpired, was that the cable system refused to wither. It kept pace technologically and that technology was more widely shared among nations than was satellite know-how. At least as far as international telephony is concerned, the result up to the end of the millennium was something of a stand-off with, if anything, the long-term advantage lying with the cables.

# COMMUNICATIONS
# SATELLITES

## SCIENTIFIC COMPETENCE AND IDEATION: THE
## COMMUNICATIONS SATELLITES

The ground of scientific competence for the communications satellite includes two fundamentals. First is the theoretical understanding of how gravity might make 'a projectile . . . revolve in an orbit, and go round the whole earth' which was outlined by Newton in the *Principia* (Lovell 1973: 9). Second is an understanding of rocketry.

The origins of the rocket are lost in time but it is noted as an instrument of war at the battle of K'ai-Feng-Foo in 1232. It became something of the weapon of the underdog, because igniting a combustible substance inside a tube requires no great theoretical knowledge nor, indeed, a very high level of technological wherewithal. Rockets were used, for example, against the British by the Sultan of Mysore in the battles of Seringapatam in 1792 and 1799. In the twentieth century, both in Russia and in a Germany constrained by the restrictions of the Treaty of Versailles, there was considerable interest in rockets (Blagonravov 1996).

From 1932, Sergev P. Korolyov was head of MosGIRD (the Moscow Reactive Propulsion Group) and in the 1950s he was in charge of the intercontinental ballistic missile (ICBM) programme which led to the launch of Sputnik. Also in 1932, the Germany army found a home at one of its proving grounds for an amateur society, *Verein für Raumschiffahrt* (the Society for Space Travel – VfR) which had been regularly launching rockets from a *Raketenflugplatz* just outside Berlin. The army gave a young VfR member and Ph.D. candidate, Wernher von Braun, facilities to pursue his research into rocket combustion. By 1937, von Braun was installed, with a staff of eighty, at Peenemunde on the Baltic coast. By 1942, his fourth *Fernraket Aggregat* (Long-range Rocket Assembly) was put into production, using slave labour, as the *Vergeltungswaffen Zwei* – Vengeance Weapon No. 2 or V-2. Those launched against Britain killed 2754 people and injured 6523 more. At the war's end, when von Braun and 118 key personnel were transferred with their families to the United States, they were working the A-10 *Aggregat,* an intercontinental version of the V-2, in fact an ICBM prototype. The Soviets induced some lesser Peenemunde lights to build them a V-2 assembly plant and used these rockets to launch a series of sub-orbital space shots between 1949 and 1952 carrying dogs. They then let 'their' Germans return to the German Democratic Republic and Korolyov used only Russian scientists to develop the Soviet first-stage ICBM boosters.

Such an ICBM device comes disguised, automatically as it were, as a satellite rocket launcher as well and the agenda in this phase of the cold war was to let the Americans know of growing Soviet capability by launching some artificial satellites. Following Jules Verne's ideas of using a rocket for probing space (*De la terre à la lune,* 1865), Everett Hale, in a short story published in 1869, had dreamed up a brick-built navigation satellite for determining longitude (Paul 1975: 105).[1] A more plausible description of an artificial satellite, albeit also in a fiction, was published in Russian by K. E. Tsiolkovskii in 1895. In the reality of the 1950s, the cover afforded by satellite research was made all the better by the fact that the world's scientists were organising an International Geophysical Year for 1957/8 and had called for governments to support artificial satellite launches as part of that work. On 4 October 1957, Korolyov and his team put Sputnik I into orbit; but, since it was so small, there was a chance that the Americans would not get the message. Indeed, the White House instantly announced that it was just 'a silly bauble in the sky' (Lovell 1973: 22; Lewis 1968: 54). Korolyov altered his plans, moving up the launch of a capsule big enough to contain a dog's' life support system. Sputnik II, with the dog Laika on board, was orbited a month later (Daniloff 1972: 103). The rocket that hoisted it aloft therefore had to be powerful enough to carry an ICBM. There were no American instant dismissals.

Von Braun took only eighty-five days after Sputnik II to launch Explorer I, the American reply. He could easily have beaten Korolyov had he not been prevented by interservice rivalries, the hostility of the aeronautic industry to his work as a non-civilian army operation and a lingering problem with his Peenemunde past. As it was, the post-Sputnik II order to launch a satellite at any cost was the first move in what was to become an unprecedented peace-time flow of largesse to the military-industrial complex. Eisenhower used Sputnik to unlock the coffers. The Sputniks and Explorer I were the very first partial prototypes of the communications satellite; but as with other technologies in this book, these devices could have been to hand earlier than they were. In fact, the V-2 was itself already a quite viable booster vehicle for a Sputnik:

[B]ecause of the German V-2, the implications of the development of control theory and practice and the development of powerful radiotelemetry – it became clear after the war (in 1946) that, with the same *Aggregat* and a perfectly plausible second stage, Peenemunde could have orbited a payload as early as 1942.

(Needell 1983: 134)

Clearly then, the Germans could have done the same thing for their new American and Russian masters in 1946 had there been a real supervening necessity for a communications or other satellite.

The earliest specific (non-fictional) reference to a passive communications satellite, one relying on mirrors reflecting sunlight, is to be found in *The Rocket into Planetary Space*, a 1926 work by Hermann Oberth, the first president of the VfR. However, Arthur C. Clarke's outline of a chain of three manned geostationary radio satellites, published in the October 1945 edition of *Wireless World*, was the first proper articulation of the 'repeater' satellite concept. Clarke had been the treasurer of the British equivalent of the VfR, the British Interplanetary Society. Before the war, the BIS mustered about a hundred members of whom the truly committed numbered about ten. The group continued to meet during the war, and on one occasion had just heard a speaker (blinded by his own side's smoke-screen) dismiss tales of large German rockets as pure Nazi propaganda when the building was shaken by a V-2 explosion. After the war, the society, with Clarke in the chair, no doubt suppressing only with difficulty its memory of the 9277 British V-2 dead and wounded, moved to confer honorary membership on Wernher von Braun as soon as his address could be discovered (Clarke 1969: 141). Clarke wrote:

> It will be observed that one orbit, with a radius of 42,000 km, has a period of exactly twenty-four hours. A body in such an orbit, if its place coincided with that of the Earth's equator, would revolve with the Earth and would thus be stationary above the same spot on the planet.
>
> Let us now suppose that . . . a station were built in this orbit. It could be provided with receiving and transmitting equipment . . . and could act as a repeater to relay transmissions between any two points on the hemisphere beneath, using any frequency that will penetrate the ionosphere . . .. A single station could only provide coverage to half the globe, and for a world service three would be required, though more could be readily utilised.
>
> (Ibid.: 193–4)

Clarke thought his space stations would have to be manned and serviced by shuttle but, in the event, developments in electronics allowed for smaller unmanned devices to perform exactly the function he outlined. However, the elegance of his case was not overwhelming. He had proposed what was to be known as a high-orbit system, the one presently used for the commercial tele-communications applications. There are other possibilities involving a greater number of satellites in lower non-synchronous orbits. In the years immediately after Sputnik the advantages of Clarke's proposal were not conclusive. High orbit meant far smaller, far more complex devices and perhaps unacceptable transmission delays of 540 milliseconds as the voices bounced through 44,750 miles of space.

In 1954, Bell opted for the low level solution. Broadband capacity for television as well as telephony, facsimile and data would be handled by a 180 lb. satellite which in turn would be put into orbit with an apogee of 3450 miles and a perigee of 575 by a specially configured air force missile. Such an orbit could give good visibility between Western Europe and the North-Eastern United States if it were inclined at 45° to the Equator (Dickieson 1963: 741). Against such ever-hardening realities and the seemingly never-diminishing power of the phone company, proponents of Clarke's high orbit vision could, in the late 1950s, offer little. Nevertheless Hughes, an aeronautics firm, was becoming interested in the practicalities of this alternative scheme, perhaps as a way of keeping the telephone company out of space. The high-orbit idea, the low-orbit alternative, and a number of split-the-difference variations were all canvassed in the US at this time. Still more schemes were also in play. Oberth, now 66 years old, was brought from Germany to the USA by von Braun in 1955 and he considered his mirror scheme reasonable enough to spend some of his time refining the calculations for its orbit (Ordway and Sharpe 1979: 426). The communications satellite idea was thus very well articulated; yet, whether it would ever work was another matter. Lobbing complex pieces of electronics into precision orbits, the necessary technological performance, remained a chancy proposition.

Even more worrying was the ionosphere. The extensive use of ionospheric waves to bounce radio signals around the world was both boon and bane to the concept of Clarke's communication satellites. The boon was that the ionosphere rendered short-wave radio communication extremely volatile. There was a need for something better. The bane was that the ionosphere was presumably imperm-eable to radio waves. Clarke had dismissed this, stating 'with certainty' that 'shorter wave lengths are not reflected back to the Earth' and he was proved to be right (Clarke 1969: 197). There is a 'window' for radio waves between 8mm and 20m which was imperfectly understood in 1945 but was subsequently demonstrated in a series of experiments. In 1946, the US Army Signal Corps bounced a radar signal (i.e. very short-wave) off the moon through the iono-sphere. Bell also bounced a signal off the moon to link East and West Coasts as did Jodrell Bank to talk to Australia (Lewis 1968: 297–8). From 1959 to 1964, the US Navy had a permanent lunar (as it were) circuit in place between Washington and Honolulu.

Other successful penetrations of the ionosphere involved a version of Oberth's mirror, the Echo 1, a 100-foot metallised balloon launched by the National Aeronautic and Space Agency (NASA) on 12 August 1960. (NASA had been created, post-Sputniks, to avoid continuing service rivalries.) In 1962 Echo 1 reflected a poor-quality television image between California and Massachusetts (Paul 1975: 22). Such passive devices as the moon or Echo I required extremely complex ground stations. Masers (the microwave amplifiers which, as we have seen, were essential to the development of the transoceanic telephone cable system) were used and an enormous hearing tube 20 feet across was built by Bell to capture the faint signals being bounced back (Fagen 1975: 271–2). When this series of mirrored balloon experiments was concluded in 1963, the Bell Lab horn, in effect the prototype ground station, was assigned to radio astronomy work. Passive devices were not the answer.

Over Christmas 1958 the DoD had orbited a smaller 'active' metal device, Score (Signal Communications by Orbiting Relay Equipment) built by RCA. Rather like Sputnik, it could only transmit, in this instance another recorded Eisenhower message which played on command from the ground. It worked for twelve days. Courier I-B was the first true repeater, an Army Signal Corps' satellite which could cope with twenty dash-dot teleprinter signals at once, albeit not in real time. It stored the signals it received and played them back on subsequent passes. Orbited on 4 October 1960, it weighed 500 lb. and was effectively powered by its 20,000 solar cells for eighteen days. With Courier, the viability of space-side communications became a demonstrated fact.


## PROTOTYPES: LOW AND MEDIUM ORBITS

The United States now actively started to evolve policy for institutionalising a satellite communications system. Previous experience, as ever, was invoked. Early in 1959, the American tradition of state-aided entrepreneurship in telecommunications was confirmed for the new technologies of space when a House Committee determined that enough was now known to mandate the immediate creation of a 'useful world-wide communication system based on the use of satellites'. Although nobody 'was prepared to envisage a point in time when Government assistance in the form of providing launching vehicles . . . and actual launching operations would not be required', nevertheless the aim should be the 'complete commercial operation of the system' (Oslund 1977: 158). Bolstered by this, AT&T, despite its continued investment in transoceanic cables, took the satellite proposal it had been working on for six years to the FCC, formally requesting permission for a system with fifty low-altitude satellites in polar orbit and twenty-six ground stations to be co-owned between itself and the foreign tele-communications organisations which were its traditional international partners.

Kennedy space policy (arising from the 'On Urgent National Needs' statement, i.e. the 'man to the moon' programme) embraced a space-side communications system but was less enthusiastic about private enterprise providing it. Fearing yet another extension of AT&T's monopolistic power, the administration ordered that all alternatives be explored (Oslund 1977: 163). So although NASA, in July 1961, agreed to launch the Bell-financed satellite designated Telstar, it also contracted RCA to build it another almost identical device but with a deeper projected orbit while Hughes Aircraft was to provide an experimental high-orbit synchronous machine. AT&T was first in the metal. Telstar, containing 2528 transistors (and not one IC), was nearly 3 feet in diameter, weighed 170 lb. and was powered by 3600 solar cells. It was launched into an elliptical path, its perigee 593 miles and its apogee 3503 miles, on 10 July 1962. It took less than $2\frac{3}{4}$ hours to circle the globe. It ceased to operate on its 1242nd orbit in November, although clever manipul-ation of its radio command signals restored it briefly in February 1963. Relay I, the satellite built for NASA by RCA had been placed in a deeper – more 'medium' – orbit, its perigee 227 miles and its apogee 1109 miles more than Telstar's. It was just under 3 feet long, weighed 172 lb., with a twelve-telephone/one-television channel capacity. These pioneering 'birds' – still prototypes – were followed by a second Telstar and Relay II.

With Bell, their traditional partner, involved, the British and French Post Offices had constructed ground stations as their part of the Telstar experiment. The British opted for a parabolic dish which was erected in Cornwall not far from Poldhu on Goonhilly Down. The French had a copy of the Bell design at Pleumeur-Bodou in Brittany. The American ground station was erected by AT&T within a natural bowl at Andover, Maine. The design was similar to that used for the Echo receiver but the listening aperture was increased from 400 square feet to 3600 square feet. The horn, which was covered with an air-inflated radome to protect it from Maine's annual 90-inch snowfall, was 90 feet long and 68 feet in diameter at the mouth.

Relay's effectiveness, and the rapidly increasing power of the booster rockets available, forced Bell Labs away from the Telstar low-orbit random solution. (In the event, because it was thought to offer greater security, only the US military were to build a low-orbit system. Launched in batches of six to eight satellites at a time, IDSCP – *I*nitial *D*efence *S*atellite *C*ommunication *P*rogramme – was com-pleted by the summer of 1967 and was used during the Vietnam War. The idea was subsequently canvassed again for mobile phone use in the late 1990s.)

The most extensive exploitation of a Relay-style medium-orbit system was by the Soviets. Given their geographical situation and the contiguity of their then primary political sphere of influence, they did not need the worldwide capabilities of either low or high systems. In April 1965 Molniya (Lighting) IA satellite was launched into an orbit which came as close as 375 miles to the earth but, over the USSR, was at 24,780 miles for eight out of every twelve hours, thereby reducing the number of satellites required to establish a constant capability. In May, television transmission was demonstrated with a film from Vladivostok about fishermen in the Sea of Japan. A second Molniya was launched in October. Over the next two years some twenty-five ground stations were built but only two had two-way capability. On 3 October 1967 the launch of Molniya IF, the sixth of the series, inaugurated the entire system designated Orbita (Paul 1975: 64).

As for the impact of these prototypes, Ed Murrow, echoing Henry Thoreau, said: 'The issue, gentlemen, is not how we deliver it but what our delivery has to say' (Lewis 1968: 172). To match the Soviet fishermen, the first Telstar image, which Goonhilly missed, was of the Andover radome, a US flag in the foreground with the 'Star-Spangled Banner' over. (It should not be forgotten that AT&T quit show business in 1926.) The British replied in kind with pictures of the Goonhilly control room, without flags and anthems, while the French transmitted eight minutes of variety on videotape. Telstar, with its rapid orbit period, was visible to both Atlantic shores for less than half an hour at a time so the era of specially created live international television began with brief shows. Two hundred million people watched the programme transmitted on 23 July 1962, the first of what was to be a short-lived genre. The system might have been a technological wonder, delivering live pictures which the transoceanic cables could not handle, but the live image of a native American turned out to look just like his filmed image and the audience promptly returned to their national television fare. Relay was responsible for the first live transmissions of actual events, i.e. occasions not specially and solely produced for this purpose, for example, the launch of the Mercury spacecraft designated Faith 7, Sir Winston Churchill's acceptance of honorary US citizenship, and the funeral of Pope John XXIII and the coronation of his successor. Despite these, Murrow's Thoreau-esque scepticism did not seem to be out of order.

## SOCIAL NECESSITY AND INVENTION: THE GEOSTATIONARY SATELLITE

Television, though, was not the issue; nor, really, was competition with the Russians. Telstar's essential function was to allow AT&T to defeat its American rivals and bring the free world's transoceanic cable system to its knees. Yet, by continuing to lay cables, AT&T was hedging its bets. The US administration, on the other hand, wanted the certainty of a satellite victory; but one which did not extend the phone company's 'monopoly'. The government's requirement was for the United States to match its post-war 'Imperial', as it were, role with an 'imperial' communications system which it owned or dominated.

Against this, the need for instant television pictures was quite minor, despite all the publicity. The logic of journalistic professionalism, bred over the century and a half since the telegraph, suggests that news personnel were the ones truly addicted to getting the pictures ever faster. This can be thought of as a sort of disease. For example, on 21 October 1957, seventeen days after Sputnik I, the BBC screened film of the Queen's arrival in the USA at Staten Island. The 15-second shot had been sent across the Atlantic frame by frame, using existing press wire picture facilities. It had taken nine hours. It would be difficult to quantify the advantages to national life of the 15 royal television seconds on the day of the arrival as opposed to the many minutes available the following day. It is equally hard to see why many minutes the same day, the Telstar breakthrough, would make much difference either. The world television audience demanded American television programming, but that demand did not require instantaneous transmission – ships or stratocruisers were quite fast enough to bring *I Love Lucy* half-hours to European and Latin American shores.

Journalistic addiction to instantaneity was as nothing compared with the governmental belief, born in the dawn of the age of electronic communications, that vital national interests are involved in the development and ownership of telecommunications systems. This notion exerted a tremendous influence on all aspects of telecommunications. It justified limitations on programme importation, such as those behind which British television flourished for decades. It allowed the American broadcasting and telephone industries to operate internally without any international competition. It governed the radio jamming policies of the pre-1989 Eastern Bloc. It accounted for the desire for autonomous systems exhibited by all new nations. The incorporeal nature of these ephemeral messages had not prevented them from attracting the most protectionist of policies. The strongest necessity for the satellite system was a certain 'imperialist' vision of American telecommunications interest. Otherwise, global telecommunications needs (except television) could have been met by transoceanic telephone cables.

The American way was always to eschew 'Post Office arrangements' in favour of private exploitation. That is why Morse got the telegraph back and why AT&T became a private regulated monopoly. It was also why private enterprise had been allowed to build the American parts of the international telecommunications system. But this had left the United States unable to combat the British, much less exercise the hegemonic role its post-World War Two position was thought to require. This continued British dominance was a crucial supervening social necessity for an American satellite-based system. A staff report to the Senate Space Committee argued that: 'To construe space telecommunications too narrowly would overlook immediate and rich potential as an instrument of US foreign policy' (Oslund 1977: 161). The civilian satellites were, then, spin-offs which would not have been realised in the metal had not they afforded the US an opportunity, denied for a hundred years and now required by her changed international position as leader of the West, to gain ascendancy over a worldwide telecommunications network through superior technology. This is what had sustained the prototype phase and it was also what was driving the technological performance NASA had asked Hughes Aircraft to accomplish.

In effect, NASA had contracted Hughes to 'invent' a geostationary satellite, Syncom. Since all supervening necessities, both major and minor, had already occurred, the 'invention' took place contemporaneously with the development of the most immediate prototypes, Telstar and Relay. Syncom had to be small enough to fit upon a known rocket and light enough to allow that rocket to lob it 22,375 miles up. Thereafter the satellite had to find and keep an exact station and had to be capable of repeating at least one telephone conversation. Hughes had been chosen for this task because it had been investigating the possibility of Clarke's idea even as AT&T was campaigning for the other solution (Galloway 1977: 36). Hughes' initial plan was to orbit a comparatively simple machine that would weigh no more than 33 lb. and would be unable to carry television. It assigned three of its designers, Williams, Hudspeth and Rosen to the puzzle and they made good progress. They decided to spin the device gyroscopically for stabilisation. They also decided on elegant miniature lightweight hydrogen peroxide and nitrogen-powered manoeuvring gas-jet engines for fine adjustments when the orbit was achieved. But the capacity to carry television became vital because of the publicity generated by Telstar's transmissions, and Syncom had to increase its weight so that it could do likewise. To achieve high orbit now required that the satellite be attached to an extra solid-fuel rocket.

As Bell Labs lost no time in pointing out, to manoeuvre the rocket from Cape at $28\frac{1}{2}°$ of latitude north to the Equator required that this 'aggregat' make a left turn and that no guidance system then in existence could accomplish such a feat. Nor were there military models to function as Score and Courier had functioned for Telstar and Relay (Lewis 1968: 310–11). (Advent, the army's first planned geostationary device contracted to GTE, had only been put on the drawing board in 1960 (Galloway 1977: 20).) Furthermore, terrestrial experiments by Bell over very long cable circuits had shown users hostile to voice delays.

This style of attack typifies the earliest stages of the operation of the 'law' of the suppression of radical potential. Overall, the international carriers, led by AT&T, with the support of the FCC, took the 'traditional' view that as the most experienced transoceanic telecommunications entities, they should own this new potential competitor. Against this, the domestic US telephone and telegraph companies (AT&T apart) took a slightly different position, suggesting the system be owned by all authorised common carriers as the 1934 Communications Act defined them, which of course included themselves. For these companies, constraining AT&T became a question of denying the superiority of the low-orbit system. RCA, despite Relay, argued that even if the high-orbit method took longer to develop it would be economically more viable. GTE went so far as to suggest that 'A random system [i.e. AT&T's] could discredit us before the world as a leader in space communications if Russia establishes a stationary satellite system' (Galloway 1977: 36). The aeronautics companies worried that Bell would get into the missile business.

The Justice Department, as had become its habit over the better part of a century, examined all these various ownership proposals for traces of 'monopoly' – that potent encoded term for 'AT&T'. It concluded that 'a project so important to the national interest should not be owned or controlled by a single private organisation' (Galloway 1977: 30). Not for the first time, the phone company needed to balance its case between a technologically based potential dominance and a more diplomatic 'Vail-tendency' (as it might be called) approach. 'Hard as it may be for some to understand,' AT&T complained, 'our sole interest is in the earliest practicable establishment of a world-wide commercial satellite system useful to all international communications carriers and agencies here and abroad' (ibid: 28). Of all the players, only Philco (again, true to *its* corporate culture) broached a radical solution, proposing that the US build a system which then be handed over for the UN to operate. (Philco, it will be remembered, wanted an 800-line television standard in 1939.)

Despite AT&T's somewhat beleaguered position, its criticism of the Hughes scheme highlighted the fact that the synchronous satellite was a communications device and Bell Labs, the acknowledged authority on telecommunications, was against it. In advance of Advent, Hughes had no guarantees that even Syncom's basic concept was going to work. In May 1962, as Congress prepared to act on satellite communications, the DoD cancelled the Advent project. Faced with these uncertainties, both political and technical, Hughes began to cool off to the point of withdrawing. In telecommunications, geostationary satellite is the systems engineering 'invention' *par excellence* with nothing to 'discover' and seemingly little or no place for intuition or emotion even of the 'will to think' kind that Shockley celebrates. It is significant to note, therefore, that Hughes' design team was deeply involved in its work. Williams was actually prepared to back his technological hunches by offering his own savings to the management so that the project might continue and, to that end, he burst into a vice-president's office and slapped a cheque for $10,000 on the desk. Hughes stuck with Syncom, even as the row about institutional frameworks intensified on the Hill.

Against the somewhat diverse views of industry, those political positions first deployed in connection with the telegraph (and first defeated in 1856) were once more being put forward. Liberal democrats sensitive to the public money poured into the space programme, put yet again the 'Post Office arrangement' argument, and claimed the system for the public. This political discourse was also affected by the possibility that the Russians might at any minute inaugurate either a high- or low-orbit system which might prove as attractive to the world as one, in the words of Senator Russell Long, 'owned by the American monopolies' (Galloway 1977: 34).

Unlike the similar American rows that had taken place about the telegraph, telephone and radio, the argument about space communications perforce involved other nations, nations which had, whatever their ideologies, tended historically to accept the 'Post Office arrangement'. International communications involved governments. Even the US government, despite its tradition of 'leaving' communications to private enterprise, had attended the first international radio frequency allocation conference in Berlin in 1906 where an International Radiotelegraph Union had also been established. (The United States had instigated the model of such organisations when in 1863, at its suggestion, the Postal Union was formed.) The Radiotelegraph Union merged, in 1932, with its telegraphic opposite number to create an International Telecommunications Union (ITU). However, ITU frequency allocation agreements, dating in their latest form from a 1947 Atlantic City meeting, made no provision for space communications. As early as 1955, the US Department of State began to prepare for the revision of these regulations at an ITU Radio Administrative Conference to be held in Geneva in the winter of 1959. In the interim, all space telecommunications, civilian and military, had to be conducted so as not to offend against the established users of the spectrum. The ITU in 1959 agreed to a thirteen-band space-side allocation for three years and determined to reconvene at an Extraordinary Administrative Radio Conference in 1963 to make more permanent arrangements.

Kennedy was as aware as anybody of the dangers of 'monopoly' (i.e. the phone company) both internally and from the foreign policy perspective. Hence the order to NASA to explore all options. The executive branch now developed a compromise proposal in which an entirely new entity would be created to run the space system. It was not, as the liberals wanted, to be organised along Rooseveltian lines as a purely governmental agency; rather it was to be a private company somewhat like the original RCA wherein established industry players were given control of a business created by government action. For the satellites, all the common carriers were to have control but were to share the new company with the public – which obviously could include electronic manufacturers and the aerospace industry. Thus the public's development dollars were to be returned in the form of an investment opportunity. And, in response to United Nations hostility to the commercialisation of space, enunciated in 1961, this new government-sponsored company could present itself as being (obviously) previously uninvolved in American capitalism. The liberal neo-populist proponents of the 'Post Office' position were sufficiently opposed, despite the fact that the company would have to obtain State Department approval for any foreign contractual agreements, to stage a four-day filibuster against the bill. Public ownership became associated with the high-orbit scheme simply because private ownership was connected to AT&T and the low-orbit solution.

In the midst of the debate Telstar flew, but it made no difference. The 'law' of the suppression of radical potential had already worked to such good effect that even AT&T itself had given up its hopes of domination. It now supported the president even while it continued actively to pursue its transoceanic cable plans. The bill was signed into law as the Communications Satellite Act on 31 August 1962. Title III established a Communications Satellite Corporation (COMSAT) in which 'Fifty per centum of the shares of stock . . . shall be reserved for purchase by authorised carriers' and at 'no time shall any stockholder who is not an authorised carrier . . . own more than 10 per centum of the shares' (TITAS 1964: 39–40). It immediately became a blue-chip stock and America's house was in order for the upcoming Administrative Radio Conference.,

By spring 1963, Syncom I, the geostationary 'invention', was ready to go. At less than half Relay' s weight, 79 lb., it was nevertheless capable of television. The engine ignited on a command from earth but immediately thereafter Syncom went dead. It was lost for a week. When rediscovered by astronomers it was found to have achieved a perigee of 21,3754 miles, an apogee of 2823 miles and a period of 23 hours 45 minutes. The basic manoeuvre had worked and it was probably an exploding gas-jet engine that had killed the bird. It was not an auspicious demonstration of the superiority of the high-orbit option. Syncom II, with specially designed peroxide engines, as opposed to the shelf-items with which its predecessor had been equipped, was launched on 23 July 1963, nine weeks after Telstar II. This one made it into a circular orbit but not on the equatorial plane. Instead it described a 'figure-of-eight' movement across the globe. Nevertheless it was visible for long periods of time and it drifted until both California and Nigeria could see it. An American warship in Lagos harbour signalled Paso Robles, 7700 miles away, a satellite distance record. The orbit, though inclined, could be adjusted to an exact 24-hour period and by 15 August daily seconds-long pulsings of gas had placed it on station. The following summer Syncom III was placed on exactly the right equatorial orbit and reached its station over the International Date Line on 11 September just in time to transmit the Tokyo Summer Olympics to America and dramatically illustrate the advantages of a stationary device. The continuous transmissions received in the United States had to be broken up into hour-long segments for retransmission to Europe by Relay II. The geostationary satellite was invented and was obviously a superior mechanism for the international transmission of television.

## SUPPRESSION: THE INTERNATIONAL NETWORK

Meanwhile, the 1963 Extraordinary Administrative Radio Conference had met in Geneva and determined wavebands for space communications. The American delegation was forty-three strong but, even so, the support of the Soviet Union was needed to beat off a French proposal that broadcasting transmissions, radio or television, from any space object be banned. Enough spectrum for 9000 voice channels and four television circuits was agreed. The permanency of the arrangement was questioned by Israel for fear that this would enshrine the USA's and USSR's 'first come, first served' dominance. Despite this, the allocations were adopted as permanent. Comsat, which had been incorporated in March 1963, now had something concrete to sell. Comsat's directors, led by the ex-chair of Esso, were at odds with the US government's vision of a utility company and thought the RCA model of autonomous entrepreneur more appropriate. They were now running a free enterprise which would simply establish and operate a system that was more extensive and cheaper than any other. The rest of the world would therefore negotiate with Comsat to use it. This was the plan they presented at meetings with the Europeans, the Canadians and the Japanese in the summer. They were disabused of this vision of their own business when the Europeans, who had established CETS (Conférence Européenne des Télécommunications par Satellites) as a forum for achieving a joint position, told an American governmental group after the Geneva radio frequency meeting that they simply would not deal with Comsat.

In the European response in the early 1960s one major theme was the protection of the generation of voice-quality cables then being laid, whose technology was not a complete American monopoly. The GPO and AT&T had augmented TAT I, the first Anglo-American voice cable, with TAT II in 1959 and TAT III in 1963. The British and their Commonwealth partners were working on COMPAC, the first transpacific cable, which would run, in a fine old British Imperial fashion, from Vancouver to Auckland and Sydney via Fiji, while the French and German Post Offices, again with AT&T, planned TAT IV for 1965. The chairman of the British space development organisation said, 'It by no means follows that the US communication system will necessarily be the best solution for others'; and in the British Parliament some felt that 'we shall finally end up by starving the transatlantic cable of telegraphic communications from America and assisting Comsat to get off the ground, and that Britain will merely end up renting a line from the Americans' (Galloway 1977: 96).

Yet this was not how it was to turn out. Congress had in effect negated the United States' best shot at achieving domination of a global telecommunications system, the reason it had pursued the matter in the first place. It had chosen between Scylla of a 'Post Office arrangement' (that is the refusal to create a government entity to run the satellites) and the Charybdis of 'monopoly' (that is, the refusal to allow AT&T to run them). As a result, by denying AT&T the space system, and in creating an alternative commercial entity which could not, because of AT&T, have monopoly powers, Congress had let the entire world off the hook. This was the reality, but it was somewhat at odds with the Information Revolution seductiveness of the technology. Most believed that by the 1970s cables would be obsolete, and that belief conditioned two needs – first, to constrain the development of the satellites until the expected obsolescence occurred, cables having a life of twenty-three or more years; and second, to make sure the world system would be in a substantive way international. Behind these needs were the sort of nationalistic worries that had animated members of Congress during the first debates on the telegraph in 1856, but now the technological boot was on the other foot. So however mesmerised they might be by space, for the Europeans the principle of national autonomy over telecommunications was too important to be swept aside, especially by a pushy American corporation. In February 1964, when next Comsat approached CETS, in Rome, it was in the company of officials from the State Department and the FCC.

Now the skeleton of a plan evolved. Obviously Comsat would have to manage the system as the only organisation with access to the requisite technological wherewithal held by NASA, but it would be subject to an international committee of control. CETS's price for this was a promised transfer of technology among the member nations of the committee so that research, development and manufacture in the long term would be more dispersed. Arrangements were made for American influence to decline as new nations joined the system. These points, which were largely acceptable to the US government, were hammered out over the next few months, resulting in a deal which would operate until 1969. An 'Agreement Establishing Interim Arrangements For A Global Commercial Communications Satellite System' was opened for signature in Washington on 20 August 1964, the day after the Syncom III launch. The insertion of the word 'commercial' was a measure of how much of the fundamental American position had been secured. Nevertheless nine other nations, as well as Vatican City, signed.

Comsat had handed over control of its projected system to an International Telecommunication Satellite Consortium, Intelsat as it came to be called. Intelsat ownership was determined by telephone usage, the United States beginning with 61 per cent. Britain came next with an 8.4 per cent interest, but all were to surrender prorated portions of these quotas to other nations as they joined. The United States was not to fall below 50.6 per cent, however. By 1969, when these arrangements ran out, seventy countries had initialled the Interim Agreement. As an engine of the 'law' of the suppression of radical potential Intelsat operated brilliantly in that, as it determined the rates charged, it prevented any undercutting of the cables. Even the dominant Comsat voice was influenced in this regard by the fact that one-third of its board were American carriers, who had large interests in cable. In effect, Intelsat functioned internationally as Comsat functioned domestically, as the agent containing the disruptive potential of the new technology.

The cost of this to American policy was that the new system did not, as was initially intended, replace the old cabled one. On the other hand, Intelsat was a success in cold war terms in that a majority of nations, including therefore many from the non-aligned group, joined. Although it treated circuits on its satellite transponders somewhat as loss leaders, regarding the real business as being in expensive ground stations, its pricing policies otherwise favoured the disadvantaged. The Soviet Union was isolated, reduced to repeating against Intelsat the very arguments used against Comsat in the congressional debate: 'How can we expect this enterprise to be unbiased and just on the international scene?' (Galloway 1977: 129). By 1968, they had a rival scheme, Intersputnik, based on the Orbita system, but only Bulgaria, Cuba, Czechoslovakia, Hungary, Mongolia, Poland and Rumania joined them in operating it.

This success aside, Intelsat ran into a number of difficulties. With Comsat as its dominant shareholder, Intelsat contracted Comsat to manage the system. Comsat handouts spoke of Intelsat as a 'unique partnership for progress' but the reality was rather different. The American corporation did not even bother to insert in the District of Columbia telephone directory a telephone number for Intelsat, which was secreted on half of the third floor of its Washington headquarters (Snow 1976: 137). Complex committee structures did not correct this and the rank-and-file members became increasingly unhappy. For example, in 1967, there was one representative on Intelsat's executive committee for the Philippines, Thailand, Singapore, India, Indonesia, Malaya and New Zealand – some 720 million people – and one for the Vatican City, population 855. Members from the developed world were also unhappy at the pace of technological transfer. Eleven European states had recently established a multinational space research organisation and a rocket development team which were designed to create a space programme. These were ignored by Comsat when it let its first Intelsat contracts.

On 6 April 1965 NASA orbited the Hughes 303, known as Early Bird or Intelsat I. It weighed 85 lb. and took 23 hours and 57 minutes, give or take 57 seconds, to circle the earth. It was equipped with 240 voice circuits or, if these were cleared down, one television channel. Vice-president Humphrey exclaimed as Early Bird was demonstrated: 'My goodness, now we'll be able to call everybody!' But he could have done that, more or less, already – there were 374 telephone lines available under the Atlantic alone. There was no rush to rent transponders on the satellite and, after the free honeymoon was over, the television networks decided they could live without the facility on a day-to-day basis since it was so expensive. It was to remain Intelsat's sole space-side asset until October 1966.

Comsat, on behalf of Intelsat, also contracted Hughes for the next generation of Intelsat IIs which were launched the following year. With these a global system was created and Clarke's dream became a reality.

Comsat's partners had viewed these early developments with a degree of equanimity, since obviously the Americans had a head start. However, with the Intelsat III series, patience was at an end. Comsat still failed even to discuss a possible launcher contract with the Europeans and decided yet again on a Hughes satellite. The third generation was to have 6000 channels and be ready in 1970 but the American government intervened, at the behest of Intelsat's other high tech members, to persuade Comsat that it would be politically more sound to introduce an interim satellite with a greater percentage of non-US components. This became the Intelsat IIIs built by TRW, with 1200 circuits, but twice as much foreign subcontracting (4.6 per cent) than had Intelsat II (2.3 per cent). The delayed Hughes birds, now designated Intelsat IVs, were built with 9000 rather than 6000 circuits and contained 26 per cent of non-American components. To achieve this, Hughes was forced to train the foreign technologists in the secrets of the hardware so that they could return home, duplicate the work and send it back to Hughes. This was still not enough and the French and Germans inaugurated the first direct internal challenge to Intelsat by planning a communications satellite of their own, Symphonie. (All other non-super-power devices had been scientific, meteorological or navigational.)

As the end of the decade approached, and with it the termination of the Interim Agreement, the stage was set for an extremely complex negotiation. Comsat had made some moves to protect itself. By 1969 nearly 10 per cent of its employees were foreign nationals, although only 2.5 per cent of its 641 managers were. The US share of Intelsat had dropped to 52.61 per cent. Thirteen per cent of research contracts were being awarded abroad, and this was increasing. The US government insisted on more – that Comsat institutionalise the inherently schizophrenic quality of its position by dividing administrative from technical management within the organisation. But the basic facts remained – of the $323 million the system had cost so far, no less than 92 per cent had been spent in the US.

The Europeans came to the table in greater disarray than in 1964. For the states among their number with lesser high tech pretensions, for instance, Spain the failure to effect a greater measure of technological transfer meant little. Protection of the cable system was more important to them (and to the UK for historical reasons). Exacerbating these differences of position was the threatened collapse of the joint Eurospace programme. Europa rockets, with stages made in different countries, had achieved eleven straight launch-pad failures, causing Britain to announce its withdrawal to go it alone, as the French had already successfully done. (It was to be years before a series of disasters with previously dependable American launchers caused Intelsat to contemplate using European rockets instead.) But this reality did not make the political situation any easier at the outset. Outside Europe, many of the less developed countries with attenuated telephone systems wanted a 'one seat, one vote' system and some even suggested a truly representative assembly to manage the operation on UN lines.

It was expected to take only weeks, or at the most months, when Washington's largest international conference to date convened in February 1969 but, in the event, two-and-a-quarter years were to pass before the 'Agreement and Operating Agreement Relating to the International Telecommunications Satellite Organis-ation', the Definitive Arrangements, were opened for signature. The time was spent in what was described as 'tedious technical negotiations', but, although they may well have been tedious, the arguments were about power, not machinery. Needless to say Intelsat emerged with a very complex governance structure but also one in which Comsat's, and therefore the US's, role was much reduced. The Americans were in effect limited to a 40 per cent share of interest and Comsat's role as operator of the system was reduced from 'manager' to 'management services contractor' working to a small permanent Intelsat staff led by a director general. But even after twenty-seven months of debate, this last was not final, being subject to review in 1979 with the possibility that Comsat be replaced entirely. (This did not happen and Comsat still manages the system.) Other battles were lost. Comsat came to the table determined to kill the Franco-German bird, Symphonie, and to obtain the right for Intelsat alone to provide navigational and other specialised services. The US government felt that Comsat's stand against so-called regional satellite systems could not be sustained and, instead, the best that could be achieved was to insist on compatibility, i.e. no Orbitas. The British resisted the navigational proposal since that would have affected traditional British dominance of such systems.

The world was able to escape from the realities of US power; it needed to talk to America but did not need Comsat to do it. This reality, however, was hidden behind a welter of 'revolutionary' hype. The arrangements were open for initial-ling on 20 August 1971 and Arthur C. Clarke, as the system's father, addressed the delegates of the fifty-four nations gathered to sign it:

> Today, my friends, whether you intend to or not, whether you wish to or not, you have just signed far more than yet another intergovernmental agreement. You have just signed the first draft of the articles of Federa-tion of the United States of Earth.
>
> (Byrne and John 1972: 657)

This for me is as perfect an expression as I have found of the complete failure of the technicists to understand what is actually afoot in the world.

The Intelsats grew in capacity to 3750 voice channels in 1971, and to 6250 in

1967. They also acquired rivals. The Franco-German Symphonie was launched by NASA,which also orbited a domestic bird for the Canadian government. Just as significantly, there was no reduction in the pace of cable-laying – from the US to Spain, from Canada to the UK, across the Pacific. Cable capacity was growing, too, from 845 voice circuits to 1840 and to 4000. The self-evident cost-effectiveness of the satellites, less significant a factor than it might have been because of national interests, was becoming less clear. Cable costs fell from the $305 per circuit mile to the $8 per mile even as the real cost of satellites, launches, lost birds, shorter lives and terrestrial investments came to be better understood. Although economists believed that above 600 miles satellites must be cheaper than these conventional, pre-fibre optic cables, it turned out to be not by so great a factor as to overwhelm nationalistic considerations.

Comsat seriously tried to resist TAT V, the 845-circuit cable to the Iberian Peninsula, arguing that it was unnecessary and would divert traffic from Intelsat, but lost. It was obvious by the early 1970s that the American carriers as well as their European opposite numbers were no longer under the spell of space. The balance between the two technologies was being maintained. Intelsat gave a more than adequate return to its investor nations (especially those few who also had interests in the lucrative ground station market), but no cable telephone entity was superseded. One reason was traffic growth. In 1927 there were 10,000 telephone calls at $75 each between the US and the UK. By 1957 there were 250,000 and by 1961 4.3 million. There were 115 million message units leaving America in 1982, about 30 per cent originating in the New York area and 37 per cent of them destined for Great Britain (Moss 1984: 11–12). By 1985 the cheapest cost for an initial transatlantic minute was $1.17 plus tax. And there was no sign that limits were being reached.

The projected growth of such business was usually described by proponents of the satellites as a 'nightmare' which only space technology could solve. It turned out to be no such thing, although different institutional arrangements, notably the appointment of AT&T as American agent rather than the creation of Comsat, might have yielded a somewhat changed result, at least in the short term. Nevertheless, in the longer term, the breakthrough into fibre optics would have tipped the balance in favour of the cables. As fibre optics came on stream in the late 1980s, the limitation of Clarke's entire concept became ever clearer. In 1988, AT&T and its traditional (if by now 'privatised') partners laid such a cable across the Atlantic. It could handle 37,800 simultaneous telephone calls and of itself doubled transatlantic capacity. The following year a consortium of thirty companies inaugurated a similar cable across the Pacific at a cost of $700 million. The fibre system used by these wires was viable even though amplification required down-converting the signal into conventional form because no optic amplifier yet existed. This became a major research and development agenda item. In the

1990s, with further optic cables of even greater capacity laid or planned, the initial belief that satellites would dominate international telecommunications was, like so many Information Revolution certainties, proved to be in error. Fibre cables have the potential to turn geostationary communications satellites into nothing but space litter by the turn of the millennium. Only their unique usefulness in television broadcasting direct to homes protects them from this fate, while low-orbit birds by the late 1990s were looking to be of use, this time to feed mobile phones.

# 16

# THE SATELLITE ERA

## DOMESTIC SATELLITES

Comsat's less than triumphal international progress was matched by its faltering advance domestically, although, initially, the company proved as attractive a stock as Congress had hoped. The 50 per cent available to the public was snapped up by 150,000 buyers and the value of their holdings, an average of twenty shares per person, doubled to $100 million. Otherwise Comsat suffered a string of defeats.

The site of the first of these was over the ground stations, then costing around $10 million each. The international ground station market had developed very much as expected with all the usual players involved – Marconi in Hong Kong and on Ascension Island; Plessey, GEC and AEI at Goonhilly; Nippon with Hughes, Mitsubishi with TRW and Bell in Japan; Siemens in Germany; ITT in Spain; RCA in Canada; Philco in Italy and Bell in France. The station in Bahrain had been built by Marconi but was not owned by the local government but by Cable and Wireless. In contrast, Comsat was not involved in this market, not even in the US, but it wanted to be. In 1966, following fruitless negotiations between it and the US carriers who had built the stations it was running, the FCC issued the Solomonic judgement that seven of the eight in question should be controlled on a fifty-fifty basis for three years. The Alaskan station was to be wholly owned by Comsat. The carriers' ownership interests in Comsat, AT&T's 25 per cent for example, complicated this matter.

The FCC found against Comsat on another important issue. The military, who permanently used some 17 per cent of the carriers' total terrestrial system, let bids for ten satellite circuits to Hawaii and points west. The FCC forbad Comsat from bidding and determined that it should be a carriers' carrier, which is to say an organisation having nothing to do with users, only carriers. Via these, the military were soon spending over $20 million a year on leasing Intelsat satellite circuits, Comsat again being forced, as it were, to share business with its part-owners.

Comsat's next defeat was over the issue of domestic satellites, a most important element of the technology's potential. The secondary supervening necessity, television transmission, became ever more important as the satellites faltered in the struggle with the cables for international voice and data traffic. Eventually, the geostationary communication satellites' best hope of survival would be in a direct television broadcast mode (DBS-Direct Broadcast Satellite) to individual homes. At the outset, though, with receiving dishes still six metres across, the domestic use of the communications satellite was a question of television networking. In 1965 ABC proposed to the FCC a scheme for an equatorial geostationary device which would allow it to network its own programs coast-to-coast. 1965 was the last year of black-and-white prime-time and it was estimated that the process of colourisation then under way was going to cost between $250 and $275 million. Prime-time colour alone required $100 million. It is obvious that ABC, as the trailing third network and the last to go to colour, would be most interested in obtaining the relief from AT&T's longline charges that the satellite promised.

All the usual paraphernalia which allows the FCC to be such an exemplary agent of the 'law' of the suppression of radical potential went into play. In March of the following year, the commission undertook to study the issue, which it did – for the next seven years. It studied to such good purpose that, with the help of the Nixon White House, it in effect froze domestic satellite distribution of network television and, as with the 1948–52 freeze on television itself, inaction allowed the players to regroup around the new technology. Clearly, since international versions of the device were in existence, the delay from first request in 1965 to the launch of a domestic satellite in 1974 could not have been technological. Nor could it have been financial, since the American networks in 1965 spent about $55 million with AT&T on the longlines ABC was proposing to bypass. It was estimated that a satellite could have done the job for $25 million.

At this point Comsat had about $200 million of surplus capital and obviously from its shareholders' point of view the application of these monies to meeting domestic needs was not only appropriate but necessary (Snow 1976: 113); but Comsat could not threaten a significant element of its biggest shareholder's – AT&T's – annual revenues. Comsat therefore petitioned the FCC for permission to establish a demonstration rather than a working domestic satellite system. AT&T, in reply, petitioned directly for its own domestic satellite. It denied ABC's claims as to the potential savings involved, a position somewhat weakened as an authoritative counter claim when, at the same time, AT&T allowed that a 35 per cent saving might be effected were it, and it alone, permitted to launch and run the system. By 1968, AT&T had revised even this opinion, claiming that satellites would be just as expensive as terrestrial links.

The Philco role, that of radical visionary, was this time played by the Ford Foundation under the guidance of ex-commercial broadcaster Fred Friendly. Commercial television of the 1950s was beginning to be regarded as a Golden Age, while current output, characterised by an FCC chair as a 'vast wasteland', was causing increasing concern. The struggling educational (i.e. non-commercial) stations were seen as a potential corrective to this. However, they had never been able to afford AT&T's longline prices and had therefore been unable to constitute themselves into a network. Public programming, watched piecemeal across the nation, never achieved a sufficiently coherent audience to impinge upon the commercial rating system, which in turn meant that, since it could not demonstrate an audience, its political clout was reduced. It was estimated that NET, a main provider of non-commercial programs, would have to spend $8 million a year with AT&T to create a network, just $2 million more than its total programme budget. Friendly saw satellites as a way out. All broadcasters would use the new system, the commercial networks paying; any profits would fund public television (Friendly 1968: 310). Such a scheme, sponsored by the Ford Foundation with technical advice from Hughes, was presented to the FCC in the summer of 1966. It attracted considerable attention, being subject to hearing by a senate subcommittee. Faced with a popular proposal that would in effect have taxed a most powerful interest group, the networks, and removed significant revenues from another, AT&T, the FCC remained mute.

By the end of 1969, the Republicans now being in the White House, the FCC was girding its loins to grant Comsat its temporary licence for a domestic satellite system. The Executive branch requested an opportunity to study the question and quickly affirmed its hostility to a monopoly supplier. It suggested that the FCC license all-comers and so the Commission, in its *First Report and Order* on this matter, established what was to become known as the domestic 'open skies' policy. Eighteen applications were received from fifteen organisations. The Ford Foundation Plan was, of course, dead. The networks were now paying AT&T some $75 million annually for longlines. Nothing was done.

In 1971, the Canadian government let a contract for the world's first domestic satellite. Despite its Inuit name, Anik (Brother), it was American built and American launched. By January 1973 it was operational, the first communications satellite to be owned by an Intelsat signatory outside Intelsat's control. (Symphonie was launched two years later.) Some of Anik's intended beneficiaries were less than pleased with it. An Inuit delegation to the CBC complained: 'Hasn't the white man caused enough trouble already? Does he now have to send us a 'brother' who does not know our problems . . ... We do not need him' (Paul 1975: 71). On the other hand, RCA was so impatient with the FCC's continued prevarications that it requested permission from it and the Canadian regulatory agency to use an Anik transponder. As expanding traffic was being frustrated by the limitations of the terrestrial infrastructure, RCA got its way. In consequence, Anik, orbited for socio-political rather than market reasons, was fated to be the first US domestic satellite and 'earned a return on capital investment that was virtually unprecedented in the telecommunications industry' (Martin 1977: 215).

Westar, the first US domestic satellite, was orbited in the summer of 1974. It was not owned by Comsat but by Western Union which, as we have seen, survived to this great age in defiance of America's supposedly *laissez-faire* communications policies through various government interventions. It had been four years since the FCC *First Report and Order,* eleven since Syncom 1. It was to be a further decade before any of the networks moved entirely to satellite distribution, this giving AT&T a more than twenty-year period in which to adjust to the loss of this business.

## DIRECT BROADCAST SATELLITES

Perhaps the most significant of Comsat's failures was its inability to establish a technological lead in the development of direct broadcast satellites. This was left to NASA and the military. NASA had specialised needs generated by the Apollo programme which generated a continuing series of satellites that were in design and capacity always one step in front of the contemporary Intelsat machines Comsat was producing. In 1968, NASA's third ATS (*A*pplications and *T*echnology *S*atellite), for example, used despun antenna for the first time. The antenna spun round at the same speed as the satellite but in the opposite direction, maintaining a position constant to earth – a necessary advance if massive satellite with huge antennae were to be built. And massive 'high-power' satellites were needed because, crudely, the bigger the satellite, the smaller the receiving station could be. ATS 3 could carry television and was used as a back-up to the Intelsat system. Prince Charles' investiture as Prince of Wales was seen in America and the Mexico City Olympics were transmitted to Europe via ATS 3. Later versions were developed by NASA in response to complaints from the Intelsat's rank-and-file signatories for satellites to be used as a development tool. [1]

As for the military, the UK and the US signed an agreement in November 1965 which involved Britain in the IDSCP being developed by Philco. The British defence establishment was to get a complete satellite-based system to replace all British military communication links worldwide. The Johnson administration, following the Tonkin Resolution of 1964, was escalating its commitment in South-East Asia and was pleased to encourage a faltering British military presence east of Suez. In addition, the British, still a major transoceanic cable player, had advanced maser technology and so could contribute meaningfully to IDSCP's development. In 1965 the Signals and Research Establishment was set up at Christchurch, Hants.

By 1966 it was working on small portable ground stations and Idex and Scot emerged. Both were a fraction the size of Intelsat's contemporary commercial receiving stations. Idex, which cost £35,000, weighed 1.3 tons but could be pulled by a Land Rover. Scot, an even smaller device 6 feet in diameter, was installed on HMS *Wakeful* and HMS *Intrepid*. The ground station was metamorphosing a dish.

Comsat was interested in such possibilities and spun-off a wholly owned subsidiary, Comsat General, to be freer than its parent in establishing specialised satellite applications. Coupled with the 'open skies' ideology at the FCC, the ploy worked. It was allowed, with IBM and Aetna Insurance, to pioneer a dedicated business information satellite, the first element in the contemporary system (using both satellite and cable) which allows for worldwide instantaneous trading. It was also licensed to build a navigation system, Marisat, initially mainly for use by the US Navy. This too was to impact on the development of the satellite dish. Their size shrank to 4 feet in diameter specifically designed for shipboard installation. By the early 1970s at the latest, experimental 'high-power' satellites could be received on dishes under 3 feet across. With the military Tascat communications system, which followed IDSCP, 1-foot dishes were used.

Yet, despite Comsat General, Comsat itself was much reduced by the 1980s. It was no longer in direct control of Intelsat and a number of signatories had broken its monopoly of space. It had lost a battle to be a common carrier and had been denied the domestic satellite system. In 1984 President Reagan decided that America's best interests would not after all be served by an international mono-poly such as Intelsat and that Comsat should not have a privileged position in the new burgeoning international business data transmission market. The Comsat Act was rewritten, removing the privileged ownership position of the carriers at their own request. They sold off their shares and relinquished their seats on the Comsat board. Satellite communications had not turned out to be such a threat that these protections were needed against it, and the carriers had determined that they were better off being free to compete openly. This echoed AT&T's withdrawal from RCA half a century earlier. It now withdrew from Comsat.[2]

The delay in developing the domestic small dish is a further clear expression of suppression. While the military were down to 1-foot, the first commercial domestic 'low power' satellites then coming on stream still required a 9-metre dish costing $80,000. The FCC only approved yet 'smaller' dishes in 1976 and even these *TV Receive-Only* (TVRO) devices were 4.5 metres in diameter. Like the Orbita stations in Russia, they could not transmit ('up-link'). Nevertheless, they sprouted at the head-ends (central distribution points) of the cable systems to produce in fairly short order a glut of television services unique to cable (p. 313). There were 500 dishes within a year and about 5400 by 1984. Their price dropped to under $5000 and they were also increasingly to be found at broadcast network affiliate stations, replacing the old landline links.

Among the more noticeable consequences of the 'low power' domestic satellite was the new daily newspaper, *USA Today,* which appeared in America in 1982. By 1983 it was being printed simultaneously via satellite in seventeen cities and was read by over one million people a day. Two decades earlier, in 1964, Arthur C. Clarke had correctly predicted that his satellites would produce such a paper: 'One of the first countries to benefit . . . will be, rather ironically, the United States, which has never possessed a really national newspaper' (Clarke 1969: 128). But, again, the limitations of technological determinism must be noted. 'Influential newspapers,' he claimed,' such as the London and *New York Times* will experience a great increase in distribution.' This has not happened since few modes of communication are more heavily culturally determined and therefore location-bound than newspapers. Most publications using the technology did not alter their editorial contents at all, correctly deducing that it was the unchanged original which would sell.[3] The Soviet Molinyas were also appropriated to produce simultaneous editions of *Pravda.*

A wholly unanticipated consequence of the technology was that ordinary Americans began to eavesdrop on this 'low-power' domestic satellite traffic, specifically the television network and cable system feeds. In advance of licensed small dish technology, according to some reports over a million Americans, as of the summer of 1985, had taken the matter into their own hands and erected TVRO dishes at between $2000 and $5000, to obtain domestic satellite television signals not designed for home reception at all. It was estimated that as many as a quarter of rural homes had either no reception or reception so limited in quality and choice as to make this sort of expenditure worthwhile. About 35,000 a month were being installed. Beyond some local ordinances forbidding the erection of home satellite receivers, the field was almost completely unregulated. Although most people bought from dealers, it was possible to build a dish with 'materials commonly found in the local hardware store; plywood, standard dimension lumber, threaded rods, nuts, bolts, washers, screen, paint and so on' (Anon 1982: 54). This unplanned exercise of the people's powers of appropriation was, of course, easily contained. The cable industry moved rapidly to remove the threat by scrambling its signals and the 1984 'deregulating' Cable Telecommunications Act, *inter alia*, made the unauthorised reception of a scrambled signal a federal offence (Senate 1984). HBO, the leading US pay cable television service (p. 312), was the first to announce it would encrypt, and various schemes to collect from the dish owners were canvassed, although none at first seemed viable. Nevertheless this was enough to blight the further uncontrolled growth of home TVROs.

Licensed attempts at introducing DBS services, properly paid for by subscribers using the small dishes which the military had been exploiting for more than a decade, also failed in the 1980s. The American cable industry was expanding too rapidly for a really significant market gap to open up for 'high-power' DBS. Moreover, the National Association of Broadcasters attempted to smother the technology at birth at the FCC and in the courts and those delays, against this background of burgeoning cable provision, initially killed the business. In 1984 a five-channel DBS satellite service was finally introduced, operated by USCI Inc, to serve the Northeast and Midwest of the US. Starting in the thirty-three counties around Indianapolis, it charged $40 a month for the service and $400 for the dish and converter box but it managed to sign up only 10,000 subscribers and was bankrupted. Comsat, CBS and Paramount were among those who announced but never started services. Rupert Murdoch, despite his successful exploitation of the technology elsewhere, repeatedly announced and then delayed a service and in the meantime created a traditional US terrestrial television network instead. In the US, between cable and VCR the space for DBS was shrinking fast.

Yet it had not totally disappeared and a niche was emerging, largely because of the misfeasances of the cable industry which, since being deregulated by the 1984 Act, had become a byword for poor service and endless rate hikes. (Indeed, so badly behaved was it that it was re-regulated by Congress in 1992 over President Bush's veto (p. 314).) This and the possibility of non-high definition digital transmission created an opening. A GE subsidiary launched DirecTV in 1994 and by the end of the following year it had about 1.5 million subscribers. Its long-term viability was enhanced when AT&T put $137 million into it. To obtaining the service required a converter box – to translate the compressed digital signal into conventional analogue for display on old-fashioned television sets – and a 48-cm dish. The capacity for digital to deliver a new high definition wide-screen standard was ignored in favour of using digital's capacity for compression to deliver a large number of channels, 125 in all.

The British government similarly suppressed digital HDTV in favour of increased numbers of standard channels with its 1997 scheme for terrestrial digital broadcasting. Thus a new television standard remained unavailable despite the abortive analogue HDTV demonstrations of the 1980s and the increasing availability of 1000+ line digital systems in the 1990s. Programming entrepreneurs appear to be interested in increasing the number of channels they transmit, actually somewhat in defiance of what is known about the commercial attractiveness of so doing (p. 317) but they appear to have little interest in selling new sets, which they do not make, and even less in buying new production equipment, which they also do not make. On the other hand, receiver and production equipment manufacturers, concentrated in the East, are interested in selling such hardware but cannot provide the programming which would make them a necessity. (Witness the curious enterprise of Sony's late 1990s attempt to market a sort of faked HDTV receiver in the old standard with a wide-screen reformatting chip.) This stand-off, a classic instance of suppression, was working in the 1990s to delay a new television standard.

None of this affected the American surge in DBS penetration. There, in a further expression of the 'law' of suppression, whereby the old interests buy into technologies which threaten them, the second largest US DBS operator, Primestar Partners, with 1.1 million subscribers in 1995, was owned by the major cable industry players. It was anticipated that by the year 2000, DBS would reach 6 per cent of American households, but that, because the absolute number of households rises constantly, this would not impact much on the overall strength of either the broadcast or the cable industry (Veronhis Suhler 1996: 129–31).

The original British plan for a 'high-power' DBS to be run exclusively by the BBC was obviously in line with the 'law' of suppression but somewhat out of step with the times. Public service broadcasters were under increasing attack and in a number of European nations had been commercialised (by being forced to take advertisements) or even fully privatised. The British DBS plan metamorphosed into a risk-spreading consortium scheme to supply programming (via Unisat) to the British cable system, should that ever emerge. The consortium was disbanded in the summer of 1985. Eighteen months later, in December 1986, the Independent Broadcasting Authority awarded a commercial company, BSC, a direct broadcast satellite licence. Murdoch's Sky, with incompatible dish and converter technology, was licensed as its competitor and in short order absorbed it, creating a BSkyB monopoly.

This was because, at this point, in the UK BSkyB faced no competition in expanded entertainment services via cable or any other technology such as lower power television Satellite Master Antenna TV (SMATV), Multipoint Multichannel Distribution Systems (MMDS), home microwave links or so-called 'wireless cables'. The situation was the reverse of the one facing Murdoch in America where all these technologies and satellite backyard dishes were in (albeit marginalised) play – and cable had 47 per cent of television homes wired up by 1987 (Veronhis Suhler 1996: 130). In the UK there was only cable, and its penetration rate was around 1.25 per cent, a quarter of a million homes, the second lowest in Western Europe (Lange and Renaud 1989: 17). Five years later, this had barely increased to 300,000 homes. In this vacuum BSkyB flourished. By 1993, some three million households, one in seven, were subscribers. Satellite services accounted for nearly 6 per cent of all viewing (Fiddick 1993: 2,13). By 1996, its cumulative audience share was around 11.4 per cent and it was taken in one in five of all homes. It was said to be producing profits of £700,000 a day and was seen as a runaway success (Horsman 1996: 19).

In the rest of Europe, the 'high-power' DBS era was inaugurated by the German TV-SAT in November 1987. The first European digital satellite, Astra I-E, was launched in 1995. By 1996 something in the order of 200 transponders were available but the substantial penetration of cable in many countries, in contrast to the UK, was an inhibiting factor. BSkyB remained Europe's most successful direct-to-home satellite broadcaster.

In the rest of the world, especially the Far East, the satellites inaugurated a new era of transnational television, not without a certain amount of cultural and political friction. The Americans were using the emerging system to distribute cable services, notably Ted Turner's news channel CNN. In 1991, the BBC, with its long tradition of international radio broadcasting (a tradition now described as a 'strong brand'), started World Service Television. It positioned itself as a global rival to CNN and was claiming 18 million homes worldwide by 1994. Via the Hong Kong based StarTV Network, which used AsiaSat, it was reaching 11 million of these in the East, including 4 million in China (*BBC Handbook* 1993/4: 61). In 1993, Murdoch bought StarTV for $525 million. Despite a rhetoric which suggested that these new channels could not be controlled by national governments, Murdoch bowed to Communist Chinese political pressures over Western news bulletins and denied the BBC space on the system. By 1995, AsiaSat 2 allowed StarTV to distribute movies, safer than news, in Mandarin, Tagalog, Cantonese, Hindi, English, Japanese and Bahasa Indonesia, presumably to the most economically privileged sectors of these societies. Singapore and Taiwan licensed Disney for both up and down links.

These developments, especially in the Far East, represented a significant globalisation of industries which had been traditionally national. Nevertheless, to what extent these multinationals were free from local national political control, especially by authoritarian regimes, remained very much an open question. Nor was it very obvious how the economies of scale, of which such multinationals are supposedly capable, impact on, much less enhance, programme production. From the earliest days of Telstar through the Eurovision Song Contests, *Jeux sans frontières* and the rest, international programming's achievements have been, shall we say, modest. Conversely, popularity attaches to authentic national material, be it the near universal acceptance of American prime-time series or, for example, in the US, *The Forsyte Saga* (a black-and-white classic series which became British television's first and most significant hit there). The long-term ideological significance of the importation of foreign television signals also remains something of a mystery. It is by no means the case that such importation reproduces the ideology of the imported programs, as the crudest version of the cultural imperialism thesis suggested.[4] The spread of Western programming by DBS intensifies the Western presence but that has always been part of the non-Western world's television experience. There is little to suggest that such intensification, of itself, will reduce the capacity of audiences to read programming against the hegemonic grain in ways that make cultural sense for them.

What is far clearer about these applications of specialised satellite services and, most significantly, direct broadcasting is that they represent the most effective use of the technology. Clarke's concept of a space-side general telecommunications system looks to be far less long-lived, especially internationally, although local uses continue to emerge. For example, there is a strong possibility that commercial 'high-power' low-orbit systems could be revived by the turn of the millennium to support the proliferation of extremely local personal mobile phones.

The mobile telephone is a development of solid-state electronics. At first, traditional free air propagation, old-fashioned point-to-point wireless, was exploited as citizen band radio in countries which, like the US, licensed such uses. It was the imposition of the 55 mph speed limit on interstate highways in 1973 which encouraged American truck drivers to install amateur two-way radio transceivers to warn of police speed traps; and caused the police to take up the technology in response. Within two years such CB (Citizen Band) radios were comparatively widely diffused, especially in rural America. The more universally adopted mobile phone followed about a decade later, the first commercial system being licensed in the US in 1983. Such devices used a system of terrestrial transmitters to establish a network of cells and complex switching technology to pass signals to and from the phones via these cells. There were one million American users by 1989 and poor reception and lack of privacy did not impede the mobile phone's diffusion in the 1990s. Phones weighing as little as 218 grams became commonplace. By 1996, and in defiance of any potential health risk caused by having radio frequencies so close to the ear, some 6.3 million mobiles were in use in the UK alone (Potter 1996: 2).[5] However, apart from digitalisation, the fundamental limitation of terrestrial radio transmissions limited the performance of the system. An extensive low-orbit satellite system would alleviate such difficulties – although radio astronomers greeted the prospect with considerable alarm.

This application apart, it is possible to see satellites as an extremely centralising technology. I would argue that, despite the efforts at every stage to constrain the development of satellite communications, from the failure to exploit the V-2 through the institutional arrangements governing Intelsat to the delayed introduction of 'high-power' devices transmitting to very small dishes, less disruption has been threatened by this technology than others here considered. The result has been that, as the systems of ownership and control slowly emerged, no national or international players were disturbed and comparatively few new players were dis- covered (and none of those was entirely without prior communications interests). The cost of this calm was simply that for the thirty years since the technology came on stream (and for the couple of decades prior to that when it was not being exploited) the full potential of the system was only slowly allowed to develop and then only insofar as it did not affect other technologies, notably cables.

The Federation of the United States of Earth will need more, much more, than balls of metal in the sky to facilitate its birth.

# 1 7

# CABLE TELEVISION

## THE RETURN OF THE WIRE: CABLE TELEVISION

As the above account reveals, the wires never really went away. The early radio and television networks were wired and the transoceanic telephone cables have kept pace with the development of the international telecommunications satellite system. Yet, more than that, cables have always been used for the distribution of radio and television signals to the home. Indeed, cable has been, from the outset, a viable alternative to free-air propagation. As Peter Eckersley, the engineer who had built the BBC's SB wireless net, suggested to Reith, it was nothing less than a complete alternative to wireless transmission (Briggs 1961: 358); but almost nowhere did this happen, nor has it developed in this way. Instead careful prevarication and delay has meant that, usually, cable has only been allowed to supplement the efforts of the broadcasters. It has taken decades to achieve even this limited function but it should be noted that at no time had this slow diffusion been occasioned by technological constraints. Cable has stood ready to supplant broadcasting from the very beginning of both radio and television; its failure so to is a further vivid example of the operation of the 'law' of the suppression of radical potential.

I have suggested that bandwidth limitations placed upon the telephone circuit were economic in origin and not primarily the result of technological constraints. Thus, higher fidelity wires for the re-transmission of radio signals were immediately developed in the 1920s and were in place almost as soon as radio was itself established. In the Netherlands, the need for signal enhancement and a taste for the importation of distant foreign stations provided the supervening necessities for radio cable systems. By 1939, 50 per cent of Dutch homes, and in some urban areas as many as 80 per cent, were wired. In Britain the 'rediffusion' of domestic radio services had begun in 1925 on the south coast where shipping signals caused enough interference to render domestic reception difficult. In the north-east too, where the BBC was comparatively slow to provide service, 'relay exchanges' sprang up. Reception in most places was excellent and constantly improving and so by 1935 only some 3 per cent of radio licence holders received service through these wires but the war increased reception problems and by 1950 some 8 per cent of radio homes were back on the wire (Hollins 1984: 35–41).

Eckersley left the corporation in 1929 to join Rediffusion, the leading relay company. Two years later he had devised a way of using the national electrical power distribution grid and mains cables to carry six radio signals. The radical potential of this proposal to break the GPO/BBC hegemony was well understood. As the *BBC Year Book* noted (1933: 72): 'Each exchange may increase to the stature of a BBC in miniature'. The GPO, in 1930, had already forbidden any 'wireless exchange' operator from originating programs. Further restrictions were imposed. No company was to have more than 100,000 subscribers drawn from any one area of 2,000,000 and none was to operate in an area as a monopoly. The threat to the BBC hegemony was translated into a potential attack on broadcasting standards. The relay system

> contains within it forces which if uncontrolled might be disruptive of the spirit and intentions of the B.B.C.'s charter. The persons in charge of wireless exchanges . . . can transmit amusing items from the British programs and replace talks and other matter of informative or experimental value by amusing items in programs from abroad and so debase their programs to a level of amusement interest only.
>
> (ibid.)

In the event, neither the attractions of foreign stations (with dance bands on Sundays) nor lacuna in the domestic transmission system were sufficient in Britain or on the Continent to allow public demand to sweep away the paternalistic objections of the postal and broadcasting authorities. Cable radio as a rival programming service withered on the branch.

The technology of the wide-band co-axial cable capable of carrying a high definition (1930s-style) picture of some 400+ lines had been developed, as we have seen, by AT&T. In Britain, the new video technology was grafted on the old radio system and the first television cable was operating in Gloucester by 1951. Fifteen years later more than one million receivers were on cable; yet the introduction of the UHF network, which began in 1963, inexorably wiped out the prime *raison d'être* for most of these systems – poor reception. As had happened with radio cable, improvements in transmission reduced cable television's attractiveness. Only municipal regulations forbidding roof antennae kept it alive, increasing its universe to a high of about 14 per cent, 2.5 million homes in 1970s, one-third of them Rediffusion subscribers.

Reception improved not just because technology became more sophisticated. It was also the result of an ideological position which saw broadcasting less as a business and far more as a centralising social force. The nemesis of the UK cable industry was GPO and BBC insistence on a form of universal service whereby, for example, the huge variety of possible UHF signals was curtailed in the interests of maximising reception. In Britain, as in most European states, the original thirteen VHF and the current sixty-nine UHF bands were used to ensure that every household received the same signals clearly. In the UK this meant three national networks, which were to become four only in 1982 with the start of Channel Four and the Welsh channel, S4C.

Contrast the United States: there, eschewing UHF, the internationally agreed thirteen VHF channels, reduced to twelve by a 1952 FCC decision, were used exactly to achieve the opposite result, i.e. a maximising of the number of different signals to create a competitive television marketplace. That objective, after all, is what ostensibly occasioned the FCC's four-year 'freeze' in licensing television stations between 1948 and 1952, though it meant disregarding fringe reception problems. In consequence, the need for signal enhancement created a viable ancillary business to the business of broadcasting. It grew out of the technical shortcomings of the free-air system, shortcomings which were not just the result of the way the VHF band was deployed but also other problems. For example, the pioneering NTSC colour system was less easily received in the home than were comparable European systems and this poor reception was exacerbated by geographical (distance and mountains) and urban (skyscrapers) factors as well. And, finally, there was the 'freeze'.

On Tuesday and Saturday nights in the late 1940s, the bars of Summit Hill, Pennsylvania would fill with people from the town of Lansford in Panther Valley below to watch Milton Berle and the boxing matches. Summit Hill was high enough to receive Philadelphia's television signals 70 miles to the south. The valleys were not and, because of the 'freeze', were prevented from having local television stations either. It was here, locked in the eastern mountain ranges, that cable television in America was born although other mountainous areas in the West came up with similar solutions (Roman 1983: 1–2). Four radio dealers in Lansford, George Bright, William McDonald, Robert Tarlton and Rudolph Dubosky, established the Panther Valley Television Company. They built a tower on Summit Hill 85 feet high, charged subscribers a $100 installation fee and thereafter a monthly $3.[1] By December 1950, the Panther Valley system had been franchised by its community. They had found a way to side-step FCC regulations which prohibited the free-air re-broadcasting of signals; the Commission had nothing to say about sending television pictures down a wire.

Although they were working with readily available equipment, it nevertheless had to be configured to the nascent cable industry's needs. Milton Jerrold Shapp started Jerrold Electronics in Pennsylvania with his army discharge money, $500, in 1948 and expanded the business by building master television antennae on apartment buildings. One of his staff told him about the Lansford system where further expansion depended upon the availability of a reliable signal amplifier. Shapp promised Tarlton, one of the Lansford four, such a device. His company quickly became the leading cable hardware manufacturer, a position it maintained for the next half-century. Among Shapp's innovations was his insistence on five-year service contracts based on an initial $5 connection fee and a monthly 25¢ service charge for each subscriber. In return Jerrolds undertook to train service personnel, replace defective units and generally keep the system running for the duration of the agreement. Such a relationship gave the early five-channel 'Ma'n'Pa' operations the technical wherewithal to offer a reliable service to the public with little know-how of their own. It also allowed Jerrolds to commandeer some 76 per cent of the early cable equipment market.

Original cable programming remained a secondary concern throughout the development period although another Pennsylvanian pioneer, Martin Malarkey, did start his own local talent showcase in Pottsville, PA; but the more significant added value came from the importation of distant broadcast signals. For instance, San Diego received three network VHF stations until in the 1960s it became the largest cable market when all seven Los Angeles stations (including the same three networks' LA affiliates) were imported (Mason et al.1971: 25). By 1982, it had, at an average of $9.50 per month, 209,000 subscribers, 70,000 more than the next biggest system on Long Island. As five-channel systems gave way to twelve channels, even well-served cities like San Diego were attached to conurbations via cable.

The FCC's VHF wavelength allocation procedures, after the end of the 'freeze', had privileged conurbations at the expense of the countryside, obviously because such a policy created the maximum audience for advertisers. In terms of VHF coverage, the cost of seven stations in New York and the other 'major markets' (as American broadcasters call cities) was that generally across the country one house in five could only get two VHF stations or less. The Commission slowly allocated further licences in the UHF band to supplement this but by the early 1970s even with these new UHF stations, 18 per cent of all homes could receive only four or fewer signals and 3 per cent none at all (Mason et al. 1971: 19).

Cable was massively aided by this marketplace approach to broadcasting. The move to colour also helped. Poor reception of VHF black-and-white in built-up urban areas meant ghosting on the picture. With colour, picture quality became even worse and cable found an opportunity to sell itself even in the privileged conurbations. NTSC UHF was little better. To the limited signal availability in rural areas and smaller towns and cities, there was now added poor colour broadcasting transmission standards everywhere.

The received rhetoric of the cable industry is that penetration grew very slowly throughout the 1950s and 1960s and that the technology's real supervening necessity was neither signal enhancement nor distant importation but additional unique entertainment services. It is claimed that the business supposedly never took off until such channels became available in the 1970s. However, on the contrary, poor reception and limited small town and rural choice were the basis of cable's steady and consistent growth throughout this period, when almost no special services were offered. By comparison with the other communication techniques, there is no objective reason for describing cable television's early growth as slow. Within the first decade 850,000 largely rural homes received service from no less than 800 providers and by 1962 there were 1325 community antenna television (CATV) systems with 1.2 million subscribers. A decade later there were 5.9 million subscribers on 2750 CATV systems, one television household in ten. (Mason *et al.* 1971: 32).

Largely ignored by the urbanised broadcasting industry and its regulators, by the early 1960s cable had grown into a sufficiently lusty infant to demand attention. In one sense it was the ultimate parasite, reselling a product, television, that was not only expensive to produce but also protected in law by copyright. The cable industry, however, paid not a cent to the broadcasters. On the other hand, if the business of commercial television is seen less as the provision of entertainment and more as the selling of audiences to advertisers, the cable industry, as long as it did not originate competitive programming, could be viewed as the broadcaster's little helper, simply increasing the number of its viewers. Throughout the 1960s, American courts were to take this latter lenient view of cable. In 1961 it was held that television stations could not restrict the use of their signals after transmission unless economic harm could be proved. In 1964, an Idaho network affiliate claimed it was being damaged because the cable company ran the same programs imported from distant stations. The Court held for the cable company (Roman 1983: 11–12). The most significant of this strand of decisions was that of the Supreme Court in *Fortnightly Corporation vs. United Artists Television* (1968). Since other stations and the networks had failed to establish their rights to the material they transmitted, in this 1967 case an original producer, United Artists, sought relief against a cable company, *Fortnightly*. The inadequacies of the common law of copyright, essentially a protection for eighteenth-century booksellers, were fiercely illuminated by this decision.

Because the common law did not admit the concept of intellectual property, copyright could be said to be based more on 'the expropriation of author's rights' than on the 'transfer of rights by contract' which systems acknowledging intellectual property enable (Anon (EJF) 1996: 6). The Court in *Fortnightly* began by holding that copyright was a limited right. For such incorporeal stuff as television signals, the relevant American statute, The Copyright Act of 1909, provided protection only against an 'exclusive right to perform' and the Court determined that re-transmitting a signal down a wire, whether for profit or not, was not a 'performance' within the meaning of this act. The cable company was more like an ordinary viewer than a television station.[2] Clearly the disruptive potential of the cable industry was not going to be contained by law. On the contrary, the courts were responding to a supervening social necessity pushing (as it were) to equalise the provision of television across the country which the broadcasters and their regulator had failed to do. In the final analysis, the broadcasters could still charge the advertisers for their viewers whether they were reached through the cable or through the air. Nevertheless, even before most of these legal decisions, the FCC, which had refused jurisdiction over cable in 1959, began to act to protect its primary clients in the broadcasting industry.

In 1963, the Commission was petitioned by a firm which wished to establish a CATV system to import signals to a distant part of Wyoming. The local broadcasting station successfully argued that it would be put out of business, its FCC licence rendered valueless. Since this fell within the principle of demonstrating economic harm, the petition was denied and when the CATV company sued, the court held that the Commission was correct in supporting the station. Research indeed demonstrated that for independent VHF stations in major markets and for network affiliates in small ones the importation of distant signals could be devastating – 30 per cent audience loss for the former and 50 per cent for the latter. Ten per cent falls were also noted for large market network affiliates (for example, in San Diego) when faced with competition from important metropolitan affiliate signals (for example, from LA) (Mason *et al.* 1971: 217–19).

Bolstered by this, the FCC asserted its right to regulate the entire cable industry and in its *First Report and Order* of 1965, it simply told the cable operators they could not import programming which duplicated that of local stations (defined as those within 60 miles of the cable system's head-ends) within thirty days of a local broadcast. The FCC also announced that it would freeze the importation of distant television signals into the top 100 markets. A year later the thirty-day rule was relaxed to a one-day prohibition but the other restrictions of cable were not lifted. After the decision in *Fortnightly*, the FCC imposed even stricter regulations on the importation of distant signals, wiping out most of the legal advantages gained by the cable industry. While they remained free to re-transmit local signals, they would now require the specific permission of copyright holders, stations, networks, producers, syndicators, etc., on a programme-by-programme basis before they could import signals – an impossibility.

If the courts were responding to supervening social need, the Commission was acting, not untypically, as an agent of the 'law' of suppression. Local re-broadcasting was to be cable's primary permitted function. Furthermore, as an additional burden and in line with the social rhetoric of the early 1970s, the

FCC now required all systems to originate material on a 'public access' basis. The earliest video-technologies, the Sony Portapak and other cheap (by broadcasting standards) equipment, were being made the basis of a call for a more democratic television culture. This was especially strong in Canada where an entire programme of the National Film Board (Challege for Change/*Pour une société nouvelle)* was transformed from a documentary film-making project into a Portapak citizens-as-videomakers project instead. The Canadian Radio and Television Commission, in 1971, required that access channels be provided by cable system operators (Engleman 1990: 16). The US Federal Communications Commission made the same order a year later (Hollins 1984: 208).

During the 1970s the game was changing. No longer were the cable system owners little 'Ma'n'Pa' enterprises, outgrowths of rural electrical appliance stores. For the whole of the previous decade cable firms had been consolidating themselves into MSOs (*M*ultiple *s*ystem *o*perators). Some key communications players had also been buying up cable systems to become MSOs. These included, until the FCC ordered them to divest, broadcasters such as CBS (Mason *et al.* 1971: 32). The cable system was being integrated into the industry behind the shield of the FCC's draconian restrictions.

Then, as the decade progressed, the FCC eased up on its requirements in part because its immediate work was done in that cable was being contained and in part because of the new rhetoric of deregulation (the reverse of the previous impulse towards public access). Copyright law was rewritten and cable operators were required to pay general licence fees which were to become, despite the modest percentage of production costs they represented, an ongoing source of friction with the broadcasters. Importation regulations and mandatory access requirements were dropped. The cable 'freeze', the period of maximum regulation, operated exactly as the television 'freeze' had twenty years earlier. It allowed the players to begin to sort themselves out while not entirely inhibiting growth. Indeed by 1974, despite these restrictions, 11.7 per cent of all American homes were cabled. (For comparison, note that this level of penetration by BSkyB in the UK in the early 1990s was generally considered to be a massive success.)

## THE IMPACT OF DOMESTIC SATELLITES

In 1972, to add to its other troubles, Wilkes-Barre, in the centre of Pennsylvania's depressed anthracite coal industry, was declared a hurricane disaster area. On 4 November that year, in the midst of another storm, 365 cable subscribers, for an extra fee over and above their basic charge, saw the very first transmission of a new cable service, Home Box Office (HBO). For their money, they received a hockey game and the feature film, *Sometime a Great Nation*, uninterrupted by commercials.

The great notion of pay-TV was not born that stormy night in North Eastern Pennsylvania; the idea of transmitting movies to the home is as old as television itself, since some of the earliest pioneers worked on it specifically for this purpose. To have people pay for such transmission, whether over the air or through a wire, simply required scrambling the picture, the technology for so doing having been first demonstrated in 1931. More extensive field trials of pay-TV formed part of Hollywood's sustained attempt to cope with the rise of New York television in the late 1940s (p. 123). HBO was the brain-child of a cable visionary, the man who had wired lower Manhattan, Charles Dolan. Dolan had sold his Sterling Manhattan Cable to Time Inc, and among his first moves in his new berth at the big organisation was a proposed pay-TV service for cable. (Anon 1982: 13). Time invested $150,000 in this which would grow to over $30 million before the service broke even, six years later.

Time Inc.'s involvement with audiovisual media stretches back to the *March of Time* newsreels which began in 1931. It had acquired its complement of television stations (all eventually sold in the 1980s to avoid 'conflict of interest' charges) and was responsible for the marketing of BBC products to the American public television system during the 1970s. Its involvement with cable became its most successful video enterprise by far. By the 1980s it was one of the largest MSOs with nearly $2\frac{1}{2}$ million subscribers in 400 systems. By the 1990s, after merging with another major media conglomerate and MSO, Warners, it was one of the world's largest multimedia companies.

After two years of effort HBO had been sold to a mere 57,000 subscribers on forty-two cable systems. This was deemed to be a quarter of the way to a financial break-even point and, although a solid enough achievement in the sorry history of American pay-TV, it was not sufficient to guarantee the business. Even if the 200,000 mark had been passed by the end of 1975, HBO would still have been a marginal enterprise. The suggestion that, by using a satellite and 'head-end' TVROs to reach these discrete (and by broadcasting standards minute) cable systems, an economically viable audience could be reconstituted, was first made shortly after the ABC domestic satellite petition to the FCC. A number of cable industry entities were therefore involved in the 'open skies' bids of 1970 and 1971 and, indeed, Dolan had mentioned the satellite option in his initial proposal to Time. In 1973, HBO, the MSO Teleprompter Corporation and the equipment manufacturer Scientific-American used Anik II to demonstrate satellite's potential to the annual cable trade convention in Anaheim.

By 1974, Westar was in business and other satellites were being launched. This fact influenced FCC attitudes to the cable industry. Up to that point it had demonstrated, at the behest of the broadcasters, a marked willingness to contain cable. To that end, apart from its general regulations, it had also denied pay-cable permission for sports events and restricted the use of feature films; but now, having finally approved domestic satellites, it was eager for them to be viable and therefore pleased to encourage cable industry use of the new birds. Time spent $6.5 million leasing two satellite transponders for five years from RCA, which had joined Western Union as a satellite owner. The satellite pay-cable rights to the Ali-Frazier heavyweight title fight in the Philippines were acquired and HBO went live with 'The Thrilla from Manila', as the bout was billed. The channel had been gaining subscribers at the rate of 15,000 a month. After the fight that figure doubled and by year's end it had reached nearly 300,000 homes via hundreds of small cable systems. Eight years later it had 12 million and, on occasion, it achieved a bigger audience than any of the three broadcast networks. By 1995, it had 25 million subscribers, over a quarter of all US television households (Veronhis Suhler 1996: 135). It also acquired direct competitors such as Viacom's Showtime in 1978 and Warner's The Movie Channel in 1979; but it became clear that there was room for only two major film-based services and in 1983, these latter channels merged. In 1995 HBO still had twice the number of subscribers.

Other satellite distributed services were offered on a non-subscription basis – so-called 'basic services' which came into the home together with the re-transmission of broadcasting signals for the monthly cable fee. Ted Turner, a yacht-racing local television station owner in Atlanta, whose family money came from outdoor advertising sites, leased satellite time in 1977 to offer cable services his undistinguished (that is to say typical smaller market independent broadcast station) programming mix of old television shows and even older movies. He could, however, now claim a national audience, for within five years the station, WTBS, was reaching a universe of 26 million cable homes. Armed with this potential audience, he still bought his programming as if for a local market but he sold his advertising time on a more national-style rate-card. The result was millions of dollars of increased profit and the cable 'superstation' was born. (Even without the satellite WTBS was a highly profitable enterprise.) With this satellite boost to his revenues, Turner spun off a flurry of services including, in 1980, the prestigious CNN 24-hour news service as well as less distinguished exercises such as a music channel, a rival to Warner's Music TV (MTV), which was off the air within weeks of its launch. WTBS aside, the profitability of many of these enterprises, including CNN, remained questionable and the whole array was nearly bankrupted by the hubristic acquisition of MGM in 1986. The MSOs bailed Turner out and he survived to launch yet another service, TNT, based on the MGM library of old films, and to bid, unsuccessfully, for CBS.

Turner's emulators included other services unique to cable, i.e. not broadcast anywhere. ESPN (the Educational and Sports Network, now entirely sports) which could be received in even more homes than Turner's superstation was owned, eventually, by ABC (itself then bought by Disney). MTV was seen as being as significant as CNN (although its audience was small even by cable's norms), while up-scale services such as Discovery (a documentary channel) were deemed to be real challengers to the public television system. By 1984, there were four domestic satellites carrying at least forty services, many of which were only part-time and highly specialised and the vast majority of which were not profitable (Hollins 1984: 145). They were, in effect 'lost leaders' to sell cable service.

By the mid-1990s, there were thirty major nationally distributed cable channels. There were early experiments in different methods of revenue raising. For example, the children's channel Nickelodeon was initially commercial-free but charged cable systems a few cents per subscriber. It could do this because it was seen as socially valuable, just the sort of offering to boost a cable company's negotiation position with a municipality; but, as the Reagan era progressed, such considerations became less pressing. Nickelodeon turned into a service carrying commercials as many, except the pay-TV ones, had been from the outset.

The degree to which cable's growth depended upon these extra services, despite the vigorous assertions of the cable industry, is debatable. Cable was, after all, a large and extremely profitable business by 1976 before add-on services significantly began to come into play. The factors that made it so – poor reception and the limited availability of broadcast signals – did not change after 'The Thrilla from Manila'; nor had the industry by that date remotely satisfied demand. It is therefore reasonable to suggest that, even without the add-on services, cable would have continued to prosper. It is equally probable that the main driving force for cable remained poor reception. An extensive survey in 1981, five years into the era of satellite distributed cable services, found that among those refusing to subscribe, 49 per cent gave 'I get good reception already' as their reason, the same percentage as those citing cost (Anon 1981).

Be all this as it may, the industry continued to grow, totally throwing off the restrictions originally imposed on it. In the 1980s, cable disentangled itself from the city franchising, just as the telephone companies had done at the beginning of the century. The 1984 Cable Telecommunications Act, which made unauthorised receipt of encrypted signals an offence, also enshrined this changed situation. In emasculating the franchising process the industry was free to pursue profit as it thought best and it did so with a will, but also without much evident commitment to service. Shortly thereafter, the Court of Appeal relieved the industry of the requirement to re-transmit local signals – the 'must-carry' rule. It can be said that, in triumph, cable did not behave well. Within the decade, complaints about service and rate hikes were flooding into Congress from the public and eventually, against the grain of the time and over President Bush's veto, legislation was passed re-regulating the industry. As we have seen, this performance also contributed to DBS's second chance in the 1990s.

Nevertheless, a majority of the American public continued to subscribe. By 1995, 92.2 million of America's 95.4 million television households were 'passed' by the cable and could be easily connected. Some 65.8 million, nearly two out of every three of these cabled households, bought basic services for an average monthly fee of $23.07 each. In addition, 46.1 million of these subscribers bought premium pay services for a further $8.68 per month. Total subscription revenues were $16.8 thousand million per annum with a further $4.8 thousand million on pay-TV. The system was deemed to be mature with much slower expansion, 1.7 per cent per year, anticipated up to the millennium (Veronhis Suhler 1996: 130–52).

## THE IMPACT ON BROADCAST TELEVISION

America was not alone in exploiting this technology but elsewhere signal enhancement has been not the only, or even the primary, supervening necessity for cable. In culturally dependent societies the importation of distant foreign signals has in some cases produced extensive cable systems. In Canada the thirst for American programming created a cable system which by the 1980s, a decade earlier than in the United States, had already passed more than 80 per cent of homes and had signed up 75 per cent – a level of penetration which America is not expected to reach before the twenty-first century. This has left the public broadcaster, CBC, peculiarly vulnerable to political attack.

In Europe, a similar taste for imported signals, already seen with radio in the Netherlands before the Second World War, drove cable developments. In Belgium, to take the most extreme example, by 1987 84.3 per cent of all homes with television were connected, a situation not unlike Canada's because penetration was driven by the importation of French and Dutch broadcast signals. But increased choice also began to play a role. By 1996, Europe's most successful television channel of any kind, with a regular 43 per cent share, was VTM, a Belgian cable service (part owned by a Dutch publishing group) transmitting mainly locally produced mainstream entertainment programming.

Other European countries with high cable penetration levels included the Netherlands (70.4 per cent), Switzerland (67.3 per cent) and Luxembourg (66 per cent). Elsewhere, for example, in Spain, cabling was just getting underway in the 1990s (Lange and Renaud 1989: 17). In the early 1980s in Britain, cable became a major source of Information Revolution hype. 'Mrs Margaret Thatcher has recently taken the most important industrial decision of her administration, and nearly all Britons are completely unaware of the fact', wrote *The Economist* of a 1982 cabinet decision to wire Britain with fibre optics. This was said to 'have as much potential for Britain as it moves into the next century as laying the railway network did in the last' (Anon 1982: 11). While the accuracy or otherwise of this assessment can be debated, there is no question that the market (to which Mrs Thatcher left the implementation of this plan) has taken a rather less hyperventilated view of the matter. Five years after this 'decision', new cable penetration, in decline from its previous high, was (as we have said) a mere 1.25 per cent, 260,000 homes. A decade beyond that, with the heavy involvement of the American Baby Bells eager to complete in telephony rather than television, it was about a million, its potential as an entertainment medium much reduced by, among other things, Mrs Thatcher's encouragement of Murdoch's DBS.

The haphazard intervention of neo-liberal governments elsewhere produced upheavals in the pattern of broadcasting, notably a sustained privatising and commercialising reform movement attacking the public broadcasters. This was often attributed to technological requirements, but, as in Britain, the technology was actually of far less significance than the ideology. For example, France, which had never really established a stable institutional frame for radio and television, sold off its public television in 1987 well in advance of any technological impact from cable or satellite. That year a mere 100,000 French homes, 0.5 per cent, were cabled (Lange and Renaud 1989: 17).

Hidden by these political upheavals and the smoke-screen of technobabble is quite another reality. These new delivery systems, cable or satellite, were in fact having far less impact on traditional television than might be thought. Traditional television has proved to be resilient.

Let us return to the world's richest television society, the USA. Overall, the new American system, still dominated by broadcasters but with a significant degree of cable distribution and programming as well as niches for satellites and other technologies, appeared to be more or less stable by the mid-1990s. Nevertheless, much is made of the fact that, largely because of cable but also – less noted – because of the continued growth in the number of independent UHF broadcast television stations, the big three American networks have suffered a precipitous decline in their audience figures. The networks' prime-time share of switched-on televisions was 93 per cent in 1971. By 1987 it had fallen to 71 per cent. In 1995 it was 59 per cent (Veronhis Suhler 1988: 32; Veronhis Suhler 1996: 95). Obviously, the networks no longer dominate as they did when their only competition was a few largely marginalised independent broadcasting stations. However, what is ignored in these percentages is the absolute increase in the number of households over these two decades. Increasing population produced a rise of some 22.5 million more homes so that, for example, the absolute number of homes watching the networks rose by 1.5 million between 1988 and 1994 (Veronhis Suhler 1995: 106). This has so softened the blow of reduced audience share that in the 1990s new terrestrial networks were being established, for the first time since the 1940s. The first of these was Rupert Murdoch's Fox, ironically a major programming source for his other global ventures in new distribution technologies.

The American cable industry, in effect, denied the broadcasters the benefits due to them from having an ever-growing population to serve. Yet cable did not, as was widely anticipated in the 1970s, destroy the broadcasters. Nor did it destroy their bottom line; that is, television's share of the advertising spend. In all 'day-parts' (not just prime time) and at all stations (not just network affiliates) the percentage share of advertising revenues has fallen far less than has the audience share. Over the decade to 1995, that declined by just over 10 per cent from 96.1 per cent to 85.8 per cent. By the mid-1990s revenues were once again expected to rise, from just over $30 thousand million in 1995 to $41 thousand million (in 1995 dollars) by the year 2000 (Veronhis Suhler 1996: 100, 104).

Conversely, cable's many commercial channels take a disproportionately lower percentage of the advertising spend. Contrast the nascent US television industry in 1952, with around one-third of homes already commanding 70 per cent of broadcast advertising dollars, with cable's performance in 1984. With more than 40 per cent of homes on the wire, cable secured a mere $400 million of advertising revenues – about 4 per cent of radio and network television's take in that year. By 1995, all cable channels, pay and commercial, had almost exactly one-third of the total television audience; but the industry banked only one-sixth of the advertising spend – $5.3 thousand million. Advertisers were simply proceeding as if one broadcast television viewer was worth two cable channel viewers. A major reason for this was that the fragmented nature of cable services made it difficult for the advertiser to spend money with the industry. By the year 2000, estimates suggest that the audience balance will have improved, now more slowly than in the past, in favour of cable. Its one-third share will become 40 per cent and its advertising revenues will nearly double to $9.8 thousand million (Veronhis Suhler 1996: 104–5).

None of this means that cable, which also had an additional $29 thousand million revenues from subscriptions in 1995, is not a massively successful industry. I am simply pointing out that, contrary to the hype, it does not produce enough revenue from these combined sources to mount full-scale entertainment channels in competition with the broadcasters. Thus it has not yet destroyed broadcast television in America. This is not just because of the advertising revenues discrepancy. There are other inhibitors. The history of cable's development, which seems to be echoed with other technologies in other countries for example, (DBS in Britain), suggests that increasing channels by whatever means does not *proportionately* increase revenues (as we have just seen), nor programming nor audiences.

Take programming: Cable's total revenues have first to sustain a vastly more expensive distribution system than that which the broadcasters use. Instead of the largely automated transmitters and TVROs of a television station, cable systems require municipal licences, way-leaves, wires, amplifiers, installers and repairers. They also need community antennae and the same sort of TVROs as the broadcasters. But what really reduces the industry's ability to compete as a programme originator is the very number of services they offer. Whereas the US networks split up a core income of some $12 thousand million in 1995 between, essentially, four players, some twenty-eight major nationally distributed advertising supported cable services shared $3.6 thousand million. This entire range of services had, therefore, about the same amount of advertising revenue as one broadcast network.

In the UK, similar ratios prevail. In homes which buy the services, satellite and cable channels have 34 per cent of the viewers, much as cable does in America with much the same economic impact on individual channel budgets. Sky One, for example, had a reported budget of £35 million as against the main commercial network's £600 million. Of course, the programming budgets overall could be improved if the number of services were reduced, but the cable/satellite indust-ries, trapped by a rhetoric of increased choice, cannot take that option. Against this is the suggestion that these are services so new and innovative that compar-isons with the old (and supposedly extremely inefficient) broadcast channels do not apply. However, this can be readily disputed.

The cable channels have almost totally failed to alter the established genres and forms of television broadcasting in any significant way, never mind add to them. The 24-hour news channels, for example, simply repeat a slowly (mostly very slowly) changing traditional news bulletin every half-hour virtually all the time. The American Weather Channel has a standard television weather bulletin repeated every few minutes. American cable's most original idea is Court TV, a cheap variant on studio talk whose gavel-to-gavel coverage of the O. J. Simpson trial is credited, together with CNN's nearly equally obsessive attention, with having increased basic cable's total 1995 rating by 1.6, a 20 per cent hike over the previous year.

Because of these economics original basic cable programming is largely news, weather, talk and shopping (a mere 1990s fad) and sport. Even the most expensive of these, sport, is cheap, when compared to drama at the Hollywood average of more than $1.5 million an hour – as is 'off-network' recycling, record company promotional materials (MTV) and endless repetition, marketed as 'convenience'. Pay channels do little better. HBO itself, despite its huge revenue streams, cannot afford original feature film production values, when movies cost an average of nearly $40 million each. With pay services such as HBO, repetition has been the answer. Each film was screened about six times a month, allowing a 24-hour programme to be sustained with about twenty new titles a month, with many films pre-sold as hit movies (as well as many more which failed theatrically and some which were totally unreleased to the cinemas). Without breaking this basic pattern, HBO and its rivals have undertaken a certain amount of production with increasing success, budgeting projects above television's $1.5 million an hour although still well below the feature film level. However, no cable channel, whether pay or advertising supported, originates non-sporting, general entertainment material at the level of the broadcasting networks.

I would argue that the high cost of traditional production is a function of techniques and industrial arrangements such as the star system. These techniques, enshrined in pre-war Hollywood practice, were very much established by the film industry exactly as barriers to entry, but they now constitute a 'language', a means of communicating between producers and audience. They produce programming recognisable as such by the audience and cannot easily be abandoned. This is why the oft-quoted analogy with magazines will not work, however multi-channelled the television environment becomes. A full-scale traditional service with a broad range of largely original programming seems to require at least 10 million homes on a regular basis. The fewer the homes, the more repeats and imported programs. Half a million readers of a magazine such as *Guns and Ammo* are simply too few to produce television revenues at a sufficient level for *Guns and Ammo* programming with acceptable production values.

This 'production-value law' is but one expression of the cultural determinants working to limit the programming possibilities of new television distribution systems. The other is that introducing channels does not produce programming, even if the money is available for it. Consider how difficult it is for the broadcasters to find material popular enough to refresh their schedules every season. Moreover, if programming is the rock for cable/satellite operators, audiences constitute the hard place. Obviously, given the continued need to work, sleep and eat, audiences do not proportionately increase their viewing time to match the number of channels they have available. In America, the gap in total viewing between the two-thirds of homes which have cable and the one-third which do not is measured in minutes. In those cabled homes, the average American spent 1020 hours per annum watching broadcast television and 469 hours tuned to basic cable services. But, as with advertising revenue, the same factor applies – cable was splitting its anyway reduced hours between many more channels. The result was that, contrary to the hype, cable audiences were minuscule – even for MTV and CNN, never mind the Nashville Network, Lifeline and Comedy Central. In 1995, MTV managed a cumulative 0.6 rating – that is, just over half a million homes. The Discovery Channel got to about a million and CNN around a million and a half. The largest basic cable service in audience terms, USA Network, essentially an off-network re-run channel, reached just over 2.4 million homes (Veronhis Suhler 1996: 135). The weakest of the big three broadcast networks was doing five to six times better than that.

There is even some evidence that audiences are confused by and not attracted to systems with dozens of channels. First, each cabled household, even when given a choice of an average thirty-six channels, the mid-1990s norm, watched only about a quarter of them for significant amounts of time – ironically, about the same number of channels as the old VHF dispensation made available in the largest conurbations. Second, previous attempts to introduce large-capacity, interactive 'two-way' addressable cable have failed, notably the Warner Cable's Qube experimental system pioneered in Columbus, Ohio in 1977 but abandoned less than a decade later as underused and uneconomic. The cultural 'fit' of 500 or more channels is not self-evident.

Thousands of channels are undoubtedly possible because of fibre. The first experimental cable television fibre trunk line was laid in 1976 and the first system was operating by November 1984 in Birmingham, Alabama. By the mid-1990s two-thirds of all cable trunk networks were fibre, but, as in the transoceanic cable, signals have to be demodulated because they cannot be amplified or distributed along 'the last mile' to the home in optic mode. Talk of a fibre-optic system in the mid-1990s was in fact premature because amplifiers and switches were not to hand. In the meantime, the US cable industry opted, in an unstructured way, for a compromise – HFC, Hybrid Fibre Coax. The 'law' of suppression was still at work. As with the UK failure to use digitised satellite signals to introduce HDTV, this hybrid also represents the limits of market logic and rationality. The US telephone companies, which had converted a mere 6 per cent of their trunk feeders to fibre by the mid-1990s, appeared thereby to be responding more appropriately to the challenge of what was still an incomplete technology. Nevertheless, cable operators can see the potential of a digitised fibre-optic network vastly to increase the number of available channels; indeed, exponentially to increase the number of conventional available channels. Yet, given the cultural determinants of production values, available programming and audience time, how these were to be filled remained obscure.

What is clear is that cable in America represents one of the consciousness industry's real triumphs as a majority of Americans now pay twice, through advertisements and subscriptions, primarily to watch television channels they used to pay for only once. This has been done in obedience to the 'law' of the suppression of radical potential whereby the new technology over a period of fifty years has been absorbed by the institutional structures of the old. This process has not only reduced cable's, and (probably) DBS's, disruptive potential, it also ensured that those same structures will remain profitable. Although taken over and somewhat battered and by no means inured to the consequences of myopic managements, nevertheless all the major American broadcasting players are still in place. Elsewhere, the new distribution technologies had much less effect on the old broadcasting structures than had neo-liberal political thinking. Unless politics intervened to prevent it, there was little to suggest that the same essential pattern of relative containment that had been seen in America would not happen in these other countries too.

# 18

# THE INTERNET

## PROTOTYPES AND IDEATION: COMPUTER NETWORKS

The history outlined in this third section demonstrates that the idea of networks is as old as telecommunications. Quite extraordinary claims were nevertheless made for the results of simply (comparatively speaking) linking distant computers together – the Internet. It is, of course, always possible that some technological development will have profoundly disturbing social effects, despite the fact that, over time, most such technologies exhibit far less radical potential. However, if a claim for radical exceptionalism (as it might be termed) is to be sustained, it would seem reasonable to suppose that the technology ought to exhibit some exceptional elements from the outset. This the Internet cannot do. The history and pattern of its development and the pace of its diffusion are, when all hyperbole is laid aside, not markedly different from the accounts given of the other networks here discussed – or, indeed, in general, from the technologies described in the earlier parts of this book.

The ground of scientific competence for the Internet includes the existence of computers and the use of machine code compilers – languages – as a basis of communicating with them. The existence of telecommunications networks, which date back into the nineteenth century, is also obviously crucial as are the theoretical tools for the design of such networks, exemplified by the development of Information Theory in the late 1940s. This theory emerged, as we have seen, from Norbert Wiener's wartime work on predictive gun-sights (which had led to the idea of 'cybernetics'); and the formulae developed in 1949 at Bell Labs by Shannon and Weaver for designing the most efficient telephone systems possible. Cybernetics was widely discussed. Norbert Wiener's best-selling popular outline of these concepts, *The Human Use of Human Beings,* appeared in 1954; but Wiener's *Cybernetics: or Control and Communication in the Animal and the Machine* was published in 1961, which spoke to its continued currency. Cybernetics and Information

Theory were important to the Internet because Information Theory commoditises information, draining it of semantic content. Encoded electronically and treated as being without meaning, messages became far more malleable than they were traditionally.

Prototype activities leading to the Internet would then include the distant operation of a single computer by telephone wire. This was first done by George Stibitz with the IBM Model 1 in 1940, so the concept of remote operation via keyboard and telephone line can be said to antedate the first true computers by a number of years. By the 1960s, both GE and a specialised firm, Tymeshare, sold systems allowing for remote access to computers via telephone links (Hardy 1996: 5). Time sharing involved programming a computer so that it could deal with numerous separate jobs at the same time without any individual user being aware of delays. The concept was applied first by proponents of main frames against supporters of minis and then by proponents of minis against supporters of PCs, in both cases effectively suppressing the building of even smaller machines. It is the creation of programming protocols to allow users to share the computing power of a single machine with maximum efficiency that is important to the development of the Internet. From this comes the use of real-time main frames linked to many distant terminals for such purposes as airline reservation systems. The first such was based on a smaller version of Whirlwind developed by IBM for American Airlines and was on stream by 1964. It was, at the time, the largest real-time system in the world (Augarten 1984: 208).

The transformation to the ideation stage of the Internet occurred when the concept of an associative system for the organisation of data impacted on the growing sophistication in the research community about the handling of electronic data within networks. Of specific importance here is the idea of breaking up continuous messages, of the sort which Information Theory addressed, into smaller discrete 'packages' of information in order to maximise efficiency further. Both of these elements were articulated early enough for the Internet to exhibit the same comparatively slow pace of development which we have noted in all other connections in this book.

Take the idea of associative databanks: in July 1945, in a popular (but nevertheless quite densely argued) article Vannevar Bush envisaged a machine which, in essence, allows for the entire compendium of human knowledge to be accessed or searched in an associative manner. It will be recalled that Bush was intimately concerned with the development of the computer. Shannon's professor at MIT, he had built the differential analyser which sat in the basement of the Moore School and had facilitated further computing developments during the Second World War from his position in the US Office of Scientific Research and Planning.[1] This article represents the first published articulation of the idea of a *web*.

Bush conceived of what he called the 'memex', essentially a microfilm/audio recording device, which would allow 'selection by association rather than by indexing':

> When data of any sort are placed in storage, they are filed alphabetically or numerically, and information is found (when it is) by tracing it down from subclass to subclass. It can only be in one place . . . . The human mind does not work that way. It operates by association. With one item in its grasp, it snaps instantly to the next that is suggested by the association of thoughts, in accordance with some intricate *web* of trails carried by the cells of the brain.
>
> (Bush 1945: 105; emphasis added)

The memex was to be a sort of multi-screened microfilm reader[2] operated by a keyboard into which a user could scan an entire personal library as well as all notes, letters and communications. Further notes and comments could be made photographically or on audio using built-in systems. 'All this is conventional,' wrote Bush, 'except for the projection forward of present-day mechanism and gadgetry.' He goes on:

> [The memex] affords an immediate step, however, to associative index-ing, the basic idea of which is a provision whereby any item may be caused at will to select immediately and automatically another. This is the essential feature of the memex. The process of tying two items together is the important thing. . . . When the user is building a trail, he names it, inserts the name in his code book, and taps it out on his key board. . . . It is exactly as though the physical items had been gathered together to form a new book. It is more than this, for any item can be joined into numerous trails.
>
> (Bush 1945: 106)

Given that this was published in advance of ENIAC's completion, it is not surprising that Bush did not envisage the computer as one of his present-day 'gadgets' – although he was one of a handful of people who knew about the Moore School's work. Nevertheless, his *Atlantic Monthly* article does clearly point the way to a conceptualisation of data arranged as webs rather than the branchings of a tree which computing power would, in fact, most easily allow.

The other basic element for the ideation transformation, the breaking up of messages within an electronic network, is not quite as old as this. It appears in the literature in the early 1960s. At that time, Paul Baran was a RAND researcher working, on behalf of the US Airforce, on the problem of military communications systems in case of nuclear attack (Baran 1964). In a 1964 paper, he proposed breaking up all messages within the system into what he called 'message blocks'. This attack on the internal integrity of the message clearly required an intellectual jump of some significance but, without wishing to belittle Baran's achievement, he was aided by the insights of Information Theory. Just as it had allowed for the design of telephone exchanges which would send calls along the least congested routes thus maximising the overall utilisation of the network, so Baran's scheme envisaged individual messages being broken up and sent in discrete packages around a network to achieve the same result – a more even flow of data through the entire network.

The same concept also occurred to the British computer pioneer Donald Watt Davies who, at the National Physical Laboratory, had helped to build Pilot Ace. Watt Davies's version of Baran's 'message blocks' was remarkably similar, even down to his proposals about optimum transmission rates and size. His notion of how these blocks of data might be routed, however, was slightly different; and he came up with a different term for them, one which was actually to prevail – 'packets' (Hafner and Lyon 1996: 64–5). Baran's 'distributed adaptive message blockswitching' became Watt Davies's 'packet switching'.

Baran's use of the term 'distributed' speaks to the initial supervening social necessity for the Internet. His proposal follows a slightly earlier concept, dating from 1962, for a distributed network of computers (nodes), designed to survive the failure or removal of one or more of them. The supervening social necessity was the need for a literally atomic-bomb-proof communication system. Here again, basic received telephone network design had already encompassed decentralised, distributed systems which could survive partial destruction. Decentralisation was critical to this and to Baran's plans, because it prevented network failure should network control be knocked out. Control was distributed. It was also a highly redundant system in that all essential functions were duplicated and reduplicated. Baran built such a principle of 'redundancy of connectivity' into his plans as well.

Significantly, the differences between Baran and Watt Davies arose because Watt Davies was being inspired by a quite different sort of supervening social necessity. By the early 1960s Britain's pretensions as a major nuclear power were not as strong as they had been and, even at the NPL, strong cold war considerations were no longer such a driving force. Watt Davies was working to an agenda in computer science, a more purely intellectual set of questions arising out of the possibilities of linking computers to explore what might be accomplished if such a thing were done. This was also a supervening necessity in the United States and it has led to a rather interesting obfuscation of the origins of the system which has significant cultural ramifications.

Among the pioneers who built the network which was to evolve into the Internet, there are those who wish to deny quite strenuously the centrality of the need for nuclear-bomb-proof communications systems and to stress instead their interests as being purely scientific. Of course, to do this requires a certain cognitive dissonance on their part as they were all working for the Pentagon or for firms contracted to the Pentagon, even if their announced purposes were not overtly military.[3] Given the current state of the public record, the links between Baran's clearly military inspired thinking and the project which actually produced the prototype ARPANET are obscure. But it is clear that the supervening necessity for networking the main frames came from the same military concerns as had caused those main frames to be built in the first instance. Given the intimate connection of the computing project in general with the cold war and, specifically, nuclear confrontation, it is scarcely surprising that thought was given to the need to back up computing systems in case of nuclear attack. Obviously the way to do this was to yoke these very large machines together.

Confusion arises because the computing science agenda, which sought to do the very same thing, was also legitimate. Indeed – as with Sputnik and the ICBM – it was legitimate enough to act as a perfect 'cover' for the military agenda. In his 1964 paper Baran had already queried a civilian dimension: 'Is it time now to start thinking about a new and possibly non-existent public utility, a common user digital data communication plant designed specifically for the transmission of digital data among a large set of subscribers?' (Baran 1964: 1179). The Internet emerges in the US in the 1970s as a species of spin-off from a (largely still classified) national security project rather than any sort of discrete 'invention' .

The enabling agency for the Internet, ARPA, was created by the DoD in 1957 as a first response to Sputnik. The Advanced Research Projects Agency was to be a species of rapid response unit to ensure that the Russians would not catch the Americans napping again. Of course, as we have seen, the real reason why the Americans were 'caught napping' was nothing more than inter-service rivalry; but it was in nobody's interest to admit this. Better to claim to have been genuinely wrong-footed and, as Eisenhower almost certainly intended, unleash unprecedented public largesse upon the military-industrial complex and its outposts in the universities. ARPA had been dreamed up in 1957 by Neil McElroy, Eisenhower's Secretary of Defence, a non-military type who had been poached from Procter & Gamble where he had been the CEO. He was not likely to cramp the President's military style. That ARPA confronted no real technological gap was not a problem for a man who understood intimately the usefulness of soap operas to the selling of soap powders. However, the agency's first largely space-based agenda was almost immediately passed to a second post-Sputnik organisation, NASA, which had the same remit to halt inter-service rivalry and a more direct claim on space. ARPA survived into the Kennedy era and prospered by becoming instead a patron of advanced earth-bound military research projects. As such, it picked up a SAGE back-up computer and a more general responsibility for blue sky computing projects.

Joseph Licklider, who, as we have seen, was one of the first to think about computer interfaces other than keyboards and screens, was appointed director of ARPA's computing projects. Between 1962 and 1964 he moved the emphasis from command and control to graphics, war-games, better languages and time sharing systems. This agenda became, within ARPA, the Information Processing Techniques Office (IPTO). A basic problem for Licklidder was the lack of language and machine standardisation. In a memo he wrote:

> Consider the situation in which several different centres are netted together, each centre being highly individualistic and having its own special language . . . is it not desirable or even necessary for all the centres to agree upon some language or, at least, upon some conventions for asking such questions as 'What language do you speak?'
>
> (Hafner and Lyon 1996: 38)

For Licklider this remained a somewhat hypothetical, if fascinating, problem since he did not believe that the computers would need to be networked except on 'rare occasions'. Could it be that a post-nuclear attack situation would be such a 'rare occasion'? He added: 'It seems to me to be important, nevertheless, to develop a capability to integrated network operation'. It is on this basis that Licklider's successors at ITPO continued to develop the idea of a network of, essentially, university computers, but only at a theoretical level. This 'academic' as it were supervening necessity was not strong enough to ensure that work in programming and in the metal would go forward.

Nor, curiously, was the other more militaristic social necessity working very well either. Although Baran made good progress as an advocate for a packet switching system with his RAND colleagues, his approaches to AT&T, thought to be necessary if the system was ever to be built, met with considerable hostility. The Telephone Company would not let Baran even have a copy of their longline maps. The Airforce took Baran's side but, the vogue for inter-service agencies still continuing, it was no longer their decision. A new Defence Communications Agency (DCA), dominated by telecommunications traditionalists, was given responsibility instead. Baran gave up. This series of failures can be seen as a phase in the suppression of computer networking's radical potential. What was underpinning these hostile attitudes, perhaps, was the establishment of an extremely extensive, highly redundant system based on more traditional telephonic approaches. This would account for AT&T's opposition. Their attitude and the attitude of the DCA makes sense only if it is assumed that they thought they had the problem solved by other means.

Thus by the mid-1960s only one prototype system was in place. It had been built by Watt Davies within the NPL and with the enthusiastic backing of the GPO. When in 1967 the nascent computer networking community met, at ARPA's behest in Ann Arbor, they did have before them at least a small-scale demonstration that packet switching and the distributed network would work; and that turned out to be enough for the ITPO team to clear the log jam of the previous years.

It became clear to them, as it had previously to Watt Davies, that the difficulties of networking wildly different machines with vastly divergent languages could not be resolved except by introducing minicomputers into the structure to act as interfaces. (The CDC PDP 8, the first mini, had been on the market since 1963.) The idea broached at Ann Arbor was to network the minis, which would share language and protocols, while each main frame team worked out how to get its monster machine to address its 'own' (as it were) mini. They christened the minis IMPs (Interface Message Processors).

This solution, which represents a final element of ideation for the network, also had another major advantage. The problem was that, at first sight, networking seemed to those who ran the main frames to be little more than an extension of time sharing. Time sharing between institutions jealous of their computing time was not necessarily perceived as a welcome goal. However, the idea of introducing a further computer to handle networking chores served to distance the concept of networking from that of time sharing as well as offering potential collaborators more computing power. It made the whole thing far more attractive.

At the end of that year, the IPTO people at ARPA finally discovered Baran's work of the early 1960s via a paper read at a conference in Tennessee by one of Watt Davies's British associates. Baran now became informally involved and ARPA seriously committed to building a network along the lines that had been emerging over the previous seven years (Hafner and Lyon 1966: 77). Although the scheme that became ARPANET was clearly focused on academic sites, this does not mean that the computer science agenda was entirely dominant. It should not be forgotten that all these machines were still closely bound into defence work of one sort or another wherever they were sited. Nor should it be forgotten that the initial ARPA contract was for four IMPS, at $360,000 each, and the programming to make them work together at a further initial cost of $640,000. Not even at the height of the cold war would the American government fork out $1 million just because some computer guys wanted to play at linking their machines together. The military hovered like Banquo's ghost over the feast.

In the summer of 1968 the prototype phase moves significantly forward towards the 'invention'. Having been rebuffed by both IBM and CDC, who claimed the minis could never be made small enough to allow the idea to work, IPTO bought the IMPS from Honeywell. They were a new model type designated the DDP-516 in (enter Banquo) a 'ruggedised' case specially designed for battlefield use. In typical DoD fashion they cost about four times as much as the CDC PDP 8s (and ten times as much as the CDC 9s which came on the market the following year).

The shadow of Banquo was also present as IPTO let the contract for the conversion of these machines, the actual building of the net and the development of the necessary programming to a firm at the heart of the military-industrial complex – Bolt, Beranek and Newman. This was a Boston consultancy company then employing 600 people which had started out in the acoustics business. On the civilian side, they had scandalously fouled up the acoustic design of the Avery Fisher Hall in New York and had then got into audiotape analysis (where, for example, they were to deal with the Watergate missing tape section). Eighty per cent of their business was for government and, eventually, in the 1970s they were to be fined $700,000 for overcharging. On the other hand, BBN had employed Licklider in the late 1950s because of his psychoacoustics background and had provided him with one of Olsen's first machines, a PDP 1. The Pentagon attended IPTO's first briefing of BBN.

## FROM NECESSITY TO DIFFUSION: ARPANET TO INTERNET

Just as the barely perceived distinction between the military and computing science supervening necessities allows some to argue that the project was not in essence a military one, so the fact that the BBN team left the main frame programmers free to deal with a number of issues, the protocols for incoming data for example, encourages the notion, even at this very early stage, that the network was democratic, not centrally controlled. The BBN team worked on the Honeywells, the routing algorithms and the protocols for the IMPs, while the main framers worried about the bridge between their machines and the IMPS. Very rapidly, the main frame teams formed themselves into a Network Working Group (NWG). This was independent of the BBN group and it became ever more significant. For example, within the first month, the team at the Stanford Research Institute (SRI) established the prompt system, now used for log-in name and password, by creating the L-O-G-I-N command. Host-to-host protocols – Telnet, Network Control Protocol (NCP), File Transfer Protocol (FTP) – were all created by the NWG independently of BBN, never mind ITPO/ARPA. Eventually this model, whereby groups of independent users affect the structure of the network, was to become by the early 1990s a crucial element in the argument that the Internet could not be controlled.

The first phase began at BBN on 1 January 1969. The first of the adapted IMPs was due at UCLA in September. The basic concept was a mixture of what Baran and Watt Davies had been proposing at the start of the decade but with far less emphasis on redundancy. The cover, computing science, was thus very much in place. The first reprogrammed IMP arrived on time at UCLA, as did the second at the SRI a month later. By the end of 1970 there were ten centres and two dedicated cross-country lines. By 1971 the system was working, albeit with downtime of a day a month. BBN developed the concept of remote diagnostics and maintenance from its node to combat problems. But, although the network worked, Licklider's hunch that it would be needed only on 'rare occasions' was apparently being borne out. After a year, it was operating at only 2 per cent of its capacity. The cover was starting to look thin.

Those involved resorted to a perfectly legitimate public relations blitz. At a 1972 Conference on Computer Communication in Washington a massive series of demonstrations was organised, most of them, it must be admitted, rather asinine – remote chess games, quizzes and an interactive programme involving a psychotic character, PARRY. PARRY was at UCLA while the 'doctor' was at BBN. But all this had the desired effect. The system acquired a name, ARPANET, and the computing community was made aware of networking possibilities. Two major initiatives emerged – international communication and, most important of all, electronic mail.

Apart from ARPANET, and the Watt Davies network at the NPL, there were by this time two other operating systems. One, christened ALOHANET, used radio links to network the University of Hawaii's computers which were sited on four different islands. A French team was establishing Cyclades. SATNET used satellite links to make good the drop-out deficiencies in contemporary transoceanic cables, albeit as a temporary solution because a large number of high-volume high-quality maser-amplified cables were being planned. But there were enough networks in existence for the idea of a network of networks to be born at this conference. Not only that, the NWG, with its endless exchange of suggestions and decisions on protocols and other operational details, offered a viable model as to how work could go forward internationally without any formal authorisation being required. Again, the cultural sense of being outside external authority was reinforced.

It might be argued that this happened because the spin-off could be allowed to spin even further as it had (from the DoD's viewpoint) the useful effect of deepening ARPANET's military cover. Be that as it may, the NWG became the INWG, the International Network Working Group. In 1973, at a conference in the University of Sussex, Vint Cerf, who had been at UCLA and was involved in the NWG from the very beginning and Bob Khan, the information theorist on the original BBN team, presented the group with draft protocols to allow networks to talk to each other. After a further year's work, these became the

*Transmission Control Protocol* (TCP), the essential programme at the heart of what was to become the Internet.

The 1973 Sussex meeting was also where the first international e-mails made their appearance. Cerf was delayed because of the birth of his child, news of which was e-mailed to the conference. (It will be recalled that the first British telegram was about the birth of one of Queen Victoria's children.) Another man had left the meeting early, forgetting his razor. From the States, he used ARPANET and a temporary satellite link, set up for the conference, to get a friend to find it for him. This was nothing but the international extension of a strand of development which had been underway for some time.

For time sharing systems on single computers, the concept of creating a designated file where messages between users could be left had been developing since the early 1960s. For example, there was a programme designated MAILBOX which had been installed at that time at MIT. Following the 1972 Washington conference, Ray Tomlinson, one of the BBN team, took the idea a stage further. His mailbox programme could receive messages from right across the ARPANET. It is to Tomlinson that we owe the '@' in e-mail addresses. Within a year, 75 per cent of ARPANET's traffic was in this e-mail form. Tomlinson had restored the net's cover but it remained one of the most expensive communication systems ever devised; and one whose real costs and purposes seemed to be almost totally hidden from those who used it. It should not be forgotten that in 1973 most computers were main frames and that even the so-called minis still cost thousands of dollars each. The Altair, that extraordinarily limited personal device, was still two years in the future. E-mail was thus the domain of a very privileged élite, made somewhat less élite by a move at this same time to cheaper 'non-ruggedised' IMPs, Honeywell 316s. To augment the limited interface available on these new machines, the BBN team set about building a TIP, or Terminal IMP, which would allow for sixty-three terminals to feed into the original ARPANET IMP. As the 1970s progressed, this sort of extended distribution of access, although still very much limited to university computer science departments, allowed for a number of other unplanned developments, spin-offs; the creation of mail lists (MsgGroup) in 1975 would be a significant example of this.

The power of such user groups grew with the network. Between 1973 and 1975 a node was added every month. There were now some 2000 users. In August 1973, for example, 3.2 million packets were being transmitted. The users contrived more than basic procedures. For example, on 12 April 1979 Kevin MacKenzie, a brand new member of the MsgGroup, invented 'Emoticons' [: -) ]. Licklider and Albert Vezza noted: 'One of the advantages of the message system over letter mail was that, in an ARPANET message, one could write tersely and type imperfectly, even to an older person one did not know very well, and the recipient took no offence' (Licklider and Vezza 1978: 1330).

Feeding the cultural sense that here was a realm barely controlled by the Powers That Be was the failure of the authorities to impose their will on these emerging structures. It was not until 1979, five years after the INWG agreed the initial TCP Internet protocol, that ARPA created an Internet Configuration Control Board, but, if only because it was so late, it had very limited success as a control mechanism (Dufour 1995: 29). As far as some INWG people were concerned the message was: '"Time to roll up your toy academic network." . . . They thought TCP . . . and Internet were just that – an academic toy' (Hafner and Lyon 1996: 247). There were also a number of scandals in the world of academic computing as a radicalised student generation realised how central the universities' computing centres were to the war effort in Vietnam and other cold war agendas. ARPANET itself was used to move illegal army intelligence files around, which caused a predictable uproar when the story broke. This sort of thing was not helped by ARPA being redesignated DARPA, the Defence Advanced Research Projects Agency, in the early 1970s.

In the event, DARPA's only successful interventions in shaping the emerging Internet were minor. The Agency managed to destroy a user group, USING, which had set itself up as a sort of lobby to monitor DARPA's activities. As the net's first historians put it: 'DARPA saw no need to share authority with a tiny self-appointed watchdog group made up of people the agency viewed as passengers on its experimental vehicle' (Hafner and Lyon 1996: 230). The other great DARPA success was the domain name system, agreed in 1986 which introduced in the US the terms 'edu' for universities, 'com' for commerce, 'mil' for military, etc. But these were the exceptions.

Overall, it is perfectly possible to see why the idea was abroad that the net was, to a degree unique in the history of telecommunications systems, in the hands of its users:

> Originally, the Internet was a post-apocalypse command grid. And look at it now. No one really planned it this way. Its users made the Internet that way, because they had the courage to use the network to support their own values, to bend the technology to their own purposes. To serve their own liberty.
>
> (Sterling 1993)

But such strident technicist rhetoric cannot disguise the fact that Banquo's ghost had not gone away. The hyperbole simply ignored the fact that, at least until the collapse of the Soviet Union and probably thereafter, the network was still, essentially, maintained for Licklider's 'rare occasion'; the noisier network users were, the louder they proclaimed their power, the better hidden this real purpose remained. By 1979, for example, only sixteen ARPANET sites were on campuses.

The remaining forty-six were buried in the military-industrial complex. (The system was costing $14 million a year to run and was transferred to the DCA in 1973. Licklider's 'rare occasion' had still not happened but it might. In 1983, the military side of the operation was spun off into MILNET, which was integrated into the recently created Defence Data Network (Hardy 1996: 7). ARPANET itself was closed down, significantly, in 1989, the year the cold war (supposedly) ended.)

I would want to go further and argue that even on the other genuine computer science agenda side, there was also a considerable measure of cognitive dissonance. The bottom line is that these networks were developed at vast expense and, for all that users were allowed to (as it were) dot the 'i's and cross the 't's on how they were operated on a daily basis, the essential power was still vested elsewhere. Consider the National Science Foundation's role.

A 1974 NSF report spoke of creating 'a frontier environment which would offer advanced communication, collaboration, and the sharing of resources among geographically separated or isolated researchers' (Hafner and Lyon 1996: 240). This became more pressing since, as we have seen, only a handful of universities were on the ARPANET and the DCA would not allow uncleared departments to hook up. By 1979, there were 120 computer science departments and most of those not yet on the net saw that as a real disadvantage when recruiting staff or pursuing research project funding. The problem was that in that year, for example, it cost $100,000 to run an ARPANET node, whether it produced traffic or not. Obviously this was well beyond the resources of most of these 'separated and isolated researchers' with whom the NSF was concerned. In May 1979 a group of non-ARPANET computer departments met at Madison and decided to build a cheaper, slower and less redundant network, to be called CSNET, the Computer Science Research Network. Nevertheless, the meeting still put a $3 million price tag on the five-year plan.

The NSF was not initially convinced but the proposal was re-submitted with a full business plan. (No trace of Banquo's ghost here.) By carefully designing different levels of service, for example, offering only an e-mail facility, it was possible to suggest that CSNET could become self-sufficient via user fees after an initial start-up period. These fees could amount to as little as $21,000 in a full year, primarily for telephone line charges. The NSF agreed and coughed up $5 million for start-up costs and CSNET was established. For the first time, the advantages of computer networking were made available to academics beyond the computer science departments. By 1983, with more than seventy sites on-line, this network was financially stable. On the back of this success, in 1985 the NSF agreed to build and manage a 'backbone' linking its five supercomputing centres. Regional nets were designed to feed into what was to become the NSFNET and the remains of ARPANET were also connected to it.

And so we come, not for the first time, to the moment when privatisation is pitted against a 'Post Office solution'.

In the 1970s estimates were beginning to be made as to the potential impact of e-mail on the traditional mail services. The White House Office of Telecomm-unications Policy and the US Post Office both commissioned studies. Consultants Arthur Little told the OTP that 30 per cent of all mail would be electronic. This, of course, has turned out to be very wide of the mark.[4] It almost goes without saying that the Post Office solution was rejected. It is also obvious that, at the moment when Justice was finally having its way with AT&T, the telephone company solution was rejected also. It is a measure of the naiveté of those involved that they thought they could transfer ARPANET from DARPA to AT&T and apparently believed that it was only the incompatibility of package technology with traditional telephony that stopped this from happening (Hafner and Lyon 1996: 232). From the late 1980s on, and despite the illusion of independence which had surrounded the enterprise almost from the outset, it was inevitable that this tax-funded and government-managed asset would be handed over to the private sector.

The National Science Foundation agreed to commercial exploitation and on-line services sprang up. CompuServe, the first of these, started in 1979 and fifteen years later claimed 3.2 million users in 120 countries and was part-owned by Time Warner. Its biggest rival, America Online, claimed 3.5 million users and had commercial relationships with the German group Bertelsmann and the French group Hachette. Prodigy belonged to IBM and Sears and claimed 1.4 million users (Dufour 1966: 32–3). In 1990 at Europe's advanced atomic particle accelerator, CERN, Tim Berners-Lee created (one hopes in his own time) the protocols to allow, finally, Vannevar Bush's vision of the memex to become a reality. His 'World Wide Web' was open for business in 1992. Meanwhile a Commercial Internet Exchange had been established in 1991 (Dufour 1995: 39). The NSF, finally, in 1995 handed the backbone and its management over to the private telecommunications giants Sprint, Ameritech and Pacific Bell which became the gatekeepers of the principal access points. Those who seriously believed they were in a brave new world of free and democratic communications were simply ignoring the reality of their situation. Those from great corporations who claimed they were engineering a revolutionary new world were engaged in something else: it might be called 'selling snake oil'.[5] Objecting to Microsoft's late attempt to break into this world in the mid-1990s on the ground that its entry introduces the mega-multimedia international conglomerate into the pure realm of Cyberspace became a curious aspect of the hype. (Cyberspace, and cyberpunk, are terms popularised by William Gibson in his seminal and endlessly misread novel, *Neuromancer,* published in 1989.) What Gates' interest represented was nothing but the last phase in a straightforwardly classic expression of the suppression of radical potential whereby the new technology is distributed among the established players to minimise the threat to their businesses.

The only outstanding issue by the mid-1990s was the extent to which the net might force the telephone entities finally to abandon their traditional and increasingly meaningless time and distance pricing structures. 'Free' local calls (where the cost is actually folded into the service rental charge) in the United States meant that the use of the network apparently cost nothing once the equipment had been purchased and a contract for services made with a local access provider. Even where local calls were charged, the net seemingly cost the user little:

> The illusion of getting away with something was entirely based on the fact that data transmission times have dropped so that it takes only 2/3rds of second, for example, to send an e-mail message from the US to Antarctica. Moreover, the Net breaks up even such super-fast messages transmitting them with scant regard to the time/distance cost structures of traditional telephone use. But, however fast and however efficient the routing, this is still not 'free'. The telephonic infrastructure is being paid for by users, but minimally. That these costs become largely invisible is because the Net itself is a very efficient user (and, indeed, abuser) of the infrastructure. To believe that the Internet is, in fact, free is exactly the same as believing that commercial television is 'free to air'. It is an example of what once was called false consciousness.
>
> (Winston and Walton 1996: 82)

It did not mean very much, either, that the established players did not initially care if, at the margins of the system, pornographers, militias and assorted deviants put out messages. These flies could be swatted at any time. For example, Operation Sun Devil was carried out in the US in May 1990, as Berners-Lee was working on his 'www' protocol. Twenty-eight raids in two weeks seized forty-two computers and confiscated 23,000 disks. By June 1995, America On-Line was cutting off six people a day for 'net abuse'. As the system became less marginal, a regime was already being forged in legislation and the courts to suppress the radical potential of the Internet as effectively as past regimes have suppressed past potentials. It was easy to discern the outlines of the solution – connection charges, usage charges, copyright charges, content codes. The same computing power that was driving the system was being turned to police it – package switching notwithstanding.

By July 1995 there were supposedly anything from 6.5 million machines worldwide to 10.3 million in the US alone connected to the net. The popular figure of Internet users of between 35 and 45 million appears to have been obtained by simply multiplying the 6.5 million by seven – perhaps because in the earliest days of the ARPANET, seven users per terminal was a norm. The range of estimates does not inspire confidence and seems, on the face of it, to be absurd. At this time, some net demographers were putting the user figure at about one-tenth of the high estimate, that is some 3 million. This would seem to be far nearer to the mark: in Britain for example, only 20 per cent of 4 million home computers were even claimed as connected in 1996 (while, at the same time, surveys claiming up to 6 million British users were regularly published without explanation as to how such a figure could be reached).

And who were these users, these 'early adopters'? 'According to the Georgia Institute of Technology, in the most comprehensive survey of Internet users to date (1994), 90% were men, 80% white, 70% North Americans, 50% spent 40 hours or more a week computing and 30% are graduates' (Winston and Walton 1996: 79).

From the very beginning it has been clear that the most unambiguously valuable facility provided by the net is e-mail. That would seem to hold for current users as it did for the ARPANET pioneers. There is no more efficient or cheaper way to communicate, especially when time zone differences are so great that no working hours are shared. It is also probably the case that, again as happened with the pioneers, shared professional or, especially, academic concerns can lead to useful multi-person exchanges. However, the radical impact of such a system on the academy, say, will be contained for the foreseeable future by traditional require-ments of authorship and publication. Other uses such as the creation of a virtual social community seem to have less, if any, purpose except as a sort of hobby.

There were several other reasons for viewing the reality of the net, as opposed to the inflated rhetoric surrounding it, with a certain cynicism. The more users, the more slowly the system went. Experience suggested that California needed to be asleep if any chance of reasonable access were to be achieved. The limited Boolean logic of the search engines constituted a further constraint on Bush's vision. Worst of all is the clutter and absurdity of most information the engines have to search. The Internet represents the final disastrous application of the concept of commoditisation of information in the second half of the twentieth century. By the mid-1990s there was talk of abandoning the whole system in favour of a second Internet which could be kept preserved from the information detritus suffocating the original.

There is also little to support the idea that the net will become a crucial method for selling goods and services. Every system for avoiding shopping from the mail-order catalogue to the cable television shopping channel has never done more than provide, albeit often profitably, niche services. One of the sillier facets of Information Revolution rhetoric is the belief that technology is urgently required to help people avoid going shopping or travelling on business. People like shopping and travelling – just as they like being told, or reading, stories. So we do not need stories to be any more 'interactive' than they have been since the dawn of time; a liking for travel is why business people have avoided the lure of the video-conference phone for nearly two-thirds of the twentieth century; and we so love shopping we have made the shopping mall (as the latest incarnation of the nineteenth century arcade) into our emblematic public space. Why the slow, cluttered and inefficient Internet should be more significant than previous distant buying systems is not clear. It seemed that in the early years the only effective marketers on the vaunted Information Highway were pornographers.[7]

All in all, I am inclined to agree with American humorist Dave Barry: 'The Internet is the most important single development in the history of human communications since the invention of "call waiting" ' (Barry 1996: 121). I would add that (to repeat a phrase from *The Telegrapher* magazine in 1866), 'as surely and as naturally as water runs down hill' the Information Highway will transform itself even more than it is at present into the Information Toll Road. The overheated claims being made for it were, even before they were fully promulgated, falling victim to the inexorable operation of the 'law' of the suppression of radical potential. Beyond the hype, the Internet was just another network. This is to say its social effects could (and would) be as profound as, for example, those of that far more ubiquitous network, the telephone. As profound . . . and as unrevolutionary.

# CONCLUSION: THE PILE OF DEBRIS

## FROM THE BOULEVARD DES CAPUCINS TO THE LENINGRADSKY PROSPECT

7 October 1976. The Ciné and Photo Research Institute (NIKFI), Leninskaya Prospest, Moscow. A demonstration of a 70mm holographic motion picture system:

> The movie consists of a full-size girl coming right through that screen, holding a bouquet in front of her face so that everyone in the audience can move around in his seat and look at the bouquet and see her face. . . . The Brightness is amazing; it is comparable to an ordinary movie. . . . The strange thing . . . is that the screen can be viewed from both sides simultaneously. Actually half the audience can sit on one side, and the other half can sit on the other.
>
> (Jeong 1977: 143)

It is still too early to say whether this presentation will be written into the technological history of communications as holography's founding moment, the equivalent of the Lumière *cinématographe* show in the Boulevard des Capucins on 23 December 1895. Alternatively, it could be that Victor Komar, the researcher responsible for this film, will be a Ronalds, a forgotten pioneer of an elegant but rejected prototype rather than a Lumière, an 'inventor'. Either way, the pattern of competence and ideation, prototype and 'invention', socially driven diffusion and suppression is holding good for holography – just as it is holding good for the Internet. I have argued above that claims for the Internet's radical exceptionalism to this pattern cannot be based on its history thus far; on the contrary, this history conforms with that of all other networks from telegraphy on. In the same way, I want to conclude by suggesting that the next possible quantitative leap in communications, holography, is also progressing in accordance with the model I outlined at the beginning of this book.

337

By the 1990s holography had been nearly two centuries in the making, its basic theory, like so much else, grounded in Young's interference experiments of 1801. These were first applied to a photographic process by Gabriel Lippmann, of the lenticular stock, to produce dye-less colour images in 1893. Lippmann created a special camera and an exceptionally fine grain film which he exposed while pouring mercury down the back of the plate. The interference caused by the incoming light waves to the waves being reflected back from the mercury enabled colour information to be registered as a standing wave pattern in the emulsion. Lippmann's 'photochromes' remain among the few iconically accurate colour photographs ever made, but can be played back only by exactly positioning a strong light behind the plate and the viewer before it. For this and much else, Lippmann received the Nobel Prize in 1908.

In an analogous fashion to the photochrome, a hologram is a photographic record of the difference between a reference beam of light and the pattern of interference created in that beam by an object. It allows for a true stereoscopic representation of the object to be recreated – true, that is, in the sense that the hologram allows the eye to look round the sides of the object just as it could in reality. This is unlike a 3D system using, say, coloured filters and double images to create an illusion of depth where every person sees the same illusion and where head movement will not reveal new facets of the scene.

In 1947, Dennis Gabor, an industrial researcher, was looking to improve the performance of electron microscopes to the point where atomic structures would be revealed. The imaging of atomic structures had an intimate relationship with such microscopes since the first images of this kind had been produced on the device in 1927 by Sir Lawrence Bragg. Gabor believed that, with a coherent light source, he could enhance the electron picture and using a high pressure mercury lamp he eventually produced miniature holograms. The development of the laser gave holographers their basic tool (Walton 1982). The laser delivers exactly the strong coherent light source needed. By splitting a laser beam, an arrangement could be made whereby half passed across the object to be recorded while the other half, via a mirror, bounced round it. The photographic plate registers the beam as it has been disturbed by the object and also the undisturbed part as a reference. When a laser is once more pointed at the plate, the object reappears in front, just as with a photochrome placing an ordinary light creates the colours.

Dr Gabor was to receive his Nobel Prize in 1971, twenty years after he had pioneered the holograph. With the coming of the laser Gabor's technique prospered. In 1963, Emmett Leith and Juris Upatnieks showed the first laser-based holograms, marking the start of time-based (or moving) holography's prototype phase. In the USSR, which was in the forefront of holographic experimentation, Yuri Denisyuk, the first exactly to copy Lippmann's technique, produced a reflection hologram which would 'play back' in ordinary incoherent light. In 1965 a holographic interferometer was introduced to industry as a way of studying stress by comparing 'before' and 'after' holograms of the object. Interferometers using standard stereoscopic photographic techniques had been developed before the turn of the twentieth century to test, by comparison, for imperfection in carpet patterns or counterfeit coins. With holographic interferometers any deviation between the hologram of the perfect original and subsequent copies shows up as a fringe or disturbance around the image. Testing does not distress the artefact. In 1968, Stephen Benton, then of Polaroid, demonstrated a white light transmission (i.e. lit from behind) hologram which also did not require a play-back laser. By 1972, RCA had a technique for embossing such holograms on plastic.

Holograms achieved full colour in the 1970s and have recorded live subjects (with pulsed lasers, since continuous ones cannot cope with any vibrations) but a basic question hovers over further developments: What use is holography? Supervening necessities are currently limited to certain industrial applications and fine art. The most widespread diffusion of the technology, as embossed logos on credit cards, is actually, according to Benton, unconvincing as a security measure. This is perhaps not surprising since that application was prompted by the plastic hologram embossed on to two million promotional packets of Reece's Pieces to publicise the film *E.T.* (Brand 1987: 84–7).

More seriously, Benton, having moved to MIT's Media Lab, worked with General Motors to produce full-scale holographic images of cars, obviating the need for the traditional expensive hand-crafted clay mock-ups. The hologram is quicker, cheaper and more easily altered. The military value of having a true three-dimensional image of terrain to be taken – a Belfast terrace, for instance – is self-evident. Holography promises the ultimate map, a Borgesian conceit corresponding at all points with reality.

But the real diffusion question is whether or not holography will acquire movement and thereby emerge as an entertainment medium. This has been slower in coming and is not aided by the tentative history of three-dimensionality in the cinema. Certainly we have had a long fascination with stereoscopic images, dating back to the Victorian Stereopticon toy. The familiar red and green coloured glasses, for use with projected still images, date back to the 1850s. These were initially used for movies in 1909, when the first of what has been a number of attempts to market stereoscopic films took place. The earliest real fad for 3-D was in 1922. It flared again in 1936. For the World Fair in 1939, Land's light polarisation principle was used in the glasses allowing for colour 3-D for the first time. There was another fad in 1953/4 when a number of Hollywood features, including *Dial M for Murder* and *Kiss Me Kate*, were released. In the 1990s, the large-screen Imax system revived the glasses once again.

The Soviets were using a different technique by applying lenticular principles to the screen. Such a 'parallax stereogramme' needed no glasses and a feature length version of *Robinson Crusoe* shot with the system played in five theatres for a whole decade after the end of the Second World War.

It is possible that these repeated efforts, which constitute the ground of scientific competence for the moving hologram, do speak to an abiding desire to achieve three dimensions since we are, as a culture, addicted to realist illusions. By this reading, it is only the inconvenience of the glasses or the faulty nature of the illusion that has been holding us back. Moving holography 'fits' and will therefore in due course be 'invented'.

The prototype moving holographic image, of a fish in an aquarium, was produced with a pulsed laser in 1969 but could be viewed by just one person at a time. (Holograms cannot easily be projected, so a screen-size holographic image requires films of large size, too.) A conventional film, 540 frames long, of a woman sitting winking and blowing a kiss, Lloyd Cross's *Kiss II* of 1974, was hologrammed to produce a few seconds of stereoscopic movement (Kac 1995: 54). This multi-plexing technique was used in 1987, by the sculptor, Alexander [sic], to produce a sort of Zoetrope device which played back an 8-minute holographic film, *The Dream*. The holograms, created in the Franco-German Defence Research Establishment, were transported in front of the play-back illumination and viewed through a little window (Alexander 1995: 187–97). A more radical application by Claudine Eizykman and Guy Fihman used actual three-dimensional holographic images to create a 5-minute piece, *Un nu*, in which a woman done up as a mummy unbandages herself. To view the hologram one entered a structure 7 feet high, 2 feet wide and 28 inches deep.

For the moment, the best claim to be moving holography's Edison (or even its Lumière) belongs to Victor Komar. He has come nearest to creating a true cinematic experience with the 47-second holographic movie of the woman and the bouquet described above. It was shot on film and viewed by as many as four people at once. In line with Russian 3-D tradition Komar used a special screen – 'an important part of the holographic projection installation' (Komar and Serov 1989: 170).This had been patented by Gabor in 1969. Komar also used a very powerful ruby laser which pulsed at one-twentieth of a second (Komar 1977: 127–143). A conferee at the 1976 Moscow meeting where Komar premiered his film wrote: 'Delegates who saw the actual results were left with the sense of having been present at an historical occasion, comparable with the classic demonstrations of past pioneers in film and television and having equally vast and perhaps unrecognised potentialities' (ibid.: 140). By 1984 Komar had produced a 5-minute colour film but the 'law' of suppression was at work. After the collapse of the Soviets he found himself without funds to continue his investigations and by 1995 he had reportedly retired.

It is possible that these experiments represent a dead end in that we will never have a photographically based, cinema-style holography. Komar's technique might be a mere prototype signpost pointing to the true invention which is yet to come. Instead of film, computer power might (and most likely will) be used to digitise the data and turn it into holographic television. This option remained just beyond reach as the millennium approached. As Stephen Benton put it: 'Unfortunately . . . the amount of information in a hologram is so large as to stymie even the most ambitious electronic or computational systems, then and now' (Benton 1991: 82). Does Campbell Swinton's vision in the early 1920s of how to make electronic television work apply to electronic moving-image holography? 'If we could only get one of the big research laboratories . . . who have large staff and any amount of money . . . they would solve a thing like this in six months.' Whether or not the formidable technical obstacles can be this easily dealt with, there is no question that those with the large staffs and any amount of money have a quite different agenda in hand, in which a new digital high definition 2-D television standard is but one item.[1]

It will be well into the next century before the transmission and reception of holographic television comes to the fore even as a research issue. And the question will still remain – will our culturally determined addiction to realism constitute a sufficient supervening necessity to ensure moving holography gets to be 'invented'? Or will holography be the ultimate redundancy, an elaborate system for re-creating the experience of the theatre and concert hall, thereby doing nothing more than mechanically returning us to the pre-electric experience of perform-ance? Until we have the answer, we will be unable to see if Komar played the role of Ronalds, Edison or the Lumières. Whatever this outcome, my point is that we are already more than half a century into this line of development – and that is if we ignore the time which has passed since Young's articulation of interference concept and Lippmann's application of it to an image-making process. As with the Internet, as with all the technologies we have considered in this book, so with holography. The pattern continues.

This book has been a history of electrical and electronic systems of commun-ications. I have used this account to mount a case against the concept of techno-logical determinism, arguing instead that social, political, economic and cultural factors are the prime determinants of technological change. In passing, as it were, I have also disputed the concept of an Information Revolution, taking particular issue with the rhetorical hyperbole it has engendered. Instead I have suggested that change is accomplished slowly. My case has been grounded in the pattern of actual development which has led to the creation and diffusion of these various tele-communications technologies over the better part of the last two centuries. Despite a rhetoric which strongly suggests the contrary, the pattern persists. I have used the model to indicate the primacy of the social sphere in conditioning the technologists' work. I have tried to show how social forces both push and hinder these developments, forcing a social 'fit' upon them in the process. This

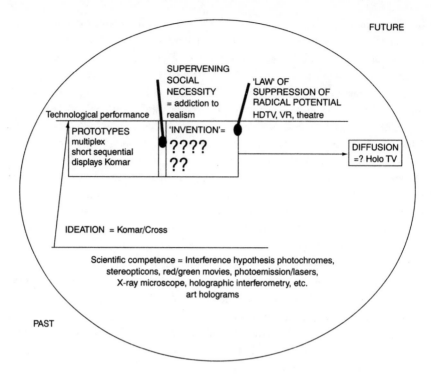

FUTURE

SUPERVENING
SOCIAL
NECESSITY
= addiction to
realism

'LAW' OF
SUPPRESSION OF
RADICAL POTENTIAL
HDTV, VR, theatre

Technological performance

PROTOTYPES
multiplex
short sequential
displays Komar

'INVENTION'=
????
??

DIFFUSION
=? Holo TV

IDEATION = Komar/Cross

Scientific competence = Interference hypothesis photochromes,
stereopticons, red/green movies, photoemission/lasers,
X-ray microscope, holographic interferometry, etc.
art holograms

PAST

*Figure 14* Moving-holograms

'fit' is essentially achieved by suppressing the disruptive power of the technology to impact radically on pre-existing social formations. I formulate this as a 'law' of the suppression of radical potential.

I hold our situation to be, basically, that business, media, alienation, nuclear families, right-wing governments, technologically induced health hazards, traffic jams, deep-fried food, dating, poverty – all these, and much else, continue as usual. No revolution – just 'the constant revolutionising of production, uninterrupted disturbance of all social conditions, ever-lasting uncertainty and agitation', as the Communist Manifesto put it.

Thus the pile of debris at the feet of Klee's *Angelus Novus* grows ever closer to the heavens. Only a good *historical* understanding of how it got there can help us clear it away.

# NOTES

## INTRODUCTION

1 This is an account of how a particular group of technologists, in history, interacted with their societies to produce a given set of devices. This enterprise is very close to Thomas Kuhn's project in the historical sociology of science. Kuhn's *The Structure of Scientific Revolutions* (1962) – 'undoubtedly one of the more influential and controversial scholarly books to emerge in the last few decades' (Gutting 1980: 117) – proposes a pattern of cause and consequence relating to changes in the basic concepts governing scientific inquiry. Kuhn offers a schematic explanation of these changes. Kuhn's schema has been extensively applied to fields well away from the history of science. Indeed by the early 1990s, it received the ultimate accolade of acceptance – and misapplication – when it became a fashion in business school to talk in Kuhnian terms – for example, 'paradigm shift'. It had become a species of 'supertheory'. Despite this, my schematic, although about science's sib, technology, does not follow Kuhn – except in that it offers a (different) schemata and is about (non-existent) revolutions.

2 'Revolution' is used here in its commonly understood sense of alteration and change, rather than in its original technical sense of recurrence or turning. This is the meaning, with its modern connotation of rapid political change, intended by those who coined the phrase 'Information Revolution'. Raymond Williams wrote:

> *Revolution* and *revolutionary* and *revolutionise* have of course also come to be used, outside of political contexts, to indicate fundamental changes, or fundamentally new developments, in a very wide range of activities. It can seem curious to read of 'a *revolution* in shopping habits' or of the '*revolution* in transport' and of course there are cases when this is simply the language of publicity to describe some 'dynamic' new product. But in some ways this is at least no more strange than the association of *revolution* with VIOLENCE, since one of the crucial tendencies of the word was simply towards important or fundamental change. Once the factory system and the new technology of the late eighteenth century and early nineteenth century had been called, by analogy with the French Revolution, the INDUSTRIAL *Revolution*, one basis for description of new institutions and new technologies as *revolutionary* had been laid.
>
> (Williams 1976: 229–30; emphasis in original)

Revolution, in whatever sense it is used, implies movement, and in these developed usages, that means movement through time. The concept of the 'Information Revolution' is therefore in essence historical.

## 1 THE TELEGRAPH

1 Navies had a long-range signalling capacity since the Duke of York, rather more effective as an admiral than he was to be as a king, instituted a code of flags during the Anglo-Dutch wars in the seventeenth century.

## 2 BEFORE THE SPEAKING TELEPHONE

1 Caveats caused considerable problems of which the Bell/Gray incident is among the most notorious. The system was abolished in 1910.
2 Maxwell's theory replaced Franklin's and became the paradigm for the next half-century. The concept of the ether was tested by the Michelson-Morley experiment of 1887 which failed to show that there was any, even infinitesimally small, slow-down or drag on the earth's rotation. However incorporeal, the ether should have exerted some drag and therefore this experiment introduced an anomaly in the Maxwell paradigm. As Kuhn explained:

> Maxwell's discussion of the electromagnetic behaviours of bodies in motion made no reference to ether drag, and it proved very difficult to introduce such drag into his theory. . . . The years after 1890 therefore witnessed a long series of attempts, both experimental and theoretical, to detect motion with respect to the ether and to work ether drag into Maxwell's theory. . . . The latter [theoretical work] produced a number of promising starts . . . but they also disclosed still other puzzles and finally resulted in just that proliferation of competing theories that we have previously found to be a concomitant of crisis. It is against this historical setting that Einstein's special theory of relativity emerged in 1905.
>
> (Kuhn 1962: 74)

## 3 THE CAPTURE OF SOUND

1 Otis had produced a safe, i.e. self-arresting, elevator by 1857 but the geared hydraulic lift specifically for passengers dates from this year.

## 4 WIRELESS AND RADIO

1 That is, if we ignore the dreams of the ancients (where Paracelsus specifically envisages a form of telepathic signalling) or the usual obscurities of the Renaissance (where della Porta – again! – writes of 'mariners compasses having the alphabet written about them' to enable communicate without wires (Marvin 1988: 155)).

2 Birkenhead also recalls that a murderer was captured using the first transatlantic cable in 1864.
3 The subsequent development of the lamp after this date is supposedly a more structured story involving a number of prominent scientists including one Nobelist who worked at the GE lab in Schenectady. In fact, the actual day-to-day search for a metal filament and improved production techniques was much the same as it had been at Menlo Park (Winston 1986: 375–6). The crucial importance of the electric bulb as a transformative social agent and a mark of modernity is dealt with by Marvin (1988: esp. 158–90).

## 6 ELECTRONICALLY SCANNED TELEVISION

1 The games were cancelled.
2 Although, as Uricchio points out, the collective viewing mode was sanctioned by socialist aspirations for the medium prior to the 1933 election (Uricchio 1990: 116). He has also communicated his view to me privately, that despite the enthusiasm created by the hype of the 1920s, people were disappointed with the reality of television in the 1930s and displayed so little appetite for it that Goebbels did not add it to his armoury of propaganda tools.
3 Exactly at this time, in what might be thought of as a final expression of the confusions between photoelectric devices for still and moving images, an American lawyer, Chester Carlson, was experimenting with a selenium-coated plate to produce a device to make copies of patent applications. The print and images in an application were impressed as a positive pattern on the plate which then attracted negatively charged toner. The pattern of the toner, now a copy of the original, was then transferred to paper and heat sealed. In 1938 Carlson patented the device, which was to be eventually marketed in the 1950s as xerography ('dry writing' in Greek).
4 Sarnoff predicted in the mid-1950s that: 'By 1963, all of America would be blanketed by colour, and each and every home will be receiving its entertainment in full colour' (Brown 1992: 123). In the event, although NBC – alone – ran a full colour schedule in 1964, it took longer than that. In that year 1.4 million colour sets were sold, enough to begin to affect the ratings. In 1965, when 20 per cent of television stations were still monochrome, CBS followed NBC; in 1966 ABC became a full colour network. Thus the Europeans, who had seemingly delayed decisions on colour for a decade, turned out to be colourising their networks at almost the same time as the Americans. The BBC's second service, inaugurated in the spring of 1964, was a full-colour channel by December 1967. American network television went fully to colour exactly fourteen years after FCC authorisation, when sales of colour receivers in the US were level-pegging with sales of black-and-white sets for the first time. By 1973, twenty years after colour had been authorised, 43,500,000 US homes, around two-thirds had colour.

## 7 TELEVISION SPIN-OFFS AND REDUNDANCIES

1 The ability of VCRs now to do many of these same tricks is an excuse for manufacturers to increase cost, such facilities being equally pointless toys. The only real cultural requirement is for an effective multi-channel, multi-day timing device and this genuinely useful addition to the VCR is actually nothing but a simple time-switch, despite its usual extremely user-hostile form.

2 For a fuller account of the development of this technology see Winston 1996: 88–108.
3 For example, Fujio 1978: 92. The identical phrase may be found in Fujio *et al.* 1980: 584.

## 8 MECHANISING CALCULATION

1 But it does certainly belong to scientific competence, and attacks claiming Babbage was forgotten and therefore unable to influence twentieth-century computer pioneers are unfounded. References to Babbage's work occur regularly from 1889 when his son, Major General H.P. Babbage, published 'Babbage's calculating engines' (Babbage 1899: Hyman 1984: 254–5).
2 In the received history, Jacquard is an elegant and visionary figure whose peripheral insight was to bear fruit half a century later. In fact he was working for the Lyons silk manufacturers to produce a machine which would eliminate operatives, especially skilled operatives. The workers burned the first Jacquard looms but he succeeded in his commission. Their skilled trade was destroyed.
3 By a Dublin accountant, Percy Ludgate, who worked on plans for an analytic machine from 1903 until his death, aged 39, in 1922. He also outlined the concept of the numerical storage address (Ludgate 1909: 71–4).
4 The Z3 is now in a Munich museum and by 1949 the Z4 was installed in the Federal Technical University in Zurich.

## 9 THE FIRST COMPUTERS

1 For example, how can the IBM SSEC be classified? IBM's response to Harvard's wartime rebuff had been to behave like nothing so much as a great ship cast adrift on an electro-mechanical sea. In complete defiance of ENIAC and the thinking coming out of the Moore School, IBM built, tested and put into operation, between 1945 and 1948, the last giant electro-mechanical machine, said to be 6000 times faster than the Harvard Mark I (ASCC). The Selective Sequence Electronic Calculator (SSEC) had 12,500 vacuum tubes and 21,400 electro-magnetic relays and something very closely resembling a stored programme.

> All instructions are given in numerical form. Each unit of the machine and each operation it can perform have been assigned a number, and the presence of this number in the instructions calls into action the associated unit or operation. This procedure permits the use of all the numerical facilities of the machine, not only for problem data *but for handling operating instructions as well.*
>
> (Eckert 1948: 221, emphasis added)

In fact, in the electronic part of the SSEC (as opposed to its electro-mechanical part), there was an eight-word store and it can be said that this was the first machine (assuming Colossus Mark II to be *hors concours*) to have anything like a stored program capacity. However, despite this, some claim that its measure of stored programmability is insufficient to justify it as a computer. Certainly the SSEC suffered the fate of the dinosaur. Without successors, it was dismantled in 1952.

## 11 THE INTEGRATED CIRCUIT

1 I have relied extensively on Braun and MacDonald 1982 for the history of solid state electronics.
2 The impetus thereby created carried on into the post-war period, effectively delimiting the range of enquiry and preventing an equally serious investigation of other metals even of the same group, IV in the periodic chart.

> But who knows what materials we might be using today if these two [silicon and germanium] had not established such a substantial lead during the war, a lead that could have been challenged only at enormous cost and which was never seriously rivalled by the dozens of compound semiconductors proposed at various times.
>
> (Braun and MacDonald 1982: 30)

This dominance continued into the present although, by the early 1980s, other substances, notably gallium arsenide, started to come into specialised use, for instance in high-speed logic circuits for super computers.
3 At the Bell Labs, as everywhere in the scientific world, all notebooks are filed and entries time-dated. This is a standard practice dating back to the beginning of modern scientific culture. 'The plotting of the ship's course and the transcription of topographic data to maps instituted the higher bookkeeping of science' (Mumford 1970: 20–1). The keeping of the ship's log, the prompt record of observed events set the meticulous pattern of the laboratory notebook. Such a tradition of meticulousness has the added advantage of allowing disclosures, a crucial element in establishing patent rights, to be properly witnessed – normally under the signed rubric, 'read and understood'.
4 Shockley subsequently achieved a certain notoriety as a eugenicist with the idea of a sperm bank for Nobel Laureates such as himself as a central plank of his thought – a sort of junction transistor for improving the race (Brooks 1976: 224).
5 It can be said even at the outset that the Swiss were not wrong-footed with electronics in the sense that they were unprepared. They had established a collective research laboratory, the Centre Electronique Horloger (CEH) in Neuchatel and by 1967 working models were being made there of sufficient quality to be entered in the traditional competitions for accuracy (Landes 1983: 346). The productivity of the Swiss industry in conventional manufacture increased significantly during the 1970s, the crucial first decade of the electronic challenge. In 1978, despite the fact that Japan was tripling its production, Switzerland, although declining sharply, still had the biggest slice of the world market, 63 million of 265 million pieces. And, after all, the Swiss had never been in the business of cheap watches and had survived the attack of Timex – the first best-selling cheap watch – throughout the 1950s.

## 12 THE COMING OF THE MICROCOMPUTER

1 Ahl left and eventually founded *Creative Computing*, one of the many magazines catering to the owners of the sort of machine Digital turned down (Augarten 1984: 266–7).
2 However, the Jobs/Wozniak initial design philosophy survived sufficiently intact for Apple Macs still to command around one-third of the professional 'paint and draw' market into the late 1990s.

## 13 THE BEGINNINGS OF NETWORKS

1 A similar Bell conservatism can be seen at work in the matter of the combined receiver/transmitter. The first such handset had been patented in the UK as early as 1877. They were issued to the US Army by the 1890s and Bell linesmen had them in 1902. Despite the widespread diffusion of the device in Europe (they were known as 'French phones'), Bell opinion was against them and as a result, Americans got the modern telephone 'station' (i.e. a one-piece transmitter/receiver cradled on a device with a numerical dial) in 1924 (Brooks 1976: 138). Perhaps Bell's slowness with automatic exchanges and handsets can be attributed to the fact that these were not, *ab initio*, Bell devices.

2 Compare Bell Lab pre-divestiture record with that of, say, the Media Lab at MIT whose only widely diffused device is the white-light hologram used on credit cards (p. 339).

3 The average telephone user has experienced improvements only at the margin, except where in the UK the cable companies were marketing telephony from the mid-1990s as a species of lost leader. Otherwise, the effect of privatisation has been to make the making of telephone calls, especially in public places and yet more especially in the USA, a lot more complicated than it used to be with strings of digits being required to access the longline service provider 'of choice' before the number can be dialled.

## 14 NETWORKS AND RECORDING TECHNOLOGIES

1 There was a spin-off benefit to these film/television marriages. If the television picture was filmed at the receiving end, the film image could then be conventionally projected. By 1933 Fernseh A.G. demonstrated a variant on its intermediate film process which allowed for the projection, via a Nipkow disk, of a 180-line picture 10 x 14 feet. The technique survived to be seriously considered by Paramount for its theatre television system in the late 1940s. In the Paramount version the camera exposed the electronic picture, presumably to be received over the UHF theatre network had that been allowed by the FCC (p. 123), and 66 seconds later the developed film dropped by chute straight into the gate of the cinema projector. (The Eidophor was also in use in these experiments, as was mentioned above (p. 123), but, although it produced a large screen image, it did so directly from the received electronic signal and was not a retrieval device.) As we have seen, theatrical television was not a meaningful supervening necessity (or rather, was not allowed to be one) and these experiments were terminated.

## 15 COMMUNICATIONS SATELLITES

1 Verne uncannily suggested Tampa, Florida as the launch site for his rocket.

## 16 THE SATELLITE ERA

1 ATS 6 was part of a fad for offering telecommunication fixes, usually at grossly inappropriate levels of technology, to the developing nations. In the 1980s Intelsat was pushing Share (Satellites for Health And Rural Education) as a sixteen-month free experiment to celebrate its twentieth birthday. Such schemes have a venerable history since the socially ameliorating effects of media hardware have long been puffed.

The magic lantern was recommended 'for all educational purposes' in 1705 (Eder 1978: 57).

2 It would be wrong to suggest that all these blows, foreign and domestic, destroyed Comsat. A prime purpose of the 'law' of suppression, it must be remembered, is to protect all established players. In the 1990s, Comsat was still a large telecom company with over 1,500 employees and nearly half a billion dollars' worth of annual revenue.

3 *The Economist*, which successfully expanded from Britain into the American market, might be an exception to prove this rule, the transatlantic orthodoxy of its neo-liberal editorial position in the 1980s perhaps facilitating the ease with which it crossed this border. More typical is the *New York Times*: New Yorkers exiled in Los Angeles wanted authentic editorial pages in their Californian edition to feed their nostalgia, so minimal editorial concessions were made.

4 As in the work of Cees Hamelink or Herb Schiller. For a discussion of the limitations of the cultural imperialism idea, see Tracey (1985: 17–56) or, more specifically, Mohammadi (1995: 370–7) on the use of audio-cassettes in the Iranian revolution. As Armand Mattelart put it: 'The messages of mass culture can be neutralised by the dominated class who can produce their own antidotes' (Mattelart 1980: 200).

5 Much the same point can be made about VDUs. The US National Institute for Occupational Safety and Health found that in the United Airlines office in San Francisco, an environment with a high density of VDTs (Visual Display Terminals, known in UK as VDUs – Visual Display Units, i.e. televisions), half of forty-eight pregnancies between 1979 and 1984 had ended in miscarriages, birth defects or other abnormalities. Working with VDTs can also increase risk of seizure in epileptics, according to the British Health and Safety Executive. The HSE also found facial dermatitis occurred in VDT work environments with low humidity. The clincher (perhaps) is that the American Electronics Association (who make the things) testified before the Congress in 1984 that there was no evidence as to the deleterious effects of television. Their spokesman said: 'Regulation of VDTs on any health and safety basis is unwarranted' (UPI 1984: 4).


## 17 CABLE TELEVISION

1 John Walson of Mahonoy City has been credited with the first cable system but this seems to be unfounded (Parsons 1996: 354–65).

2 The technological naiveté of this decision is perhaps matched only by the Court having failed, for half a century, to acknowledge that telephone wire-tapping constituted an invasion of privacy grievous enough to be protected by the Fourth Amendment of the Constitution against illegal physical searches of property. The Justices also did not do too well, initially, in the matter of copywriting the algorithms in computer programs (Winston 1995: 275).


## 18 THE INTERNET

1 He also thought ICBMs would never be targetable.

2 Eastman Kodak part funded the investigation into digital devices Bush conducted at MIT in the 1930s.

3 In *When Wizards Stay Up Late*, Bob Taylor, the man who first commissioned the work which was to produce ARPANET, the forerunner of the Internet, wants it clearly understood that the 'rumours' which 'had persisted for years that ARPANET had

been built to protect national security in the face of nuclear attack' were a 'myth' (Hafner and Lyon 1996: 10). Within pages, however, he is discovered driving to his office which 'was on the third floor, the most prestigious level in the Pentagon' (ibid: 11) and, a page later, that when he travelled he 'carried the rank of one-star general'. He left the Pentagon in 1968 for the University of Utah having 'burned out' trying to damage control the Vietnam body count controversy of that year (ibid: 152).

4 The real threat to the traditional Post Office actually emerged in the late 1980s in the form of rival, but equally traditional private mail carriers. Once again these were encouraged by the neo-liberal *Zeitgeist* which had a more profound effect than did the technology. Another thought: It is one of the more perplexing mysteries of late twentieth-century life as to why (1) people would think accountants (aka 'consultants') had enough imagination to undertake this sort of assessment; and (2) why their collective almost complete failure ever to predict anything correctly has little or no impact on their 'consultancy' business.

5 I take the term from one of the earliest, albeit anecdotal, books to call the Internet's bluff: Clifford Stoll's *Snake Oil: Second Thoughts on the Information Highway* (1996).

6 John S. Quatermain, described as an Internet Demographer of Austin Texas in the *Los Angeles Times*, of 5 August 1994, then estimated users worldwide at 2 to 3 million.

7 Even more marginal activities such as American audio CD dealers selling against the grossly inflated European CD prices – but since their suppliers are, more or less, those responsible for these same European mark-ups it is not hard to see how that trade can be stopped the moment it becomes noticeable.

## CONCLUSION

1 All this is to discount the effects of virtual reality systems which create the illusion of the third dimension, as did the Stereopticon, by filling the entire field of vision with a small image. However, the essential dangers of bringing the eye so close to the radio frequency emissions of two tiny television screens, which is what current VR proposals involve, is likely to have some inhibiting effect on the diffusion of this technique.

# REFERENCES

Abramson, A. (1955) 'A short history of television recording', *Journal of the SMPTE*, vol. 64 (in Shiers *q.v.*).

—— (1973) 'A short history of television recording: Part II', *SMPTE Journal*, vol. 82 (in Shiers *q.v.*).

Addeo, E.G. (n.d.) *The Ampex Story*, Ampex Corporation: internal document (in Nmungwen *q.v.*).

Aitken, H.H. (1964) 'Proposed automatic calculating machine', *IEEE Spectrum*, August (in Randell (1973) *q.v.*).

Alexander 1995 'Development of integral holographic motion picture', *SPIE*, vol. 2333.

Andrews, E.G. (1963) *Bell Journal*, vol 42, no.2, March.

Anon (1940), 'Color television demonstrated by CBS engineers', *Electronics*, October (in Shiers *q.v.*).

—— (1945) 'Garrigues likes 1050-line video', *Broadcasting*, 23 April.

—— (1981) 'Sony does it again in HDTV', *Broadcasting*, 4 May.

—— (1982) *Coop's Satellite Digest*, October.

—— (1984) *Listener*, 24 May.

—— (1994) *Oxford Magazine*, Spring.

—— (1996) *Journalism and Authors' Rights: Policy Statement of the European Federation of Journalists*, Brussels: European Federation of Journalists, December.

Arlen, G., Prince, S. & Trost, M. (1987) *Tomorrow's TV: A Review of New TV Set Technology, Related Video Equipment and Potential Market Impacts, 1987–1995* (Com/Tech Report Series), Washington: National Association of Broadcasters Research and Planning Department, January.

Atanasoff, J.V. (1973) 'The use of high speed vacuum tube devices for calculating (privately circulated memorandum, August 1942) (in Randell (1973) *q.v.*).

Augarten, S. (1984) *Bit by Bit: An Illustrated History of Computers*, New York: Ticknor and Fields.

Babbage, H.P. (1889) *Babbage's Calculating Engines*, London: E. & F.N. Spon.

Backus, J. (1980) 'Programming in America in the 1950s – some personal impressions (in Metropolis *et al. q.v.*).

Baran, P. (1964) 'On distributed communications networks', *IEEE Transactions on Communications Systems*, 1 March.

Barnouw, E. (1975) *Tube of Plenty*, New York/Oxford: Oxford University Press.

Barry, D. (1996) *Dave Barry in Cyberspace*, New York: Crown.

Beck, A.H.W. (1967) *Words and Waves*, London: Weidenfeld & Nicolson.

Bell, A.G. (1908) *The Deposition of Alexander Graham Bell in the Suit Brought by the United States to Annul the Bell Patents*, Boston: American Bell Telephone Company.

Benjamin, L. (1994) 'In search of the Sarnoff 'radio music box' memo', *Journal of Broadcasting and Electronic Media, vol.*37, no.3: 325–35.

Benjamin, W. (1969) 'Theses on the philosophy of history', *Illuminations*, New York: Schocken Books.

Bennett, A.R. (1895) *The Telephone Systems of the Continent of Europe*, London: Longmans, Green & Co.

Benton, S. (1991) 'Elements of holographic video imaging', *SPIE - International Symposium on Display Holography,* vol. 1600.

Berke, A.A. and Meons, G.C. (1932) *The Modern Corporation and Private Property*, New York: Commerce Clearing House.

Bigelow, J. (1980) 'Computer development at the Institute for Advanced Study' (in Metropolis *et al. q.v.*).

Birkenhead, First Earl of (n.d.) *Famous Trials of History*, London: Hutchinson.

Birkoff, G. (1980) 'Computer developments 1935–1955, as seen from Cambridge, USA', (in Metropolis *et al. q.v.*).

Biting, R.C. (1965) 'Creating an industry', *Journal of the SMPTE,* vol. 74 (in Shiers *q.v.*).

Blagonravov, A. A. (ed.) (1966) *Iz istorii raketnoi teknhniki*, Moscow: Historical Institute for Natural Science and Engineering (trans and ed. by H.I. Needler, *Soviet Rocketry - Some Contributions to its History*, Jerusalem: Programme for Scientific Translations).

Blake, G.G. (1928) *History of Radio Telegraphy and Telephony*, London: Chapman and Hall, 1928.

Boddy, W. (1990) *Fifties Television: The Industry and Its Critics*, Urbana: University of Illinois Press.

Bohn, T. (1968) 'Broadcasting national election returns: 1916–1948', *Journal of Broadcasting,* XII: 3, summer.

Bond, B. (1996) 'The big idea', *Television*, April/May.

Brand, S. (1987) *The Media Lab: Inventing the Future at MIT*, New York: Viking.

Braudel, F. (1981) *Civilisation and Capitalism 15th–18th Century Volume 1: The Structures of Everyday Life, The Limits of the Possible,* New York: Harper & Row.

Braun, E. (1980) 'From transistor to microprocessor' (in Forester *q.v.*).

Braun, E. and MacDonald, S. (1982) *Revolution in Miniature: The History and Impact of Semiconductor Electronics*, Cambridge: Cambridge University Press.

Briggs, A. (1961) *The History of Broadcasting in the United Kingdom, Vol. II: ' The Golden Age of Wireless'*, Oxford: Oxford University Press.

—— (1979) *From Iron Bridge to Crystal Palace*, London: Thames & Hudson.

Bright, C. (1893) *The Story of the Atlantic Cable*, New York: D. Appleton and Company.

Brock, G.W. (1981) *The Telecommunications Industry*, Cambridge MA.: Harvard University Press.

Brock, W.R. (1973) *Conflict and Transformation: The United States 1844–1877*, Harmondsworth: Penguin Books.

Brooks, J. (1976) *Telephone*, New York: Harper & Row.

Brown, L. (1992) *Encyclopaedia of Television*, Detroit: Gail Research.

Brush, J. and Brush, D. (1981) *Private Television: Into the Eighties*, Berkeley Hights, New Jersey: International Television Association.

Bryan, G.S. (1926) *Edison: The Man and His Work*, New York: Knopf.

Burks, A.W. (1980) 'From ENIAC to the stored programme computer: two revolutions in computers' (in Metropolis *et al. q.v.*).

Burks, A.W., Goldstine, H.H. and von Neumann, J. (1973) *Preliminary Discussion of the Logical Design of an Electronic Computing Instrument, Part 1*, Princeton: Institute for Advanced Studies, vol.1, 28 June 1948 (in Randell (1973) *qv.*).

Burtt, E.A. (1967) *The Metaphysical Foundations of Modern Physical Science*, London: Routledge & Kegan Paul.

Bush, V. (1945) 'As we may think', *The Atlantic Monthly*, July.

Bylinsky, G. (1975) 'Here comes the second computer revolution', *Fortune*, November (in Forester *q.v.*).

Byrne, D. and John, L. (1972) 'Telecommunications', *Year Book*, Chicago: Encyclopaedia Britannica.

Carey, J and Moss, M. L. (1985) 'The diffusion of new telecommunications technologies: telecommunication policy', New York University: unpublished manuscript, June.

Chanan, M. (1995) *Repeated Takes: A Short History of Recording and Its Effects on Music*, London: Verso.

Chapius, R.J. (1982) *100 Years of Telephone Switching: Part One*, Amsterdam: North Holland.

Cherry, C. (1961) *On Human Communication*, New York: John Wiley.

Chesher, C. (1996) 'CD-ROM's identity crisis', *Media Information Australia*, no. 81, August.

Chew, V.K (1981) *Talking Machines*, London: HMSO.

Chu, J.C. (1980) 'Computer development at Argonne National Laboratory' (in Metropolis *et al. q.v.*).

Churchill, W.S. (1951)*The Second World War: volume four*, London: Cassell.

Clarke, A.C. (1969) *Voices from the Sky*, London: Mayflower.

Cole, G.D.H. and Postgate, R. (1961) *The Common People 1746–1946*, London: Methuen.

Congress of the United States, Joint Economic Committee (1964) *Invention and the Patent System*, Washington: United States Goverment Printing Office.

Czitrom, D.J. (1982) *Media and the American Mind*, Chapel Hill: University of North Carolina Press.

Daniloff, N. (1972) *The Kremlin and the Cosmos*, New York: Knopf.

Deavours, C.A. (1981) 'Untitled response to Rejewski' (*q. v.*) *Annals of the History of Computing*, vol. 3, no 3.

De Forest, L. (1942) *Television Today and Tomorrow*, New York: Dial Press.

Dickieson, A.C. (1963) 'The *Telstar experiment*', *Bell Journal*, vol. 42, no. 4, part 1, July.

Dinsdale, A. (1932) 'Television in America today', *Journal of the Television Society*, vol. 1 (in Shiers *q.v.*).

Dufour, A.(1995) *Internet*, Paris: Presses Universitaires de France.

Dummer, G.W.A. (1983) *Electronic Inventions And Discoveries*, Oxford: Pergamon.

Dyos, H.J. and Aldcroft D.H. (1974) *British Transport*, Hardmondsworth: Penguin Books.

Eckert, J. Presper Jr (1980) 'Thc ENIAC' (in Metropolis *et al. q.v.*).

Eckert, W.J. (1948) 'Electrons and computation', *Proceedings of the IEEE*, vol. 67. no. 5, November (in Randell (1973) *q.v.*).

Eder, J-M. (1978) *Geschichte der Photographie* (trans E. Epstean, *History of Photography*), New York: Dover.

Eisenstein, E.L. (1983) *The Printing Revolution in Early Modern Europe*, New York: Cambridge University Press.

Elsner, M., Muller, T. and Spangenberg, P. (1990) 'The early history of German television:

the slow development of a fast medium', *Historical Journal of Film, Radio and Television*, vol. 10, no.2.

Elton, M. (1984) private communication. (I am grateful to Martin Elton for providing me with this data.)

Engleman, R. (1990) 'The origins of public access cable television', *Journalism Monographs*, no. 123, October.

Evans, D.S. (ed.) (1983) *Breaking Up Bell*, New York: North Holland.

Everett, R.R. (1980) 'WHIRLWIND' (in Metropolis *et al. q.v.*).

Everson, G. (1949) *The Story of Television. The Life of Philo T. Farnsworth*, New York: W.W. Norton.

Fagen, M. D. (ed.) (1975) *History of Engineering and Science in the Bell System: The Early Years 1875–1925*, Bell Laboratories.

Fahie, J.J. (1884) *A History of the Electric Telegraph to the Year 1837*, London: E. & F.N. Spon.
—— (1901) *A History of Wireless Telegraphy*, New York: Dodd Mead.

Falk, H. (1968) 'Electronics', *Year Book of the Events of 1967*, Chicago: Encyclopaedia Britannica.

Felker, J.H. (1952) 'Regenerative amplifier for digital computer applications', *Proceedings of the Institute of Radio Engineers*, vol. 40 no. 11, November.

Fiddick, P. (1993) 'Research', *The Guardian*, 21 June.

Fink, D.G. (ed.) (1943) *Television Standards and Practice* (in Shiers *q.v.*).
—— (1945) 'Television broadcast practice in America – 1927 to 1944', *Proceedings of the Institute of Electrical Engineers*, vol. 92, part III (in Shiers *q.v.*).
—— (1955) 'Color television v. color motion picture', *SMPTE Journal*, vol. 64, June.
—— D. (1980) 'The future of high definition television: first portion of a report of the SMPTE study group on high definition television', *SMPTE Journal*, vol. 89, February.

Fiske, John (1987) *Television Culture*, London: Routledge.

Flichy, P. (1991) *Une historie de la communciation moderne: Espace public et vie privée*, Paris: La Découverte.

Forester, T. (ed.) (1980) *The Microelectronic Revolution*, Oxford: Basil Blackwell.

Friedel, R. and Israel, P. (1986) *Edison's Electric Light: Biography of an Invention*, New Brunswick, New Jersey: Rutgers University Press.

Friendly, F. (1968) *Due to Circumstances Beyond Our Control*, New York: Vintage.

Fujio, T. (1978) 'A study of high-definition TV system in the future', *IEEE Transactions on Broadcasting*, vol. BC-24, no. 4, December.

Fujio, T., Ishida, J., Komoto, T. and Nishizawa, T. (1980), 'High-definition television system – signal standard and transmission', *SMPTE Journal*, vol. 89, August.

Galloway, John (1977) 'Domestic economic issues' (in Pelton and Snow *q.v.*).

Garratt, G. R. M. and Mumford, A. H. (1952) 'The history of television', *Proceedings of the Institution of Electrical Engineers*, vol. 99, Part IIIA ( in Shiers *q.v.*).

Gelatt, R. (1977) *The Fabulous Phonograph 1877–1977*, London: Cassell (quoted in Chanan *q.v.*).

Gibas, H. (1936) 'Television in Germany', *Proceedings of the Institute of Radio Engineers*, vol. 24 (in Shiers *q.v.*).

Goldstine, H.H. (1972) *The Computer from Pascal to von Neumann*, Princeton: Princeton University Press.

Goldwyn, E. (1978) 'Now the chips are down', *The Listener*, 6 April.

Good, I.J. (1980) 'Pioneering work on computers at Bletchley' (in Metropolis *et al. q.v.*).

Gorokhov, P.K. (1961) 'History of Modern Television', *Radiotekhnika* (in Shiers *q.v.*).

Gow, J. (1989) *The Development and Suppression of the Radical Potencial of DAT*, State College, PA: Penn State School of Communications Working Papers.

Graham, M. (1986) *RCA and the VideoDisc: The Business of Research*, New York: Cambridge University Press.

Greb, G. (1958–9) 'The golden anniversary of broadcasting', *Journal of Broadcasting*, vol. III, no. 1, winter.

Greenwald, W.I. (1952) 'The impact of sound upon the film industry: a case study in innovation', *Explorations in Entrepreneurial History*, vol. 4, no. 4, 15 May.

Gutting G. (1980) *Paradigms and Revolutions*, Notre Dame: University of Notre Dame Press.

Hafner, K. and Lyon, M. (1996) *Where Wizards Stay Up Late: The Origins of the Internet*, New York: Simon & Schuster.

Hamming, R.W. (1980) 'We would know what they thought when they did it' (in Metropolis *et al. q.v.*).

Handel, S. (1967) *The Electronic Revolution*, Harmondsworth: Penguin Books.

Hanson, D. (1982) *The New Alchemists*, New York: Avon.

Harding, A. (1966) *A Social History of English Law*, Harmondsworth: Penguin Books.

Hardy, H. (1996) 'The history of the net', MA Thesis, Grand Valley State University, Michigan: umcc.umich.edu/pub/seraphim/doc/nethist8.text

Hazard, P. (1964) *The European Mind 1680–1715*, Harmondsworth: Penguin Books.

Hempel, C.G. (1942) 'The function of general laws in history', *Journal of Philosophy*, 34: 1, January.

Hempel, M. (1990) 'German television pioneers and the conflict between public programming and weapon wonders', *Historical Journal of Film, Radio and Television*, vol. 10, no.2.

Henderson, W.O. (1969) *The Industrialisation of Europe*, London: Thames & Hudson.

Hilmes, M. (1990) *Hollywood and Broadcasting: From Radio to Cable*, Urbana: University of Illinois Press.

Hodges, A. (1983) *Alan Turing - The Enigma*, New York: Simon & Schuster.

Hollins, T. (1984) *Beyond Broadcasting: Into the Cable Age*, London: BFI.

Horner, Steve (1993) 'Smile! This will have you in a spin', *The Independent*, 1 February.

Horsman, M. (1996) 'The rise and rise of BSkyB', *The Independent*, 30 July.

Hubbell, R.W. (1942) *4000 Years of Television*, New York: Putnam.

Hurd, C.C. (1980) 'Computer development at IBM' (in Metropolis *et al. q.v.*).

Hyman, A. (1984) *Charles Babbage: Pioneer of the Comptuter*, Oxford: Oxford University Press.

Iams, H., Morton, G.A. and Zworykin, V.K. (1939) 'The image iconoscope', *Proceedings of the Institute of Radio Engineers*, September.

Ishida, J., Nishizawa, T. and Kubota, K. (1982) 'High definition television broadcasting by satellite', *IEEE Transactions of Broadcasting*, vol. BC-28, no. 4, December.

Ives, H.E. (1927) 'Television', *Bell Journal*, October (in Shiers *q.v.*).

—— (1929) 'Television in Colors', *Bell Laboratories Record*, vol. 7 (in Shiers *q.v.*).

Ives, H.E., Gray F. and Baldwin, M.W. (1930) 'Two way television' *Proceedings of the Institute of Electrical Engineers*, vol. 49 (in Shiers *q.v.*).

Jenkins, C.F. (1927) 'Radio vision', *Proceedings of the Institute of Radio Engineers*, vol. 15 (in Shiers *q.v.*).

Jensen, A.G. (1954) 'The evolution of modern television', *Journal of the SMPTE*, vol. 63 (in Shiers *q.v*).

Jeong, T.H. (1977), 'Postcript' (to Komar: *q.v.*).

Jewes, J., Sawers, D. and Stillerman, R. (1958) *The Sources of Invention*, London: Macmillan.

Jurgen, R. (1989) 'Chasing Japan in the HDTV race', *IEEE Spectrum*, October.

Kac, E. (1995), 'Beyond the spatial paradigm: time and cinematic form in holographic art', *Blimp: Zeitschrift für film*, no. 32.

Karuppiahya, L. (1996) *International Broadcasting and the BBC World Service – Speaking to the World In Foreign Languages*, Unpublished MA Thesis, University of Wales, Cardiff.

Kingsbury, J.E. (1915), *The Telephone and Telephone Exchanges*, London: Longmans, Green & Co.

Kline, M. (1980) *Mathematics - The Loss of Certainty*, New York: Oxford University Press.

Knuth, D.E. and Pardo, L.T. (1980) 'The early development of progamming languages' (in Metropolis *et al. q.v.*).

Komar, V.G. (1977) 'Progress on the holographic movie process in the USSR', *SPIE - Three Dimensional Imaging*, vol. 120.

Komar, V.G. and Serov, O.B. (1989) 'Works on the holographic cinematography in the USSR', *SPIE - Holography 89*, vol. 1183.

Kuhn, T. (1962) *The Structure of Scientific Revolutions*, Chicago: University of Chicago Press.

Lafferty, W. (1983) 'The Blattnerphone: an early attempt to introduce magnetic recording into the film industry', *Cinema Journal*, vol. 22, no. 4, summer.

Landes, D.S. (1983) *Revolution in Time*, Cambridge MA: Harvard University Press.

Langdon, W. C. (1935) *The Early Corporate Development of the Telephone*, New York: Bell Telephone.

Lange, A. and Renaud, J-L. (1989) *The Future of the European Audovisual Industry*, Manchester: European Institute for the Media.

Lavington, S. (1980) *Early British Computers*, Manchester: Manchester University Press.

Leapman, M. (1983) *Companion Guide to New York*, London: Collins; Englewood Cliffs NJ: Prentice-Hall.

Lewis, R. S. (1968) *Appointment on the Moon*, New York: Viking.

Licklider, J. and Vezza, A. (1978) 'Applications of Information Technology', *Proceedings of the IEEE, vol.* 66, no. 11.

Limbacher, J. (1968) *Four Aspects of the Film*, New York: Brussel & Brussel.

Lovell, B. (1973) *The Origins and International Economics of Space Exploration*, Edinburgh: Edinburgh University Press.

Ludgate, P.E. (1909) 'On a proposed analytical machine', Royal Dublin Society, (in Randell 1973 *q.v.*).

McChesney, R. (1990) 'The Battle for the US airways, 1928–1935', *Journal of Communication*, vol. 40, 4, autumn.

—— (1991) 'Press–radio relations and the emergence of network, commercial broadcasting in the United States, 1930–1935', *Historical Journal of Film, Radio and Television*, vol. 11, no. 1.

MacDonald, S. and Braun, E. (1977) 'The transistor and attiude to change', *American Journal of Physics*, vol. 45, 11, November.

McGee, J.D. (1950) 'Distant electrical vision', *Proceedings of the Institute of Radio Engineers*, vol. 38 (in Shiers *q.v.*).

Markoff, J. (1997) 'Hollywood Goes DVD, Cautiously', *International Herald Tribune*, 10 January, p. 13/17.

Martin, J. (1977) *Future Developments in Telecommunications*, Englewood Cliffs: Prentice-Hall.

Marvin, C. (1988) *When Old Technologies Were New: Thinking about Communication in the Late Nineteenth Century*, New York: Oxford University Press.

Mason, E. (with the Sloan Commission on Cable Communications) (1971) *The Cable: Television of Abundance*, New York: McGraw-Hill.

Mattelart, A. (1980) *Mass Media, Ideologies and the Revolutionary Movement*, Sussex, Harvester (in Fiske *q.v.*).

Mauchly, J.W. (1942) 'The use of high speed vacuum tube devices for calculating', privately circulated memorandum, August (in Randell *q.v.*).

—— (1948) 'Preparation of problems for EDVAC-type machines', *Annals of the Computation Laboratory of Harvard University*, vol. 16 (in Randell (1973) *q.v.*).

—— (1980) 'The ENIAC' (in Metropolis *et al. q.v.*).

Maxwell, J. C. (1865) 'A dynamic theory of electromagnetic field', *Philosophical Transactions,* vol. 155.

Merryfield, C.W. (1878) 'Report of the Committee . . . appointed to consider the advisability and to estimate the expense of constructing Mr. Babbage's Analytical Machine, and of printing tables by its means', (in Randell (1973) *q.v.*).

Metropolis, N. (1980) 'The MANIAC' (in Metropolis *et al. q.v.*).

Metropolis, N. and Worlton, J. (1972) 'A trilogy on [sic] errors in the history of computing', First USA-Japan Computer Conference, Session 21–2.

Metropolis, N., Howlett, J. and Rota, G-C (eds) (1980) *A History of Computing in the Twentieth Century*, New York: Academic Press.

Millman, S. (ed.) (1983) *A History of Engineering and Science in the Bell System – Physical Sciences (1925–1980)*, Bell Laboratories.

Mohammadi, A. (1995), 'Cultural Imperialism and Cultural Identity', in Downing, J., Mohhamadi, A. and Sreberny-Mohhamadi, A. (eds) *Questioning the Media: A critical introduction*, Thousand Oaks CA: Sage.

Moncel, Le Compte du (1879) *The Telephone, the Microphone and the Phonograph*, New York: Harper & Brothers.

Morison, E. E. (1968) *Men, Machines and Modern Times*, Cambridge MA: Massachusetts Institute of Technology Press.

Moss, M. (1984) 'New York isn't just New York anymore', *Intermedia*, autumn.

Mumford, L. (1966) *The City in History*, Harmondsworth: Penguin Books.

—— (1970) *The Pentagon of Power*, New York: Harcourt, Brace Jovanovitch.

Murdock, G. (1992) 'Citizens, consumers, and public culture', in Michael Skovmand and Kim Christian Schrøder (eds) *Media Cultures: Reappraising Transnational Media,* London: Routledge.

Nagel E. and Newman, J.R. (1958) *Godel's Proof*, New York: New York University Press.

Nakajima, H. and Kosaka, M. (1986) 'The DAT Conference. Its activities and results', *IEEE Transactions on Consumer Electronics*, vol. CE-32, no.3, August.

Needell, A.A. (ed.) (1983) *The First Twenty-Five Years in Space*, Washington: Smithsonian Institute Press.

Neumann, J. von (1945) 'First Draft of a report on the EDVAC Contract no. W-760–RD-4926', Philadelphia: Moore School of Electrical Engineering, University of Pennsylvania, 30 June (in Randell (1973) *q.v.*).

Nmungwun, Aaron (1989) *Video Recording Technology: Its Impact on Media and Home Entertainment*, Hillsdale NJ: Lawrence Erlbaum.

Noble, D.F. (1984) *Forces of Production*, New York: Knopf.

Norman, B. (1984) *Here's Looking at You*, London: BBC/Royal Television Society.

Noyce, R.N. (1977) 'Microelectronics', *Scientific American*, vol. 237 no.3, September (in Forester *q.v.*).

Ordway III, F.I. and Sharpe, M.R. (1979) *The Rocket Team*, New York: Thomas Y. Crowell.

Oslund, J. (1977) 'Open shores to open skies' (in Pelton and Snow *q.v.*)

Owen, C.H. (1962) 'Television broadcasting', *Proceedings of the Institute of Radio Engineers*, vol. 50, May (in Shiers *q.v.*).

Parsons, P. (1996) 'Two Tales of a City: John Walson, Mahonoy City and the "founding" of cable television', *Journal of Broadcasting and Electronic Media*, No. 40: 3.

Paul, G. (1975) *Die dritte Entdeckung der Erde* (trans by A. Lacy & B. Lacy as *Satellite Spin-Off*), Washington DC: Robert B. Luce.

Pelton, J.N. and Snow, M. (eds) (1977) *Economic and Policy Problems in Satellite Communications*, New York: Praeger.

Pepys, S. (1953) *Diaries: Vol, III*, London, J.M.Dent.

Percy, J.D. (1952) 'John L. Baird: the founder of British television', *Journal of the Television Society*, (in Shiers *q.v.*).

Phillips, Vivian (1980) *Early Radio Wave Detectors*, London: IEE & Peter Peregrinus.

Post, E.I. (1936). 'Finite combinatory processes - Formulation 1', *Journal of Symbolic Logic*, vol 1, no. 3, September.

Potter, B. (1996) ''Ear, what's all this fuss about mobile phones', *The Guardian: On Line*, 14 November.

Prescott, G.B. (1972) *Bell's Electric Speaking Telephone*, New York: Arno.

Preston, S.J. (1953) 'The birth of a high definition television service', *Journal of the Television Society*, vol. 7 (in Shiers *q.v.*).

Rajchman, J. (1980) 'Early research on computers at RCA' (in Metropolis *et al. q.v.*).

Randell, B. (ed.) (1973) *The Origins of Digital Computers: Selected Papers*, Berlin: Springer-Verlag.

—— (1980) 'The COLOSSUS' (in Metropolis *et al. q.v.*).

Rejewski, M. (1981) 'How Polish mathematicians deciphered the enigma', *Annals of the History of Computing*, vol. 3, no. 3, July.

Rhodes, F.L. (1929) *Beginnings of Telephony*, New York: Harper & Brothers.

Robertson, J.E. (1980) 'The ORDVAC and the ILLIAC' (in Metropolis *et al. q.v.*).

Robertson, J.H. (1947) *The Story of the Telephone: A History of the Telecommunications Industry of Britain*, London: Pitman & Sons.

Rodgers, W. (1969) *Think*, New York: Stein & Day.

Rolt, L.T.C. (1970) *Isambard Kingdom Brunel*, Harmondsworth: Penguin Books.

Roman, J.W. (1983) *Cable Mania*, Englewood Cliffs: Prentice-Hall.

Sandbank, C.P. and Moffat, M.E.B. (1983) 'High definition television and compatibility with existing standards', *SMPTE Journal*, May.

Sarnoff, D. (n.d.) *Collected Speeches*, RCA.

Scannel, P. and Cardiff, D. (1982) 'Serving the nation: public service broadcasting before the war' in Waites, B., Bennett, T. & Martin, G. (eds) *Popular Culture, Past and Present*, London: Croom Helm.

Schiller, H. (1976) *Communication and Cultural Domination*, White Plains, New York: International Arts and Science Press.

Schindler, G.E. (ed.) (1982) *A History of Engineering and Science in the Bell System - Switching Technology (1925–1975)*, Bell Laboratories.

Schlafly, H.J. (1951) 'Some comparative factors of picture resolution in television and film industries', *Journal of the SMPTE*, January.

Schwartz, B. (1959) 'Antitrust and the FCC: the problem of network dominance', *University of Pennsylvania Law Review*, vol. 1097, no. 6.

Selsdon, Lord (ch.) (1935) *Report of the Television Committee*, Television Advisory Committee, London: HMSO Cmd. 4793 (The Selsdon Report).

Senate (1950) Report, *Document no. 197*, 31st Congress (2nd Session).

——— (1984) Section 5.b.i, *Congressional Record*, 11 October, S14297.

Shannon., C. (1938) 'A symbolic analysis of relay and switching circuits', Transactions of the American Institute of Electrical Engineers, vol. 327.

Sheldon, J.W. and Tatum, L. (1951) 'The IBM card-programmed electronic calculator', paper given at joint AIEEE-IRE Computer Conference, 12 December (in Randell (1973) *q.v.*).

Shiers, G. (ed.) (1977) *Technical Development of Television*, New York: Arno.

Shockley, W. (1976) 'The path to the conception of the junction transistor', *IEEE Transactions on Electronic Devices*, vol. ED-23, no 7, July.

Slutz, R.J. (1980) 'Memories of the Bureau of Standards' SEAC' (in Metropolis *et al. q.v.*).

Snow, M.S. (1976) *International Commercial Satellite Communications*, New York: Praeger.

Sola Pool, I. de (1983) *Technologies of Freedom*, Cambridge MA: Belknap Press.

Soma, J.T. (1976) *The Computer Industry*, Lexington MA: D.H.Heath.

Stehman, J.W. (1925) *The Financial History of the American Telephone and Telegraph Company*, Boston: Houghton Mifflin.

Sterling, B. (1993) 'Literary freeway – not for commercial use', Speech to National Academy of Science Convocation on Technology and Education, 10 May, Computer Underground Digest, vol. 5 no. 54 (in Hardy *q.v.*).

Stibitz, G.R. (1980) 'Early computers', (in Metropolis *et al. q.v.*).

Stoll, C. (1996) *Silicon Snake Oil: Second Thoughts on the Information Highway*, London: Pan.

Sturmey, S.G. (1958) *The Economic Development of Radio*, London: Gerald Duckworth.

Thompson, E.P. (1968) *The Making of the English Working Class*, Harmondsworth: Penguin Books.

Thompson, R.L. (1947) *Wiring a Continent*, Princeton NJ: Princeton University Press.

Thompson, S. (1912) *Journal of the Rotgen Society*, January.

Tiltman, R.F. (1933) *Baird of Television*, London: Seeley Service.

TITAS (1964) *Communications Satellite System COMSAT*, Washington DC: Treaties and Other International Acts Series 5646, 20 August.

Tomash, E. (1980) 'The start of an ERA: Engineering Research Associates, Inc., 1946–1955' (in Metropolis *et al. q.v.*).

Torres Y Quevedo, L. (1915) '*Essais sur l'automatique*', *Revue Generale des Sciences Pures et Appliquees*, 15 November (in Randell (1973) *q.v.*).

Toumlin, S. (1984) 'Fall of a genius', *New York Review of Books*, 19 January.

Tracey, M. (1985) 'The poisoned chalice? International television and the idea of dominance', *Dædalus*, vol. 114, no.4, autumn.

Tropp, H.S. (1980) 'The Smithsonian computer history project and some personal recollections' (in Metropolis *et al. q.v.*).

Turing, A.M. (1936) 'On computable numbers with an application to the *Entscheidungsproblem*' *Proceedings of the London Mathematical Society*, vol. 42, November.

——— (1937) 'On computable numbers - with an application to the *Entscheidungsproblem*. A correction', *Proceedings of the London Mathematical Society*, vol. 43.

Udelson, J.H.(1982) *The Great Television Race*, Tuscaloosa: University of Alabama Press.

Ulam, S.M. (1980) 'Von Neumann: the interaction of mathematics and computing' (in Metropolis *et al. q.v.*).

UPI (1984) *Daily* (Kingston NY) *Freeman*, 16 March.

Uricchio, W. (1990) 'Introduction to the history of German television, 1935 – 1944, *Historical Journal of Film, Radio and Television*, vol. 10, no.2.

Veronhis Suhler (1988) *The Veronis, Suhler and Associates Communications Industry Forecast*, New York: VSA.

—— (1995) *The Veronis, Suhler and Associates Communications Industry Forecast*, New York: VSA.

—— (1996) *The Veronis, Suhler and Associates Communications Industry Forecast*, New York: VSA.

Waldrop, F.C. and Borkin, J. (1938) *Television: A Struggle for Power*, New York: William Morrow.

Walton, P. (1982) *Space Light*, Sydney: Doubleday/London: Routledge & Kegan Paul.

Watson, T.A. (1926) *Exploring Life*, New York: Appleton.

Weaver, W. and Shannon, C. (1949) *The Mathematical Theory of Communication*, Urbana: University of Illinois Press.

Webb, H.L. (n.d.) *The Development of the Telephone in Europe*, London: The Electric Press.

Weizenbaum, J. (1980) 'Once more, the computer revolution' (in Forester, q.v.).

Wiener, N. (1954) *The Human Use of Human Beings*, New York: Doubleday.

Wile, F.W. (1926) *Emile Berliner: Maker of the Microphone [sic]*, Indianapolis: Bobbs-Merrill.

Wilkes, M.V. (1956) *Automatic Digital Computers*, London: Methuen.

—— (1980) 'Early programming developments in Cambridge' (in Metropolis *et al. q.v.*).

Williams, F.C. and Kilburn. T. (1948) 'Electronic digital computers', *Nature*, vol. 162, no. 487, September (in Randell (1973) *q.v.*).

Williams, R. (1976) *Keywords*, New York: Oxford University Press.

Wilmotte, R. (1976) 'Technical frontiers of television', *IEEE Transactions on Broadcasting*, vol. BC-22, no. 3, September.

Wilson J .C. (1935) 'Twenty five years change in television', *Journal of the Television Society*, vol. 2 (in Shiers *q.v.*).

Winston, B. (1986) *Misunderstanding Media*, London: Routledge & Kegan Paul.

—— (1993) 'The *CBS Evening News*, 7 April 1949', in J.E.T. Eldridge (ed.) *Getting The Message*, London: Routledge.

—— (1995) *Claiming the Real: The Documentary Film Revisited*, London: BFI.

—— (1996) *Technologies of Seeing: Photography, Cinematography and Television*, London: BFI.

Winston, B. and Walton, P. (1996) 'Netscape: virtually free', *Index on Censorship*, vol. 25, no. 1, issue 168, January/February.

Wolff, M.J. (1976) 'The genesis of the integrated circuit', *IEEE Spectrum*, August.

Wulforst, H. (1982) *Breakthrough to the Computer Age*, New York: Charles Scribner.

Zuse, K. (1980) 'Some remarks on the history of computing in Germany' (in Metropolis *et al., q.v.*).

Zworykin, V.K. (1929) 'Television with cathode-ray tube for receiver', *Radio Engineering*, vol. 9 December, (in Shiers *q.v.*).

—— (1934), 'Television', *Journal of the Franklin Institute*, vol. 217 (in Shiers *q.v.*).

# INDEX